T0154036

Discovery and Distinction in the Early Middle Ages

John J. Contreni

Medieval Institute Publications is a program of
The Medieval Institute, College of Arts and Sciences

 WESTERN MICHIGAN UNIVERSITY

Discovery and Distinction in the Early Middle Ages

STUDIES IN HONOR OF JOHN J. CONTRENI

Edited by
Cullen J. Chandler
and
Steven A. Stofferahn

MEDIEVAL INSTITUTE PUBLICATIONS
Western Michigan University
Kalamazoo

Publication of this book was supported by a grant from Indiana State University.

Library of Congress Cataloging-in-Publication Data

Discovery and distinction in the early Middle Ages : studies in honor of John J.
Contreni / edited by Cullen J. Chandler and Steven A. Stofferahn.
    pages cm
  Includes bibliographical references and index.
  ISBN 978-1-58044-170-4 (clothbound : alk. paper)
    1. Carolingians. 2. France--History--To 987. 3. Italy--History--Carolingian
rule, 774-887. 4. Germany--History--To 843. 5. Germany--History--843-918. 6.
Europe--Court and courtiers--History--To 1500. 7. Europe--Intellectual life--To
1500. 8. Europe--Church history--600-1500. 9. Christianity and other religions-
-Judaism--History--To 1500. 10. Judaism--Relations--Christianity--History--To
1500. I. Chandler, Cullen J., author, editor of compilation. II. Stofferahn, Steven
A., 1971- author, editor of compilation. III. Contreni, John J., honouree.
  DC70.D57 2013
  944'.014--dc23

                                                              2013013762

Contents

Preface

It is a commonplace in volumes such as this to wax poetic on the merits of the scholar honored in its publication, and indeed from this project's very beginning, the broad outpouring of goodwill toward the subject has been remarkable—if not altogether surprising. Those who know John J. Contreni know a man of quiet dignity whose dedication, grace, and resolve have earned him the esteem of scholars around the world. It has therefore been our great pleasure to have joined with them in celebrating his career. In doing so, it would be all too easy for an introduction to lapse into panegyric. But while that may be deserving in this case, it would hardly resonate with the character of the man. In that spirit we shall strive instead to hearken more closely to the honoree's own characteristic modesty, precision, and economy of style.

Although he did not declare a history major until his junior year (first having pursued political science and then economics) at St. Vincent College in Latrobe, Pennsylvania, John Contreni exhibited a deep appreciation for the subject from an early age. He grew up in a house full of books, unusual for the modest neighborhood in which he lived in Englewood, New Jersey, and especially remembers reading through *The Champlin Encyclopedia* (1948), whose first entry, mirabile dictu, is "Aachen." It was during his junior year at St. Vincent that he first came to appreciate the multilayered appeal of medieval history, inspired in part by eclectic reading in Johan Huizinga, Norman Cantor, and Karl Morrison. His early interests were in intellectual history, specifically philosophy. As an undergraduate he added Copleston's *History of Philosophy* to his library and subscribed to his first academic journal, the *Journal of the History of Ideas*. (His *first* subscriptions were to *Field & Stream* and *Outdoor Life*.)

Clio brought him to Michigan State University, specifically to Richard E. Sullivan, whose example as a historian doing history both in the seminar room and in the massive undergraduate survey—where Contreni apprenticed as a teaching assistant—inspired his own teaching and professional development. Richard Sullivan famously insisted that his students try to situate the particular problems on which they happened to be working within "the total stream of history." When he read Pierre Riché's *Éducation et culture dans l'Occident barbare, 6ᵉ–8ᵉ siècles* (1962) for a Sullivan seminar, Contreni knew he had found a way to ground the history of ideas in the history of societies and cultures. Schools provided the crucible in which intellectual traditions were creatively molded to contemporary, malleable, and often conflicting demands.

"Why don't you go study with Pierre Riché?" was all the encouragement he needed from his mentor to write to Paris, where Riché directed the Maison de l'Inde on the Boulevard Jourdan in addition to holding an academic post at the new campus of the University of Paris in Nanterre, a western suburb. Nanterre in 1969–70 was a gritty American-style campus still energized by the tumultuous events of 1968. Contreni enrolled in the university (for the equivalent of $20, he has often reported) and took all of Riché's courses. When another student identified Bede as a monk of Cluny, he knew he might survive in a French classroom. His real learning took place in the Bibliothèque Nationale, as it was then called, on the Rue de Richelieu, where Riché took him on a whirlwind tour of the Salle de Travail and the Cabinet des Manuscrits, introducing him to the librarians who would help him mine the BN's incomparable resources. It was Pierre Riché who suggested that the manuscripts of Laon might be worth studying and who took him on a memorable trip to Laon, stopping along the way to point out sites associated with the occupation and resistance of the 1940s. After sixteen months working at the BN and the Bibliothèque municipale of Laon, with weekly meetings at the Maison de l'Inde and at Nanterre when classes were in session, Contreni returned to East Lansing with a dissertation in progress, two articles in press, and a second daughter.

The dissertation, published on the recommendation of Bernhard Bischoff by Arbeo Gesellschaft in 1978 as *The Cathedral School of Laon from 850 to 930: Its Manuscripts and Masters*, went on to win the Medieval Academy's John Nicholas Brown Prize in 1982. This important work, along with his widely appreciated translation of Riché's *Education and Culture in the Barbarian West* two years earlier, established its author's place in the field of early medieval intellectual culture. Contreni's abiding interest in education went on to manifest itself in myriad subsequent investigations of just how Carolingian students and masters undertook their spirited labors in what was once routinely dismissed as a dull age of compil-ers. These works, along with other innovative articles appearing in *Speculum*, *Le Moyen Âge*, *Scriptorium*, and *Studi medievali* formed the pillars of a distinguished academic career.

Yet this accounts for only one avenue explored by a most engaging mind. Exhibiting the characteristics of the ninth-century polymaths often lauded in his own classes, Contreni has likewise branched out in other directions over the years. Building upon his early work with the Laon manuscripts (one of which appeared in a facsimile edition through his efforts), he brought novel attention to the now-familiar figures of Martianus Hiberniensis, John Scottus Eriugena, and Haimo of Auxerre, while also highlighting Irish contributions to Carolin-gian culture. Picking up those threads, a number of studies on computus, Bede's scientific works, the school of Auxerre, monastic culture, and even the intriguing *Visio Baronti* followed. All along the way, however, Contreni never lost sight of the fact that for the Carolingians, the most important text of all was the Bible. Early medieval literary culture *was* biblical culture, and to study manuscripts remained the surest route to understanding the scholars who produced them—core recognitions that have long served him as a reliable compass. The resulting body of scholarship has ensured that for experienced and novice scholars alike, Contreni's works—the insightful and wide-ranging essay in the *New Cambridge Medieval History* comes immediately to mind—have become standard reading for those wishing to learn more about the Carolingian intellectual revival.

It is therefore no small task to recount the quantity, quality, and influence of John Contreni's accomplishments to date. Widely known and respected for his many works on early medieval literary, intellectual, and political culture, he has made a lasting impression over the past four decades, particularly in the realm of manuscript studies. Indeed, the Medieval Academy of America clearly recognized this influence when he was elected a Fellow of the Academy in 2003. While the essays offered here thus feature a number of new perspectives on themes of enduring consequence to early medievalists, those same scholars may find the accompanying select bibliography of Contreni's published works of great interest as well. Quite aside from the fact that this register represents only a portion of his published work (which to date includes six books and editions, forty-eight articles and chapters, eighteen notes, seventy-three reference-work entries, thirty-five invited addresses, thirty-six conference presentations, and no fewer than 143 book reviews!), one clearly discerns in it a robust curiosity. In addressing a variety of topics reflecting Contreni's own wide-ranging interests, the following essays, hailing from leading and emerging historians from the United States, Canada, England, France, and Germany, seek to highlight those familiar intellectual currents: Authors and Audi-ences, Schools and Scholars, Context and Connections, and Visions and Voices.

Fellows and friends have often remarked how the trajectory of John Contreni's career very much mirrored that of Richard E. Sullivan, who served as department head, dean, and provost at Michigan State University. A career is one's own, of course, but the similarities would nonetheless be hard to miss. Contreni's leadership roles at Purdue University therefore ought to come as little surprise. Whether as a professor, head of the Department of History, dean of the Graduate School, and the first Justin S. Morrill Dean of the College of Liberal Arts, or simply as a good friend, he has earned a reputation on and off the Purdue campus for service, generosity, perspicacity, and a genuine desire to show how much the seemingly esoteric side of medieval history has to offer as we strive to understand our own place in the modern world. But perhaps most telling of all, John has excelled in the earnest imparting of wisdom. His inclusion among the inaugural cohort of faculty registered in Purdue's Book of Great Teachers will long bear witness to his dedication to both undergraduates and (as we with gratitude attest) his graduate students.

It is our hope that in celebrating the accomplishments of so distinguished a figure as he prepares for a well-earned retirement (getting back to *Field & Stream* and *Outdoor Life*, no doubt), this volume may also bring to light even more discoveries about an age illumined so well and for so long by John himself.

Acknowledgments

Our sincere thanks go to the volume's contributors for their earnest and timely participation in this endeavor, and to those presiders, presenters, and attendees at the sessions and dinner in John's honor at the 2008 International Congress on Medieval Studies. We would also like to express our appreciation to those who have so readily contributed to this effort, including Patricia Hollahan of Medieval Institute Publications, Amy Livingstone, Gordie Thompson, Karl Morrison, Kathleen Mitchell, John Lepley, and the College of Arts and Sciences and Department of History at Indiana State University. Finally, we owe a special debt of gratitude to Amy Chandler and Maggie Dalrymple for their patience, support, and steadfast encouragement in seeing this project through to its joyful conclusion.

Abbreviations

CCCM	Corpus Christianorum Continuatio Mediaevalis
CCSL	Corpus Christianorum Series Latina
CSEL	Corpus scriptorum ecclesiasticorum Latinorum
MGH	Monumenta Germaniae Historica
Auct. ant.	Auctores antiquissimi
Capit.	Capitularia regum francorum
Capit. episc.	Capitula episcoporum
Conc.	Concilia
Epp.	Epistolae (in Quart)
Epp. sel.	Epistolae selectae
Fontes iuris	Fontes iuris Germanici antiqui in usum scholarum separatim editi
Formulae	Formulae Merowingici et Karolini aevi
Poetae	Poetae Latini medii aevi
Schriften	Schriften der Monumenta Germaniae Historica
SS	Scriptores (in Folio)
SS rer. Germ.	Scriptores rerum Germanicarum in usum scholarum separatim editi
SS rer. Merov.	Scriptores rerum Merovingicarum
PL	Patrologia Latina

John J. Contreni
A Select Bibliography
1972–2012

1972

"A propos de quelques manuscrits de l'école de Laon au IXᵉ siècle: Découvertes et problèmes." *Le Moyen Âge* 78:6–39.

"The Formation of Laon's Cathedral Library in the Ninth Century." *Studi medievali*, 3rd ser., 13: 919–39. Reprinted in *Carolingian Learning, Masters and Manuscripts*, ch. 13.

1973

"Le Formulaire de Laon: Source pour l'histoire de l'école de Laon au début du Xᵉ siècle." *Scriptorium* 27:21–29. Translated and revised in *Learning and Culture in Carolingian Europe: Letters, Numbers, Exegesis, and Manuscripts*, ch. 10.

1974

"A New Manuscript of the *Sermones de Epistolis Dominicarum* of Guilelmus Peraldus." *Manuscripta* 18:166–72.

1975

"Haimo of Auxerre, Abbot of *Sasceium*, (Cessy-les-Bois), and a New Sermon on 1 John V, 4–10." *Revue bénédictine* 85:303–20. Reprinted in *Carolingian Learning, Masters and Manuscripts*, ch. 7.

1976

"The Biblical Glosses of Haimo of Auxerre and John Scottus Eriugena." *Speculum* 51:411–34.

"A Note on the Attribution of a Martianus Capella Commentary to Martinus Laudunensis." In *Catalogus translationum et commentariorum: Medieval and Renaissance Latin Translations and Commentaries*, ed. Paul Oskar Kristellar, F. Edward Cranz, and Virginia Brown, 3:451–52. 9 vols. to date. Washington, DC: Catholic University Press of America, 1960–2011.

"The Study and Practice of Medicine in Northern France during the Reign of Charles the Bald." In *Studies in Medieval Culture VI and VII*, ed. John R. Sommerfeldt and E. Rozanne Elder, 43–54. Kalamazoo, MI: Medieval Institute Publications. Revised and expanded version published as "Masters and Medicine in Northern France during the Reign of Charles the Bald." In *Charles the Bald: Court and Kingdom*, ed. Margaret Gibson and Janet Nelson, 330–50. British Archaeological Reports, International Series, 101. Oxford: British Archaeological Reports, 1981. Revised version published ibid., 2nd rev. ed., 267–82. London: Variorum, 1990.

"Three Carolingian Texts Attributed to Laon: Reconsiderations." *Studi medievali*, 3rd ser., 17:797–813.

[Translated]. Pierre Riché. *Education and Culture in the Barbarian West, Sixth through Eighth Centuries*. Columbia: University of South Carolina Press.

1977

"The Irish Colony at Laon during the Time of John Scottus Eriugena." In *Jean Scot Érigène et l'histoire de la Philosophie*, ed. René Roques, 59–67. Paris: Centre national de la recherche scientifique. Reprinted in *Carolingian Learning, Masters and Manuscripts*, ch. 8.

"A New Description of the Lost Laon Manuscript of the *Collectio Hispana Gallica*." *Bulletin of Medieval Canon Law* 7:85–89. Reprinted in *Carolingian Learning, Masters and Manuscripts*, ch. 14.

1978

The Cathedral School of Laon from 850 to 930: Its Manuscripts and Masters. Münchener Beiträge zur Mediävistik und Renaissance-Forschung 29. Munich: Arbeo-Gesellschaft. John Nicholas Brown Prize of the Medieval Academy of America, 1982.

1980

"Inharmonious Harmony: Education in the Carolingian World." *Annals of Scholarship: Metastudies of the Humanities and Social Sciences* 1:81–96. Reprinted in *Carolingian Learning, Masters and Manuscripts*, ch. 4.

"Two Descriptions of the Lost Laon Copy of the *Collection of Saint-Maur.*" *Bulletin of Medieval Canon Law* 10:45–51. Reprinted in *Carolingian Learning, Masters and Manuscripts*, ch. 15.

1981

"John Scottus, Martin Hiberniensis, the Liberal Arts, and Teaching." In *Insular Latin Studies: Papers on Latin Texts and Manuscripts of the British Isles, 550–1066*, ed. Michael Herren, 23–44. Toronto: Pontifical Institute of Mediaeval Studies. Revised version printed in *Carolingian Learning, Masters and Manuscripts*, ch. 6.

1982

"Codices Pseudo-Isidoriani: The Provenance and Date of Paris, B. N., lat. 9629." *Viator* 13:1–14. Reprinted in *Carolingian Learning, Masters and Manuscripts*, ch. 16.

"The Irish in the Western Carolingian Empire (According to James F. Kenney and Bern, Burgerbibliothek 363)." In *Die Beudeutung der Iren für Mission und Kultur in frühmittelalterlichen Europa bis ins 11. Jahrhundert*, ed. Heinz Löwe, 2:758–98. 2 vols. Stuttgart: Klett-Cotta. Reprinted in *Carolingian Learning, Masters and Manuscripts*, ch. 9.

1983

"Carolingian Biblical Studies." In *Carolingian Essays: Patristics and Early Medieval Thought*, ed. Uta-Renate Blumenthal, 71–98. Washington, DC: Catholic University of America Press. Reprinted in *Carolingian Learning, Masters and Manuscripts*, ch. 5.

1984

"The Carolingian Renaissance." In *Renaissances before the Renaissance: Cultural Revivals of Late Antiquity and the Middle Ages*, ed. Warren Treadgold, 59–74, 184–91, 213–16. Stanford: Stanford University Press. Reprinted in *Carolingian Learning, Masters and Manuscripts*, ch. 3.

"Introduction." In *Codex Laudunensis 468: A Ninth-Century Guide to Virgil, Sedulius, and the Liberal Arts*, 5–25. Armarium Codicum Insignium 3. Turnhout: Brepols.

1986

"The Irish Contribution to the European Classroom." In *Proceedings of the Seventh International Congress of Celtic Studies Held at Oxford, from 10th to 15th July, 1983*, ed. D. Ellis Evans, John G. Griffith, E. M. Jope, 79–90. Oxford: D. Ellis Evans. Reprinted in *Carolingian Learning, Masters and Manuscripts*, ch. 10.

[Contributor]. *Insular and Anglo-Saxon Illuminated Manuscripts: An Iconographic Catalogue, c. A.D. 625 to 1100*. Compiled and ed. Thomas H. Ohlgren. New York: Garland.

1987

"From Polis to Parish." In *Religion, Culture and Society in the Early Middle Ages*, ed. Noble and Contreni, 155–64.

"Preface." In *Religion, Culture and Society in the Early Middle Ages*, ed. Noble and Contreni, 13–17.

[Edited, with Thomas F. X. Noble]. *Religion, Culture and Society in the Early Middle Ages: Studies in Honor of Richard E. Sullivan*. Kalamazoo, MI: Medieval Institute Publications.

[Review essay] "Prosopography of Medieval Elites." *Medieval Prosopography* 8:73–80.

1988

[Plenary address] "Learning in the Early Middle Ages." Twenty-third International Congress on Medieval Studies, Medieval Institute, Western Michigan University, Kalamazoo, MI, 6 May.

1989

"The Carolingian School: Letters from the Classroom." In *Giovanni Scoto nel suo tempo: L'Organizzazione del sapere in età carolingia*, Atti del XXIV Convegno storico internazionale Todi, 11–14 ottobre 1987, 81–111. Spoleto: Centro italiano di studi sull'alto medioevo. Reprinted in *Carolingian Learning, Masters and Manuscripts*, ch. 11.

"Education and Learning in the Early Middle Ages: New Perspectives and Old Problems." *International Journal of Social Education* 4:9–25. Reprinted in *Carolingian Learning, Masters and Manuscripts*, ch. 2.

"The Egyptian Origins of the Irish: Two Ninth-Century Notes." in *St. Kilian: 1300 Jahre Martyrium der Frankenapostel*, ed. Klaus Wittstadt, 51–54. Würzburger Diözesan-Geschichtsblätter 51. Würzburg: Bistum Würzburg. Reprinted in *Carolingian Learning, Masters and Manuscripts*, ch. 17.

[Bibliography] "Medieval Studies to A.D. 1200." In *New Catholic Encyclopedia*. Vol. 18, *Supplement*, 291–302. Washington, DC: Catholic University of America Press.

1990

"The Tenth Century: The Perspective from the Schools." In *Haut Moyen Âge: Culture, éducation et société*; Études offertes à Pierre Riché, ed. Claude Lepelley et al., 379–87. La Garenne-Colombes: Éditions européennes Erasme. Reprinted in *Carolingian Learning, Masters and Manuscripts*, ch. 12.

1991

"Haimo of Auxerre's Commentary on Ezechiel." In *L'École carolingienne d'Auxerre de Murethach à Remi, 830–908*, ed. Dominique Iogna-Prat, Colette Jeudy, and Guy Lobrichon, 229–42. Paris: Beauchesne.

1992

Carolingian Learning, Masters and Manuscripts. Collected Studies Series CS363. Aldershot: Variorum, 1992.

"Learning in the Early Middle Ages." In *Carolingian Learning, Masters and Manuscripts*, 1–21.

1995

"The Carolingian Renaissance: Education and Literary Culture." In *The New Cambridge Medieval History*. Vol. 2, *c. 700–c. 900*, ed. Rosamond McKitterick, 709–57. Cambridge: Cambridge University Press.

"Images of Power and Culture in the Carolingian and Monastic Periods from the Eighth to the Twelfth Centuries." In *Creating French Culture: Treasures from the Bibliothèque nationale de France*, ed. Marie-Hélène Tesnière and Prosser Gifford, 3–16. New Haven, CT: Yale University Press.

"The Pursuit of Knowledge in Carolingian Europe." In *"The Gentle Voices of Teachers": Aspects of Learning in the Carolingian Age*, ed. Richard E. Sullivan, 106–41. Columbus: Ohio State University Press. Reprinted in *Learning and Culture in Carolingian Europe: Letters, Numbers, Exegesis, and Manuscripts*, ch. 2.

Bibliography: "Church History and Intellectual History, 300–1050." In *The American Historical Association's Guide to Historical Literature*, 3rd ed., ed. Mary Beth Norton and Pamela Gerardi, 1:678–82. 2 vols. New York: Oxford University Press.

1996

"Carolingian Biblical Culture." In *Iohannes Scottus Eriugena: The Bible and Hermeneutics*, ed. Gerd Van Riel, Carlos Steel, and James McEvoy, 1–23. Ancient and Medieval Philosophy, De-Wulf-Mansion Centre, Series 1 20. Leuven: Leuven University Press. Reprinted in *Learning and Culture in Carolingian Europe: Letters, Numbers, Exegesis, and Manuscripts*, ch. 7.

1997

"From Benedict's *Rule* to Charlemagne's Renaissance: Monastic Education in the Early Middle Ages—and Today." *American Benedictine Review* 48, no. 2:186–98.

[Edited, with Pádraig P. Ó'Néill]. *Glossae divinae historiae: The Biblical Glosses of John Scottus Eriugena*. Millennio Medievale 1, Testi 1. Florence: SISMEL: Edizioni del Galluzzo. Sections 7f and 10 revised and reprinted in *Learning and Culture in Carolingian Europe: Letters, Numbers, Exegesis, and Manuscripts*, ch. 6.

[Review Essay] "An Eriugenian Triptych": John Scottus, *Iohannis Scotti Eriugenae Periphyseon (De divisione naturae) Liber Quartus*, ed. Édouard Jeauneau, with the assistance of Mark Zier, English translation by John J. O'Meara and I. P. Sheldon-Williams, Scriptores Latini Hiberniae 13 (Dublin: Institute for Advanced Studies, 1995); John Scottus, *Iohannis Scotti seu Eriugenae Periphyseon Liber Primus. Editionem nouam a suppositiciis quidem additamentis purgatam, ditatam uero appendice in qua uicissitudines operis synoptice exhibentur*, ed. Édouard A. Jeauneau, Corpus Christianorum Continuatio Mediaevalis 161 (Turnhout: Brepols, 1996); Édouard Jeauneau and Paul Edward Dutton, *The Autograph of Eriugena*, Corpus Christianorum, Autograph Media Aevi 3 (Turnhout: Brepols, 1996). *Peritia: Journal of the Medieval Academy of Ireland* 11:373–78.

2002

"'By lions, bishops are meant; by wolves, priests': History, Exegesis, and the Carolingian Church in Haimo of Auxerre's *Commentary on Ezechiel*." *Francia: Forschungen zur westeuropäischen Geschichte* 29:29–56. Reprinted in *Learning and Culture in Carolingian Europe: Letters, Numbers, Exegesis, and Manuscripts*, ch. 3.

"Charlemagne and the Carolingians: The View from North America." *Cheiron: Materiali e strumenti di aggiornamento storiografico* 37:111–54.

"Counting, Calendars, and Cosmology: Numeracy in the Early Middle Ages." In *Word, Image, Number: Communication in the Middle Ages*, ed. John J. Contreni and Santa Casciani, 43–83. Micrologus' Library 8. Florence:

SISMEL: Edizioni del Galluzzo. Reprinted in *Learning and Culture in Carolingian Europe: Letters, Numbers, Exegesis, and Manuscripts*, ch. 5.

"John Scottus and Bede." In *History and Eschatology in John Scottus Eriugena and His Time*, ed. James McEvoy and Michael Dunne, 91–140. Ancient and Medieval Philosophy, De Wulf-Mansion Centre, Series 1 30. Leuven: Leuven University Press. Reprinted in *Learning and Culture in Carolingian Europe: Letters, Numbers, Exegesis, and Manuscripts*, ch. 8.

"Reading Gregory of Tours in the Middle Ages." In *The World of Gregory of Tours*, ed. Kathleen Mitchell and Ian Wood, 419–34. Cultures, Beliefs and Traditions: Medieval and Early Modern Peoples 8. Leiden: Brill.

[Edited, with Santa Casciani]. *Word, Image, Number: Communication in the Middle Ages*. Micrologus' Library 8. Florence: SISMEL: Edizioni del Galluzzo.

2003

"'Building Mansions in Heaven': The *Visio Baronti*, Archangel Raphael, and a Carolingian King." *Speculum* 78:673–706. Reprinted in *Learning and Culture in Carolingian Europe: Letters, Numbers, Exegesis, and Manuscripts*, ch. 1.

"Glossing the Bible in the Early Middle Ages: Theodore and Hadrian of Canterbury and John Scottus (Eriugena)." In *The Study of the Bible in the Middle Ages*, ed. Celia Chazelle and Burton Van Name Edwards, 19–38. Medieval Church Studies 3. Turnhout: Brepols.

"What Was Emperor Augustus Doing at a Carolingian Banquet (Anth. Lat.² 719ᶠ)?" *Rheinisches Museum für Philologie*, n.s., 146, nos. 3–4:372–94. Reprinted in *Learning and Culture in Carolingian Europe: Letters, Numbers, Exegesis, and Manuscripts*, ch. 9.

2005

"Bede's Scientific Works in the Carolingian Age." In *Bède le Vénérable: Entre tradition et postérité/The Venerable Bede: Tradition and Posterity*," ed. Stéphane Lebecq, Michel Perrin, and Olivier Szerwiniack, 247–59. Lille: CEGES— Université Charles-de-Gaulle—Lille 3. Reprinted in *Learning and Culture in Carolingian Europe: Letters, Numbers, Exegesis, and Manuscripts*, ch. 4.

2006

"'And Even Today': Carolingian Monasticism and the *Miracula sancti Germani* of Heiric of Auxerre." In *Medieval Monks and Their World: Ideas and Realities, Studies in Honor of Richard E. Sullivan*, ed. David Blanks, Michael Frassetto, and Amy Livingstone, 35–48. Brill's Series in Church History 25. Leiden: Brill.

[Remembrance, with Karl F. Morrison and Thomas F. X. Noble]. "Richard E. Sullivan." *Speculum* 81:976–78.

2011

"Gregorius Turonensis." In *Catalogus translationum et commentariorum: Medieval and Renaissance Latin Translations and Commentaries*, vol. 9, ed. Virginia Brown, 9:55–71. Washington, DC: Catholic University of America Press.

Learning and Culture in Carolingian Europe: Letters, Numbers, Exegesis, and Manuscripts. Variorum Collected Studies Series. Farnham: Ashgate.

2012

"'Old Orthodoxies Die Hard': Herwagen's *Bridferti Ramesiensis Glossae.*" *Peritia: Journal of the Medieval Academy of Ireland* 22/23:15–52.

"The Patristic Legacy to c. 1000." In *The New Cambridge Medieval History of the Bible.* Vol. 2, *From 600 to 1450*, ed. Richard Marsden and E. Ann Matter, 505–35. Cambridge: Cambridge University Press.

"Reckoning Time at Reichenau and St Gall (Computistics)." In *Carolingian Culture at Reichenau and St. Gall: Tours of the Libraries of Reichenau and St. Gall.* UCLA Digital Library http://www.stgallplan.org/en/tours_time.html

In Press

"Getting to Know Virgil in the Carolingian Age: The *Vita Publii Virgilii.*" In *Rome and Christianity in the Early Middle Ages: Studies in Honor of Thomas F. X. Noble*, ed. Valerie Garver and Own Phelan.

"Gregory's Works in the High Medieval and Early Modern Ages." In *A Companion to Gregory of Tours*, ed. Alexander Callender Murray. Leiden: Brill.

"Learning for God: Education in the Carolingian Age." In *Sciences in the Carolingian World*, ed. Bruce S. Eastwood. Studies in the Early Middle Ages 11. Leiden: Brill.

"'Let Schools Be Established . . . ' For What? The Meaning of *Admonitio Generalis*, cap. 70 (*olim* 72)." In *Music in the Carolingian World: Witnesses to a Metadiscipline*, ed. Graeme Boone. Columbus: Ohio State University Press.

"Women in the Age of Eriugena." In *Eriugena and Creation*, ed. Willemien Otten and Michael I. Allen.

PART 1

Authors and Audiences

CHAPTER 1

Reading Roman History in the Early Middle Ages

ROSAMOND McKITTERICK

Early medieval manuscripts of the *Chronicon* of Eusebius, translated and continued by Jerome, present a dramatic visual confirmation of the triumph of Rome. The text, which runs from Abraham to AD 378, is set out in columns, with the years since Abraham and Olympiads as well as regnal years of kings, judges, archons, and emperors. Events such as wars, the deaths of rulers, the fall of Troy, or the birth of Christ are recorded on a highly selective basis in the relevant column, whether pertaining to Medes, Persians, Assyrians, Hebrews, Scythians, the Argives (or Greeks of Argos), Athenians, Macedonians, or Egyptians. The method creates marvelous juxtapositions, such as the coincident careers of the judge Deborah and King Midas. The Latins first appear after the sack of Troy, and the provinces of Rome and the Romans become increasingly prominent from the foundation of the city and Romulus and Remus onwards. Once Titus has destroyed Jerusalem in AD 71 even the Hebrews' column, the final one to remain alongside the Romans after the fading of all the other empires, disappears and thereafter the story is entirely centered on the Roman world into which events of Christian history are integrated. These are set against a background of a succession of Roman emperors and their campaigns. The historical map created by the extraordinary layout of this text was apparently taken over from the late antique exemplars, or so comparison between a fifth-century copy such as Oxford, Bodleian Library, Auct.T.II.26 and ninth-century manuscripts of Eusebius-Jerome's *Chronicon* such as Leiden, Universiteitsbibliotheek, MS Scaliger 14 or Oxford, Merton College Library, MS Coxe 315 would suggest.[1] Even so, scribes brought their own perceptions of the importance of particular aspects of a text to the task of copying. The moment of Troy's fall, for example, takes up almost the entire page in MS Scaliger 14, a book possibly owned by Charlemagne himself. This book's scribe was also so concerned with Rome's history that he extended the *Chronicon* with detail from Eutropius's *Breviarium ab urbe condita* and continued his brief record of events up to 645. Other Carolingian manuscripts of the *Chronicon*, such as Leiden, Universiteitsbibliotheek, Voss. lat. Q.110, display Troy's fall in a similarly emphatic fashion.

Manuscripts of Jerome-Eusebius's *Chronicon* like Scaliger 14, Leiden, Voss. lat. Q.110, or Merton College's Coxe 315 offer an obvious reflection of a reader's response to his exemplar, even if only at the level of its reproduction, rearrangement, and extension into later periods for further readers. These books symbolize one of my concerns in this essay, namely, the potential influence on any reader a particular copy of a text can exert and how one might be able to reconstruct the processes as well as the consequences of reading history in the early Middle Ages. But the peculiar presentation of Roman history within the *Chronicon* of Eusebius-Jerome signals my principal theme, namely, the evidence it offers of its authors' own reading of Roman history and their subsequent presentation of it in order to integrate Christian history into its wider historical and cultural context, offered with a strong moral about the fate of human vainglory to a wider audience. Because so many of my examples, whether of compilations and compositions of texts or of manuscript copies thereof are from the Carolingian period, I shall also consider the significance and some of the consequences of this concentration of interest in Roman history in the late eighth and the ninth centuries. I offer it all as a heartfelt gesture of admiration, affection, and gratitude to John Contreni for his friendship, his scholarship, and his unfailing generosity to fellow scholars.

What in any case do I mean by Roman history, given that I have started with the possibly unexpected *Chronicon* of Jerome-Eusebius rather than the classical narratives of Roman history by Caesar, Livy, Pompeius Trogus, and the *Epitome* of Justinus, Sallust, Suetonius, Tacitus, Velleius Paterculus, and Virgil, and the later epitomes and continuations by Florus, Aurelius Victor, Eutropius, and the *Scriptores historiae Augustae*? Certainly the events recounted in the works of these classical authors, not least Virgil's epic narrative of Aeneas's flight from Troy and the foundation of Rome, became essential elements of the understanding of the classical past in the early Middle Ages. But Roman history, as suggested by the *Chronicon* of Eusebius-Jerome and its continuations, was also incorporated into histories of the early Christian church, including Eusebius-Rufinus's *Historia ecclesiastica* and the *Historia ecclesiastica tripartita* of Cassiodorus-Epiphanius, into Josephus's Jewish wars and Jewish antiquities written in Flavian Rome, and into Orosius's seven books of history against the pagans. In the early Middle Ages, especially in the Carolingian period, Rome's past was integrated into universal chronicles such as those of Frechulf of Lisieux, Ado of Vienne, and Regino of Prüm.[2] These post-classical texts inherited a strong understanding of the complexity and diversity of Rome's past, in which religion played a crucial role. They intertwine Roman sacred and Roman secular and imperial history. On all these—knowledge of them and their circulation in western Europe on the evidence of extant manuscripts and references in both library catalogues and the writings of eighth- and ninth-century authors—I have commented elsewhere.[3] Many other categories of text which offer distinctive perspectives on the history of Rome could be added, such as historical martyrologies or compilations of Roman and canon law,[4] though study of them and their implications for the reading and reception of Roman history in the early Middle Ages will have to wait for another occasion.

Although evidence of reading and readers in the early Middle Ages, and indeed perhaps in any period, is notoriously difficult to assemble, there are some obvious categories of evidence to consider.

Annotations and Glosses

First, there are annotations, where scribbles by a reader signal attention to and even engagement with the text. The Palatine Virgil may serve as an example from many possible. It is a late fifth-century copy of the *Aeneid*, *Eclogues*, and *Georgics* of Virgil, annotated probably at the Rhineland monastery of Lorsch in the first half of the ninth century and subsequently, ca. 850 in a milieu, perhaps Lyon, which used proto-Romance-flavored Latin as well as Old High German.[5] The codex contains three series of annotations and corrections from late antiquity and the Carolingian period in ink. Over seven hundred further glosses made in drypoint in the middle of the ninth century were discovered twenty years ago by Michael McCormick. These were written in both Tironian notes, the antique system of shorthand maintained by the Franks, and in Caroline minuscule, and in Latin and Old High German. The glosses are primarily lexical in character; they simplify the text in order to explain it. Words are provided with synonyms or an etymologically related word, for example, folio 83v *opaca* is glossed 'obscura' (*Aeneid* 2.725). Constructions are clarified with the addition of modifiers, and some proper names are labeled *homo, mons, insula, fluvius*, or otherwise explained: thus the *Argivae* are glossed as "Greci," *Xanthi* is a "flumen," *Eryx* is glossed "rex," *Cassandra* is "Troiana," *Pyrrus* is "filius Ahcillis [sic!]," and so on. A few glosses are grammatical. The majority of the glosses appear to be spontaneous.

There is always the possibility that even the apparently spontaneous glosses had themselves been copied from some other exemplar by a scribe who recognized their usefulness as aids in the process of reading. There is no consensus at the moment about the question of whether early medieval glossaries are new creations which occasionally make use of an ancient source, but their very existence seems to be more than simply a fascinating vehicle for the transmission of knowledge.[6] They are also vital evidence for the recognition of the demands made by reading texts from different cultural milieux and the challenges they offered to understanding. The most extensive glossary from the Carolingian period is the *Liber glossarum*, from the scriptorium producing "a-b" script. But some of the palatine Virgil's Carolingian glosses are clearly the consequence of consulting Servius's commentary on Virgil. Because of the light the glosses throw on ninth-century readings of both Servius and Virgil, this does require some comment here.

The grammarian Servius wrote his commentary on Virgil's poetry in the fourth century. Servius himself was one of a long line of commentators, but he supposedly based his own work in particular on an earlier but lost commentary by the grammarian Donatus, some of which has been identified in a seventh- or eighth-century edition of Servius which expanded Servius's text with material from Donatus. Servius's commentary takes the standard classical commentary form of a lemma (a word or phrase) and comments thereon on grammatical issues, aspects of rhetoric and poetics, and the cultural context. The commentary self-evidently has an ideology of its own as well as being a quarry for readers "to excavate for use in constructing their own readings of the texts."[7] Commentaries can work to add support for a reader's own understanding. They may themselves have possessed *auctoritas* in the mind of the reader, though modern scholars who have worked extensively on Virgil commentaries have suggested that these commentaries could also be rejected if they did not suit. Yet they also potentially add greatly to a reader's knowledge, because of the constant references to other authors' use of similar words and phrases, or the citing of authorities on particular points. Thus reading a text with commentary or glosses adds not only to the readers' intellectual arsenal but also expands their mental horizons and engages them in a series of dialogues with the past. Servius's commentary is also a didactic text, offering basic explanations of words as well as more sophisticated observations. We can probably envisage it being used alongside Virgil as well as in its own right, either directly or indirectly through its extensive use by the seventh-century Spanish encyclopedist Isidore of Seville in his *Etymologiae*.

Servius was known in England in Aldhelm's day, and the earliest manuscript of the commentary is in fact a fragment written in a southwest English script dating from the first half of the eighth century, but with associations with Fulda. The transmission history of the Servius commentary is intricate, with Carolingian copies of both the seventh-century revised version from Fulda, Fleury,

Laon, and Tours on the *Aeneid*, and of the so-called pure Servius, also primarily on portions of the *Aeneid*. The multiplicity of variant readings and families have greatly upset editors in the traditional mold, whereas precisely because they differ, all these manuscripts offer the potential for understanding the reading of the *Aeneid* in the ninth century by individuals at many different levels. The Laon codex, Bibliothèque municipale, MS 468, with commentary on the *Bucolics* and the *Aeneid*, is a case in point. In his magnificent facsimile edition of this codex, John Contreni identified it as a schoolbook written in the second half of the ninth century, designed to introduce students to certain Latin texts, and compiled under the direction of the Laon schoolmaster Martin the Scot of Laon, who also contributed to the copying of the text.[8] The copying itself seems to have been part of the didactic process of learning to write. Martin's interventions are most often corrective or clarificatory, not least in the filling in of words or syllables the copyist himself could not read in the exemplar, the spacing of words on the page, adjusting abbreviations and orthography, and adding vernacular equivalents for words on occasion. Martin's contributions are at their densest in the introduction to the life and works of Virgil and on the origins of the Trojans. Contreni suggested that the exemplar (probably from Soissons) for the Laon copy of the glosses was filled with Tironian notes as well as some insular abbreviation symbols that the baffled apprentice scribe did not understand. Many glosses are explicitly taken over from Servius but others, while following his method, are independent. The glosses to the *Aeneid* start on folio 35v and are very basic in character. They explain that the man who is the subject is Aeneas, that Troy is a city in Ilium, that Latium is in Italy, that the ancient city (*urbs antiqua*) is Rome, that Carthage is in Africa, and so on. The compiler had set himself the task of enabling the reader to understand not only Roman history but also the cultural context. The codex includes a short vita of Virgil and a two-page summary of the plot of the *Aeneid* at the beginning of the book. The life appears to be the *Vita Bernensis* at the beginning but also to have gathered added details from the Donatus *Life* and from Jerome-Eusebius's references to Virgil in the *Chronicon*.[9] The compiler explains that Virgil intended to imitate Homer and praise Augustus. As further reading aids, glossaries of sibyls, magi, philosophers, gods, and goddesses are added.

Epitomes and Continuations

Further evidence for the reading of Roman history and its reflection of changing views of Roman antiquity and the history of the empire is provided by epitomes and continuations of authors such as those by Aurelius Victor and Eutropius, who rewrote the earlier sections in order to give them a particular twist. Jordanes's *Historia romana* in the sixth century, for example, wrote about "how the Roman empire began, how it grew, how it subjected virtually the whole world to its dominion, and how it continues to hang on to its hegemony (at least in pretense) even now . . . so that when you (the reader) understand the devastation of various nations you may long to be freed from all worldly tribulation and turn to God, who is true freedom."[10] Paul the Deacon's *Historia romana*, composed in the later eighth century, endeavored to establish Italy as the sacred, cultural, and historical center of Roman identity. He added substantially to his principal source, Eutropius, in order to make Christ and Emperor Augustus the focal point of the narrative, to stress military prowess as an imperial virtue. As Benjamin Cornford has argued, Paul's narrative makes it clear that the terminology and basic assumptions of late antique authors were still an important part of the conceptual framework for this eighth-century Italian writer.[11] Like Eutropius's *Breviarium*, Paul's *Historia romana* was adapted, paraphrased, and abbreviated in its turn. Bamberg, Staatsbibliothek, MS Hist. 3, for example, written in Halberstadt ca. 1000, is a wonderful example of histories of Rome gathered together, adapted, and paraphrased in a Latin containing many vernacular forms. It contains the *Epitome de Caesaribus* of ca. 400, the *Excidium Troiae*, Jordanes's *Romana* and *Getica*, the *Liber historiae francorum* of the eighth century which begins with the Trojan origins of the Franks, Bede's *Ecclesiastical History* and his world chronicle from the *De temporum ratione* (itself an adaptation and continuation of Eusebius-Jerome's *Chronicon*), and Paul the Deacon's *Historia romana* and the *Historia langobardorum*, as well as various texts to do with Alexander the Great. In particular, the paraphrased version of Paul the Deacon's *Historia romana* in this codex offers in part a Christian reading of Roman history and adds new material to integrate the history of the Christians. It also simplifies aspects of the politics and political structure of Rome and clarifies many points that the compiler presumably thought needed clarifying for his new audience.[12]

Textual Parallels

So far I have been discussing various manifestations in early medieval manuscripts of responses to a text and attempts to clarify it. One other obvious form of evidence for the reading of texts can also be mentioned, for it has received the most attention and documentation. This is the identification of textual parallels, whether in the form of a direct quotation or echoing of a phrase, unusual word, or even whole sentences or passages from other authors. Such textual parallels are ostensibly the most secure way of establishing that an author has had access to a particular text, but their usefulness is tempered of course by the possibility that the author is simply reproducing the quotation from another text which itself quotes the words or phrase in common. The use by grammarians of particular phrases by classical authors to illustrate particular points of grammar, or an author's citation by patristic authors and various medieval writers such as Cassiodorus and Isidore of Seville, can mean that early medieval authors may only be able to be credited with second- or even thirdhand knowledge of particular texts. There are many pitfalls in making claims for the knowledge of particular texts for particular authors, as those who have debated whether or not Bede, for example, knew Virgil or Pliny directly have discovered to their cost.[13] Textual parallels and verbal echoes may indicate, for example, that the author of the revised sections of the *Annales regni francorum* had read Livy,[14] that Ermold the Black was familiar with the *Aeneid*, and the creators and/or commissioners of the frescoes in the palace at Ingelheim described by Ermold had learned their history from the *Chronicon* of Jerome-Eusebius.[15] Further, Tacitus's *Germania* had been read by Rudolf of Fulda and by the author of the *Annales Fuldenses*. Manitius's efforts to find textual parallels between the works of Tacitus and Einhard, however, proved unconvincing, and could either be coincidence or even taken from other texts where similar combinations of words occur.[16]

Structure and Form

Reliance on such possible textual parallels to prove knowledge of a text may be misplaced, for it does not allow for the possibility of one text inspiring particular trains of thought, prompting emulation in a particular context, or leading to the adoption or adaption of the form of another text. In the last section of this study, therefore, I should like to turn to a different category of evidence for the reading of Roman history, namely texts that make ideological use of Roman history for new purposes. They themselves are inspired by Roman history and emulate it in both structure and an emphasis in subject matter in order to establish their own subjects within a particular cultural and ideological context. I propose to offer three brief examples (two of which I have explored in detail elsewhere), one from the sixth century and the others from the late eighth and ninth centuries. The first is Alcuin's poem on the destruction of Lindisfarne in 793. The second is in any case Roman history, for it is the *Liber pontificalis*, or *Book of the Popes*. The third is the *Vita Karoli*, or *The Life of Charlemagne*, by Einhard.[17]

Alcuin's poem on hearing of the Danish attack on Lindisfarne in June 793 has long been famous as one of the earliest records of a Danish raid on the British Isles. Although Alcuin is not an eyewitness, Mary Garrison has established how the poem enables us to assess the literary and theological repercussions of Viking violence. The poem is the only contemporary reference to the Lindisfarne raid, but it is also at one level singularly uninformative. Only a dozen or so of the

240 lines of the poem narrate the attack. These say only that a pagan warband arrived by ship from the ends of the earth and wreaked havoc in an unspecified holy place and possibly killed a few people. The remainder of the poem, however, is offered as a consolatory reflection on sin, perplexity about why God has permitted the disasters and suffering that has befallen mankind, the fall of many empires, and the workings of God's justice. The historical examples Alcuin invokes in his poem (Babylon, Persia, Alexander the Great, Rome now in ruins, Jerusalem destroyed by the Roman army of Titus, the Gothic invasion of Italy, the Huns ravaging in Gaul, the advance of the Saracens and conquest of Spain by the Arabs) are clearly inspired by the *Chronicon* of Jerome-Eusebius for the earlier empires, and no doubt the later references are due to the *Chronicon*'s continuation in chapter 66 of Bede's *De ratione temporum* as well. Highly allusive these historical examples may be, but they are crucial indicators of the way Alcuin's knowledge of history, including Roman history, has shaped his own perception of the inevitability of disaster in the long course of human history.[18] How the influence of Roman history might interact with other interpretative modes, such as biblical typology, among Carolingian scholars, would be an interesting topic to explore, though it is not feasible within the compass of this essay.[19]

The *Liber pontificalis*, the first and second edition of which was produced in the 540s and 550s respectively,[20] can be seen as a reaction to the dramatic political changes of the late fifth and early sixth centuries, largely written in the Ostrogothic period of rule in Italy. But this early portion of the *Liber pontificalis* also played a role in shaping perceptions of this period as a whole, and indeed, the entire history of the papacy, in subsequent years. As is well known, the text takes the form of a series of biographies, greatly varying in length and detail. The possible and most usual topics for the *Life* of each pope include a note of the pope's name, family, and origin, accompanied by the record of the secular rulers (emperors and/or consuls) in his time, and the precise length of his reign in years, months, and days. Where appropriate there follows a note of the career before he became pope and an account of the immediate context of his election (often with details of the opposition and rival candidates), details of his pontificate in terms of political actions, innovations to the liturgy or to canon law, gifts to the church and building activity, death and place of burial, and the ordinations he performed. The last entry is usually a note about the length of time the see remained vacant.

The models for the pope's lives and possible sources of information included in them have been conflated. Although there is every likelihood of the famous Calendar of 354 and early martyr narratives supplying information for the biographies of each pope,[21] the structural models are far more significant for our understanding of the text as a whole. Sacred and biblical biographical narrative and hagiography have customarily been regarded as the precedents for the format for the *Liber pontificalis*. I suggest that a far more influential model, both in structural and ideological terms, however, was Roman secular and serial biography, most especially the lives of the Caesars. The basic structure of each emperor's *Life* in Suetonius's *Lives of the Twelve Caesars* and even more strikingly of the texts that are effectively his continuators—the so-called *Kaisergeschichte*, Aurelius Victor's *De caesaribus*, and the *Historia Augusta*—are very similar to the structure of the lives in the *Liber pontificalis*. The *Kaisergeschichte*, for example, offered the emperor's name and origin, remarks on his life before he became emperor, the process of becoming emperor, including an account of rival contenders for the throne, his career as emperor (often including the uprisings of those who tried to oust the emperor), legislation, public and building works, death and burial, and the length of the reign.[22] His contemporary Eutropius, writing ca. 369, in his charting of Rome's progress towards dominance of the world was far more preoccupied with military affairs and the Senate. Yet his accounts of the procession of emperors also conform to the basic structure of the biography, with brief notes on their careers.[23] Similarly, the *Historia Augusta*, now thought to be the work of one author writing ca. 395, provides notes about the ancestry of each emperor and his life before he acceded to the imperial throne. His policies and the events of his reign, his personal habits and appearance, his death and honors received after death are all described. Not all these topics are given equal weight. Like Suetonius's *Lives of the Twelve Caesars*, gossip, anecdotes, and occasional documents are included. Rome is a constant theme of every *Life*, with its topography and buildings and the role of the Senate very prominent.

However different the development of themes by these authors, all ring the changes of a basic structure inherited from Suetonius. All wrote history in the form of serial biography and so did the authors of the *Liber pontificalis*. Unfortunately it cannot be proven that any of these texts were indeed available to the authors of the *Liber pontificalis*, for no manuscript witnesses place any of these texts in Rome in the sixth century. Nevertheless, the *Liber pontificalis* in itself and in its adoption of this form of history writing is a clear indication of knowledge of these classical and late antique texts.

The manuscript history of the *Liber pontificalis* raises further questions about the possible contexts of reception and adaptation of the text of the *Liber pontificalis*, not so much as a collection of biographies, or even as single lives, but as a composite text with a particular message about the history of Rome. There are many things that could and should be said about all the surviving manuscripts of the *Liber pontificalis* up to the beginning of the ninth century, but for my purposes in this essay I wish simply to make two obvious points. First, it looks as if the text of the *Liber pontificalis*, at least to ca. 735, was disseminated as a whole in the early Carolingian period. It may be that the Naples and Turin fragments of the late seventh century indicate that the whole text, as originally conceived in its second recension of the mid-sixth century, was also once transmitted in its entirety. As I have stressed elsewhere, the great majority of extant manuscripts, most of them from north of the Alps, go no further than *Life* 94 (Stephen II) and the circulation of later portions of the *Liber pontificalis* appears to have been very limited.[24] Secondly, the famous Lucca codex containing the *Liber pontificalis* also includes Eusebius-Rufinus's *Historia ecclesiastica*, Jerome-Gennadius's *De viris illustribus*, the chronicle of Isidore, and the historically arranged canon law collection known as the *Sanblasiana*, which includes the Symmachan apocrypha.[25] The *Liber pontificalis*, moreover, certainly emphasizes martyrs, but in this respect was locating Rome within the framework of history already provided by Jerome-Eusebius's *Chronicon*. Eusebius had interwoven the fortunes of Jews and Christians with the histories of the Assyrians, Persians, Greeks, and Romans, and the fortunes of secular rulers with religious events and ideas. Gradually the chronicle's narrative focuses on the Roman Empire and the summary of Christian events against the backdrop of a succession of emperors and their campaigns. The later association of the *Chronicon* and the *Liber pontificalis* in the Lucca codex, therefore, is an indication of the successful Christianization of the history of Rome. Later manuscript compilations that included portions of the *Liber pontificalis* offer still more reorientations of Roman and papal history by juxtaposition. Vienna, Österreichische Nationalbibliothek, cod. 473, for example, is a codex, written ca. 869, which embedded the *Liber pontificalis* in a history book about the Franks and the Carolingian rulers. Here it appears alongside the *Liber historiae francorum* and the *Annales regni francorum*, as well as an extract from Einhard's *Vita Karoli*.[26] The composition and dissemination of the *Liber pontificalis* in relation to other histories being written both at the time of the earliest redaction and in the period from which the earliest surviving manuscripts survive (that is, the sixth century on the one hand and the late eighth and early ninth centuries on the other) together corroborate the new and Christian historiographical context in which the *Liber pontificalis* was understood in both Lombard Italy and Francia. The new Roman history embodied in the *Liber pontificalis* could be harnessed to new ideological programs of historical writing.

Both in its original conception, therefore, as well as in its subsequent inclusion with other history texts in composite codices, the *Liber pontificalis* provides important indications of an added dimension to the possible reading and understanding of Roman history in the early Middle Ages. In relation to other histories written or available in the fifth and sixth centuries, the *Liber Pontificalis* offered an alternative history of Rome. The particular perception of the Christian past it reflects represents a determined effort to change its audience's understanding of Roman history. The history of Rome itself was Christianized and reshaped by transforming the historiographical genre of serial biography. As Christian, and Christianized, Roman history, the *Liber pontificalis* triggered many new associations and emulators.[27]

My third example is Einhard's *Vita Karoli*, which has proved to be the most seductive and influential of the representations of Charlemagne ever written. Einhard states in his preface that the *Vita Karoli* was composed in order to celebrate the king's life, his way of life (*vita et conversatio*), his many accomplishments (*res gestas*), and his deeds and habits (*actus et mores*).[28] Einhard was moved to write the *Life* "of the most splendid and greatest of all men" out of gratitude to the king he regarded as his *nutritor*. He risked criticism for his inadequacies, but this was to be preferred over neglecting the memory of one so great. Einhard stressed his personal knowledge of his subject (which can be corroborated from other sources)[29] but acknowledged its limits in that he knew too little about the king's early life to write about it.

Although this text is so well known, it may be helpful to repeat its principal topics here.[30] Einhard offers a brief account of how Pippin took the throne of Francia from the feeble Merovingians, whose last long-haired king was reduced to one estate and traveling in an oxcart. He then provides a summary of Charlemagne's conquests of Aquitainians, Lombards, Saxons, Saracens, Bretons, Bavarians, Slavs, Avars, and Danes. This is rounded out with an ethno-geographical account of the Carolingian Empire.[31] Einhard also echoes the emphasis of the final sections of the *Annales regni francorum* in his use of embassies and gifts Charlemagne received from other rulers in the far west, the south, and the east—from Ireland, the Asturias in Spain, the Persians, and Byzantium—to symbolize the king's power. He adds a description of the building work at Aachen, Mainz, Ingelheim, and Nijmegen that Charlemagne undertook to "improve and beautify the kingdom." Einhard is not only concerned with Charlemagne as mighty conqueror, however. He also offers a sketch of Charlemagne's character, his family life, his religious devotion, and his friendship with the pope. Einhard reports that the king knew Latin and Greek, had an interest in learning (his favorite reading allegedly being Augustine's *City of God*) and that he summoned scholars to him to serve as his teachers. The description of the king's slightly odd appearance is famous: he was very tall, had the beginnings of a paunch, a small head, and a surprisingly high voice. He loved swimming in the hot springs at Aachen, preferred to wear straightforward Frankish clothes, slept fitfully at night, and was fond of eating red meat. Even within the household he gave his attention to ruling and the administration of justice. Some reference is made to the king's attention to law and to the creation of a grammar of his mother tongue, as well as to the ruler's piety and devotion to St. Peter and Rome. The final section of the *Life* deals with arrangements for the succession, Charlemagne's last illness, portents of his death, and full details of his will, death, and burial.[32]

Einhard himself clearly exploited other written information and narrative sources such as the *Annales regni francorum* (in both its original and revised versions) to compile his account, as well as drawing on his memory of what he had seen or what he had been told. Those for whom he wrote would also have their own memories. The relationship between Einhard's own account and existing historical narrative and memories raises the crucial question, therefore, of how Einhard's text might have functioned and how it was intended initially to function. What kind of historical text was it if it was possibly never intended to serve as a comprehensive biography?

Einhard's inspiration from classical texts, which went far beyond emulating their Latin style, is well known, though this is not the place to engage fully with the great diversity of discussion about Einhard's *Vita Karoli* or Einhard himself, and he has become in any case the focus of renewed attention from a number of different perspectives.[33] These include the content of the text as historical evidence, Einhard's language and command of Latin so clearly influenced by Cicero,[34] his place in the "Carolingian Renaissance," Einhard's piety and personal position, his other writings,[35] and the dissemination of the *Vita Karoli* in manuscript and print throughout the Middle Ages and early modern period.[36]

It is clear that Einhard also followed, to a greater or lesser extent, the ideal form of history implied at various points by Cicero in his *Orator* and *De oratore*: chronological arrangement, geographical precision, a clear narrative of doings and sayings, an exposition of causes and consequences, biographical details about the character's life, and a notion of what the author himself approved.[37] By so doing, Einhard placed his *Vita Karoli* within the rhetorical traditions of the praise of famous men, panegyric and laudations. The Greek rhetor Menander had outlined the ideal topics to be addressed and these were subsequently adapted by such Roman rhetors as Quintilian and Cicero: fatherland, family, birth and upbringing, deeds (starting with war), bravery, justice and temperance, the king and his enemies, his battles, appearance, other successes, wisdom, philanthropy and justice, deeds in peace (including government), and concern for the succession.[38] Cicero specifies suitable topics to be employed in praise, such as family, good looks, bodily strength, resources, riches and other gifts of fortune, as well as mercy, justice, kindness, fidelity, and courage in common dangers. Einhard actually invokes the particular topics Cicero recommends for the panegyrist in his preface to the *Vita Karoli*, namely, the deeds (*facta*) and the achievements (*res gesta*).[39] These are inspirations from texts, but visual representations of Roman imperial power and achievements were also available, on such monuments as the

Arch of Titus and Trajan's column in Rome that Einhard presumably saw when he visited Rome in 806.[40]

Einhard's indebtedness to Suetonius's *Lives of the Twelve Caesars*, and especially the lives of Augustus, Nero, and Caligula has, thanks to Isaac Casaubon (1559–1614) long been recognized. These are not only verbal echoes but also direct borrowings in the discussion of the clothes, family, personal devotion to learning, linguistic abilities, and religious faith, the omens and portents before death, the last illness and death, the will, and even to the liking of a nap after lunch.[41] Suetonius was not the only Roman historian Einhard knew or had read in entirety (or at least in extracts and quotations). David Ganz has noted, for example, that Einhard used the rare word *dicaculus* (talkative) from the *Life* of Hadrian in the *Scriptores historiae Augustae*.[42] Given the existence of a Fulda or Hersfeld copy of the *Scriptores historiae Augustae* copied in the second quarter of the ninth century from a north Italian manuscript of the first half of the ninth century, it is possible that Einhard at some stage had direct access to this late antique set of imperial biographies as well. There is in fact a striking resemblance between the structure and topics covered in the *Vita Karoli* and those of the various lives in the *Scriptores historiae Augustae*, notably the *Life* of Hadrian: the spoof author Aelius Spartianus crammed it with information and incident. The *Life* starts out with an account of the original home and details about members of the family of Emperor Hadrian and refers to the autobiography of Hadrian himself as a source of information. It recounts Hadrian's birth, how he became devoted to Greek studies, entered military service, and became too fond of hunting. He was then trained for rulership within the army and the civil service, held the quaestorship, tribuneship, and praetorship and was legate in Lower Pannonia and governor of Syria. The text confirms Hadrian's legitimacy by stating that he was adopted by Trajan as his heir. As emperor "he devoted his attention to maintaining peace throughout the world . . . and to many communities [21.7] he gave Latin citizenship." Maintaining peace was a task that involved a great deal of war-making, from Britain to the land of the Parthians, and from Germany to Africa. Hadrian deified Trajan but out of modesty he refused the title of *pater patriae* for himself; he overcame domestic plots against him, paid special attention to justice, administration, and property, and was responsible for many public building works, especially in Rome. In Gaul and Britain in particular, Hadrian reformed the army, cultivated cordial relations with members of the Senate, and rewarded many who had served him well. His personal habits and character are described, his liking for camp picnics, his lack of ostentation in his dress, his excellent memory and intellectual abilities, his interest in poetry, literature, arithmetic, geometry, and painting, flute playing and singing, his debates with professors and philosophers, his love for the writings of Cato, Ennius, Caelius Antipater, Homer, and Plato, and his patronage of scholars and the arts. This chaotic biography concludes with Hadrian's arrangements for the succession, a description of him and his favorite palace at Tivoli, portents of his death, and the building of a temple for him after his death by Antoninus Pius, his heir.[43] Thus the role of the *Scriptores historiae Augustae* was far greater than that of a supplier of arcane vocabulary for Einhard: it appears to have acted as another source of ideas for the presentation of the life of an emperor.

A further source of inspiration for the initial composition of the *Vita Karoli* is the *Agricola* of Tacitus.[44] Too great a preoccupation with finding verbal echoes has led to this text being ignored hitherto in relation to Einhard's *Vita Karoli.* Not only was the *Agricola* (completed AD 97–98) a precursor of Suetonius, it also offers stronger parallels in its form and intention, for it offered what became the standard structure of a secular biography of a political and military leader as well as the demonstration of such a tribute as a postmortem prose panegyric.

As I have made a detailed case for this connection elsewhere, I shall here simply summarize the main points.[45] Tacitus was conscious of joining a tradition of writing about the works and ways, deeds and habits, of famous men ("clarorum virorum facta moresque"). He set out to write a vita of his father-in-law Gnaeus Julius Agricola out of filial piety.[46] Similarly, Einhard stated that he was writing about his lord and *nutritor* and that he had decided to describe "the life and character and many of the accomplishments of . . . Charles, that most outstanding and deservedly famous king." Tacitus had proceeded with a short account of Agricola's family, grandfathers, and father (ch. 4)[47] and his early career as a soldier in Britain (ch. 5). There is some personal detail offered in the account of his virtues and his marriage (ch. 6), while there is also the reporting of the murder of his mother, his loss of estates, and the problems of serving under different emperors (ch. 7). Agricola's governorship of Britain and military campaigns against the British tribes in the aftermath of Boudicca's rebellion form the bulk of the text (chs. 18–39). Agricola's British campaign, conducted year after year, can also be compared with Charlemagne's long drawn-out series of campaigns against the Saxons, the subjection of different groups or tribes, strategic tactics, taking of hostages, large-scale displacement and deportation of the people and their conversion, as well as the establishment of new Frankish garrisons.[48] Agricola spent the winter of AD 79 supervising the Romanization of the province, encouraging in particular the development of urban centers and the spread of Latin education. So too, in Einhard's portrait Charlemagne's conquest of the Saxons brings them within the Frankish fold. Tacitus's sections on the ethnography and history of Britain (chs. 10–12, 13–17) and his digression on the ethnography of Britain bear direct comparison with the two ethno-geographical digressions of Einhard on the peoples of the Baltic. So too the assimilation of Britain into the Roman empire, which is the mark of Agricola's success, can be compared with Einhard's summary of the territorial extent of Charlemagne's conquests and the peoples brought under Frankish rule.[49] The end of the text records Agricola's last illness and death and his will, in which Emperor Domitian was named as coheir. This again is paralleled by Einhard in his preservation of Charlemagne's will. Tacitus then added a description of Agricola's personal appearance and concluded with a lament for the loss of Agricola and how his deeds, whose story is told by Tacitus, will outlive death.[50]

The earliest extant manuscript of Tacitus's *Agricola* is associated with Fulda. It also contains Dictys Cretensis, *Bellum Troianum* as well as the *Germania* and *Agricola* of Tacitus, Formerly Jesi 8, and lost sight of during the Second World War, the codex is now in the Biblioteca nazionale centrali di Roma, cod. Vitt. Em. 1631.[51] Only the leaves containing the *Agricola* are Carolingian, and the script is usually dated to the second quarter of the ninth century, so it was presumably codex Vitt. Em. 1631's exemplar that was known to Einhard and may have inspired him.[52] This codex text and its exemplar, a third copy of which appears to have been the source of corrections, also suggest that the *Agricola* was once not so rare as it now seems.

The date of composition of Einhard's *Life of Charlemagne* is disputed. I maintain that if the context in which the text is to be understood, the purpose for which it was written, and its probable function are all considered, then an early date soon after the death of Charlemagne, perhaps by 817, makes the best sense.[53] The sheer power of the text and the degree to which it might have functioned effectively as a funerary oration, panegyric, and celebration of the king soon after his death needs to be acknowledged, not least because this all helps to explain so many of the emphases in the text.

Einhard, Alcuin, and the authors of the *Liber pontificalis*, therefore, like the many anonymous annotators and compilers of excerpts and historical miscellanies among their contemporaries, read Roman history. The evidence for their reading is in the task they initially set themselves and the form it took. In the case of writers of new historical works, the style in which they wrote them, the topics they chose to address, and the textual parallels and verbal echoes reflect their various sources of inspiration. The particular contours of Einhard's representation of Charlemagne in particular were the consequence of his reading of Roman history. The recognition of his implicit comparisons by other readers of Roman history would have enhanced their appreciation of the text, but it was not necessary for an understanding of it.[54] The survival of so many Carolingian manuscripts of Roman history, often the earliest copies now extant, as well as the other forms of evidence for reading Roman history, suggest rich and many-layered appreciation and perceptions of the Roman past in the early Middle Ages which merit still further investigation.

Notes

Earlier versions of this essay were presented at the University of Glasgow as the Edwards Lecture in Palaeography and Manuscript Studies 2008, the University of Cambridge to the Wolfson College Humanities Seminar 2008, and to the Centres d'études médiévales in Poitiers University in 2009. I am grateful to my audiences on these occasions as well as to the editors of this volume and the anonymous publisher's reader for their comments and suggestions and to Heda Padgen for her meticulous copyediting and helpful comments.

1. *Chronici canones: Latini verti, adauxit, ad sua tempora produxit S. Eusebius Hieronymus*, ed. John K. Fotheringham (London, 1923), and *Eusebius Werke*, vol. 7, pt. 1: *Die Chronik des Hieronymus*, ed. Rudolf Helm, 2nd ed., Die griechischen christlichen Schriftsteller der ersten drei Jahrhunderte 47 (Berlin, 1956), and the digital version of Oxford, Merton College Library, MS Coxe 315 available on the Internet at Early Manuscripts at Oxford, http://image.ox.ac.uk (last accessed November 2011). Printed versions from Josef Scaliger's edition onwards have endeavored to reproduce the layout offered in the fifth century.

2. Ado of Vienne, *Chronicon*, PL 123 (repr. of Paris 1561 edition), cols. 23–138; Frechulf, *Chronicon*, in *Frechulfus Lexoviensis episcopi opera omnia*, ed. Michael I. Allen, CCCM 169 (Turnhout, 2002); Regino of Prüm, *Chronicon*, ed. Friedrich Kurze, MGH SS rer. Germ. 50, and trans. Simon MacLean, *History and Politics in Late Carolingian and Ottonian Europe: The Chronicle of Regino of Prüm and Adalbert of Magdeburg* (Manchester, 2008).

3. Rosamond McKitterick, *Perceptions of the Past in the Early Middle Ages* (Notre Dame, IN, 2006).

4. Rosamond McKitterick, "History, Law and Communication with the Past in the Carolingian Period," in *Comunicare e significare nell'alto medioevo*, Settimane di studio del Centro italiano di studi sull'alto medioevo 52 (Spoleto, 2005), 941–79.

5. Michael McCormick, *Five Hundred Unknown Glosses from the Palatine Virgil (The Vatican Library, MS Pal. lat. 1631)*, Studi e testi 343 (Vatican City, 1992).

6. See the various essays in Rolf H. Bremmer and Kees Dekker, eds., *Foundations of Learning: The Transfer of Encyclopaedic Knowledge in the Early Middle Ages*, Storehouses of Wholesome Learning 1 (Paris, 2007), and Rosamond McKitterick, "Glossaries and Other Innovations in Carolingian Book Production," in Erik Kwakkel, Rosamond McKitterick, and Rodney Thompson, *Turning Over a New Leaf: Change and Development in the Medieval Book*, Studies in Medieval and Renaissance Book Culture (Leiden, 2012), 21–78, 171–93.

7. Don Fowler, "The Virgil Commentary of Servius," in *The Cambridge Companion to Virgil*, ed. C. Martindale (Cambridge, 1997), 74–75. See also L. D. Reynolds, *Texts and Transmission: A Survey of the Latin Classics* (Oxford, 1983), 385–88.

8. John J. Contreni, *Codex Laudunensis 468: A Ninth-Century Guide to Virgil, Sedulius, and the Liberal Arts*, Armarium Codicum Insignium 3 (Turnhout, 1984).

9. On medieval lives of Virgil see Jan M. Ziolkowski and Michael C. J. Putnam, *The Virgilian Tradition: The First Fifteen Hundred Years* (New Haven, CT, 2008), 181–89, 199–201, and 250.

10. Jordanes, *Historia romana*, ed. Theodor Mommsen, MGH Auct. ant. 30; trans. by James J. O'Donnell, "The Aims of Jordanes," *Historia* 31 (1982): 223–40.

11. B. Cornford, "The Idea of the Roman Past in Early Medieval Italy: Paul the Deacon's *Historia romana*" (PhD dissertation, University of Cambridge, 2003), and B.

Cornford, "Paul the Deacon's Understanding of Identity, His Attitude to Barbarians, and His 'Strategies of Distinction' in the *Historia romana*," in *Texts and Identities in the Early Middle Ages*, ed. Richard Corradini et al., Forschungen zur Geschichte des Mittelalters 12, Denkschriften der Österreichischschen Akademie der Wissenschaften, Philosophisch-historischen Klasse 344 (Vienna, 2006), 47–60.

12. Marek T. Kretschmer, *Rewriting Roman History in the Middle Ages: The "Historia romana" and the Manuscript Bamberg, Hist.3*, Mittellateinische Studien und Texte 36 (Leiden, 2007).

13. On Bede's sources see M. L. W. Laistner, "The Library of the Venerable Bede," in *Bede, His Life, Times and Writings: Essays in Commemoration of the Twelfth Centenary of His Death*, ed. A. Hamilton Thompson (Oxford, 1935), 237–66, and Scott DeGregorio, ed., *Innovation and Tradition in the Writings of the Venerable Bede* (Morgantown, WV, 2006).

14. For example, *Annales regni francorum*, s.a. 784, ed. Friedrich Kurze, MGH SS rer. Germ. 6, 69.

15. Ermold, *In honorem Hludowici christianissimi Caesaris Augusti*, vv. 264–67, in *Ermold Le Noir: Poème sur Louis le Pieux et épitres au roi Pépin*, ed. E. Faral (Paris, 1964), 157–58.

16. M. Manitius, "Einhards Werke und ihr Stil," *Neues Archiv* 7 (1882), 527–28, continued in *Neues Archiv* 11 (1886): 67; C. Mendell, *Tacitus: The Man and His Work* (New Haven, CT, 1957), 234–36, 284–85. But compare Mary F. Tenney, "Tacitus through the Centuries," *University of Colorado Studies* 22 (1935): 347–52; F. Haverfield, "Tacitus during the Late Roman Period and the Middle Ages," *Journal of Roman Studies* 6 (1916): 196–201; David Schaps, "The Found and Lost Manuscripts of Tacitus's *Agricola*," *Classical Philology* 74 (1979): 28–42. I am very grateful to Richard Pollard for discussion of this issue and for providing these references.

17. Louis Duchesne, ed., *Le Liber pontificalis*, 2 vols. (Paris, 1886–92). For the detailed argument concerning the *Liber pontificalis* see Rosamond McKitterick, "La place du *Liber pontificalis* dans les genres historiographiques du Haut Moyen Âge," in *Liber, gesta, histoire: Écrire l'histoire des évêques et des papes de l'antiquité au XXᵉ siècle*, ed. M. Sot (Turnhout, 2008), and Rosamond McKitterick, "Roman Texts and Roman History," in *Rome across Time and Space, c. 500–c.1400: Cultural Transmission and Exchange of Ideas*, ed. Claudia Bolgia, Rosamond McKitterick, and John Osborne (Cambridge, 2011). On Einhard, see Rosamond McKitterick, *Charlemagne: The Formation of a European Identity* (Cambridge, 2008), 7–20.

18. *Alcuini Carmen*, 9, ed. Ernst Dümmler, MGH Poetae latini aevi Carolini, 1:229–35, and compare epp. 18–22, *Poetae aevi Karolini (II)*, ed. Ernst Dummler, MGH Epp. 4, 2:49–60. See also the illuminating discussion by Mary Garrison in "Alcuin and His World" (PhD dissertation, University of Cambridge, 1995), 62–129, and Mary Garrison, "Alcuin Carmen IX and Hrabanus ad Bonosum: A Teacher and His Pupil Write *Consolatio*," in *Poetry and Philosophuy in the Middle Ages: A Festschrift for Peter Dronke*, ed. John Marenbon (Leiden, 2001), 63–78.

19. For Alcuin's biblical typology, for example, see Mary Garrison, "The Bible and Alcuin's Interpretation of Current Events," *Peritia* 16 (2002): 68–84.

20. See H. Geertman, "Documenti, redattori e la formazzione del testo del Liber Pontificalis," in *Il Liber pontificalis e la storia materiale*, ed. H. Geertman, Mededelingen van het Nederlands Instituut te Rom (Assen, 2003), 267–84 (repr. in H. Geertman, *Hic fecit basilicam: Studi sul Liber pontificalis e gli edifici ecclesiastici de Roma da Silvestro a Silverio* [Leuven, 2004], 149–68).

21. For a useful summary of Louis Duchesne's reconstruction of the stages of production and further discussion of the sources drawn on, see K. Blair Dixon, "Memory and Authority in Sixth-Century Rome: The *Liber pontificalis* and the *Collectio Avellana*," in *Religion, Dynasty and Patronage in Early Christian Rome, 300–900*, ed. Kate Cooper and Julia Hillner (Cambridge, 2007), 59–76. On the Calendar of 354 see M. R. Salzman, *On Roman Time: The Codex Calendar of 354 and the Rhythms of Urban Life in Late Antiquity* (Berkeley and Los Angeles, 1990).

22. See also G. Bonamente, "Minor Latin Historians of the Fourth Century AD," in *Greek and Roman Historiography in Late Antiquity, Fourth to Sixth Century AD*, ed. Gabriele Marasco (Leiden, 2003), 85–125.

23. See A. R. Birley, "The *Historia Augusta* and Pagan Historiography," in *Greek and Roman Historiography*, ed. Marasco, 127–50.

24. McKitterick, *Perceptions of the Past*, 46–51; and McKitterick, "La place du *Liber pontificalis* dans les genres historiographiques du Haut Moyen Âge."

25. Lotte Kéry, *Canonical Collections of the Early Middle Ages (ca. 400–1140): A Bibliographical Guide to the Manuscripts and Literature*, History of Medieval Canon Law (Washington, DC, 1999), 29–31.

26. H. Reimitz, "Ein fränkisches Geschichtsbuch aus Saint-Amand und der Codex Vindobonensis palat. 473," in *Text-Schrift-Codex: Quellenkundliche Arbeiten aus dem Institut für Österreichische Geschichtsforschung*, ed. Christoph Egger and Herwig Weigl, Mitteilungen des Instituts für Österreichische Geschichtsforschung Ergänzungsband 35 (Munich, 2000), 34–90, and Rosamond McKitterick, *History and Memory in the Carolingian World* (Cambridge, 2004), 121–23.

27. Michel Sot, "Local and Institutional History (300–1000)," in *Historiography in the Middle Ages*, ed. Deborah M. Deliyannis (Leiden, 2003), 89–114; and McKitterick, "Roman Texts and Roman History."

28. Einhard, *Vita Karoli*, in *Eginhard: Vie de Charlemagne*, ed. Louis Halphen (Paris, 1947), and *Einhardi Vita Karoli Magni*, ed. Oswald Holder-Egger, MGH SS rer. Germ. 25, trans. Paul E. Dutton, *Charlemagne's Courtier: The Complete Einhard* (Peterborough, ON, 1998), and David Ganz, *Two Lives of Charlemagne: Einhard and Notker the Stammerer* (Harmondsworth, UK, 2008).

29. See for example the *Annales regni francorum*, s.a. 806.

30. Full details can be found in McKitterick, *Charlemagne*, 7–20, on which this section is based.

31. See also David Ganz, "Einhard's Charlemagne: The Characterization of Greatness," in *Charlemagne: Empire and Society*, ed. J. Story (Manchester, 2005), 38–51.

32. See Matthew Innes, "Charlemagne's Will: Piety, Politics and the Imperial Succession," *English Historical Review* 112 (1997): 833–55. Einhard, *Vita Karoli*, c. 17 (ad regni decorem et commoditatem pertinentia) and c. 22–33, ed. G. Waitz, repr., R. Rau, ed., *Quellen zur karolingischen Reichsgeschichte* 1 Note 32 (Darmstadt, 1974), 186, 192–210; English translation Paul E. Dutton, *Charlemagne's Courtier: The Complete Einhard* (Peterborough, ON, 1998), 26, 30–39.

33. Hermann Schefers, ed., *Einhard: Studien zu Leben und Werk* (Darmstadt, 1997).

34. For a useful summary see M. S. Kempshall, "Some Ciceronian Aspects of Einhard's *Life of Charlemagne*," *Viator* 26 (1995): 11–38. See also Lupus, ep. 1, in *Loup de Ferrières Correspondance*, ed. Léon Levillain, 2 vols. (Paris, 1935), 1:8.

35. See, for example, J. M. H. Smith, "Einhard: The Sinner and the Saints," *Trans-*

actions of the Royal Historical Society, 6th ser., 13 (2003): 55–77; Karl H. Krüger, "Neue Beobachtungen zur Datierung von Einhards *Karlsvita*," *Frühmittelalterliche Studien* 32 (1998): 124–45.

36. Matthias M. Tischler, *Einharts Vita Karoli: Studien zur Entstehung, Überlieferung und Rezeption*, MGH Schriften 48.

37. See, for example, Cicero, *Orator*, 19.66 and 34.120, in *Cicero, Brutus, Orator*, ed. H. M. Hubbell (Cambridge, MA, 1962), 354 and 394. On the Carolingian witnesses to Cicero's texts on rhetoric see Reynolds, *Texts and Transmission*, 102–9.

38. Charles E. V. Nixon and Barbara Saylor Rodgers, *In Praise of Later Roman Emperors: The Panegyrici Latini*, introduction, translation, and historical commentary with the Latin text of R. A. B. Mynors (Berkeley and Los Angeles, 1994), 12–13.

39. Cicero, *De oratore*, 2.84–85, ed. E. W. Sutton and H. Rackham (Cambridge, MA, 1976), 458–63.

40. See n. 31, above.

41. Compare Einhard, *Vita Karoli*, 18, ed. Halphen, 54; and Suetonius, *Augustus*, 89, in *Suetonius*, ed. J. C. Rolfe (Cambridge, MA, 1970), 256–58.

42. Ganz, "Einhard's Charlemagne," 49.

43. H. W. Berrano, *A Commentary on the "Vita Hadriani" in the "Historia Augusta"* (Ann Arbor, 1980). *Historia Augusta, Hadrian* 5.5 (per orbem terrarum paci operam impendit) and 21.7 (Latium multis civitatibus dedit), ed. and trans. David Magie, 3 vols. (Cambridge, MA, 1921–32), 1:14–15 and 64–65.

44. Tacitus, *Agricola, Germania and Dialogus*, ed. and trans. R. M. Ogilvie, E. H. Warmington, and M. Winterbottom, revised from M. Hutton and W. Peterson's translations (Cambridge, MA, 1970), 19.

45. McKitterick, *Charlemagne*, 15–20.

46. Tacitus, *Agricola*, 3, ed. Ogilvie, Warmington, and Winterbottom, 30.

47. Ibid., 1–4, ed. Ogilvie, Warmington, and Winterbottom, 26–33.

48. Ibid., 21, ed. Ogilvie, Warmington, and Winterbottom, 66.

49. Ibid., 10–12, ed. Ogilvie, Warmington, and Winterbottom, 42–50; and Einhard, *Vita Karoli*, 15, ed. Halphen, 44–46.

50. Tacitus, *Agricola*, 45–46, ed. Ogilvie, Warmington, and Winterbottom, 110–14.

51. See the useful summary by R. Pearse at Tacitus and His Manuscripts, http://www.tertullian.org/rpearse/tacitus/.

52. Reynolds, *Texts and Transmission*, 410. Heiric of Auxerre also made some excerpts; see M. Ihm, "Beiträge zur Textgeschichte des Sueton," *Hermes* 36 (1901): 343–63.

53. For detailed argument see McKitterick, *Charlemagne*, 9–20.

54. See also the valuable comments offered by Matthew Innes, "The Classical Tradition and Carolingian Historiography: Encounters with Suetonius," *International Journal of the Classical Tradition* 3 (1997): 265–82.

 CHAPTER 2

An Unedited Letter
in the Laon Letter Collection and
Another New Carolingian Letter

DAVID GANZ

Paris, Bibliothèque nationale de France, MS lat. 11379 is a composite manuscript which includes a collection of the surviving letters of Einhard, save for his letter to Lupus of Ferrières. The letters are copied in a black ink, and the opening initial of each letter is ornamented with blue and red washes. In its present form the collection of documents was completed at Laon, incorporating materials brought from the monastery of St-Bavo at Ghent. After the Viking attack on the monastery of St-Bavo in 851 the abbot transferred the relics of the saint to Laon, and the community, originally established at Nivelles, moved to Laon, where two successive abbots died.[1] The manuscript was consulted at Laon by Sirmond and Pertz, but shortly after 1829 it was acquired by the Bibliothèque nationale de France. It has been restored, and the letters have been treated with chemical reagents to make them more legible, as a result of which some words have been erased.[2] The manuscript is too tightly bound to be easily foliated, but it seems important to identify the separate parts. The St-Bavo collection of Einhard's letters occupies folios 3–18, which measure ca. 214 × 160 mm in thirty-three lines and was copied in the second half of the ninth century.[3] Possible changes of hand occur on folio 4r. Changes of pen occur on folios 7r, 10v, and 11r. Einhard's letter 40 is headed INCIPIT EPISTULA; letter 63 is headed STIONE; letter 64 is headed . . . ATIONE PRECANDO. The collection ends EXPLICIT DEO GRATIAS AMEN. This section also includes on folio 17v a remarkable letter by a vassal written to the empress Irmingard[4] occupying thirty-four lines, and it ends with letters relating to the abbey of St-Bavo at Ghent.[5]

The collection of Einhard's letters and additional letters from Ghent is now bound with leaves from other manuscripts to create a composite volume. Folio 18r contains a text listing the names of the Old Testament patriarchs accompanied by scriptural quotations and in the lower margin a Christian inscription.[6] Folio 20 is a separate leaf which contains the copy of Einhard's letters to Louis the Pious and to Lothar, the second of which is also included in the St-Bavo collection. It is written in a very fine Caroline minuscule hand, which Bischoff considered comparable with the script of the Aachen court. Folios 21r to 23r are entitled *Praedicatio* and contain two sermons of St. Effrem. Folio 24r is a computistical fragment including a poem on the date of Easter which circulated in the computus of Hrabanus Maurus[7] and was copied into manuscripts of Bede.[8] At the base of this folio the same hand has copied a poem on virtues and vices also found in Verona 85.[9] Folio 26r–v contains the beginning of Priscian's treatise on the first lines of the *Aeneid*[10] and several poems.[11] Folios 21–24 and 26 are similar and seem to use the script of the Rhineland: like folio 20 they are earlier than the Einhard letter collection. Folios 24–28 measure 211 × 157 mm. The final quire (folios 29r–36v) is a copy of a letter of Hincmar concerning the election of Hedenulf of Laon in 876.[12] This is copied in sixteen lines with large lower margins, into a quire measuring ca. 195 × 150 mm. Bischoff suggested in a letter to Pierre Gasnault that since Hincmar's letter is not copied in Reims script, it may have been copied at Laon.

In the late ninth or early tenth century the volume received additional texts entered on folios 2v,[13] 15r–v, 16r–v, 24v, 26v, 27r–v, and 28r–v. The texts are known as the Laon formulary, edited by Zeumer and studied by John Contreni;[14] they include several letters to the cathedral at Laon. Contreni believed that these letters were copied by three hands, one of which Contreni identified with Adelelm, dean and later bishop of Laon, who died in 930.[15] The Laon letters include a letter from St-Mary Reims announcing the death of two brothers, a letter from St-Remigius Reims about a prayer alliance with Laon, a letter from a monastery dedicated to Saints Peter and Paul announcing the deaths of two monks, a letter from the monastery of St-Germanus at Auxerre announcing the death of a monk, three short letters from Laon replying to death notices and noting the death of the dean Bernard in 903, and a *littera formata* from Bishop John of Cambrai 866–79 for a priest of Laon.[16]

At the same date quire signatures were added on folios 10r, ii on 18v, iii on 23v, and v on 36v. The front flyleaf folio 2r contains a list of payments for services owed, set out in three columns and cut down, which was localized at St-Bavo at Ghent by Pierre Gasnault, because the persons listed all have Germanic names and the dues include beer.[17] On the verso of this leaf is a letter from Bishop Heidilo of Noyon to Bishop Dido of Laon composed in 892.[18] I think folios 24 and

28 are conjoint, and folios 25, 26, and 27 are singletons. A stub is visible between folios 20 and 21 and between folios 27 and 28.

Both Teulet and Zeumer decided not to edit the first of the additional letters, which occupies the verso of folio 15. Zeumer believed that the first five letters in his edition, on folios 15v, 16r, and 16v, were copied by the scribe of the Einhard and St-Bavo letters,[19] and since they lack any pointers to localization, they may have been composed at Ghent rather than at Laon. Though the first and last words of many lines have been lost by the efforts of the restorer, and the text is corrupt, I print what was visible on a sunny day.[20] Lines are numbered, and lacunae at the beginning of lines are indicated. The punctuation reproduced here is found in the manuscript.

1 Dilectissimo venerando amabilis amabilissimo diligendo magistro meo ill. humilis

2 vestrae tamen sanctitati in omnibus mellifluam patre salutem.[21] Gratias omnipotenti agitur

3 exoro quatenus huius miserabilis vitae prospera aeterna dignetur vobis caelestia

4 gaudia. Ceterum noverit desiderabilis[22] multumque amabilis paternitatis beatitudinis vestrae

5 quia[23] postquam novissime vestrae nobbilitatis proditum de mihi conflictam saepissime

6 habebitis. Protinus magister quo pacto mihi praecipitis quid agam postularem vobis

7 apices vestras continuo cum agerem deberem ita vis fatiam auctius tribuat vobis pater

8 ...nitatem utique opto vobis.[24] Auceps viam quae ducit ad vitam[25] aucto mabam pro certe sic agat

9 ....lege secularum fidelis vestrae sum ac diem cotidie decant psal[terium?] pro vobis scitis profecto in ser..

10 .... promptus sum. Namque nusquam clērc non fuisse si vestra pietas non egerat

11 ....omnipotens [omnipresens?] copulo vobis in perpetuum ex utraque parte concitatio actumque fuit

12 .... homines vestrum actum vegitatum utique non tamen scitis die cotidie in serviti

13 .... seniorem meum. Ac verbis vestris resultare in secula dignis educa

14 ....minis habebitis vestram eruditionem inluminati vel locutionem

15   ....[unc] depraeco vobis unum lecinnarium adminiculum
       mihi trib

16   ....vobis placet et quid vos vultis ego didicere ago vos scitis

17   ....[in]sistere patrem meum de mihi inefficax erit et in

18   ....est mihi facere . per vestram benignitatem ad seniorem

19   ....vel provenna deprecasti maiori vestro ille

20   ....mid fuit non audio mihi dare conte quam venit a vobis

21   ....inem si mox de ore vestro non precipitis iterum non
       fatiat quicquam

22   .... praepositum. Ad ipsum praepositum subsidium mihi
       daretis obse[..]

23   .... Iubetis dare utique valde opus habeo. Gle.. scere

24   ....caeli honorem agitis gña vus sufficit mihi. Domine

25   .... quicquid non scio optime vobis debetis corrigere

26   ....am benignitatem saepe mihi opem fertis mox depreco

27   ....daretis de munusculis ad magistris meis quid possum

28   ....que moram mihi praecipitis praeparatus sum in servitio
       vestro

29   ....mor doctus habere fidem ubicumque permanebis noscat
       vobis

30   ....in vobis et in alios *cler* catazizonem posuisti

31   .... de culmine caeli natus et altithroni spiritus aeterni veniat
       sanctissimus

32 Mi .... Iure deus fatiat mentem sanctae [*scaē* = sancta est ???] ill. ad
       regnum Christi faciat vos pervenire[26]

33 Quia [*Quae*?] bona sunt atquae coronatus. Ibis ad aeterni pulcher . quod
       iugiter postulat assiduis precibus

34 Cuncti potens Dominus cuncti temporibus et ubbis [*vobis* ??] post obitum
       intra sanctorum atque chorum[27]

35 Deo...Amen [written in Tironian Notes]

The letter is written to a teacher who has sent a letter advising a pupil what to do. He affirms that he is the master's *fidelis*, and daily sings psalters for him. Letters to masters, addressed as magister, some of whom may also be bishops, are found in MGH Formulae from Salzburg, nos. 24, 27, 29, and 31, on pages 445–46, and in a Paris manuscript, BnF lat. 4841, on pages 531 and 532. John Contreni discussed some of these letters in an article of 1989.[28]

    A second unedited letter is offered as providing a text slightly easier to understand. Cambridge University Library, MS Dd. xii. 54 is a ninth-century manuscript of all of the poetical works of Wandalbert of Prüm. Because the nineteenth-century manuscript catalogue of the Cambridge University Library dated it to the thirteenth century it was not used by Ernst Dümmler for his MGH edition of Wandalbert's poems, and it does not seem to have been examined by anyone.[29] The flyleaf is a sheet of parchment which, on closer examination, proves to be a Carolingian letter, which has texts about the Egyptian days and the ides and nones entered on the verso in ninth-century script. Measuring ca. 152 × 240 mm, it has been trimmed by the binder, but what can be read is transcribed here. The punctuation of the original (a single point at the end of sentences) is reproduced. The lines of the manuscript are replicated in this transcription: on the lower portion there is a clear left hand margin.

> ..timo ac reverentissimo pontifici ill .. ex coenobio alm
> confessoris Cristi francorumque apostolici Remigii indignus sacerd
> ..monachus . fidele servitutis obsequium cum devotis oratio
> precum . Cum nullis apud vos sanctissime presul beneficiorum
> ..ratis . fisus tamen proprietate vestre insite generositatis. Opera praet
> vestre dirigere celsitudini apices mee fidelitatis. quibus signi
> quanto impense servitutis obsequio propensius vestre varies
> sororis anime absolutione hactenus laboraverimus Na tu
> rei veritas manifestetur. paucis quidem vestre sellentiae qua
> pro illa oratum sit intimabitur. Siquidem exec em not que
> pie memorie sororum condita fuit in nostra ecclesia ...
> ....sce me domno ill regi us... lx hod.

The next lines are presumably concealed behind the nineteenth-century binding of the manuscript.

> ....unt devote ment
> in altaris supra coru illius cotidiana missarum perso
> ficiamque pro vestra amore libentissime. quo adu talis a
> ne. Ceterum supplico vestre ruretenus clementi
> quodam paupere consanguineo filio uidelicet....
> viri fidelis ill nomine ill. Audivi enim dicere
> relatu quod illi terram quam suus genitor et exit progen
> iuert abstuleritis. Unde obnixe flagitamus tan
> sui propinqui in nostro coenobio degentes simulque to. a
> nostra ut pro urum omnium petitionem piam et clementem apu
> paternitatem sentiat bonitatem . restituendo illi qd
> mus humillime. Valere nos optamus unianimiter

Paleographically this text is copied in the script of Reims, in contrast to the manuscript which it now covers. The letter was apparently written by a monk from the monastery of St-Remigius to a bishop who is left unnamed. The use of *ill* for the name of the *vir fidelis* and the lack of a name for the bishop to whom the letter is directed may suggest that this is a draft, rather than the letter which was sent. The manuscript came to Cambridge from the collection of the French numismatist J. B. Hautin (1580–1640), who owned manuscripts from Le Mans, Bourges, and Saint-Denis.

Appendix

Letter of Bernhard Bischoff to Pierre Gasnault (undated)

Ms. Lat. 11379 . . . ist schwierig zu beurteilen. Denn es scheint, dass, nachdem man alles, was sicher französischen Ursprungs ist, abgezogen hat, Teile verschiedener (palaeographischer) Herkunft übrigbleiben, die nicht zu gewaltsam summiert werden dürfen.

Zeitlich rückwärtsgehend ist die jüngste Schicht, die zuerst abzuziehen ist, die von einer französischen Hand saec.X (wie ich glaube) eingetragene Sammlung von Formeln, die den "einhardischen" und den "hincmarischen" Teil der heutigen Hs. bereits vereinigt ausnützen konnte: auf foll. 2v, 15r zum Teil, 18v, 19rv, 24v, 27rv, 26v zum Teil, 28rv 25r= Formulae cod. Laudun., capp. 16, 11–13, 6–8, 9,10, 14, 15, 17.

Die Schrift des Hinkmar-Briefes, der wohl in einem (heute unvollständigen) eigenen Quinio kopiert war, ist sicher noch zu Hinkmars Lebzeiten geschrieben, nicht in Reimser Schrift; auch wenn die Schrift nicht aus einem der leicht erkennbaren Scriptorien hervorgegangen ist, muss sie doch in jener Gegend— vielleicht in Laon— lokalisiert werden.

Es bleiben foll. (1), 2; 3–10, 11–18, 19–20, 24 und 26–28. Diese können von 3 an wohl früh vereinigt gewesen sein, worauf die Lagenzahlen schleissen lassen können, aber einheitlicher Entstehung sind sie offenbar nicht. Jaffe (zitiert bei Hampe, S. 105) hielt fol. 20 "für den Rest eines anderen verlorenen Codex," aber est ist immerhinzu beachten, dass die beiden unvollständigen Lagen foll. 19–23 und 24–28 (ohne 25) einen anderen Schriftspiegel aufweisen, fol 20 also kaum allein zu betrachten ist. Leider habe ich von der Lage 19–23 nicht das Schema notiert.

Leider erkenne ich jetzt, dass ich auch noch einige Schriftproben bestellen muss, um, fern von der Handschrift, die palaeogräphische Beurteilung noch etwas sichern zu können. Schon jetzt aber möchte ich für wahrscheinlich halten, die Schriften von foll. 20-24, 26–28 dürften alter sein als der Teil mit den Einhart-Briefen und den Formeln capp. 1–5, und ich möchte sie in das II. Viertel des IX. Jhs. setzen. Von ihnen sind nach Photos bezw. Notizen jene von 24r und 26rv vielleicht rhenisch (sie lassen an Lorsch denken, aber ich möchte sie nicht zu eng festlegen); jene von fol. 20 ist von einer wirklich ungewöhnlichen Qualität (ob eine Verbindung mit dem Aachener Hofskriptorium denkbar ist, wage ich noch nicht zu sagen, est ist ja auch fur den Augenblick weniger wichtig).

Je mehr ich nun aber die mir vorliegende Schriftprobe des wohl einheitlich geschriebenen Hauptteiles des Einhart-Briefe (foll.4r–16v Mitte) betrachte, sehe ich ein, dass sie ein schwächeres Abbild des zB. in der II Bibel Karls des Kahlen vollendet gemeisterten Saint Amand Stiles des dritten oder vierten Jahrhundert-Viertels ist, und das passt naturlich sehr viel besser zu Gent als zu irgendeinem rheinischen Zentrum. Ein positiver Vergleich mit Gent ist, soweit mir bisher bekannt ist, nicht möglich, da wir von dort aus jener Zeit keine Handschriften besitzen oder kennen.

Es ist nun wahrscheinlich, dass die nicht-hinkmarischen Teile schon vereinigt von Gent nach Laon (vgl. Schatzverzeichnisse I, 38) mitgebracht wurden, und wohl gut möglich, dass fol. 2 als Umschlag diente. Die Schrift kann wohl etwa gleich alt sein wie die Briefe. oder s. IX med.

Notes

I am grateful to Pierre Gasnault for his help with this manuscript and its structure, and for his kindness in letting me see his correspondence with Bernhard Bischoff about this volume. His note on the text on the flyleaf was published in the *Bulletin de la Société nationale des antiquaires de France*, November 25, 1970, 310–18.

1. *Annales S. Bavonis Gandensis*, MGH SS 2, 187; Philip Grierson, *Les Annales de Saint-Pierre de Gand et de Saint-Amand*, Recueil de textes pour servir à l;histoire de Belgique 4 (Brussels, 1937).

2. Alexandre Teulet, *Oeuvres d'Eginhard*, 2 vols. (Paris, 1840–43), lxxv: "Malheuresement le temps et l'humidité ont attaqué indistinctement tous les feuillets de ce manuscript. . . . A partir du neuvième feuillet, les marges extérieures sont tantot rongées jusqu'au tiers de la page, tantot recouvertes d'un enduit noir et épais qui ne permet de distinguer l'écriture qu'avec une extreme difficulté."

3. Most recently edited by Karl Hampe, MGH Epp. 5, 105–41. There is an excellent English translation by Paul Dutton, *Charlemagne's Courtier: The Complete Einhard* (Peterborough, ON, 1998), 131–64.

4. MGH Epp. 5, 343–45. On this letter, see Janet Nelson, "The Search for Peace in a Time of War: The Carolingian Brüderkrieg, 840–843," in *Träger und Instrumentarien des Friedens im hohen und späten Mittelalter*, ed. Johannes Fried (Sigmaringen, 1996), 87–114 (102–4).

5. Edited at the end of Hampe's edition of Einhard's letters, MGH Epp. 5, 142–45. Ep. 68 refers to St-Bavo property. Though Hampe prints the headings of these letters in capitals, they are not in capitals in the manuscript.

6. MGH Poetae 1, 103; *Inscriptiones Christianae urbis Romae II*, ed. G. B. de Rossi, 2 vols. (Rome, 1857–88), 1:165; MGH Poetae 4, 1083.

7. Hrabanus Maurus, *De Computo*, ed. Wesley Stevens, CCCM 44 (Turnhout, 1997), 305.

8. MGH Poetae 4, 670.

9. MGH Poetae 4, 585.

10. *Grammatici latini*, ed. Heinrich Keil, vol. 3, *Prisciani grammatici*, ed. Martin Hertz (Hildesheim, 1961), 459–60. The manuscript is included in Marina Passalacqua, *I codici di Prisciano* (Rome, 1978), 245–46.

11. MGH Poetae 1, 103.

12. The letter was edited by Sirmond from this manuscript: *Hincmari Archiepiscopi Remensis Opera*, vol. 2, *Opuscula et epistolae* (Paris, 1645), 339–40 (repr. PL 126, 271–76). Cf. Martina Stratmann, "Zur Wirkungsgeschichte Hinkmars von Reims," *Francia* 22, no. 1 (1995), 1–43; Martina Stratmann, *Hinkmar von Reims als Verwalter von Bistum und Kirchenprovinz*, Quellen und Forschungen zum Recht im Mittelalter 6 (Sigmaringen, 1991), 18 and 68.

13. The letter of Bishop Heidilo of Noyon to Bishop Dido of Laon composed in 892 and a medical recipe, copied by Adelhelm according to Contreni.

14. MGH Formulae, 512–20; John J. Contreni, "Le formulaire de Laon, source pour l'histoire de l'école de Laon au début du Xe siècle," *Scriptorium* 27 (1973): 21–29; Alice Rio, *Legal Practice and the Written Word in the Early Middle Ages: Frankish Formulae, c. 500–1000* (Cambridge, 2009), 139–40.

15. Contreni, "Le formulaire," with plate of fol. 15, and *The Cathedral School of Laon, from 850 to 930: Its Manuscripts and Masters* (Munich, 1978), 152–56. The most recent discussion of the collection known to me, which questions Contreni's division of the hands in the *formulae*, is G. Declercq, "Een karolingisch Lekenabt in Gent: Einhard en de Gentse abdijen van Sint-Pieters en Sint-Baafs," *Handelingen der Maatschappij voor Geschiedenis en Oudheidkunde te Gent* 55 (2001): 73–74.

16. For a full listing of the contents of the manuscript see Rio, *Legal Practice*, 260–62.

17. Gasnault edited these accounts; see *Bulletin*, 316–17.

18. MGH Formulae, 519.

19. MGH Formulae, 512.

20. Karl Hampe, "Reise nach Frankreich und Belgien," *Neues Archiv* 23 (1898): 278, also noted how sunlight revealed more.

21. Cf. PL 96, 1373: "Melliflua verba."

22. Cf. MGH, 211, letter 2, 14, to Desiderius of Cahors: "Desiderabilis pater." Lupus of Ferrières, *Correspondance*, ep.70, starts a letter to Marcward of Prüm with "Desiderantissimo M."

23. These first lines were edited by A. Teulet, *Einhardi opera II* (Paris, 1840), 143: "comme elle n'offre pour le fond aucune espece d'interet, nous avons du renoncer à publier un texte dont la presque totalité demeurait inintelligible." Zeumer shared this view in MGH Formulae, 513n1.

24. "Opto vobis" in the letter of Bishop Franco of Le Mans to the bishop of Sens.

25. "Angustam viam quae ducit ad vitam," *Regula Benedicti*, ch. 5: "unde Dominus dicit: *Angusta via est quae ducit ad vitam*."

26. Cf. "a ad regna caelestia faciat pervenire" in the Gelasian sacramentary.

27. Cf. MGH Formulae, 522: "et in futuro in angelorum choro. Sacramentarium Missa Votiva ut dignus sit in perpetuum sanctorum tuorum chorum adstare."

28. John J. Contreni, "The Carolingian School: Letters from the Classroom," in *Giovanni Scoto nel suo tempo: L'organizzazione del sapere in età carolingia*, Atti dei convegni dell'Accademia tudertina e del Centro di studi sulla spiritualità medievale, n.s., 1. (Spoleto, 1989), 81–111. Further Carolingian letters have been edited and discussed by Bernhard Bischoff, *Salzburger Formelbücher und Briefe aus Tassilonischer und Karolingischer Zeit* (Munich, 1973); Bernhard Bischoff, "Briefe des neunten Jahrhunderts," *Anecdota novissima* (1984): 127–38; Martina Stratmann, "Briefe an Hinkmar von Reims," *Deutsches Archiv* 48 (1992): 37–81; Martina Stratmann, "Die Briefsammlung des Bischofs Herfrid von Auxerre (887–909)," *Deutsches Archiv* 50 (1994): 127–44; Hartmut Hoffmann, "Das Fragment einer karolingischen oder ottonischen Briefsammlung," *Deutsches Archiv* 50 (1994): 145–47; Mark Mersiowsky, "Regierungspraxis und Schriftlichkeit im Karolingerreich: Das Fallbeispiel der Mandate und Briefe," in *Schriftkultur und Reichsverwaltung unter den Karolingern*, ed. Rudolf Schieffer (Opladen, 1996), 109–66; Michel Parisse, *La correspondance d'un eveque carolingien: Frothaire de Toul (ca 813–847), avec les lettres de Theuthilde, abbesse de Remiremont* (Paris, 1998); and most recently M. Mersiowsky, "Preserved by Destruction: Carolingian Original Letters and Clm 6333," in *Early Medieval Palimpsests*, ed. G. Declercq, Bibliologia 26 (Turnhout, 2007), 73–99. On the general context of medieval letters, see Giles Constable, *Letters and Letter-Collections*, Typologie des Sources du Moyen Âge Occidental 17 (Turnhout, 1976).

29. I am most grateful to Michael Gullick for drawing my attention to this manuscript, and to the photographic services of Cambridge University Library for supplying me with a photograph taken by ultraviolet light. The digitized Paris manuscript is now available on the BnF's Gallica website.

 CHAPTER 3

"The Hunt Belongs to Man": Some Neglected Treatises Related to Hunting and Falconry from the Court of Louis the German

ERIC J. GOLDBERG

In the preface to his monumental *Book on the Art of Hunting with Birds*, Emperor Frederick II (d.1250) explained that he had penned his work

> to correct the mistakes of many authors who, when writing on the subject without the requisite skill, degraded the art by copying false and poorly written books of other writers on the subject. We therefore composed the material in this book to bequeath to posterity a more accurate account. Although we had proposed a long time ago to produce the present work, we delayed putting it down in writing for almost thirty years because we did not think ourselves up to the task. However, we never read that anyone preempted us and fully treated the material in our book. To be sure, there were several short works by various persons, but they were known only for their utility and composed without skill. We therefore investigated this art for a long time and with great attention and enthusiasm, using both our intellect and hands-on experience, so that at long last we might be able to write down in a book everything that our experience, and the experience of others, had taught us.[1]

In other words, in his own day Frederick II could not find any comprehensive treatises on falconry, only "several short works" that slavishly quoted from other "false and poorly written books." Although the Hohenstaufen emperor was referring to manuals about hunting with raptors, his words reflect a more general dearth of surviving treatises on hunting before the twelfth and thirteenth centuries.[2] This situation has suggested to some historians the relative primitiveness

31

of aristocratic hunting during the early Middle Ages. Frank Barlow, for example, who has written on Anglo-Norman hunting, concluded that the absence of hunting treatises before the twelfth century "in itself suggests that hunting was still essentially for the pot and that the methods were basic and little affected by sophisticated ritual."[3] Reflecting this attitude, recent studies of premodern hunting have tended to focus on the central and later Middle Ages as well as the early modern era.[4]

Like Frederick II who spent "almost thirty years" researching the art of falconry, John Contreni has dedicated the better part of three decades to studying "with the greatest attention and enthusiasm" the intellectual, religious, and political culture of early medieval Europe and the Carolingian era in particular. In his numerous publications, Contreni time and again has challenged the inherited view, reflected in Barlow's offhand comment above, that sophisticated aristocratic culture and literate court societies were somehow underdeveloped and primitive—if not to say altogether absent—before the central Middle Ages. In this article I hope to contribute to John Contreni's career-long efforts to bring to light the dynamism and creativity of Carolingian literate culture by exploring several neglected treatises related to hunting and falconry from the court of Frederick II's distant predecessor, Louis the German (840–76). That the Franks and their Carolingian kings were avid hunters is well known. Yet scholars heretofore have believed that, with the possible exception of a short veterinary treatise, the Carolingians did not commission any surviving works on hunting.[5] This article seeks to revise this view by investigating two, and possibly a third, overlooked Latin treatises from Louis the German's court that demonstrate this king's interest in hunting and falconry.[6] These works commissioned by Louis the German are significant as the earliest surviving medieval treatises related to hunting, although, as we will see, they differ considerably in style, content, and length from Frederick II's much more comprehensive *Book on the Art of Hunting with Birds*. More generally, an investigation into these treatises sheds new light on the literary culture of the Carolingian court, the political and ideological significance of the hunt as a royal ritual, and Louis the German's personal interests as an avid huntsman, learned king, and careful reader. This article therefore seeks to situate the east Frankish king and his court within the important recent scholarship on early medieval court culture and lay intellectuals.[7]

Historians of early medieval Europe have long recognized the importance of hunting for the culture and identity of elites.[8] As Franz Irsigler argued, by the sixth century hunting had become the defining badge of Frankish nobility, perhaps even surpassing warfare in its cultural significance for the aristocracy.[9] Odo of Cluny's description of the education of Count Gerald of Aurillac (ca. 855–909) was probably typical of many nobles who came of age under the ninth-century

Carolingians. Odo wrote that Gerald "applied himself to the study of letters, but by the will of his parents only to the extent of going through the Psalter. Then he was taught worldly exercises as is the custom for noble boys: to train Molossian hounds, to become an archer, and to fly falcons and hawks with skill."[10] Frankish authors and poets highlighted the hunting prowess of Charlemagne, Louis the Pious, and Charles the Bald (as did Asser for Alfred the Great and Widukind for Henry I), and the Carolingian rulers developed a number of court officials whose duty it was to oversee the royal hunt and care for the king's dogs and falcons.[11] Régine Hennebicque (Le Jan) has emphasized that the region around Aachen and the Ardennes Forest was particularly rich in royal hunting grounds, thus helping explain the Carolingians' frequent sojourns in that area.[12] Louis the German likewise seems to have been an active huntsman: on several occasions we hear of him and his sons hunting, and three of Louis's favorite residences, Frankfurt, Regensburg, and Ranshofen, had walled hunting parks nearby.[13] With the end of Frankish military expansion in the 790s, the hunt emerged as a key political ritual and ceremonial proxy for war.[14] Royal hunts put on display the military prowess of the king and his sons, forged consensus among the ruler and the magnates, symbolized the peace and stability of the empire, and helped cultivate the image of the monarch as lord of both man and nature.[15]

The first treatise for Louis the German is an intriguing short tract on hunting and dietary laws penned by an anonymous author. (See the appendix, below, for an English translation.) The circumstances surrounding the composition of this work have remained uncertain. It survives in a single late tenth-century manuscript from Mainz.[16] Ernst Dümmler published two editions of the text, although he remained somewhat hesitant about ascribing its author, royal recipient, and date of composition.[17] Dümmler's uncertainty stemmed from the fact that the surviving copy omits the author's opening salutation, and the author does not identify himself or his royal recipient elsewhere. Nevertheless, at the conclusion the author spoke of "famine's unprecedented want" (famis inaudita penuria) that was ravaging his region (per omnem nostram . . . regionem), and Dümmler interpreted these words as a probable reference to the serious famine along the Rhine reported in the year 850.[18] This in turn made Louis the German the likely recipient.[19] As for the author, Dümmler thought that Hrabanus Maurus might have penned it, although he cautioned that "this assumption is not necessary, since in Louis's milieu there probably was no lack of other educated men who were equal to this task."[20] Thus when Dümmler edited this treatise in fifth volume of the MGH Epistolae (1899), he described the author simply as "a cleric or abbot," the recipient as "a certain king (Louis the German?)," and its date as "850?"[21] Dümmler's lingering uncertainties help explain why recent scholars largely have ignored this fascinating text.[22]

Dümmler's case for Louis the German as the royal recipient and 850 as the date of composition can be strengthened in several ways. First, the report of the 850 famine in the *Annals of Fulda* closely echoes several of the topics discussed in the anonymous treatise. The treatise discusses the question of how the dietary restrictions of Scripture and penitential books applied to the eating of certain animals. The *Annals of Fulda*, which at this point seem to have been penned by the Fulda monk Rudolf,[23] notably addressed this exact same issue when describing the 850 famine. In reporting the suffering of poor families along the Rhine, Rudolf narrated how one father reluctantly set out to slaughter his young son in a forest to fend off starvation for himself and his wife. Just as he was about to slay his child, however, he spied the carcass of a deer killed by wolves and thus was able to feed his family with the meat. Rudolf concluded this story by commenting that the parents and their son were "driven by necessity to strengthen themselves by feeding on the meat which the Law prohibits."[24] Here Rudolf referred to the same biblical dietary prohibition discussed in the 850 treatise: Leviticus 17:15, which forbids the eating of carrion or an animal that has been killed by another beast. Rudolf's language also echoes a penitential book ascribed to Archbishop Theodore of Canterbury (d. 690), the so-called Penitential of Theodore (*iudicia Theodori*), which allows that one might eat unclean meat such as a carcass torn by wild beasts "if driven by necessity, that is, a famine."[25]

It was not only the famine that made the topic of dietary restrictions a pressing matter in 850. That very same summer, Louis the German had scheduled an important hunting trip. In the midst of the famine, Louis held a summit with his elder brother Lothar I (840–55) in July at Cologne and struck a treaty with him, and afterward the two brothers made a high-profile hunting trip together to the Osning Forest near Aachen. The *Annals of Xanten* reported: "That same year there was such peace between the two brothers, Emperor Lothar and King Louis, that they went hunting for many days with a few men in the Osning Forest. Many were astonished by this fact, and the brothers took leave of each other in peace."[26] The coincidence of this royal hunting trip with the famine seems to have made the issue of dietary restrictions and hunting a topic of discussion and debate at Louis the German's court. Indeed, the author of the treatise explicitly stated that many people were asking questions (*querunt etiam multi*) about this subject.[27] It is possible that the king and his subjects worried that the eating of prohibited kinds of meat had brought about the famine. As Rob Meens has emphasized, Carolingian thinkers believed the stability of the realm depended on the moral behavior and ritual purity of the people and especially the king and his court.[28] People therefore often interpreted astrological phenomena, political upheavals, and natural disasters as signs of God's anger for transgressions of sacred boundaries and taboos, such as eating unclean food. These views were popularized by such works as Pseudo-

Cyprian's *On the Twelve Abuses of the World*, a copy of which belonged to Louis the German's long-time archchaplain and archchancellor, Grimald of St.-Gall, about whom we will have more to say.[29] The *Annals of Fulda* make clear that the famine of 850 came at the end of several years of turmoil in Louis the German's kingdom and throughout the empire: Slavic rebellions, Viking incursions, Frankish defeats, a Muslim attack on Rome, demonic possession, heresy, and a false prophetess.[30] The author of the 850 treatise believed that these recent calamities were divine punishment for their transgressions. "Every day the enemy army thunders around us with arms," he wrote, "the continuous expenditures of goods wear us down, and famine's unprecedented want stalks throughout our region. We are worn out by these and innumerable other calamities because of our sins."[31]

The piece of evidence that clinches the argument for Louis the German as the recipient is the second treatise this article will consider. Louis the German commissioned that second treatise from Archbishop Hincmar of Reims in 865.[32] As we will see, in that work Hincmar recounted conversations he had recently had with Louis the German, and those conversations were about the very same topics and scriptural passages discussed in the 850 treatise. Taken together, then, this evidence confirms Dümmler's argument for Louis the German as the recipient of the anonymous treatise and 850 as its date of composition.

As for the author, however, his identity must remain uncertain. Hrabanus almost certainly did not pen the treatise. The author's prose is staccato with short sentences and changing verb tenses, which is very much unlike Hrabanus's polished style.[33] Moreover, toward the end of the treatise the author expresses his willingness to submit to the teaching (*magisterium*) of anyone who offers a more persuasive opinion on the topic.[34] Such a statement seems highly unlikely to have come from Hrabanus in 850, since as archbishop of Mainz he was the head of the east Frankish church and thus the supreme arbiter of *magisterium* in his large eastern archdiocese.[35] We can, however, draw several positive conclusions about the author. To begin, he seems to have been relatively well educated: not only is his Latin clear enough, but he echoes the Roman poet Horace and quotes Augustine's *Confessions*.[36] He also employs the uncommon words *caraxare* (to write) and *idolothita* (foods sacrificed to idols), terms that appear nowhere in Hrabanus's (or Rudolf's) writings but that show up in Anglo-Saxon sources, including the works of Aldhelm, Stephan's *Life of St. Wilfrid*, and the correspondences of Boniface and Lull.[37] The author's use of these uncommon terms therefore suggests Anglo-Saxon influence, presumably through east Frankish cultural centers like Fulda and Mainz where Insular traditions were strong from the legacies of transplanted English churchmen and women.[38]

The most revealing section about the author is the last paragraph, in which he appealed directly to Louis the German for patronage.[39] In that passage the author reveals that he was a cleric or monk (a "devoted man of prayer"), that he lived in a region hard-hit by the famine (i.e., Germany), and that the king personally had asked him to write the work. Moreover, the author laments his "continuous expenditures of goods" (continua rerum dispendia) in conjunction with the famine.[40] This comment again suggests a connection to Rudolf's account of the 850 famine in the *Annals of Fulda*. Rudolf wrote that Hrabanus spent significant resources to feed the poor: "In that same year a severe famine struck the German people, especially those living along the Rhine. At Mainz one measure of corn was sold for ten shekels of silver. At that time Archbishop Hrabanus was staying at an estate in his diocese called Winkel. Receiving the poor from all over, he daily fed more than three hundred, in addition to those who regularly dined in his presence."[41] Hrabanus's feeding of the poor at Winkel presumably would have required the cooperation of churches and monasteries in his diocese, and thus the author's comment about his expenditures suggests that he was a cleric or monk in the diocese of Mainz who contributed to the archbishop's hunger-relief efforts. The manuscript evidence supports the theory that the author had connections to the archbishop, since the treatise survives in a Mainz codex.

Geography dictated that Louis would have traveled through the middle Rhine region on his way to meet with Lothar at Cologne in the summer of 850.[42] This gives us a plausible setting in which the king could have commissioned the work from this learned churchman in the circles around Hrabanus. Indeed, the east Frankish king issued three diplomas at Tribur (just ten miles southeast of Mainz) in the first half of June (on June 6, 12, and 14), although the fact that the royal scribe Reginbert made mistakes in the dating clauses means that these charters can only be dated with certainty to 848x850.[43] While Paul Kehr tentatively favored a date of 849, they fit equally well in June 850, and the latter dating has the advantage of coinciding exactly with Louis's known itinerary, since the king was with Lothar at Cologne on July 1, 850.[44] If the dating of Louis's three diplomas to June 850 is accepted, then it is noteworthy that the one he issued on June 6 was for Archbishop Hrabanus himself, who had come to the king at Tribur.[45] Intriguingly, the preamble of this diploma expresses the hope that "what is given to God . . . cannot be unfruitful [infructuosum]." This is the only time Louis's diplomas employ the term *infructuosum*, which suggests the king and archbishop's concern about the unfruitful harvests of 850 and their desire to regain God's favor. One is tempted to suggest a monastic author from Fulda, where Hrabanus had earlier been abbot before becoming archbishop, which would explain the author's Anglo-Saxon terminology and apparent connections to Hrabanus and Mainz. Indeed, a diploma of Lothar I dated July 1, 850, reveals that Abbot Hatto of Fulda sent a group of monks with Louis the German to Cologne, and it is conceivable that the anonymous author was one of these Fulda *fratres* in the king's entourage.[46]

Behind the 850 treatise lay Louis the German's questions about the mixed messages the Bible and penitential books gave about hunting, eating meat, and the fundamental nature of Creation. According to the book of Genesis, after creating animals on the sixth day, "God saw everything He had made, and indeed it was very good" (Genesis 1:31). Indeed, Hrabanus had made the theme of the goodness of Creation the central thesis of his twenty-two volume encyclopedia, the *De rerum naturis*, a copy of which he sent to Louis in the mid-840s. In the introductory first chapter of that work, Hrabanus argued that all Creation was good because God himself, the Highest Good, had created it, and he highlighted this overarching theme in his dedicatory letter to the king.[47] Genesis went on to sanction the eating of all kinds of meat, since after the flood God proclaimed to Noah: "Every moving thing that lives will be food for you, just as I gave you the green plants" (Genesis 9:3). Yet the book of Leviticus seemed to contradict the goodness of Creation and man's permission to eat any animal through its long lists of clean and unclean animals and the prohibition of eating blood (Leviticus 11, 17:10–14). In the 830s Hrabanus had addressed this very problem in his commentary on Leviticus. Noting that Leviticus 11 seemed to contradict the goodness of Creation, he solved this riddle through a spiritual interpretation, arguing that the unclean animals represent sinners, while the clean signify those people who are devoted to God's Law.[48]

But other questions remained. What about the eating of animals killed by other animals, the prohibition Rudolf had referred to in his description of the 850 famine? Because hunters often captured their game with the help of hounds, hawks, and falcons, this seemed to go against the command that no one should eat an animal "captum a bestia" (torn by a wild beast) (Leviticus 17:15). As is well known, St. Paul broke decisively with Judaism over the necessity for Christians to observe the Mosaic Law, teaching that faith in Christ alone leads to salvation: "You who want to be justified by the Law have cut yourselves off from Christ; you have fallen away from grace. . . . For in Christ Jesus neither circumcision nor uncircumcision counts for anything; the only thing that counts is faith working through love" (Galatians 5:2-6). Yet the early Christians' abandonment of Jewish dietary restrictions had not been absolute. Early Jewish Christians, like those in Jerusalem led by Jesus's brother James, argued that the Mosaic Law should be maintained by all Christians. The Acts of the Apostles alleges that Paul and James reached a compromise over this thorny issue at the so-called Council of Jerusalem (ca. AD 49). After discussing the matter they decreed that gentile converts were freed from most aspects of the Jewish Law (including circumcision), but that they were to "abstain from what has been sacrificed to idols, from blood, from what has been strangled [suffocatum], and from fornication" (Acts 15:19–20, 28–29). While this decision sought to establish a middle ground between early Jewish and gentile Christians, eight centuries later Louis the German apparently found its significance puzzling. What exactly did the peculiar term *suffocatum* actually mean? And how did this term apply to animals killed while hunting?[49]

Early medieval penitential books compounded the confusion about how dietary restrictions applied to the hunt. As Rob Meens has demonstrated, food regulations in penitentials were important markers for delineating the "spheres of the unclean and the sacred" in early medieval society.[50] Yet there were a large number of penitentials circulating in ninth-century Europe, and they often did not agree with each other about the specific boundaries between pollution and the holy. To give an example related to the *Annals of Fulda*'s account of the 850 famine: the penitential known as *Oxoniense II*, perhaps written by St. Willibrord (d. 739), decreed that a person who ate unclean food, even if out of ignorance, was a sinner and had to perform penance.[51] In contrast, as already noted, the Penitential of Theodore was more lenient, stating that "if driven by necessity, that is, famine, one may eat unclean flesh and a carcass torn by beasts, because what is lawful is one thing, what necessity requires is another."[52] It was because of this confusion among penitentials that Ebbo of Reims in ca. 830 commissioned Bishop Halitgar of Cambrai to compose a new, authoritative penitential that went back to the earliest rulings of the church. Halitgar's "Roman" penitential was never universally accepted, however, so it in fact simply contributed to the diversity among ninth-century penitentials.[53]

With regard to hunting, penitentials offered rulings that, if heeded, would have severely curtailed the techniques hunters could use if they wanted to eat the game. For example, the Penitential of Theodore prohibited the eating of "animals that are torn by wolves or dogs," thereby making it almost impossible to hunt with canines in the traditional manner unless the huntsman somehow prevented his dogs from attacking their quarry.[54] The following chapter of the Penitential of Theodore decreed that birds and other animals killed by a hawk likewise could not be eaten, "because the Acts of the Apostles commanded to abstain from four principal things: from fornication, from blood, from that which is strangled, and from idolatry."[55] This ruling in effect proscribed the eating of any birds captured through the sport of falconry, since hawks and falcons often kill their prey immediately upon impact, the former relying on their deadly talons and powerful feet and the latter using their great swooping velocity.[56] Halitgar of Cambrai's penitential offered similar obstacles to hunters. In a chapter titled "On Strangled Animals," Halitgar argued that game killed by dogs or hawks fell under the category of *suffocatum*, again proscribing the eating of hunted animals unless the hunter himself had delivered the coup de grâce using a weapon with an iron tip or edge.[57] In effect, therefore, penitentials such as those of Theodore and

Halitgar outlawed the eating of most birds taken through falconry and seriously curtailed the eating of game taken with dogs. As Raymund Kottje has demonstrated, by the 840s manuscripts of Halitgar's penitential circulated at Fulda, Wissembourg, and Mainz, thus making the text available to Archbishop Hrabanus and Louis the German's archchaplain, Grimald of St.-Gall, who was also abbot of Wissembourg.[58] It was to resolve such apparent contradictions between hunting and dietary laws that Louis the German commissioned the anonymous author to compose the 850 treatise.

In contrast to the penitentials, our anonymous author took a much more flexible position that was sympathetic to hunters and their techniques. He began by reconsidering exactly what the term *suffocatum* meant. In contrast to Theodore and Halitgar, the author drew a firm distinction between trained dogs, hawks, and falcons on the one hand and wild *bestiae* on the other. He argued that the term "strangled" applied only to animals killed by the latter: "We call an animal strangled if it has been choked to death or torn open by a wolf, bear, or other wild beast. We say that meat of this kind must be avoided and not eaten as food."[59] Yet an animal seized by a dog, hawk, traps, or nets could legitimately be consumed, he explained, since it was the hunter's cleverness (*ingenium, calliditas*), skilled labor (*artificiosa industria*), and art (*ars*) that lay behind the capture of the animal. He summed up this position with the dictum "hominis est venatio" (the hunt belongs to man): "This is because the hunt belongs to man, whom the dog accompanies. Man uses the dog's keen sense of smell and swift speed to capture the animal, and thus the capture is ascribed not to the dog but to the man."[60]

The author went on to give a similar defense of falconry: "The method in fowling should be understood to be similar. If a dove, crane, goose, or any other bird is seized and torn apart by a hawk or 'capus,' that is, a trained falcon that returns to a man's hand, it should not be called strangled, since it is captured by the man whom the falcon's rational nature serves in capturing birds."[61] Although Scripture does not refer to falconry (the sport was introduced to the Roman elite by the Germanic peoples in the fourth century),[62] our author noted that the prophet Elijah had eaten meat brought to him by crows in the desert (1 Kings 17:6), thereby perhaps suggesting a scriptural precedent for falconry.[63] The author touched on other methods of hunting as well, such as using traps and nets, driving game into rivers, and fishing, the latter of which had been enjoyed by Louis the German's father, Louis the Pious.[64] He also mentioned the hunting of wild asses (*onagri*), a practice enjoyed by the Muslim caliphs and Byzantine emperors.[65] It is noteworthy that the anonymous author repeatedly employed the word "capture" (*captio, capere, captum*) to describe the dog or hawk's seizing of the hunted animal, thereby sidestepping the thorny issue of whether the hunter had actually killed it with his own weapon. He summarized his position, "Thus it is proper to conclude generally that whatever is captured by man's exercise, art, or cunning ought not to be reckoned among those things strangled, nor should he be guilty of any crime, as long as he takes it with thanksgiving."[66]

In the next section of the work, the author turned to what Scripture has to say about food and especially meat.[67] Here the author concurred with Hrabanus's position in *De rerum naturis* regarding the fundamental goodness of all God's Creation, stating, "Thus let there be in us the knowledge in which we know that all things are good." Taking as his point of departure Titus 1:15, "All things are pure to the pure," he emphasized that it was a person's internal, spiritual state that dictated whether eating meat was sinful. Thus the eating of hunted game and other foods was permissible, he argued, as long as it was accepted with thanksgiving and free from gluttony. In making these remarks, the author not only supported his arguments with numerous biblical passages but he demonstrated his erudition by quoting from two Roman authors, Augustine and Horace. His quote from Augustine came from the *Confessions*: "I fear not impurity of food, but impurity of desire" (10.31.46). This quotation comes from Augustine's longer discussion about the allures of food and drink and the importance of moderation, a passage in which Augustine notably cited many of the scriptural passages invoked in this treatise—and thus suggesting where our author got some of his material.[68] A few lines earlier the author echoed a line from Horace: "A jar will long retain the odor of what it was dipped in only once when new."[69] Horace's words appropriately came from a letter about the importance of men learning to control their desires while still young, and it is perhaps not coincidence that the specific passage of Horace invoked the imagery of the hunt: "A hunting pup can hunt in the woods from the moment it barks at a deer's hide in the hall. Now while you are still a boy, drink in my words with a youthful heart and trust your betters. A jar will long retain the odor of what it was dipped in only once when new."

To defend his position about the goodness of Creation, the author gave a brief excurse on the history of the early church to explain why the apostles had prohibited the eating of strangled animals as reported in Acts 15. He explained that the apostles made this decree as a concession to the Jewish Christians, who found it difficult to abandon completely the Law of the Torah: "So that they might not be upset and the new faith scandalized, the holy apostles, wanting to remove the yoke of the Law from the gentiles, abolished the greatest restrictions but permitted limited aspects of the Law to be observed by them, instructing that they abstain from strangled animals, as the Law commands, stating, 'You shall not eat an animal already dead or torn by a wild beast' [Leviticus 17:15]." The author therefore concluded that the restriction against eating strangled animals was a customary prohibition (*consuetudine prohibente*) rooted in the early history of the church—a prohibition that should be respected because of its antiquity, but not one that contradicted the goodness of God's Creation.

The author struck a notably defensive tone throughout the work, again hinting at a lively debate around Louis the German's court about dietary restrictions and hunting. At one point the author interjected, "Let me say what I think, and if it has limited authority, at least it will not be wholly foolish." A few lines later he added, "Truly I do not write these things arrogantly to defend my own personal opinion. Rather, I am prepared to give way to a better understanding, bestow the palm of victory upon him whom God will have inspired more correctly, and freely submit myself to his teaching." As we have seen, the penitentials of Theodore and Halitgar offered different judgments about what kinds of hunted game could be eaten, and the author may have anticipated objections from adherents to different schools of thought.

The second text related to hunting and falconry is a treatise that Archbishop Hincmar of Reims wrote for Louis the German in 865 concerning the kind of bird referred to in St. Jerome's translation of Psalm 104:17: "[The cedar of Lebanon] is home to the *herodius*, their leader."[70] The few historians who have commented on this treatise (myself included) have done so only in passing, interpreting it simply as proof of Louis's interest in obscure scriptural puzzles.[71] Yet a closer investigation reveals that Hincmar's treatise focused on a number of the same issues raised in the 850 treatise about hunting and dietary laws. Once again Louis the German personally requested this work, this time during a summit with Charles the Bald at Tusey in February 865. During this meeting, the east Frankish king had an unfinished discussion about Scripture with Hincmar and Bishop Altfrid of Hildesheim.[72] Hincmar began his treatise by vividly recounting their interrupted conversation, giving us a rare glimpse of the oral debates about Scripture at Louis the German's court. He wrote:

> Not long ago in Tusey when you held talks with my lord King Charles, your only brother, as you well remember, one day in my presence you summoned the venerable Bishop Altfrid according to the wisdom God gave you. You then began to ask questions about certain obscure and difficult passages of holy Scripture and to investigate them carefully. I made an effort to answer your questions, as far as the Lord enabled me and time and place permitted. But your investigation got only as far as considering and examining that all the works of God are very good, as the truth of Scripture states in Genesis [1:31]. The apostle confirms this, saying: "All things are pure to the pure" [Titus 1:15] and "Nothing should be rejected as long as it is received with thanksgiving" [1 Timothy 4:4]. You then asked why certain animals are described in the Law as unclean and not to be eaten by the people of God [Leviticus 11].[73]

What is striking here is that Louis the German was discussing the exact same issues raised in the anonymous treatise composed fifteen years earlier: hunting, clean and unclean animals, and the goodness of Creation. Indeed, Hincmar notably referred to several key scriptural verses cited in the 850 treatise (Genesis 1:31, Titus 1:15, 1 Timothy 4:4, Leviticus 11). These specific echoes clinch the argument for Louis the German as the recipient of the anonymous 850 treatise, and they indicate that he continued to be curious about these issues and talked about them during his discussion with Hincmar and Altfrid in 865. It was perhaps not by chance that Louis brought up these topics again in that year. The previous year he had injured his ribs when he fell from his horse while hunting in a game park, forcing him to convalesce in a nearby monastery for several days.[74] Indeed, the year 864 saw a number of royal hunting mishaps: Charles the Bald's son suffered a serious head wound while hunting with his companions in the forest of Cuise; Emperor Louis II was gored by a stag while hunting in the mountains of Italy; and Louis the German's own son Carloman escaped from his father's custody by pretending to go hunting.[75] As with the famine of 850, it is conceivable that all these misfortunes in 864 rekindled concerns in Louis's mind that eating certain kinds of game was offensive to God, who was punishing him and his relatives for their sins.

After reaffirming the goodness of God's Creation with Hincmar and Altfrid, Louis then turned to a specific question he had about the seventeenth verse of Psalm 104. Hincmar continued his recollection of their discussion:

> When this question seemed answered in light of Catholic tradition, you then asked why it is stated in the Psalms: "It is home to the *herodius*, their leader" [Psalm 104:17]. Anticipating my own response, the venerable Bishop Altfrid—who because of his Saxon race and natural intelligence speaks more quickly than I—cited the interpretation of the Septuagint translation: "It is home to the coot [*fulica*], their leader." At that point I began to respond that there are two kinds of *herodii*, just as there are two kinds of pelicans. . . . But at that moment my lord King Charles, your only brother, came up and urged you to make a speech to your faithful men, which was the purpose of your meeting. As you were leaving, you urged me to heed your wishes and promise to write down and send to your lordship what I ought to have responded then.[76]

In the remainder of the work, Hincmar gave a long discussion of the literal and mystical meanings of Psalm 104:17, citing the commentaries of Jerome, Augustine, Prosper of Aquitaine, Cassiodorus, Isidore of Seville, and Gregory the Great.[77]

Louis's question about the precise kind of bird meant by the Latin word *herodius* in Psalm 104:17 was not simply a point of obscure scriptural vocabulary, however. Leviticus 11:19 listed the *herodius* among the birds that could not be eaten, and the topic therefore was germane to their discussion about clean and unclean animals. The Hebrew word for *herodius* is *kws*, apparently meaning a small owl,[78] but Carolingian scholars did not know Hebrew and had to rely on Jerome's Vulgate translation of the Torah as well as the older Vetus Latina translation from the Greek Septuagint. As the passage above indicates, Hincmar and Altfrid immediately sought a solution to the meaning of *herodius* by considering the Vetus Latina translation and thus came up with *fulica* 'coot', a black-feathered waterfowl related to the moorhen. This was the translation of *herodius* that Hincmar supported in his 865 treatise for Louis.[79]

Yet the source of Louis's curiosity about the meaning of *herodius* seems to have gone deeper and to have been bound up with his interest in hunting and especially falconry. In his *De rerum naturis*, Hrabanus had devoted an entire chapter to the subject of birds, largely basing his discussion on Isidore of Seville's *Etymologies*.[80] Like Hincmar and Altfrid, Hrabanus had followed the Vetus Latina and equated the *herodius* with the coot.[81] A few pages later in a section on raptors, however, Hrabanus mistakenly stated that *herodius* was another name for falcon. He wrote: "The hawk [*accipiter*] is a bird armed more with courage than with talons, possessing great strength in its little body. This bird took its name from 'obtaining' [*accipiendo*], that is, from 'capturing' [*capiendo*]. It is avid in capturing other birds and thus called an *accipiter*, that is, a raptor . . . The *capus* in the Italian tongue gets its name from *capiendo*. Our people call this bird a falcon, which is known by another name, the *herodius*."[82] As we have seen, Hrabanus had sent Louis a copy of his encyclopedia in the 840s, and the king presumably paid special attention to this section on hawks and falcons. Thus we discover the root cause of Louis's curiosity about the meaning of *herodius*. It arose not only from the king's desire to understand the book of Leviticus and the obscure vocabulary of its dietary restrictions but also from his deep interest hunting and falconry and thus his confusion that Hrabanus had translated *herodius* both as "coot" and "falcon." In the dedicatory letter of his *De rerum naturis*, Hrabanus had expressed his hope that Louis and his "keen readers" (sagacissimi lectores) would read, discuss, and, if necessary, correct his twenty-two volume encyclopedia.[83] At Tusey in 865 we find the east Frankish king doing precisely that during his conversation about Scripture with Hincmar of Reims and Altfrid of Hildesheim. In these discussions Louis not only revisited the question about hunting and scriptural dietary laws that the 850 treatise had addressed but he also wanted to sort out a confusing error Hrabanus had made concerning hawks, falcons, and *herodii* in the eighth book of his *De rerum naturis*.

A possible third piece of evidence for interest in hunting and falconry at Louis the German's court comes from another neglected text. This is the *Liber accipitrum* or "Book of Hawks," which survives in a single eleventh-century copy in a manuscript from Poitiers.[84] The *Liber accipitrum*, which consists of thirty chapters, is not a manual on falconry but rather a list of hawks' various ailments (skin diseases, lack of appetite, fever, fungus, respiratory difficulty, lethargy, etc.) and the recipes for their putative cures. The ingredients of the medicinal reme-dies are often exotic, although it seems unlikely that most of them actually would have cured a sick bird. Particularly notable is the work's careful attention to the measurement of the recipes' ingredients, and it concludes with a chapter that standardizes the different weights and measures used throughout the treatise.[85] One chapter (seventeen), however, gave some basic practical advice about the training of hawks during the autumn and winter:

> To nourish a hawk so that it will be strong and muscular, it should be well fed from the day it is captured until the first day of January. Moreover, it should eat different kinds of meat, and you will see it grow strong and hardy. When you take it on the day just mentioned [January 1], incite it to hunt and give it a third of what it catches [?]. There will not be any bird whose flesh it will not be able to eat. It will not fear wind or snow, since it was nourished to be strong, and in this way you will be able to control it.[86]

The main clues for the compiler and date of the *Liber accipitrum* come from its opening words: "Here begins the little work of Grimaldus, the tutor and count of the sacred palace, on the diet and raising of hawks for King Charles."[87] The reference to *Karulus rex* seems to indicate a Carolingian royal recipient, even though the recipes appear to be several centuries older in their original Latin composition.[88] An Smets, who published an edition of the *Liber acciptrum*, con-cluded that the most likely identity for the compiler, "Grimaldus baiulus et comes sacri palatii," is none other than Grimald of St.-Gall, whom we have already met as Louis the German's archchaplain and chancellor between 833 and 870.[89] In turn, this would seem to indicate that the recipient *Karulus rex* was Louis the German's half-brother, the west Frankish king Charles the Bald (840–77).

Louis the German's personal interest in treatises related to hunting and falconry strengthens Smet's argument for Grimald of St.-Gall as the compiler of the *Liber accipitrum*. Of course, Grimald was Louis's archchaplain and high chancellor and not his count of the palace, and thus one would have to believe that a later copier of the *Liber accipitrum* incorrectly changed his title from *capel-lanus* to *comes*.[90] Yet the description of Grimald of St.-Gall as a tutor (*baiulus*) is appropriate, since one contemporary described him as the teacher (*preceptor*) of the young boys (*infantuli*) at Louis the German's palace.[91] It is wholly conceivable that Grimald of St.-Gall gave Charles the Bald a copy of the *Liber accipitrum*.

As this article has demonstrated, Louis the German's meetings with other rulers included hunting trips, learned discussions about hunting, and the dedication of treatises about the hunt. Seen in this context, it is believable that Grimald of St.-Gall gave Charles the Bald a copy of the *Liber accipitrum* as a diplomatic present from the east Frankish court, perhaps during one of the many meetings between the east and west Frankish kings. If the argument for Grimald of St.-Gall's authorship is accepted, this would make his *Liber accipitrum* the earliest surviving Latin treatise on falcons and falconry.[92] It would also suggest that Grimald had his own copy that perhaps circulated at the east Frankish court.

In conclusion, these neglected texts from Louis the German's court indicate the centrality not only of the hunt for Carolingian political culture but also of learned debates about hunting and falconry. These courtly conversations about hunting involved both the spoken and written word, with discussions sometimes leading to the commissioning of Latin treatises, and then those treatises sparking further oral discussions and written works. Unlike Frederick II four centuries later, Louis the German and his contemporaries seem not to have desired comprehensive treatises on hunting techniques, skills that in the early Middle Ages were passed by word of mouth from generation to generation.[93] Instead, the Carolingians appear to have been more interested in reading works on theological, scriptural, philosophical, and veterinary aspects of hunting: the relationship between hunting and dietary regulations, what hunting revealed about the nature of Creation, the precise meaning of relevant Latin words in Scripture, and, if Grimald of St.-Gall indeed compiled the *Liber accipitrum*, medicinal remedies for hunting animals. What is particularly striking about these courtly discussions about hunting is their close connections to the careful reading of texts: the Latin Bible (both Jerome's Vulgate and the Vetus Latina), penitential books, Hrabanus's massive *De rerum naturis*, veterinary recipes, as well as newly commissioned treatises on specific questions of the king. In short, Louis the German's palace was a court society that took seriously vigorous hunting, thoughtful reading, and learned debate. The absence of comprehensive hunting manuals before the twelfth and thirteenth centuries therefore does not point to the absence of sophisticated hunting and highly literate court societies in the Carolingian era. Rather, it suggests the different intellectual interests of Carolingian and later medieval elites. Louis the German and Frederick II both were avid huntsmen, but they seem to have been fascinated by different aspects of the chase.

Appendix

An Anonymous Treatise on Hunting and Dietary Laws for Louis the German (850)[94]

We call an animal strangled that has been choked to death or torn open by a wolf, bear, or some wild beast. We say that meat of this kind must be avoided and not eaten as food. However, we do not reckon among things strangled that which is captured by a dog. This is because the hunt belongs to man, whom the dog accompanies. Man uses the dog's keen sense of smell and swift speed to capture the animal. Thus the capture is ascribed not to the dog but to the man. For when we write, we attribute the writing not to the pen with which the letters are written but to the hand of the writer. In the same way traps, snares, and other devices of this kind should be understood: human cleverness and skilled industry invented all these things. Thus it is proper to conclude generally that whatever is captured by man's exercise, art, or cunning ought not to be reckoned among those animals that are strangled. Nor is a person who takes food of this kind guilty of a crime, as long as he does so with thanksgiving.

Many people also inquire whether an animal killed in water ought to be called strangled, or if it is permissible to have it as food. For it often happens that a wild ass, deer, or some other edible animal, chased by the barking of pursuing dogs, throws itself into a dangerous river and dies in that foreign element, that is to say, in water. But in this case it is still not reckoned as strangled, since man is the cause and the hunt is his. For when a fish is taken from the water, it too dies in a foreign element, that is to say, in air. Nevertheless, it is not called strangled or forbidden for human consumption. Not dissimilar should be understood the method of fowling. If a dove, crane, goose, or any other bird is captured and torn apart by a hawk or "capus," that is, a trained falcon, that returns to the man's hand, it should not be called strangled, since it is captured by the man whom nature's intelligence serves in capturing birds. And whatever is captured by means of a trap, nets, or hidden bird lime is also exempt from the term "strangled" and may be eaten without sin.

For food is sanctified by faith and by the sanctification of the divine name. About these things comes to mind what the apostle [Paul] says: "All things are pure to the pure" [Titus 1:15]; and elsewhere: "All Creation is good, and to the faithful nothing God created should be thought unclean, as long as it is received with thanksgiving" [1 Timothy 4:4]. Since the apostle decrees that all things are pure to the pure and defines all Creation as good, then it is manifestly clear that nothing in itself is impure. Thus no food should be condemned or rejected.

But why then, if all things are pure and good, do the holy apostles prohibit us from animals that have been strangled? Let me say what I think, and if it has limited authority, at least it will not be wholly foolish. When the church was in its infancy, there were many Jews who believed but nevertheless still wanted to keep the Law. They said that circumcision, the Sabbath, and other institutes of the Law ought to be kept by those gentiles who believed, and that they should live according to their custom. For they could not suddenly forget that which they had long held and quickly unlearn the wisdom of which they had once drunk. So that such people might not be upset and the new faith scandalized, the holy apostles, wanting to remove the yoke of the Law from the gentiles, abolished the greatest restrictions but permitted limited aspects of the Law to be observed by them, instructing that they abstain from strangled animals, as the Law commands, stating: "You shall not eat an animal already dead or torn by a wild beast" [Leviticus 17:15]. For when the apostle speaks of sacrifices to idols, that is, those things that are burned before idols, he says: "If an unbeliever invites you to a meal and you are inclined to go, eat whatever is set before you without raising any question on the grounds of conscience" [1 Corinthians 10:27]; and elsewhere: "Eat whatever is sold in the market and without raising any question on the grounds of conscience" [1 Corinthians 10:25].

From these words it is manifestly clear that what is received with faith and thanksgiving is good and does not at all make the person eating it guilty of a crime—as long as there is not the greed and desire of gluttony, which is the sole cause and origin of sin. About this the apostle says: "Make no provision for the flesh to gratify its desires" [Romans 13:14]. And blessed father Augustine says: "I fear not impurity of food, but impurity of desire" [Confessions 10.31.46]. Furthermore, in paradise Adam, the first parent of mankind, did not eat meat but the forbidden fruit, and he was condemned and thrust into exile in this world. In the desert Elijah ate meat, but he did not offend God because he did so out of necessity, not greed [1 Kings 17:6]. And so it is permissible to use these things in nature, which is good, but not to abandon completely customary prohibitions. For if I see someone eating these or other foods that custom rejects, I would curse him, depart, and call him contaminated and loathsome because of the food he ate.

Thus let there be in us the knowledge in which we know that all things are good. Let there be in us the charity through which we yield to the custom of many and accept their ways. Truly I do not write these things arrogantly to defend my own personal opinion. For I am prepared to give way to a better understanding and bestow the palm of victory upon him whom God will have inspired more correctly, and I freely will desire to submit myself to his teaching. For if indeed we have [written] nothing good from good things, we should not love anything of our own creativity unless the truth ordains it.

Now, my most desired lord, beloved with my whole heart, I beseech your majesty, since I (not ignorant of my own insignificance) strove to carry out your command, that you consider my urgent situation, overlook my shyness, pardon my ignorance, and favor my devotion. Modesty does not hinder me from freely admitting our misery. Every day the enemy army thunders around us with arms, the continuous expenditures of goods wear us down, and famine's unprecedented want stalks throughout our region. We are worn out by these and innumerable other calamities because of our sins, and we pray that you continually deign to extend your most generous hand to us. If you adorn us with your generosity, it will increase your name and glory, and you will win us as your faithful servant and devoted man of prayer for all eternity.

Notes

I would like to thank Lynda Coon, Mayke de Jong, Rob Meens, Robin S. Oggins, and Björn Weiler for helpful comments on early drafts of this article.

1. Frederick II, *De arte venandi cum avibus*, ed. Carl Arnold Willemsen (Leipzig, 1942), 1:1. A loose English translation is available in Casey A. Wood and F. Marjorie Fyfe, trans., *The Art of Falconry, Being the "De arte venandi cum avibus" of Frederick II of Hohenstaufen* (Stanford, 1943), 3. On Frederick II and hunting, see David Abulafia, *Frederick II: A Medieval Emperor* (Oxford, 1988), 267–70; Wolfgang Stürner, *Friedrich II*, 2nd ed., 2 vols. (Darmstadt, 2003), 2:429–47.

2. Bernhard Bischoff, "Die älteste europäische Falkenmedizin (Mitte des zehnten Jahrhunderts)," in *Anecdota Novissima: Texte des vierten bis sechzehnten Jahrhunderts*, ed. Bernhard Bischoff (Stuttgart, 1984), 171–82 (171–72); Robin S. Oggins, *The Kings and Their Hawks: Falconry in Medieval England* (New Haven, CT, 2004), 1–2; Martina Giese, "Graue Theorie und grünes Weidwerk? Die mittelalterliche Jagd zwischen Buchwissen und Praxis," *Archiv für Kulturgeschichte* 89 (2007): 19–59 (20, 31).

3. Frank Barlow, *William Rufus* (New Haven, CT, 2000), 121. See further Frank Barlow, "Hunting in the Middle Ages," *Transactions of the Devonshire Association* 113 (1981): 1–11.

4. Only a handful of examples can be cited here: Marcelle Thiébaux, *The Stag of Love: The Chase in Medieval Literature* (Ithaca, 1974); John Cummins, *The Hound and the Hawk: The Art of Medieval Hunting* (London, 1988); Richard Almond, *Medieval Hunting* (Stroud, 2003); Oggins, *Kings and Their Hawks*; Werner Rösener, *Die Geschichte der Jagd: Kultur, Gesellschaft und Jagdwesen im Wandel der Zeit* (Düsseldorf, 2004); Jacques Bugnion, *Les chasses médiévales: Le brachet, le lévrier, l'épagneul, leur nomenclature, leur métier, leur typologie* (Gollion, 2005); Thomas T. Allsen, *The Royal Hunt in Eurasian History* (Philadelphia, 2006).

5. The one possible exception to which I refer is the *Liber accipitrum* of Grimaldus, which I will discuss toward the end of this article: *Le "Liber accipitrum" de Grimaldus: Un traité d'autourserie du Haut Moyen Âge*, ed. and trans. An Smets (Nogent-le-Roi, 1999).

6. For recent scholarship on Louis the German and his court, see: J. M. Wallace-Hadrill, *The Frankish Church* (Oxford, 1983), 329–45; Stuart Airlie, "True Teachers and Pious Kings: Salzburg, Louis the German, and Christian Order," in *Belief and Culture in the Middle Ages: Studies Presented to Henry Mayr-Harting*, ed. Richard Gameson and Henrietta Leyser (Oxford, 2001), 89–105; Wilfried Hartmann, *Ludwig der Deutsche* (Darmstadt,

2002), esp. 212–41; Wilfried Hartmann, ed., *Ludwig der Deutsche und seine Zeit* (Darmstadt, 2004); Boris Bigott, *Ludwig der Deutsche und die Reichskirche im Ostfränkischen Reich (826–876)* (Husum, 2002); Eric J. Goldberg, *Struggle for Empire: Kingship and Conflict under Louis the German, 817–876* (Ithaca, 2006), esp. 165–85.

7. Catherine Cubitt, ed., *Court Culture in the Early Middle Ages*, Studies in the Early Middle Ages (Turnhout, 2003); Patrick Wormald and Janet L. Nelson, eds., *Lay Intellectuals in the Carolingian World* (Cambridge, 2007).

8. The scholarship on hunting in antiquity and the early Middle Ages is extensive. Important discussions include: Régine Hennebicque, "Espaces sauvages et chasses royals dans le nord de la France: VIIème–IXème siècles," *Revue du Nord* 62 (1980): 35–57; Jörg Jarnut, "Die frühmittelalterliche Jagd unter rechts- und sozialgeschichtlichen Aspekten," *L'uomo di fronte al mondo animale nell'alto medioevo*, Settimane 31 (Spoleto, 1985), 765–808; J. K. Anderson, *Hunting in the Ancient World* (Berkeley and Los Angeles, 1984); Lutz Fenske, "Jagd und Jäger im früheren Mittelalter: Aspekte ihres Verhältnisses," in *Jagd und höfische Kultur im Mittelalter*, ed. Werner Rösener (Göttingen, 1997), 29–93. For the related subject of banqueting, see: D. A. Bullough, *Friends, Neighbours and Fellow-Drinkers: Aspects of Community and Conflict in the Early Medieval West*, H. M. Chadwick Memorial Lectures 1 (Cambridge, 1990); Bonnie Effros, *Creating Community with Food and Drink in Merovingian Gaul* (New York, 2002); Matthew Innes, "'He Never Even Allowed His White Teeth to Be Bared in Laughter': The Politics of Humour in the Carolingian Renaissance," in *Humour, History and Politics in Late Antiquity and the Early Middle Ages*, ed. Guy Halsall (Cambridge, 2002), 131–56; Chris Wickham, *Framing the Early Middle Ages: Europe and the Mediterranean, 400–800* (Oxford, 2005), 195–97 and n. 110.

9. Franz Irsigler, "On the Aristocratic Character of Early Frankish Society," in *The Medieval Nobility: Studies on the Ruling Classes of France and Germany from the Sixth to the Twelfth Century*, trans. Timothy Reuter (New York, 1979), 105–36 (119–20).

10. Odo, *De vita Sancti Geraldi Auriliacensis comitis libri quattuor*, ch. 4, ed. Migne, PL 133:645a. In contrast to laymen, clerics and monks were prohibited from hunting, keeping dogs and falcons, and carrying weapons. Yet the fact that Carolingian church councils often restated such prohibitions indicates that some churchmen refused to give up their aristocratic way of life: Friedrich Prinz, *Klerus und Krieg im früheren Mittelalter* (Stuttgart, 1971), 83–85; Hubertus Lutterback, "Die für Kleriker bestimmten Verbote des Waffentragens, des Jagens sowie der Vogel- und Hundehaltung (500–900)," *Zeitschrift für Kirchengeschichte* 109 (1998): 149–66.

11. Einhard, *Vita Karoli magni*, chs. 19, 22, 30, ed. Oswald Holder-Egger, MGH SS rer. Germ. 25, 23, 27, 34–35; Thegan, *Gesta Hludowici*, ch. 19, ed. Ernst Tremp, MGH SS rer. Germ. 64, 200–201, 204–5; *Karolus Magnus et Leo Papa*, lines 137–325, ed. Ernst Dümmler, MGH Poetae 1, 369–74; Ermoldus Nigellus, *In honorem Hludowici imperatoris*, book 4, lines 481–565, ed. Ernst Dümmler, MGH Poetae 2, 71–74; the latter two of which are partly translated in Peter Godman, ed. and trans., *Poetry of the Carolingian Renaissance* (Norman, OK, 1985), 204–7, 256–57. Reports of royal hunts in the *Annales Bertiniani* are conveniently indexed in *Annals of St-Bertin*, trans. Janet L. Nelson (Manchester, 1991), 33–35, 40, 46–47, 111–12, 120, 152, 162, 170–71, 175, 180, 185. For poetic representations of the Carolingian hunt see further: Peter Godman, *Poets and Emperors* (Oxford, 1987), 82–92; Peter Godman, "The Poetic Hunt: From Saint Martin to Charlemagne's Heir," in *Charlemagne's Heir: New Approaches to the Reign of Louis the Pious*, ed. Peter Godman and Roger Collins (Oxford, 1990), 565–89, esp. 576–86. For Alfred and Henry

I, see: Asser, *De rebus gestis Ælfredi*, chs. 22, 74–76, ed. William Henry Stevenson, repr. ed. (Oxford, 1959), 20, 55, 58–59; Widukind, *Res gestae Saxonicae*, 1.39, in *Quellen zur Geschichte der sächsischen Kaiserzeit*, ed. Albert Bauer and Reinhold Rau, Ausgewählte Quellen zur deutschen Geschichte des Mittelalters 8 (Darmstadt, 1977), 78–79. For Carolingian court officials responsible for hunting, see: Hincmar von Reims, *De ordine palatii*, ch. 4, ed. and trans. Thomas Gross and Rudolf Schieffer, MGH Fontes iuris 3, 64–67.

12. Hennebicque, "Espaces sauvages et chasses royals," 35–57; Rosamond McKitterick, *Charlemagne: The Formation of a European Identity* (Cambridge, 2008), 166–67, 170.

13. References to Louis the German hunting: *Annales Xantenses*, s. a. 850, ed. Bernhard von Simson, MGH SS rer. Germ. 12, 17; *Annales de Saint-Bertin*, s. a. 864, ed. Félix Grat, Jeanne Vielliard, and Suzanne Clémencet (Paris, 1964), 114–15. For the hunting parks near Frankfurt, Regensburg, and Ranshofen, see: Karl Hauk, "Tiergärten im Pfalzbereich," in *Deutsche Königspfalzen: Beiträge zu ihrer historischen und archäologischen Erforschung*, Veröffentlichungen des Max-Plank-Instituts für Geschichte 11.1 (Göttingen, 1963), 30–74, esp. 35–38; Michael Gockel, *Karolingische Königshöfe am Mittelrhein* (Göttingen, 1970), 72–87 (and maps 1–2), 205.

14. For the end of Frankish military expansion in the 790s and its consequences for the politics and culture of the Carolingian court, see: Timothy Reuter, "The End of Carolingian Military Expansion," in *Charlemagne's Heir*, ed. Godman and Collins, 391–405; Matthew Innes, "Charlemagne's Government," in *Charlemagne: Empire and Society*, ed. Joanna Story (Manchester, 2005), 73–76; McKitterick, *Charlemagne*, 48–56.

15. Janet L. Nelson, "The Lord's Anointed and the People's Choice: Carolingian Royal Ritual," in *Rituals of Royalty: Power and Ceremonial in Traditional Societies*, ed. David Cannadine and Simon Price (Cambridge, 1987), 137–80, esp. 166–72 (repr. in Janet L. Nelson, *The Frankish World, 750–900* [London, 1996], 99–132, esp. 120–24). For hunting as a symbol of political stability, see: Nelson, "The Last Years of Louis the Pious," in *Charlemagne's Heir*, ed. Godman and Collins, 154–55. Paul Edward Dutton, "Charlemagne, King of Beasts," ch. 2 in *Charlemagne's Mustache and Other Cultural Clusters of a Dark Age* (New York, 2004), 43–68, emphasizes the motif of mastery over nature in Carolingian royal ideology.

16. Vienna, Österreichische Nationalbibliothek 956 (theol. 320), fols. 105v–106v. This manuscript was copied at Mainz in the late tenth century: Hartmut Hoffmann, *Buchkunst und Königtum im ottonischen und frühsalischen Reich* (Stuttgart, 1986), 264–65; Raymund Kottje, *Die Bußbücher Halitgars von Cambrai und des Hrabanus Maurus* (Berlin, 1980), 77–78 (no. 64). The codex contains an array of theological treatises and biblical commentaries, a number of them by Carolingian authors, including Alcuin's *De virtutibus et vitiis*, Smaragdus's *Via regia*, the only surviving copy of Einhard's *De adoranda cruce*, and (the latest datable text in the codex) a letter to Bishop Dado of Verdun (880–923) concerning the Magyar invasions: Michael Denis, *Codices manuscripti theologici Bibliothecae Palatinae Vindobonensis Latini aliarumque occidentis linguarum*, vol. 1 (Vienna, 1793), cols. 1031–54; Ernst Dümmler, "Ein Nachtrag zu Einhards Werken," *Neues Archiv der Gesellschaft für ältere deutsche Geschichtskunde* 11 (1886): 232–38, esp. 233–35. Otto Eberhardt, *Via regia: Der Fürstenspiegel Smaragds von St. Mihiel und seine literarische Gattung*, Münstersche Mittelalterschriften 28 (Munich, 1977), 125–26, suggests that this tenth-century codex with its intriguing combination of texts was intended for a royal audience.

17. Ernst Dümmler, "Ein theologisches Gutachten für Ludwig den Deutschen," *Neues Archiv der Gesellschaft für ältere deutsche Geschichtskunde* 11 (1886): 457–59; *Ad epistolas*

variorum supplementum, no. 10, ed. Ernst Dümmler, MGH Epp. 5, 633–35. Throughout this article I refer to the MGH edition.

18. *Annales Fuldenses*, s.a. 850, ed. Friedrich Kurze, MGH SS rer. Germ. 7, 40–41; *Annales Xantenses*, s.a. 850, MGH SS rer. Germ. 12, 17; Dümmler, "Ein theologisches Gutachten," 457. Here Dümmler was tentatively accepting the earlier suggestion of Denis, *Codices manuscripti theologici*, vol. 1, col. 1041: "Famis mentio scriptum istud anno 850 adfigere videtur."

19. Dümmler, "Ein theologisches Gutachten," 457: "Wenn dies [i.e., Denis's dating of 850] richtig ist, so kann unter dem zuletzt angeredeten Herrn offenbar nur Ludwig der Deutsche verstanden werden, dessen Theilnahme für wissenschaftliche, namentlich theologische Fragen und Schriften hinlänglich bekannt ist."

20. Dümmler, "Ein theologisches Gutachten," 457. Ernst Dümmler, *Geschichte des ostfränkischen Reichs*, 2nd ed., 3 vols. (1887–88; repr. Hildesheim, 1960), 2:418, described this work as "ein anderes theologisches Gutachten eines unbekannten Verfassers (vielleicht Rabans)."

21. *Ad epistolas variorum supplementum*, no. 10, MGH Epp. 5, 633–35.

22. One scholar who has touched briefly on this text is Rob Meens, "Pollution in the Early Middle Ages: The Case of the Food Regulations in Penitentials," *Early Medieval Europe* 4 (1995): 3–19 (17 and n. 79).

23. For Rudolf's probable authorship of the *Annals of Fulda* between 838 and 863, see Goldberg, *Struggle for Empire*, 14–15, 173–75.

24. *Annales Fuldenses*, s.a. 850, MGH SS rer. Germ. 7, 41.

25. *Penitential of Theodore, Discipulus Umbrensium*, 1.7.6, in *Die Canones Theodori Cantuariensis und ihre Überlieferungsformen*, ed. Paul Willem Finsterwalder, Untersuchungen zu den Bussbüchern des 7., 8. und 9. Jahrhunderts 1 (Weimar, 1929), 299: "Qui manducat carnem immundam aut morticinam dilacertam a bestiis XL dies peniteat. Si enim necessitas cogit famis, non nocet, quoniam aliud est legitimum, aliud quod necessitas cogit." Cf. *Annales Fuldenses*, s.a. 850, MGH SS rer. Germ. 7, 41: "Ambo tamen de carnibus lege prohibitis necessitate coacti se recrearunt." See further the *Paenitentiale pseudo-Theodori*, 16.1, in *Die Bussordnungen der abendländischen Kirche*, ed. F. W. H. Wasserschleben (1851; repr. Graz, 1958), 601: "Qui manducat carnem inmundam, aut morticinam, aut dilaceratam a bestiis, XL dies poeniteat, si necessitate famis cogente, multo levius." Concerning this text, see Carine van Rhijn and Marjolijn Saan, "Correcting Sinners, Correcting Texts: A Context for the *Paenitentiale pseudo-Theodori*," *Early Medieval Europe* 14 (2006): 23–40, who date it to ca. 820 x ca. 850.

26. *Annales Xantenses*, s.a. 850, MGH SS rer. Germ. 12, 17. For the identification of *in Hosninge* as the Ardennes Forest near Aachen, see Heinrich Kaspers, *Comitatus nemoris: Die Waldgrafschaft zwischen Maas und Rhein* (Düren, 1957), 89–93. Pertz incorrectly identified *in Hosninge* as the Osning Mountains in Saxony (*Annales Xantenses*, 17n11), a mistake that I unfortunately perpetuated (*Struggle for Empire*, 155). For the political context of these events, see: Dümmler, *Geschichte des ostfränkischen Reichs*, 1:346–47; Goldberg, *Struggle for Empire*, 153–56.

27. *Ad epistolas variorum supplementum*, no. 10, MGH Epp. 5, 633–34.

28. Rob Meens, "Politics, Mirrors of Princes and the Bible: Sins, Kings and the Well-Being of the Realm," *Early Medieval Europe* 7 (1998): 345–57.

29. Ibid., 353.

30. *Annales Fuldenses*, s.a. 846–50, MGH SS rer. Germ. 7, 36-40.

31. *Ad epistolas variorum supplementum*, no. 10, MGH Epp. 5, 635.

32. Hincmar, *Epistolae*, no. 179, ed. Ernst Perels, MGH Epp. 8.1, 167–72.

33. I am indebted to Mayke de Jong for advice on this point (personal correspondence).

34. *Ad epistolas variorum supplementum*, no. 10, MGH Epp. 5, 635.

35. For Hrabanus's career and scholarship, see especially: Raymund Kottje und Harald Zimmerman, eds., *Hrabanus Maurus: Lehrer, Abt und Bischof* (Mainz, 1982); Mayke de Jong, "Old Law and New-Found Power: Hrabanus Maurus and the Old Testament," in *Centres of Learning: Learning and Location in Pre-Modern Europe and the Near East*, ed. Jan Willem Drijvers and Alasdair A. MacDonald (Leiden, 1995), 161–76; Mayke de Jong, "The Empire as *Ecclesia*: Hrabanus Maurus and Biblical *Historia* for Rulers," in *The Uses of the Past in the Early Middle Ages*, ed. Yitzak Hen and Matthew Innes (Cambridge, 2000), 191–226; Goldberg, *Struggle for Empire*, 159–64, 174–76; Franz J. Felten and Barbara Nichtweiß, *Hrabanus Maurus: Gelehrter, Abt von Fulda und Erzbischof von Mainz* (Mainz, 2006).

36. *Ad epistolas variorum supplementum*, no. 10, MGH Epp. 5, 634 and nn. 1–2.

37. J. F. Niermeyer, *Mediae latinitatis lexicon minus* (Leiden, 1984), s.v. *charaxare* and *idolothytum*, 174, 508. For the appearance of *caraxare* and *idolothitum* in Anglo-Saxon sources, see: Aldhelm, *Opera*, ed. Rudolf Ehwald, MGH Auct. ant. 15, 64, 251, 273, 299, 304, 479, 497, 529; Stephan, *Vita Wilfridi*, chs. 49, 50, ed. and trans. Bertram Colegrave, *The Life of Bishop Wilfrid by Eddius Stephanus* (Cambridge, 1927; repr. 2007), 100, 102; Boniface and Lull, *Epistolae*, nos. 5, 6, 14, 98, ed. Ernst Dümmler, MGH Epp. 3, 114, 239, 242, 263, 385, 403. The word *caraxantur* also appears in a number of Anglo-Saxon charters; e.g., P. H. Sawyer, *Anglo-Saxon Charters: An Annotated List and Bibliography* (London, 1968), nos. 166, 567, 658, 695, 792, 922, 1175.

38. For "English missionaries on the Continent," see Ian N. Wood, *The Missionary Life: Saints and the Evangelisation of Europe, 400–1050* (Harlow, 2001), 57–122, and his cautionary words on 91–92.

39. *Ad epistolas variorum supplementum*, no. 10, MGH Epp. 5, 635.

40. The anonymous also mentioned recent attacks of the "enemy army," probably a reference to the Northmen who sacked Dorestad earlier in 850: *Annales Xantenses*, s.a. 850, MGH SS rer. Germ. 12, 17; *Annales Fuldenses*, s.a. 850, MGH SS rer. Germ. 7, 39.

41. *Annales Fuldenses*, s.a. 850, MGH SS rer. Germ. 7, 40–41.

42. For Louis's itinerary and frequent sojourns around Mainz and Frankfurt, see Goldberg, *Struggle for Empire*, 224–25.

43. *Die Urkunden Ludwigs des Deutschen*, nos. 55–57, ed. Paul Kehr, MGH Diplomata regum Germaniae ex stripe Karolinorum 1, 75–79. Based on the confused regnal years and indictions of the dating clauses, Kehr argued for a date of 848/49 for no. 55 and for 849/50 for nos. 56–57. However, the fact that all three were issued at Tribur and in early June strongly suggests that all of them should be dated to the same year. All of Reginbert's diplomas from these years (nos. 48, 50, 53–57) have problems in their dating clauses, which Kehr discusses with palpable frustration on pp. xxii, 73.

44. Lothar issued a diploma for Fulda on July 1: *Die Urkunden Lothars I.*, no. 111, ed. Theodor Schieffer, MGH Diplomata Karolinorum 3, 259–61. Kehr's dating of Louis's diplomas nos. 55–57 to June 849 presents its own potential problems, since Louis reportedly fell seriously ill in the summer of 849, apparently while in Bavaria. Louis's illness made him unable to lead an army against the Bohemians in person, and he therefore sent it under the command of his generals. The sources reporting the 849 Bohemian campaign

(*Annales Xantenses*, s.a. 849, MGH SS rer. Germ. 12, 16; *Annales de Saint-Bertin*, s.a. 849, ed. Grat et al., 58) indicate that the ailing Louis sent his army from *de Beioaria*, which creates difficulties for dating the three Tribur diplomas to June 849. Admittedly it is possible that the king was at Tribur in June 849 and then subsequently returned to Bavaria where he fell ill.

45. *Urkunden Ludwigs des Deutschen*, no. 55, MGH Diplomata reg. Germ. 1, 75–76. This charter was for Hrabanus's monastery of Klingenmünster in the Speyergau. This is Louis's only surviving diploma for Hrabanus. It is perhaps significant that the previous day, June 5, had been the feast of Saint Boniface, which suggests that the king and archbishop had observed the feast of Mainz's patron saint together at Tribur.

46. *Urkunden Lothars I.*, no. 111, MGH Diplomata Karolinorum 3, 259–61.

47. Hrabanus, *De rerum naturis*, 1.1, PL 111, cols. 13A–17C; Hrabanus, *Epistolae*, no. 37, MGH Epp. 5, 473.

48. Hrabanus, *Expositionum in Leviticum libri septem*, 3.1, PL 108, cols. 351A–351D. For Hrabanus's commentary on Leviticus, see Raffaele Savigni, "Purità rituale e ridefinizione del sacro nella cultura carolingia: L'interpretazione del *Levitico* e dell'*Epistola agli Ebrei*," *Annali di storia dell'esegesi* 13 (1996): 229–55, esp. 232–46.

49. The presence of Jews in the Carolingian empire may have exacerbated Christians' concerns about strangulation, since Jews considered strangled (*iugulatum*) any animal that was slaughtered by more than three cuts. According to Agobard of Lyons, the Jews disparagingly called improperly slaughtered animals "Christian beasts" (*Christiana pecora*) and sold such "unclean" meat to their Christian neighbors: Agobard, *De insolentia Iudeorum (ad Ludovicum)*, in *Agobardi Lugdunensis opera omnia*, ed. L. Van Acker, CCCM 52 (Turnhout, 1981), 191–95 (193).

50. Meens, "Pollution in the Early Middle Ages," 19. See further his "Politics, Mirrors of Princes and the Bible," 346–48; "Penitential Questions: Sin, Satisfaction and Reconciliation in the Tenth and Eleventh Centuries," *Early Medieval Europe* 14 (2006): 1–6; and "Penitentials and the Practice of Penance in the Tenth and Eleventh Centuries," *Early Medival Europe* 14 (2006): 7–21.

51. Meens, "Pollution in the Early Middle Ages," 9 and n. 26.

52. *Penitential of Theodore, Discipulus Umbrensium*, 1.7.6, in *Canones Theodori Cantuariensis*, ed. Finsterwalder, 299; Meens, "Pollution in the Early Middle Ages," 9 and n. 27. The English translations in *Medieval Handbooks of Penance*, trans. John T. McNeill and Helena M. Gamer (New York, 1938), here at 191, should be used with caution.

53. Kottje, *Büßbücher Halitgars von Cambrai*; Roger E. Reynolds, "The Organization, Law and Liturgy of the Western Church, 700–900," in *The New Cambridge Medieval History*, vol. 2, *c.700–c.900*, ed. Rosamond McKitterick (Cambridge, 1995), 587–621 (615).

54. *Penitential of Theodore, Discipulus Umbrensium*, 2.11.1, in *Canones Theodori Cantuariensis*, ed. Finsterwalder, 325: "Animalia quae a lupis seu canibus lacerantur, non sunt comedenda nec cervus nec capra si mortui inventi fuerint nisi forte ab homine adhuc viva occidentur sed porcis et canibus dentur."

55. Ibid., 2.11.2, 325: "Aves vero et animalia cetera si in retibus strangulantur non sunt comedenda hominibus nec si accipiter oppresserit si mortua inveniuntur quia IIII capitula actus apostolorum ita praecipiunt abstinere a fornicatione, a sanguine, et suffacoto et idolatria." Cf. the mistranslation in *Medieval Handbooks of Penance*, trans. McNeill and Gamer, 207.

56. Oggins, *Kings and Their Hawks*, 11, emphasizes this point.

57. Halitgar, *Liber poenitentialis*, PL 105, col. 704A: "De suffocatis: Si canis, aut vulpes, sive accipiter, aliquid mortificaverint; sive de fuste, sive de lapide, sive de sagitta, quae ferrum non habet, mortuum fuerit: haec omnia suffocata sunt: non manducentur. Et qui manducaverint, ieiunet hebdomadis vii." (Once again, the English translation in *Medieval Handbooks of Penance*, trans. McNeil and Gamer, 297–314, should be used with caution.)

58. Kottje, *Büßbücher Halitgars von Cambrai*, 88–89, 101–2, 200.

59. *Ad epistolas variorum supplementum*, no. 10, MGH Epp. 5, 633.

60. Ibid.

61. Ibid., 634.

62. Kurt Lindner, *Beiträge zu Vogelfang und Falknerei im Altertum* (Berlin, 1973), 111–56. More generally, see Oggins, *Kings and Their Hawks*, for royal hawking in central and late medieval England.

63. *Ad epistolas variorum supplementum*, no. 10, MGH Epp. 5, 634.

64. For Louis the Pious's periodic *piscatio atque venatio*, see Astronomer, *Vita Hludowici imperatoris*, chs. 46, 52, ed. Ernst Tremp, MGH SS. rer. Germ. 64, 466–67, 492–93. The *Waltharius* poet similarly depicted the hero Walter as a skilled fowler and angler: *Waltharius*, lines 420–25, in *"Waltharius" and "Ruodlieb,"* ed. and trans. Dennis M. Kratz (New York, 1984), 22–23.

65. Garth Fowden, *Qusayr 'Amra: Art and the Umayyad Elite in Late Antique Syria* (Berkeley, 2004), 85–114; Liudprand of Cremona, *Legatio*, chs. 37–38, in *Die Werke Liudprands von Cremona*, ed. Josef Becker, MGH SS rer. Germ. 3, 194–95.

66. *Ad epistolas variorum supplementum*, no. 10, MGH Epp. 5, 633.

67. Ibid., 634.

68. Ibid., 634n2; Augustine, *Confessions*, 31.43–47, trans. Henry Chadwick (Oxford, 1991), 204–7.

69. *Ad epistolas variorum supplementum*, no. 10, MGH Epp. 5, 634n1; Horace, *Epistolae*, 1.2.65–71, ed. H. W. Garrod, in *Q. Horati Flacci Opera* (Oxford, 1901, repr. 1989), 208–9.

70. Hincmar, *Epistolae*, no. 179, MGH Epp. 8.1, 167–72. This treatise survives in a single manuscript, Munich, clm 14738, fols. 82r–88r, apparently copied at St.-Gall in the second half of the tenth century. For this manuscript, see Bernhard Bischoff, "Bücher am Hofe Ludwigs des Deutschen und die Privatbibliothek des Kanzlers Grimalt," in *Mittelalterliche Studien: Ausgewählte Aufsätze zur Schriftkunde und Literaturgeschichte*, 3 vols. (Stuttgart, 1981), 3:187–212 (191 and n. 23).

71. Dümmler, *Geschichte des ostfränkischen Reiches*, 2:113; Hartmann, *Ludwig der Deutsche*, 214; Hartmann, "Ludwig der Deutsche," 20; Goldberg, *Struggle for Empire*, 166.

72. The classic study of Hincmar is Jean Devisse, *Hincmar, archevêque de Reims, 845–882* (Geneva, 1975–76). For Altfrid, see Hans Goetting, *Das Bistum Hildesheim*, vol. 3, *Die Hildesheimer Bischöfe von 815 bis 1221 (1227)*, Germania Sacra, n.s. 20 (Berlin, 1984), 84–115.

73. Hincmar, *Epistolae*, no. 179, MGH Epp. 8.1, 168. Concerning the Tusey meeting, see: *Hludowici et Karoli pactum Tusiacense*, no. 244, ed. Alfred Boretius and Viktor Krause, MGH Capit. 2, 165–67; Dümmler, *Geschichte des ostfränkischen Reiches*, 2:111–14.

74. *Annales de Saint-Bertin*, s.a. 864, ed. Grat et al., 114–15.

75. Ibid., 105, 114–15.

76. Hincmar, *Epistolae*, no. 179, MGH Epp. 8.1, 168.

77. Ibid., 168–71.

78. Ludwig Koehler and Walter Baumgartner, *Hebrew and Aramaic Lexicon of the Old Testament* (Leiden, 1995), s.v. *kws*, 2:466.

79. Hincmar, *Epistolae*, no. 179, MGH Epp. 8.1, 169: "Sed in eisdem libris legi quae subiungere procurabo, unde puto, sicut et vos poteritis conicere, quia communis edito fulicam pro herodio transtulit." Adding to the confusion, Dümmler, *Geschichte des ostfränkischen Reichs*, 2:418, translated *herodius* as *Reiger*, "heron," and this is the meaning also suggested by Niermeyer, *Mediae latinitatis lexicon minus*, s.v. *herodius*, 487.

80. Hrabanus, *De rerum naturis*, 8.6, PL 111, cols. 240D–255D; cf. Isidore of Seville, *Etymologiarum sive originum libri xx*, 12.7, ed. W. M. Lindsay (Oxford, 1911).

81. Hrabanus, *De rerum naturis*, 8.6, PL 111, col. 248C. Hrabanus quoted the Vetus Latina translation of Psalm 104.17: "Fulice domus dux eorum est."

82. Ibid., cols. 253A–B.

83. Hrabanus, *Epistolae*, no. 36, MGH Epp. 5, 472–73.

84. Poitiers, Médiathèque François-Mitterand 184 (288), fols. 70r–73v. For an edition, French translation, and analysis of the manuscript and text, see *Le "Liber accipitrum" de Grimaldus*, ed. Smets. This edition must be used with caution, however: see the review by Klaus-Dietrich Fischer, *Mittellateinisches Jahrbuch* 39 (2004): 118–21. See further An Smets, "The *materia medica* in the *Liber accipitrum* of Grimaldus: A Rich Collection of Simples of the Early Middle Ages," *Scientiarum historia* 27 (2001): 27–45.

85. The Latin terminology and orthography of the recipes suggest that they ultimately go back to the fifth or sixth century, when they apparently were translated from Greek into Latin in Italy, perhaps at Ravenna: *Le "Liber accipitrum" de Grimaldus*, ed. Smets, 34; Smets, "*Materia medica* in the *Liber accipitrum*," 30–31; Fischer, review of *Le "Liber accipitrum" de Grimaldus*, ed. Smets, 118–19, 120. How the *Liber accipitrum* author acquired these late antique prescriptions is unclear, but apparently they were circulating in the Carolingian empire.

86. *Le "Liber accipitrum" de Grimaldus*, ch. 17, ed. Smets, 65. The Latin text is unclear where indicated in my translation.

87. Ibid., 53: "Incipit opusculum Grimaldus [sic] baiuli et comitis sacri palatii ad Karulum regem de dieta ciborum et nutritura ancipitrum. Incipit liber †m† acciptrum."

88. Giese, "Graue Theorie," 31, 35, describes the *Liber accipitrum* as "vielleicht karolingerzeitlich." Fischer, review of *Le "Liber accipitrum" de Grimaldus*, ed. Smets, 118–19, stresses the seeming late antique original date of the recipes.

89. Smets bases this on a consideration of the eight known Grimalds between the seventh and tenth centuries: *Le "Liber accipitrum" de Grimaldus*, ed. Smets, 35–40; Smets, "*Materia medica* in the *Liber accipitrum*," 29–30. Smets unnecessarily questions her own conclusion about Grimald of St.-Gall's authorship on the grounds of the church's prohibitions of clerical hunting. It is one thing for a cleric to compile a learned medical treatise about falcons, quite another to flout canon law and actually hunt with falcons. For Grimald's career and considerable book collection, see: Josef Fleckenstein, *Die Hofkapelle der deutschen Könige*, 2 vols. (Stuttgart, 1959), esp. 1:168–83; Bischoff, "Bücher am Hofe Ludwigs des Deutschen," 187–212; Dieter Geuenich, "Beobachtungen zu Grimald von St. Gallen, Erzkapellan und Oberkanzler Ludwigs des Deutschen," in *Litterae medii aevi: Festschrift für Johanne Autenrieth zu ihrem 65. Geburtstag*, ed. Michael Borgolte and Herrad Spilling (Sigmaringen, 1988), 55–61; Goldberg, *Struggle for Empire*, 71–72, 169–71.

90. Smets incorrectly equates the Carolingian offices of (arch)chancellor and count of the palace: *Le "Liber accipitrum" de Grimaldus*, ed. Smets, 38; Smets, "*Materia medica* in

the *Liber accipitrum*," 29. For the identity of Louis's counts of the palace, see Goldberg, *Struggle for Empire*, 209 and n. 115.

91. Ermanrich, *Epistola ad Grimaldum abbatem*, MGH Epp. 5, 536, 553. For the meaning of *baiulus* as a tutor, especially of a junior ruler, see Niermeyer, *Mediae latinitatis lexicon minus*, s.v. *bajulus*, 78.

92. The next oldest one would be the so-called Anonymous of Vercelli, dating to the mid-tenth century: Bischoff, "Die älteste europäische Falkenmedizin," 171–82.

93. Giese, "Graue Theorie," 20, 27, emphasizes the oral transmission of hunting techniques before the twelfth and thirteenth centuries.

94. Vienna, Österreichische Nationalbibliothek, MS 956 (theol. 320), fols. 105v–106v; Latin edition from *Ad epistolas variorum supplementum*, no. 10, MGH Epp. 5, 633–35.

CHAPTER 4

Otto of Lucca, Author of the *Summa sententiarum*?

MARCIA L. COLISH

Aptly characterizing the *Summa sententiarum* as "the Place de l'Étoile of early twelfth-century theological literature," David Luscombe anatomized the debates surrounding its authorship in 1969. Acknowledged as a major source of Peter Lombard, this text (1138–41) is eclectic. Its author is familiar with and critical of Peter Abelard and stands in the tradition of Anselm of Laon and, above all, of Hugh of St. Victor. Having weighed the evidence for Otto—or Odo—bishop of Lucca, among others, Luscombe concludes that its author is best described as the Victorine Anonymous.[1] Without responding to Luscombe's reservations, Ferruccio Gastaldelli reopened the case in an essay published in 1980, crediting the SS to Otto. Otto, he says, studied theology in France and then taught it at Lucca's cathedral school, with the Lombard as his star pupil, before becoming bishop (1138–46). In support of this claim, and of the very existence of a cathedral school teaching theology in early twelfth-century Lucca, repeated in the reprint of his essay without *retractationes* in 2000, Gastaldelli observes that some manuscripts of the SS ascribe it to an "Odo" and that Gilbert of Poitiers gave a copy of the *De trinitate* of Hilary of Poitiers to the canons of the cathedral of St. Martin in Lucca.[2]

A major concern animating this debate has been the wish to establish a personal bond between the author of the SS and the Lombard, with Otto as the link. Our first historical reference to Peter is in a letter of Bernard of Clairvaux of ca. 1134–36, citing the bishop of Lucca's praise of Peter and recommending him to Gilduin, prior of Saint-Denis. In 2001, Richard Southern gave this theme its most elaborate, not to say baroque, orchestration. According to Southern, the bishop commending Peter was Otto. Educated at some length in Paris and environs, he returned to Lucca as master of theology in its cathedral school. Otto taught Peter Lombard, urged him to go north to complete and refine his thought, and redacted the SS during his episcopal reign.[3] Without revisiting the evidence, between 1996 and 2007 Raffaele Savigni, Philipp Rosemann, Constant Mews, and Enrico Spagnesi accepted this position as settled.[4] But it is not settled. In 1982 Lauge Olaf Nielsen reviewed the sources, rejected Gastaldelli's thesis, and supported Luscombe's, as did Riccardo Quinto in 1996 and 2010 and Patrizia Stoppacci in 2007.[5] This essay seeks to shed fresh light on what has thus reemerged as an open question.

What, in fact, do the manuscripts tell us about the authorship of the SS or about theological education in early twelfth-century Lucca? Several manuscripts of the SS do indeed credit it to an Odo. But others, including one now in Munich ascribed to *Bernardi abbatis*, cite other authors or no author at all.[6] As we know all too well, misattributions abound in medieval manuscripts. A classic case, far from unique, is the *Liber de sex principiis* not deleted from Gilbert of Poitiers' *curriculum vitae* until the 1950s and 1960s.[7] And what does Gilbert's Hilary donation tell us? Gilbert was an avid book collector with a known partiality to Hilary. He owned, and donated, multiple copies of his predecessor's *De trinitate*, as well as other patristic works, focusing his generosity on institutions to which he was personally, pedagogically, or professionally connected: Chartres Cathedral; the cathedral chapter of St. Peter in Poitiers; and the abbey of St. Martin in Luçon, which then belonged to the diocese of Poitiers. He retained the copy of Hilary which he brought inter alia to defend his views at the Council of Reims in 1148.[8] There are no known Italians in the coterie of disciples not fazed by Gilbert's abstruse teachings and rebarbative terminology.[9] In any case, the SS shows little sympathy with Porretan theology and philosophy. The author rejects Gilbert's arguments on the Trinity and Christology and the semantic theory undergirding his methodology.[10] The inventory of Lucca's cathedral library through Otto's reign reveals that Gilbert's gift was a one-off. The only other accession in the eleventh and early twelfth centuries remotely connected with the schools of northern France is a *vita eius* donated by Odelricus, *prepositus* of Reims. All other donations came from the cathedral canons, from local nobles, and from a single German knight. Their contents, when specified, are exegetical and liturgical, not works of dogmatic theology.[11]

How, then, can we explain Gilbert's gift? What follows is a hypothesis that, if not demonstrable, is suggestive. Lucca is situated on what was a major road connecting France with Rome and Italy with Santiago de Compostella, the Via Francigena, the southern gateway to the Appenines. Lucca commanded the northern outlet to this road and its crossing over the Arno. Well aware of its importance to merchants, pilgrims, and those with other ecclesiastical business, Lucca battled with Pisa for control of the Via Francigena and founded an unusually large number of hospices for travelers, especially after 1000.[12] In the eleventh century, Lucca became an important pilgrimage site itself, owing to its possession of the Volto Santo. This cult object is a life-size crucifix. Its present corpus is a twelfth- or early thirteenth-century replacement of the original, which was thought to have been sculpted by a contemporary of Christ able to limn an accurate portrait of him. The Volto Santo was believed to have been brought to Lucca from the Holy Land by an eighth-century pilgrim, and attracted Europe-wide devotion.[13] It is possible that, on his first trip to Rome in 1133, Bernard of Clairvaux stopped in Lucca for that reason, there making the incumbent bishop's acquaintance. It is certain that Hugh of St. Victor visited Lucca in the early 1130s. He sent a thank-you note to the community of Augustinian canons of St. Frediano, with whom he lodged there. A manuscript of Hugh's *Sententie*, dated to 1140, was presented to the library of the church of Anghiari, some twenty-eight kilometers northeast of Arezzo,[14] a place with no known school. Did Gilbert also receive hospitality in Lucca and donate a Hilary manuscript in thanks to his hosts?

What is known about Gilbert's itinerary obviates a conclusive answer to this question. While, in Giovanni Santini's words, the Via Francigena was a "strada dei manoscritti" for legal texts, works written and used by early scholastic theologians are found haphazardly in Italian libraries in the early twelfth century, turning up in places whose personnel had no known associations with the schools of northern France.[15] In any case, there is no automatic correlation between the contents of medieval libraries and the educational programs at their host institutions. In the collection of the abbey of Mont-Saint-Michel in Normandy, for instance, the books copied in the eleventh and early twelfth century are indeed a function of its school, then in its heyday. But, long after the school's eclipse, the library grew exponentially, thanks to the aggressive and well-budgeted acquisitions policy of late medieval abbots, who relied mostly on purchases of up-to-date scholastic theology and law from Paris booksellers. There is no evidence that anyone in the community read these books.[16] Some manuscripts in that period were deposited merely as a *mis en gage* in connection with other transactions.[17] Commenting on the lack of intersection between books donated to Balliol College, Oxford, and its curriculum at the time, R. A. B. Mynors reminds us that medieval manuscripts were "like plate, one of the recognized ways of holding capital in portable and negotiable form, . . . an inescapable medium of benefactions in an age when gifts and bequests were made in kind as much as in money."[18] With this fact in mind, the notion that Gilbert's gift of Hilary to Lucca proves the existence of a school of theology there, especially one led by a second-generation Victorine, looks to be overstated.

But Gastaldelli also asserts that local documentary evidence supports his claim as well. His citation of Enrico Coturri as his main authority on this point is, however, problematic, for Gastaldelli omits or misreads that author's most important findings as well as other studies based on documentary evidence available to him before 1980, and certainly before the republication of his essay in 2000.[19] Coturri investigated schooling in medieval Lucca in order to learn when formal teaching began there in medicine. He cites Carolingian documents testifying to the existence of a school and schoolmasters, which do not specify what they taught. There were literate notaries, most likely educated in royal or ducal schools, not the cathedral school. Documentary evidence of schools of any kind evaporates in the ninth century, inspiring two directives from Rome adjuring Lucca's bishops to provide for the education of their clergy. Nor does Coturri or anyone else find documentary evidence of a cathedral school in Lucca in the tenth, eleventh, or early twelfth centuries. The earliest charters documenting one date to 1194 and 1199. There is evidence, in the cathedral's charters, of twelfth-century masters. Some fifteen clerics and seventeen laymen with that title are mentioned. Reference to the subjects they taught occurs for only three of them: a grammarian, Enrico, who died in 1167; Guglielmo, later bishop of Lucca (1170–94), who taught the *artes* and who commented on Pseudo-Dionysius's *On the Divine Names*; and, launching the topic on which Coturri then focuses, a Ranieri who died in 1134 and who taught medicine. There is no evidence of a master named Otto and no reference to any master interested in theology before Guglielmo. Gastaldelli nonetheless maintains that the documentary record shows that Otto taught theology in Lucca and that his work remained in force later in the century, influencing Guglielmo. As a writer hospitable to the negative theology of the Pseudo-Dionysius, however, Guglielmo departs from the position on theological language found in the SS and those it influenced. His curriculum is also unusual in a period when Italian schooling in the *artes* typically prepared students for legal careers and in which Italian secular clerics made few contributions to scholarly fields besides law and polemical literature.[20]

Moving beyond these issues, other kinds of evidence not hitherto brought to bear on this debate can help to shed light on it. Two questions are pertinent here. First, what does Lucca's church history tell us about the qualities sought in the election of its bishop in the early twelfth century, and did Otto possess them? And, what does internal evidence in the SS tell us about its author?

The church history of Lucca in the late eleventh and early twelfth centuries yields valuable information, particularly about its bishops, its cathedral chapter, and their relations with each other, the local economy, the emerging commune, and the Gregorian reform movement.[21] From the Carolingian age onward, the canons of St. Martin had been a privileged and well-connected group. Drawn from families that supplied Lucca's judges, advocates, and notaries, the cathedral chapter as such received immunities, jurisdictional rights, and donations from emperors and local nobles, even in contradistinction to those enjoyed by its bishops. In addition to their independent rights to lands, tithes, and patronage in the *contado*, the canons managed the cathedral and church building programs throughout the diocese. They played a role vis-à-vis their bishop well exceeding that of the typical cathedral chapter.[22] While in these respects they acted collegially, the canons resisted repeated proposals that they live in common. Some canons married. Whether or not they did, they maintained private residences and private property, which they bought and sold and passed on to their heirs. Their right to do so was sanctioned by the papacy. Their generous use of their private wealth appears in donations made by individual canons to the chapter in 1042, 1057, 1065, 1076, and 1081. Canons, such as the brothers Lamberto and Blancardo, rank among the chief benefactors funding the raising of Lucca's new cathedral between 1060 and 1070, outstripping the bishop in their munificence.[23] These activities prompted the chapter to advance to positions of responsibility within their ranks members with local knowledge and administrative skills. These were the figures whom the charters name as *primacerius*, archpriest, deacon, subdeacon, and cantor, acting on the chapter's behalf.[24]

If worldly, the canons of St. Martin did not give scandal or engage in lifestyles of the rich and famous, but devoted themselves and their substance to the service of church and community. If secular priests wanted to embrace a common life of celibacy and austerity, they were free to become Augustinian canons. The cathedral canons saw no reason to change their own ways. But in the late eleventh century they were confronted by outsider bishops, Anselm I (1051–73) and his nephew Anselm II (1073–86), Milanesi thrust on them by the emperors, determined to reform the canons. Obnoxious for this reason to start with, neither bishop went the distance in reforming himself. Both alienated episcopal property to the advantage of relatives and supporters. Anselm I was a pluralist, retaining the bishopric of Lucca after he became Pope Alexander II. In addition to acquiring the see through nepotism, Anselm II incensed the canons and citizens of Lucca to such a degree that they ejected him from the city in 1080 and elected an anti-bishop, Pietro (1086–91). Anselm II, who had been invested by Emperor Henry IV, had a *crise de conscience* and sought investiture from Pope Gregory VII. Perhaps making a virtue of necessity, he withdrew to do penance at the abbey of St. Gilles in Provence. Although Gregory repeatedly ordered him back to his see, he basically abandoned it, spending the rest of his life in exile.[25] A later bishop of Lucca, Rangerio (1097–1112), himself an intransigent defender of Gregorian reform, wrote an adulatory metrical vita of Anselm II. But even in this puff-piece Anselm II emerges, willy-nilly, as a dead-end figure disastrously out of step with Lucca. For his own part, Rangerio, whose literary style suggests schooling in France, looks to be out of touch as well, since he seems unaware of the settlement of the Investiture Controversy in England and France in 1107.[26]

The bishops who followed Rangerio in our target period have a different profile, a function of the fact that the canons seized the opportunity at hand to reassert their control over episcopal elections. This was a general trend occasioned by the confusion brought on by the Investiture Controversy. But in Lucca it was clearly a response to recent local history as well. In 1122, Pope Calixtus II confirmed the chapter's right to elect the bishop, a right exercised until its replacement by the policy of papal provisions at the turn of the thirteenth century.[27] Bishops Rodolfo (1112–18), Benedetto I (1118–28), Uberto (1128–35), and Guido II (1135–38) were all decidedly insiders. Most of these men were members of important Lucchese families and had gained administrative experience as officers of the chapter before their elevation. Benedetto had been its archdeacon. Uberto, the likely promoter of the Lombard mentioned by Bernard of Clairvaux, also a friend of St. Norbert, was subdeacon in 1125–26 and *primacerius* in 1126, and was probably related to a dynasty of Lucchese judges. Guido was a former cathedral canon.[28]

Guido is the only bishop in this group of Otto's immediate predecessors whose reign has yielded no surviving documentation. All the others reveal in their episcopal *acta* their local know-how and executive skills honed in the chapter. Two themes stand out in their policies. One is their sagacious conduct of the ongoing conflict with Pisa, not only for control of the Via Francigena but also on a wider political and jurisdictional canvas, Pisa being Ghibelline and Lucca Guelf.[29] The second involves lands and rights in the *contado*. In the eleventh century, it had been the canons who were proactive in regaining and consolidating lands and rights that had been lost to the bishop and chapter in the post-Carolingian age, recovering them not only from secular but also from other ecclesiastical proprietors. Starting with Rodolfo, however, we now find collaboration between bishop and chapter in the recuperation of lands and rights and the extension of diocesan authority in the *contado*. Care of more immediate civic interests is also visible in Benedetto's reconstruction of the Volto Sacro chapel in the cathedral.[30]

On the death of Guido II, the canons had every reason to continue the momentum of episcopal reigns since 1112. They accomplished this objective with the election of Otto. His career before 1138 is completely undocumented.[31] But there is one thing crystal clear about Otto as bishop: he responded to local needs and knew how to address them. His *acta* show that he was zealous in prosecuting the conflict with Pisa. He continued the policy of reclaiming and extending diocesan lands and rights in the *contado*. His leadership in addressing Lucca's pastoral needs is seen in his confirmation of the ministry of deaconesses,[32] in an age when support for this office was waning. He looks to be a Lucchese insider, an energetic and capable administrator, cut from the same bolt of cloth as the bishops whom the canons had made a point of electing since 1112.

How likely is it that the Otto who emerges from his episcopal *acta* was also a theologian who had spent many years steeping himself in the scholasticism of Paris and environs, teaching it in Lucca, and taking time out from his busy episcopal career to write the SS between 1138 and 1141? It is remarkable how few participants in the debate in the authorship of the SS have turned to that text itself to ascertain whether the Victorine Anonymous and Otto of Lucca have anything in common. Luscombe appears to be the only one of them who has actually studied the theology of the SS, his prime concern being to situate it vis-à-vis Abelard and his school. But in what follows, we will see that internal evidence within this text enables us to place its author doctrinally, and geographically, and well outside of the diocese of Lucca.

As with other early scholastic theologians, the author of the SS presents authorities who support alternative positions on contested issues before giving his own solution. Comparison of the ways in which contemporary masters do so illuminates their individual approaches, whether they accent moral rigorism, pastoral sensitivity, the defense of tradition, departure from tradition, or simply the wish to organize logically the material covered.[33] On the sacraments, the author of the SS offers his own clear operative principle: if customs differ, we should follow the local custom prevailing in our own province of the church. In this connection, he repeatedly presents himself as a member of the *ecclesia Gallicana*. Within that church, its own customs suffice, even if he can also adduce theological or logical support for this rule of thumb.

A good general introduction to his approach is his handling of a debate on single as opposed to triple immersion in baptism opened by a follower of Gilbert of Poitiers. Both the SS and the Porretan master cite a letter of Gregory the Great to Leander of Seville, who had found both practices in his diocese. They apply its message differently. Gregory states that both baptismal practices have valuable symbolic significance, and that both are acceptable. The Porretan wields this authority to sweep aside triple immersion in favor of its global replacement by single immersion, on grounds of pastoral utility. The SS advocates no such policy. There no longer exist any local churches in which single immersion is practiced, he notes. While he can agree, with Gregory, that diverse customs do not obstruct the church's unity of faith, "quod in una fide nihil officit Ecclesia consuetudo diversa," and while this authority would validate single immersion if it were still practiced anywhere, the issue is hypothetical. In reality, triple immersion is the universal rule, and the principle he invokes is that it we should follow standard custom: "Ecce quod ex ista auctoritate licet semel mergere tantum, nobis tamen videtur quod magis est usus Ecclesia sequentus."[34]

In the foregoing case, the rule upheld by the SS is one followed everywhere in the early twelfth-century church. But doctrine and practice were not universal in all cases. The French school and the Gallican Church were at odds on various issues with the Italian school and the Roman Church. This opposition is visible particularly in their respective positions on two sacraments, penance and marriage. The French school typically focused on the inner intentionality of the recipient as decisive. The Italian school held that the expression of inner intentions in external, physical, or institutional forms was normative. These perspectives informed the contritionist vs. confessionist debate on penance and the consent vs. consummation debate on marriage formation.[35]

After citing both the confessionist and contritionist authorities on penance, the SS aligns its author with the contritionists. The penitent's contrition of the heart rectifies his status in God's sight. If the penitent then confesses to a priest, all the priest does is to declare a transaction that has already taken place between the penitent and God. Priests do not share in, or mediate, God's power, for it is God alone who remits sins: "Et ita verum est quod solus Deus peccata dimittit." The author concedes that, while God remits the eternal punishment for sin, completion of the satisfaction imposed by a priest remits the temporal punishment for sin. But, should a penitent drop dead immediately after contrition, he will be fully cleansed, "plene mundatus"; all punishment for sin will be waived by God. This happy outcome, says the author, is confirmed by reason, "quod etiam ratione confirmatur."[36] The position confirmed by reason is the position on this matter advocated by the French school. But the author of the SS does not therefore rule out the practice of auricular confession to a priest.

Our author flies the French school flag much higher in treating marriage formation. Here, he does not even bother to cite the consummationist authorities, moving at once to those who define marriage as formed by the spouses' present consent alone. Even absent a dowry, a priestly blessing and other wedding ceremonies, and absent its consummation, a marriage is made by the voluntary consent of persons having a legal right to marry: "Credimus igitur sufficere duarum idonearum personarum legitimum de conjunctione consensum . . . etiam cum ipso coitu celebrata frustrantur. . . . Consensum praedicto modo diffinitum sufficere credimus ad contrahendum conjugium, licet dos defuerit et sacerdotalis benedictio et alia nuptiarum solemnia, vel etiam sexuum commisto . . . sicut ex conjugio virginis Mariae et Joseph evidenter est declaratum."[37]

This sturdy defense of marriage by consent alone, anchored with the French school's clinching conviction, the sacramentality of the *mariage blanc* of Mary and Joseph, leads to the question of who possesses the legal right to marry.

A complication coloring this debate was that the authorities on which the Italian school rested its case read *servus* as "slave" in the sense of Roman law, the law in force in the patristic age and still operative in much of Italy. In this tradition, slaves have no legal rights. Adherents of the French school tended to read *servus* as "serf," denoting people who are semi-free and who do have certain legal rights, including, in their view, the right to marry. The author of the SS puts his cards on the table. He acknowledges that Justinian's *Novels*, and the early authorities citing it, are his opponents' grounds for denying *servi* the right to marry. This rule, he observes, does apply in areas governed by Roman law. But the Gallican Church is not governed by Roman law. While the equal right of *servi* and free persons to marry is compatible with the fact that we are all children of the same heavenly father, the determining principle is local legal custom: "Itaque ex his auctoritatibus [i.e., those informed by Roman law] datur intelligi quod inter servam personam et liberam non fiat conjugium, in quibuscunque Ecclesiis illud est prohibitum et communiter confirmatum; sed in illis Ecclesiis quae nondum illam institutionem susceperunt, bene fit inter tales personas conjugium, sicut in multis ecclesiis Gallicanis fit frequenter." Each party in such a marriage retains his or her own legal status; and marriage between two *servi*, following Gallican practice, is also accepted in that church.[38]

Another position of the Gallican teaching on marriage frames the discussion in the SS of the subsequent fate of spouses whose marriage cannot be consummated and hence may be canonically dissolved. The Italian school took a hard line here, asserting that the former spouses should continue to live together as brother and sister. The French school was more lenient, allowing the functional spouse, and sometimes both former spouses, to take new marital partners. Here, explicitly rejecting the authorities on the negative and dismissive side of the debate, our author not only lays down the law governing the Gallican Church but even poses the very question in a manner forecasting his solution: "De iis, qui, legitime juncti, postea nequeunt carnaliter misceri, se alter eorum vel quod uterque reclamaverit, ideo quod nequeant sibi carnis debitum reddere: gallicana judicat Ecclesia (juxta tenorum legum et quorumdam decretorum) ut inde suscepta fide et legitima probatione discedant, et aliis si velint se conjugant."[39] The permissive custom of the Gallican Church here prevails in its own area, assuming that the case is tried and proved in good faith and correct form. Here, as on other debated topics, the author of the SS does not propose to Gallicanize the Roman Church on the argument that its practice is better grounded theologically or is more reasonable. Rather, he defends the institutions of the Gallican Church, to which he gives his allegiance, wherever its writ runs.

It is true that there are scholastics in this period not born in France—witness Hugh of St. Victor and Peter Lombard—who championed the theology of the French school. But it is difficult indeed to grasp why the author of the SS would defend the positions he does, and relativize those of the Roman Church as he does, unless he regarded the Gallican Church as his professional home. It is even more difficult to imagine why a sitting bishop of Lucca, an area where Roman law was the law of the land, would be so willing to limit or even to dismiss its binding force. With respect to Otto of Lucca, and what we can know about him and the canons who elected him, this possibility approaches the vanishing point. With respect to the identity of the author of the SS, we can agree with Luscombe and his followers that the better part of valor is to describe him simply as the Victorine Anonymous. We may not be able to give him a name. But, with some certitude, we can give him a habitation, a Gallican Church located geographically, and intellectually, well north of early twelfth-century Lucca.

Notes

1. David E. Luscombe, *The School of Peter Abelard: The Influence of Abelard's Thought in the Early Scholastic Period* (Cambridge, 1969), 45, 94, 198–213, 226, 231–32, 234–35, 309–10 (198). See also David E. Luscombe, "The 'Cur deus homo' and the 'Ysagoge in theologiam,'" in *Cur deus homo: Atti del congresso Anselmiano internazionale, Roma, 21–23 maggio 1998*, ed. Paul Gilbert, Helmut Kohlenberger, and Elmar Salmann, Studia Anselmiana 128 (Rome, 1999), 73–89 (73, 74, 86).

2. Ferruccio Gastaldelli, "La *Summa sententiarum* di Ottone di Lucca: Conclusione di un dibattito secolare," *Salesianum* 42 (1980): 537–46 (repr. in Ferruccio Gastaldelli, *Scritti di letteratura, filologia, e teologia medievale* [Spoleto, 2000], 165–74); for Gilbert's donation, see 544; for the manuscript evidence, see 539–41.

3. Richard W. Southern, *Scholastic Humanism and the Unification of Europe*, vol. 2, *The Heroic Age* (Oxford, 2001), 138–44. See Bernard of Clairvaux, ep. 410, in *Opera*, ed. Jean Leclercq, Charles H. Talbot, and Henri Rochais, 8 vols. (Rome, 1957–77), 8:391. The bishop of Lucca in question is not named. Peter Lombard, *Sentences*, trans. Giulio Silano, 4 vols. (Toronto, 2007–10), 1:ix–x; Silano translates this letter and cites alternative possibilities for its dating. He describes Southern's argument as "elegant" but goes no farther as to its accuracy.

4. Raffaele Savigni, *Episcopato e società cittadina a Lucca da Anselmo II (†1086) a Roberto (†1225)*, Accademia lucchese di scienze, lettere ed arti, Studi e testi 43 (Lucca, 1996), 128–29, 275; Philipp W. Rosemann, *Peter Lombard* (Oxford, 2004), 228n6; Constant J. Mews, *Abelard and Heloise* (Oxford, 2005), 230–31; Enrico Spagnesi, "*Distinguere, compilare, componere*: Metodo teologico e metodo canonistico nel XII secolo," in *Pietro Lombardo: Atti del XLIII convegno storico internazionale, Todi, 8–10 ottobre 2006*, Atti dei convegni del Centro italiano di studi sul basso medioevo—Accademia tudertina e del Centro di studi sulla spiritualità medievale, n.s., 20 (Spoleto, 2007), 193–224 (216n59).

5. Lauge Olaf Nielsen, *Theology and Philosophy in the Twelfth Century: A Study of Gilbert Porreta's Thinking and Theological Exposition of the Doctrine of the Incarnation during the Period 1130–1180*, Acta theologica danica 15 (Leiden, 1982), 196n13; Riccardo Quinto, "*Trivium* e teologia: L'organizzazione scolastica nella seconda metà del secolo dodicesimo e i maestri della *sacra pagina*," in *Storia della teologia nel medioevo*, vol. 2, *La grande fioritura*, ed.

Giulio d'Onofrio (Casale Monferrato, 1996), 435–68 (458–59); Riccardo Quinto, "Stephen Langton," in *Mediaeval Commentaries on the "Sentences" of Peter Lombard*, vol. 2, ed. Philipp W. Rosemann (Leiden, 2010), 35–77 (66n117); Patrizia Stoppacci, "La *Glossa continua in Psalmos* di Pietro Lombardo: *Status quaestionis*, studi progressi e prospettive di ricerca," in *Pietro Lombardo*, 289–331 (329–30).

     6. Luscombe, *School of Abelard*, 86, 234.

     7. Nielsen, *Theology and Philosophy*, 45; Osmund Lewry, "The *Liber sex principiorum*, a Supposed Porretan Work: A Study in Ascription," in *Gilbert de Poitiers et ses contemporains: Aux origines de la logica modernorum*, ed. Jean Jolivet and Alain De Libera (Naples, 1987), 251–78.

     8. Jean Leclercq, "L'Éloge funèbre de Gilbert de la Porrée," *Archives d'histoire doctrinale et littéraire du Moyen Âge* 19 (1952): 183–85; H. C. Van Elswijk, *Gilbert Porreta: Sa vie, son oeuvre, sa pensée* (Leuven, 1966), 15–16, 29–30, 35–37, 99, 110–11; Nikolaus M. Häring, "Epitaphs and Necrologies on Bishop Gilbert II of Poitiers," *Archives d'histoire doctrinale et littéraire du Moyen Âge* 36 (1969): 57–87 (which prints texts of the three necrologies mentioned); Nielsen, *Theology and Philosophy*, 29, 34–35.

     9. Van Elswijk, *Gilbert Porreta*, 29.

     10. Ibid., 282–83, 334–35; Nielsen, *Theology and Philosophy*, 194, 229–34, 346n236.

     11. Pietro Guidi and Ermenegildo Pellegrinetti, ed., *Inventari del vescovato della cattedrale e d'altri chiese di Lucca* (Rome, 1921), 119–20.

     12. Renato Stopani, *La Via Francigena: Una strada europea nell'Italia del medioevo* (Florence, 1988), provides the fullest treatment. See also Charles W. Previté-Orton, "The Italian Cities till *c.* 1200," in *Cambridge Medieval History*, ed. J. B. Bury et al., vol. 5, *Contest of Empire and Papacy*, ed. J. R. Tanner (Cambridge, 1964), 208–41 (227–28); Daniel Waley, *The Italian City Republics* (New York, 1969), 119, 122; Duane J. Osheim, *An Italian Lordship: The Bishopric of Lucca in the Late Middle Ages* (Berkeley and Los Angeles, 1977), 6–7; Thomas Szabó, "Xenodochia, Hospitäler und Herbergen: Kirchliche und kommerzielle Gastung im mittelalterlichen Italien (7. bis 14. Jahrhundert)," in *Gastfreundschaft, Taverne, und Gasthaus im Mittelalter*, ed. Hans Conrad Peyer (Munich, 1983), 61–92; Gaja Simonetti, *La storia di Lucca* (Livorno, 1991), 26–29; Savigni, *Episcopato e società*, 122–23. On Lucca's economy and its competition with Pisa in this area, see most recently Richard A. Goldthwaite, *The Economy of Renaissance Florence* (Baltimore, 2009), 14–16, 20–23, 30.

     13. The fullest treatment of this legend is Raoul Manselli, "La repubblica di Lucca," in *Storia d'Italia*, ed. Giuseppe Galasso, vol. 7, pt. 2, *Comuni e signorie nell'Italia nordorientale e centrale: Lazio, Umbria et Marche, Lucca*, ed. Girolamo Arnaldi et al. (Turin, 1987), 607–743 (621–23). See also Simonetti, *Storia di Lucca*, 26–29; Vito Tirelli, "Il vescovato di Lucca tra la fine del XI e i primi decenni del XII secolo," in *Allucio da Pescia (1070–ca. 1134), un santo laico dell'età postgregoriana: Religione e società nei territori di Lucca e della Valdinievole*, ed. Cinzio Violante (Rome, 1991), 55–146 (56–57); Savigni, *Episcopato e società*, 376–84; Herbert Kessler, *Seeing Medieval Art* (Peterborough, ON, 2004), 74. On the importance which the Volto Santo gave Lucca to travelers, see also Goldthwaite, *Economy of Renaissance Florence*, 19.

     14. F. E. Croyden, "Notes on the Life of Hugh of St. Victor," *Journal of Theological Studies* 40 (1939): 232–53; the thank-you note is printed at pp. 250–52.

     15. Giovanni Santini, "Le condizione dello studio del diritto in Toscana nell'alto medioevo," in *Atti del 5° congresso internazionale di studi sull'alto medioevo: Lucca, 3–7*

ottobre 1971 (Spoleto, 1973), 389–447 (415); on theological texts, see Luscombe, *School of Abelard*, 87–90.

16. Geneviève Nortier, *Les bibliothèques médiévales des abbayes bénédictines de Normandie* (Paris, 1971), 3–4, 64–74.

17. Ibid., 71–72.

18. R. A. B. Mynors, ed., *Catalogue of the Manuscripts of Balliol College, Oxford* (Oxford, 1963), xii–xiii.

19. Gastaldelli, "La *Summa sententiarum*," 543n46; cf. Enrico Coturri, "La scuola vescovile di Lucca (secoli VIII–XIII) e l'insegnamento della medicina," in *Atti della IX bicennale di studi sulla storia di medicina* (Fermo, 1971), 125–36 (repr. in Enrico Coturri, *Pistoia, Lucca e la Valdinievole nel medioevo: Raccolta di saggi*, ed. Giampolo Francesconi and Federica Iacomelli, Biblioteca storica pistoiese 3 [Pistoia, 1988], 111–23). See also Cesare Lucchesini, *Opere edite e inedite*, vol. 15 (Lucca, 1833), 21–86; Donald Bullough, "Le scuole cattedrali e la cultura dell'Italia settentrionale prima dei comuni," in *Vescovi e diocesi in Italia nel medioevo*, Italia sacra 5 (Padua, 1964), 111–43; Renzo Papini, "Paolo Barsanti e la storia delle scuole in Lucca," *Actum Luce* 10 (1981): 153–59 (154); Savigni, *Episcopato e società*, 147–48, 424, 430, 433–34, 436, 446, 452, 455, 457, 465, 467, 470, 471 (who, at p. 404, is noncommittal on whether Otto was a theologian); Philip Jones, *The Italian City-State: From Commune to Signoria* (Oxford, 1997), 126–27. For Guglielmo of Lucca on music, see Gino Arrighi, ed., "La 'Summa musice artis' di maestro Guglielmo vescovo di Lucca," *Actum Luce* 4 (1975): 105–11; for his work on rhetoric, see John O. Ward, *Ciceronian Rhetoric in Treatise, Scholion, and Commentary*, Typologie des Sources du Moyen Âge Occidental 58 (Turnhout, 1995), 124–26; for his work on logic, showing Abelard's influence, see ibid., 226, and most recently Yukio Iwakuma, "Are Argumentations Propositions?," in *Medieval Theories on Assertive and Non-assertive Language*, ed. Alfonso Maierù and Luisa Valente (Florence, 2004), 80–110 (90–99).

20. For the purported influence of Otto on Guglielmo as a theologian, see Ferruccio Gastaldelli, ed., *Wilhelmus Lucensis Commentum in tertium ierarchiam Dionisii que est de divinis nominibus* (Florence, 1983), vii–xcii (repr. in Gastaldelli, *Scritti di letteratura*, 317–405, with references to the author's other studies on this figure). For background on mid-twelfth-century debates on theological language, see Marcia L. Colish, *Peter Lombard*, 2 vols. (Leiden, 1994), 1:91–154. On the writings of Italian secular clerical authors in this period, see Alberto Varvaro, "Language and Culture," in *Italy in the Central Middle Ages*, ed. David Abulafia (Oxford, 2004), 197–211, who points out that the Investiture Controversy tended to suck the oxygen out of the room.

21. The most important single study is Savigni, *Episcopato e società*, esp. 12, 16–20, 24, 27–53, 107–10, 115, 119–29, 137–56, 241–44, 248–56, 283–86, 301, 395, 401, 403, 404–5, 408, 411–73. On the bishops of Lucca see also Almerico Guerra and Pietro Guidi, *Compendio di storia ecclesiastica lucchese dalle origini a tutto il secolo XII* (Lucca, 1921), 181–91; Umberto Nicolai, *I vescovi di Lucca* (Lucca, 1966), 14–18; Osheim, *Italian Lordship*, 129–30; Giovanni Tabacco, *The Struggle for Power in Medieval Italy: Structures of Political Rule*, trans. Rosalind Brown Jensen (Cambridge, 1989), 166–76; Tirelli, "Il vescovato di Lucca"; Hagen Keller, "Le origini sociali e famigliari del vescovo Anselmo," in *Sant'Anselmo vescovo di Lucca (1073–1086) nel quadro delle trasformazioni sociali e della riforma ecclesiastica*, ed. Cinzio Violante (Rome, 1992), 27–50; Maureen C. Miller, *The Bishop's Palace: Architecture and Authority in Medieval Italy* (Ithaca, 2000), 97, 115–16, 141–42, 144, 269, 271.

22. On the canons, in addition to titles in the previous note, see Erich Kittel, "Der Kampf um die Reform der Domkapitels in Lucca im 11. Jahrhundert," in *Festschrift Albert Brackmann*, ed. Leo Santifaller (Weimar, 1931), 207–47; Martino Giusti, "Le canoniche della città e diocesi di Lucca al tempo della riforma gregoriana," in *Studi gregoriani per la storia di Gregorio VII e della riforma gregoriana*, ed. Giovanni B. Borino (Rome, 1947), 3:321–67 (323, 325–37); Martino Giusti, "Notizie sulle canoniche lucchesi," in *La vita comune nei secoli XI e XII: Atti della settimana di studio, Mendola, settembre 1959*, Miscellanea del Centro di studi medioevale 3, Pubblicazioni dell'Università Cattolica del Sacro Cuore 3, Scienze storiche 2, 2 vols. (Milan, 1962), 1:434–54; Osheim, *Italian Lordship*, 15–19, 21, 27, 45, 119; Cosimo Damiano Fonseca, "Il capitolo di S. Martino e la riforma canonicale nella seconda metà del sec. XI," in *Sant'Anselmo*, ed. Violante, 51–64; Amleto Spiccani, "L'episcopato lucchese d'Anselmo da Biaggo," ibid., 65–70; Kathleen G. Cushing, *Papacy and Law in the Gregorian Revolution: The Canonistic Work of Anselm of Lucca* (Oxford, 1998), 58–63; Kathleen G. Cushing, *Reform and Papacy in the Eleventh Century: Spirituality and Social Change* (Manchester, 2005), 96–97. For charters in which officers of the chapter act as parties representing the chapter, with— and without—the bishop between 1112 and 1143, see Pietro Guidi and Oreste Parenti, ed., *Regesta del capitolo di Lucca*, Regesta chartarum Italiae 6, 4 vols. (Rome, 1910–39), 1:304–426.

23. Kittel, "Der Kampf," 207–8, 209–14, 236, 239, 240; Osheim, *Italian Lordship*, 119; Romano Silva, "La recostruzione della cattedrale di Lucca (1060–1070)," in *Sant'Anselmo*, ed. Violante, 297–309 (300).

24. Guidi and Parenti, *Regesta del capitolo*, 1:304–426; Osheim, *Italian Lordship*, 119. For a document of the nascent commune witnessed by chapter officers including the *primacerius*, deacon, subdeacon, and cantor, see Thomas W. Blomquist and Duane J. Osheim, "The First Consuls at Lucca: 10 July 1119," *Actum Luce* 7 (1978): 310–40 (37) (repr. in Thomas W. Blomquist, *Merchant Families, Banking, and Money in Medieval Lucca* [Aldershot, 2005], no. 7).

25. Although all the historians cited in note 21, above, tell this story, the best concise biographies of these two bishops are by Cinzio Violante, "Alessandro II" and "Anselmo di Biaggo," in *Dizionario biografico degli italiani*, 67 vols. (Rome, 1960–2006), 2:176–83, 3:397–404. On why Anselm II chose St. Gilles, its appeal lay in its recent adoption of the Cluniac observance, a movement late out of the gate in Tuscany; see Enrico Coturri, "I monasteri e la vita monastica intorno a Lucca fino al XIV secolo," *Atti dell'Accademia lucchese di scienze, lettere ed arti* 2, nos. 15–16 (1983): 231–60 (repr. in Coturri, *Pistoia, Lucca, e la Valdinievole*, ed. Francesconi and Iacomelli, 159–85 [173–75]).

26. On Rangerio's *vita metrica*, his possible origins, and schooling, the best study is Gabriella Severino, "La *vita metrica* di Anselmo da Lucca scritta da Rangerio: Ideologia e genere letterario," in *Sant'Anselmo*, ed. Violante, 222–68; on Rangerio's pro-Gregorian polemic, see Mario Nobile, "Il 'Liber de anulo et baculo' del vescovo di Lucca Rangerio, Matilde, e la lotta per le investiture negli anni 1100–1111," ibid., 185–94; Leidulf Melve, *Inventing the Public Sphere: The Public Debate during the Investiture Contest (1030–1122)*, 2 vols. (Leiden, 2007), 2:620–21.

27. On this general development, see Robert L. Benson, "Election by Community and Chapter: Reflections on Co-Responsibility in the Historical Church," in *Who Decides for the Church: Studies in Co-Responsibility*, ed. James A. Coriden (Hartford, CT, 1971), 54–80 (54–64); on electoral rights in Lucca, see Martino Giusti, "Le elezioni dei vescovi

di Lucca specialmente nel secolo XII," *Rivista di storia della chiesa in Italia* 6 (1952): 205–30 (210); Osheim, *Italian Lordship*, 45.

28. On these careers and connections, see Osheim, *Italian Lordship*, 130; Savigni, *Episcopato e società*, 47–53, 126–28, 404.

29. Osheim, *Italian Lordship*, 6–7; Savigni, *Episcopato e società*, 126.

30. On these trends in general, see David Herlihy, "The Agrarian Revolution in Southern France and Italy, 801–1150," *Speculum* 33 (1958): 23–41 (30–36); David Herlihy, "Church Property on the European Continent, 701–1200," *Speculum* 36 (1961): 81–105 (93–99). On Lucca in this connection, the leading study is Amleto Spiccani, *Terre di Lucca: Saggi di storia medioevale della Valdinievole (secoli XII–XIII)* (Pisa, 2003), 20–22, 26, 36–40; see also Nicolai, *I vescovi di Lucca*, 15–17; Osheim, *Italian Lordship*, 19–29, 70–73; Duane J. Osheim, "Rural Italy," in *Italy in the Central Middle Ages*, ed. Abulafia, 161–81; Tirelli, "Il vescovato di Lucca," 55–75, 86–146; Savigni, *Episcopato e società*, 28–47, 108–10, 126.

31. This factual blackout is confirmed by Osheim, *Italian Lordship*, 130: "We know nothing of him or his origins"; Savigni, *Episcopato e società*, 128–29.

32. Nicolai, *I vescovi di Lucca*, 17.

33. On these general tendencies, see Marcia L. Colish, "Systematic Theology and Theological Renewal in the Twelfth Century," *Journal of Medieval and Renaissance Studies* 18 (1988): 135–56; Marcia L. Colish, "Authority and Interpretation in Scholastic Theology," in *Religious Identity and the Problem of Historical Foundation: The Foundational Character of Authoritative Sources in the History of Christianity and Judaism*, ed. Judith Frishman, Willemien Otten, and Gerald Rouwhorst (Leiden, 2004), 369–86 (repr. in Marcia L. Colish, *Studies in Scholasticism* [Aldershot, 2006], nos. 1 and 2).

34. *Summa sententiarum*, 5.3, PL 176, cols. 42D–174A (col. 130A, col. 130B) (hereafter SS). For the Porretan, see Nikolaus M. Häring, ed, "Die *Sententie Magistri Gisleberti Pictavensis episcopi* I," *Archives d'histoire doctrinale et littéraire du Moyen Âge* 45 (1978): 7.13–14; 83–180 (149).

35. For more on the contemporary debates on penance and marriage discussed in this essay, see Colish, *Peter Lombard*, 2:588–600, 602–4, 628–58, 673–89.

36. SS, 6.10–11, PL 176, cols. 146C–149B (6.11, cols 148A and 148C–D, respectively).

37. SS, 7.1–7, PL 176, cols. 155B–160C (7.6, cols. 158C–159C).

38. SS, 7.14, PL 176, cols. 165B–166B (col. 165D). On marriage rights of *servi* in the twelfth century see Anders Winroth, "Neither Slave nor Free: Theology and Law in Gratian's Thought on the Definition of Marriage and Unfree Persons," in *Medieval Church Law and the Origins of the Western Legal Tradition: A Tribute to Kenneth Pennington*, ed. Wolfgang P. Müller and Mary E. Sommer (Washington, DC, 2006), 97–109.

39. SS, 7.20, PL 176, cols. 170C–171A (col. 170C).

PART 2

Schools and Scholars

 CHAPTER 5

Benedict of Aniane as Teacher

M. A. CLAUSSEN

Among that first great generation of individuals whose efforts we name the Carolingian Renaissance, among all those writers and poets, clerics and monks, bishops and abbots, among even the occasional layman or woman who appears, none perhaps has a drearier reputation than Benedict of Aniane.[1] This is quite in contrast to Alcuin, for whom almost all scholars seem to have warm feelings of affection, often brought to the fore by his famous encomium to his cell—"in you the gentle voices of teachers could once be heard / expounding with their hallowed lips the books of wisdom"[2]—or the serio-comic lament addressed to the wayward pupil he names Corydon—"all things were accessible to you: / whatever the fathers discovered in ancient times / your noble intelligence revealed to you."[3] Alcuin speaks directly to us, or so it seems, he shares our interests and our concerns, our frustrations and delights, or so it seems. Most scholars, on the other hand, find it hard not to bristle up whenever Benedict of Aniane is mentioned. C. H. Lawrence, in his survey of medieval monasticism, describes him as Louis the Pious's "agent"; his monastery at Inde as "a kind of ascetical staff college, where abbots and monks would be sent to learn the approved practices."[4] Benedict, whom Lawrence describes as a "zealot" twice in two paragraphs, sought to impose a "straight-jacket" of "rigorism."[5] In the slightly less charged words of Walter Horn and Ernest Born, Benedict attempted to bring a "restrictive asceticism" to the variegated and diverse practices of monasteries across Francia.[6] Luckily, he was stymied, at least to a degree, by the resistance of "a more liberal group[!]."[7] Perhaps the usually discreet Dom David Knowles best sums up the general sense most succinctly, when, in *The Monastic Order in England*, he says that for monks, "Benedict of Aniane has never been a spiritual guide."[8] In his apparently relentless desire to organize, impose, and regulate, Benedict seems to have the gentle voice of a Soviet apparatchik or a Maoist cadre.

When it comes to examining Benedict as a teacher, these images hold. While no one has denied Benedict has teachings—doctrinal ones like the *Disputatio adversus Felicianum*,[9] written against the adoptionist Felix of Urgel and included in Benedict's *Munimenta fidei*,[10] an odd compilation of texts that includes creeds, hymns, and dialogues—few have thought of him as a teacher. And so we are left with the image of Benedict as the zealous rigorist, the Carolingian version of a Dickensian schoolmaster, enforcing his harsh and inflexible discipline with a rule book in one hand and a hickory switch in the other. But Benedict's contemporaries seem to have thought differently. Alcuin, in his fifty-sixth letter, writes to Benedict with unusual warmth, thanking Benedict for his help in either restoring to health a sick brother whom Alcuin had sent to Aniane, or, perhaps more likely, bringing this same man to spiritual health.[11] Alcuin reports that Benedict has consoled this man with his words and his deeds, and says that he yearns to speak with Benedict in person, noting towards the end of the letter that their conversations always bring Alcuin "the sweetness of love" (dulcedinem . . . dilectionis).[12] It was probably Alcuin who stood behind Benedict's work in the mission against Adoptionism, and, writing of this work in Septimania and the Spanish March, Alcuin later commends Benedict to Nibridius of Narbonne as a good shepherd of the flock of Christ.[13] Of course, Alcuin is notoriously amicable, and seems to have liked almost everyone he ever met.[14] Theodulf of Orléans, a southerner like Benedict, is an altogether more prickly character; yet his poem to Benedict (*Carmen* 30) is overflowing with both praise and warmth of feeling.[15]

But whether either of these two actually had experience of Benedict as a teacher is doubtful. Both were friends, both were learned, and both were equals. We do have a couple of letters from the two Reichenau monks, Tatto and Grimald (their transcription of the so-called Aachen *Normalexemplar* is our best copy of the *Rule* of Benedict),[16] who had a more traditional relationship with Benedict. The first of these letters is addressed to their monastery's librarian, Reginbert, and describes their painstaking method of making a copy of the rule.[17] The second is addressed to Haito, bishop of Basel and abbot of Reichenau, and describes, rather briefly, the time the two spent at Inde, sent there to learn "whatever we could of the most worthy practices of the way of the rule, [by living] with that venerable abbot."[18] And although the two monks imply that Haito was skeptical of the value of the new-fangled innovations that Benedict was promoting, Tatto and Grimald are most enthusiastic: they write of the "verissimae res et exempla" they have seen, which their words, they say, can barely describe.[19]

And we have another text as well: a letter of Benedict himself, addressed
to a wayward pupil of his own, a certain Guarnarius.[20] The manuscript that contains this letter is late, dating, according to its editor, from the twelfth century,
but the style is very closely matched by the authentic works of Benedict, and is
marked by his fondness for Latin alliteration.[21] The immediate goal of the letter
is unclear, for it has three different sections. In the first, Benedict admonishes
Guarnarius for having apparently left his monastery. It opens most pathetically:
"O my son, listen, I beg, to the voice of a parent entreating behind this letter . . .
so that you might hear what I bring forth."[22] This opening plaint, a clear echo
of the first line of the *Rule* of Benedict, allows our author to do several things.
First of all, it consciously draws attention to itself. Almost anyone who had read
the *Rule* would recognize this allusion, and if the addressee is in fact a former
monk, the resonance would virtually be assured. Second, revising and revoicing
the opening of the *Rule* in his own words allows Benedict of Aniane to further
his gradual conversion into Benedict of Nursia.[23] But beyond simply rewriting
and ventriloquating the earlier rule, Benedict of Aniane instills the phrase with
the passion of emotional distress; it is as if the author is so distraught that he cannot even recollect accurately the most famous part of a text which he had dedicated his life to understanding.[24] Guarnarius, "who in the beginning hastened to
his inheritance, now lacks a blessing," says Benedict, quoting from Proverbs, for
he has forsaken wisdom because of his own foolish inclination.[25] After weaving
together a series of biblical passages on this theme, Benedict urges him to "yield
your will to the will of God."[26] The second part of the letter opens with the sort
of alliteration Benedict seems to relish: "uti sane exinde federe fidei federeris,
formam fidei te exposcente decerpsi"—roughly, "in order that you might join the
league of faith, I have gathered together a creed."[27] He speaks of the traps that
await those not strengthened with a proper understanding of the faith, which he
then provides with a series of quotations drawn from the New Testament. And
he states that having been instructed in these teachings, the teacher (*eruditor*)
will lead the many to justice, himself forever illumined by a holy fire.[28] After the
creed, the final section of the letter contains a rather philosophical discussion
of the meaning of *usia* and *ipotases*. Before a very warm valediction, the letter
concludes with a paragraph-long attack on the *modernos scolasticos*, who have
confounded many with their syllogisms.[29] Whatever its actual purpose, whether
to convince Guarnarius to return to his monastery, or to correct some errors in
his thinking, the letter uses a variety of tactics. It opens in the grand style, as
Augustine would have it, with a plea both familial and emotional.[30] Most of the
argument in the first part of the letter is based on tradition and authorities, with
citations from Isidore, Augustine's *De Trinitate*, and Scripture, the latter quoted
almost twenty times. The second part, on the creed, offers eleven quotations from

the Bible (eight of which are from Paul) and then a conclusion based on dialectic and philology. Altogether, Benedict's method does not seem all that different from many other Carolingian teachers: the letter recognizes the importance of personal ties between master and pupil, it shows the proper respect for and deference towards biblical and Christian tradition, and it highlights the idiosyncratic contribution that its author makes in his use of Greek.[31]

So much for the obvious evidence—an altogether rather thin dossier.[32] But there are a few other texts that can be examined to gain a better understanding of Benedict as a teacher. Ardo, Benedict's biographer, tells us that he compiled two great collections of monastic rules, the *Codex regularum* and the *Concordia regularum*.[33] The *Codex* is a collection of some thirty monastic texts, mainly rules, that span several centuries and three continents; at the head of the only surviving manuscript of the *Codex* is the so-called pure text of the *Rule* of Benedict (RB).[34] Ardo tells us that the purpose of the *Codex*, which was to be read every morning in Chapter, was to show the superiority of RB in every respect.[35] The *Concordia* is the more interesting text, for it offers a sort of commentary on RB—the glosses being provided by other rules, themselves generally found in the *Codex*. According to Ardo, the purpose of the *Concordia* is to show to the contentious that RB had nothing silly or empty in it, but rather that it was supported and sustained by the other rules.[36] He adds that his Benedict composed the book by first taking the statements (*sententiae*) of RB, and one by one joining to them harmonious counterparts from the other rules.[37]

While there is no preface to our manuscript of the *Codex*, we do have two different prologues, one in prose and the other in dactylic hexameters, to the *Concordia*.[38] Benedict's explanation of the book's origins in the first prologue rather differs from that which Ardo provides. He writes that he has been asked by monks and abbots how other rules compare to RB, and that they have said to him, "What applies to me that I have not undertaken to read?"[39] So from the very start, the immediate cause of the *Concordia* is not to convince the contentious, as Ardo would have us believe, but rather to answer the sincere questions of his perplexed monastic brethren. He opens his response in a classically Carolingian way:[40] "While carefully reflecting on the common advantage [*communi utilitate*] I sought how I might be most useful [*utilius*] to all."[41] This concern with the role of scholarship and learning in seeking and implementing the common good is of course one of the hallmarks of the Carolingian Renaissance.[42] To undertake this task, Benedict says that he began to read the lives of the saints and the rules of the Fathers, and noticed that many of the rules featured the same sense, and sometimes even the same words, as the RB. He writes that from this he concluded that Benedict "adopted his rule from others, and, as it were, from many smaller handfuls vigorously assembled his own handful."[43] In other words, Benedict of

Aniane believed, as most scholars do today, that the *Rule of the Master* preceded *RB*, and that Benedict's rule is based on and derived from it.[44] Benedict goes on to note that since contemporary monks and abbots do not know about the complex textual relationships he has discovered among the various rules, he has brought together all the sayings (*sententiae*) that agree with Benedict for the sake, he tells us, of charity (*caritatis causa*).[45]

The verse preface takes another tack. Instead of discussing the prosaic origins of the *Concordia*, Benedict offers a very sensual account of the cosmological origins of monasticism in general, and monastic rules in particular. "The Judge ordered the constellations to rise up together," he begins, "in order that the shadows of the world might be driven out."[46] Fifteen lines later, the church appears: "an apostolic meeting echoing through the crossroads of the world with thundering words."[47] The martyrs arrive almost immediately, "clothed in rose vestments, shining ruddily with their very blood," followed hard on their heels by the monks, thousands and thousands of them, clothed in white and living in the desert, on high cliffs, in deep valleys, or inside mountain caverns.[48] But although they seem, from Benedict's description, to be living outside society, "they show by their works and by their words" the way for all to ascend to heaven.[49] Among this great crowd, however, a select few, taught by Christ himself, sketch out the heavenly road most clearly: "Benedict [of Nursia], Isidore [of Seville], Basil [of Caesarea] stand out as chosen," Benedict writes, "whose words shine through all the earth."[50] Benedict of Aniane has gathered their testimony like flowers and is presenting it to monks as a fragrant garland of salvation, for "they all teach one faith and one spirit, they draw the way to one fatherland, and one path leads there."[51] The *Concordia* he describes as a "sweet flowing nourishment of honey" that will "grant to the blessed to live without end with Christ, and to deserve worthiness for free!"[52] Comparing Benedict's own words with Ardo's narrative, we can see that once again Ardo has it wrong: rather than being a necessary disciplinary corrective to detractors and murmurers, the *Concordia* offers to all the dulcet hope of eternal salvation.

In certain ways, Benedict is setting forth in these two prefaces a program for the Carolingian monk. The first preface stresses the textual history of monasticism, and Benedict explains that his effort, usefully undertaken for the common good, has uncovered a rich and complex story that has been forgotten or ignored. Benedict, in other words, makes clear the Carolingian supposition that learning and scholarship can lead to a clearer understanding of the past, and hence to a better sense of how to amend the present.[53] But more important than his own archival activity, Benedict tells us in the second prologue why monasticism is important. Not only are monks the heirs of the martyrs, their splendid white robes a gleaming monument to their holiness and devotion, but they also play a central role in Christian society, for by their efficacious words and pious deeds, they point out the path of salvation to all.

The *Concordia* has thus long been generally misunderstood. For instance, Karl Ferdinand Werner has argued that both compilations—the *Concordia* as well as the *Codex regularum*—are texts that seek to promote a uniformity of observance and cult.[54] One would think that just the opposite is true. Both offer, after all, abundant evidence of a diversity of tradition, practice, observance, and discipline, and this multiplicity is sanctioned not only by the collection of texts that Benedict had assembled, but by the authority of the authors who are represented. Basil, Augustine, Caesarius, Isidore, Columbanus, Cassian, Leo the Great: these are all writers whose works were taken most seriously by Carolingian scholars, and all of them (along with many others) appear in Benedict's works, offering ways of ordering the monastic life that differ, sometimes a little, sometimes a great deal, from those in *RB*.[55] And even a cursory glance at the *Concordia* might indicate that the texts and rules that Benedict of Aniane uses to gloss *RB* do not concord. Almost everything seems to be in dispute, from the election and authority of the abbot and the role of his subordinates, to what psalms are to be chanted at what hour, to the uses of "alleluia" during the various seasons of the liturgical year.[56] If the *Concordia*, then, does not show the superiority of *RB* or its advantages or its benefits, what is its purpose?

This question returns us to Benedict of Aniane as a teacher. Benedict, both as a monk and eventually as an abbot, belonged to the long tradition of monastic education that had its roots in late antiquity.[57] By the eighth century, learning to read, to write, and perhaps do some arithmetic was generally a pedagogical goal, but only a secondary one; the primary purpose of monastic schooling was spiritual formation.[58] Nevertheless, there were some immediately pressing educational matters to be dealt with in a Carolingian monastery. Oblates, young monks, and perhaps older novices had to be taught how to chant their offices, read their Bibles, and pray their psalms.[59] This would allow them to participate in the daily round of prayers by which monks secured the blessings of God for themselves, their families and friends, their patrons and benefactors, and their kingdoms.[60] More importantly, literacy would give the novice access to Scripture, which was a primary preoccupation of Carolingian society in general, and Carolingian monks in particular.[61] But the second goal, the greater one, of monastic education was what St. Benedict calls in his rule a *conversatio morum*. Although this is sometimes translated as "conversion of manners," it really seems to mean a "transformation of life."[62] For Carolingian masters, one way to achieve this transformation of their young monastic charges was through the close and careful processes of *custodia* and *disciplina*, *correctio* and *emendatio*.[63] But beyond observation and control by their *seniores*, beyond learning grammar and reading from their *magistri*, young monks learned how to be monks and discovered how to attain their *conversatio* by the day-to-day practice of living in a monastery, by imitating their superiors, by following customs, and by asking questions.[64] While we do not have texts that tell us this, we perhaps do have a clue about how this was done in the way many monastic rules are composed. About half of the rules in the *Codex* and *Concordia* are written either as dialogues or as letters addressing a specific request for guidance. The most overtly dialogical rules are from late antique Lérins. For instance, the *Rule of the Four Fathers* begins: "While we were sitting around together seeking wholesome knowledge, we asked our Lord that he might grant us his Holy Spirit, who would instruct us on how we might order the *conversatio* of the brethren and their rule of life."[65]

While few other of the monastic rules are presented so conversationally, it is worth recalling that the rules of Basil, Augustine, Paul and Stephen, and the Master are clearly presented as dialogue between a *magister* (a master or teacher) and a disciple, as are the instructions of Pachomius and his successor Horsiesius. Even *RB* opens with direct speech aimed at a single individual, the *filius* addressed in the famous opening line, "obsculta o fili praeceptum magistri." To these authors, it seems a written rule acted as a sort of substitute for the direct encounter between a teacher and a student.[66] Benedict of Aniane, in the *Concordia*, does something similar. He places the texts of the various rules in dialogue as well, and thus allows the masters of the monastic tradition to speak to one another across the centuries and continents. While *RB* might be the dominant voice since it opens each chapter, it is met with a polyphony of responses. In the *Concordia*, Benedict of Aniane has reawakened the gentle voices of teachers from the past, allowing them once again to whisper their words of wisdom and experience to him and to the monks of Francia.

But there is perhaps a little more that we can adduce from the *Concordia*. Discussing the role of the ever-problematic Bible in education, John Contreni has written that "the drive to preserve orthodoxy and exegetical integrity in the face of a text that could supply multiple interpretations to many different readers was one of the dynamic elements of early medieval culture."[67] Benedict perhaps found himself in a similar situation after he had begun the research he describes in the prose preface to the *Concordia*. As mentioned earlier, perhaps the most striking feature of the collection is the great diversity of monastic traditions represented in these rules, and Benedict must have realized, simply as a practical matter, that either a particular tradition had to be chosen, or a new one constructed based on the traditions handed down in the rules.[68] But how would an abbot, or a teacher, choose which tradition to privilege? One could plausibly argue that *Concordia* is a sort of textbook, one that confronts the reader or student with a set of problems regarding monastic history; like the Bible, it presents a variety of traditions, stories, and practices, and it is up to the reader, or student, to decide which one to choose.[69] An analogy to seeing the *Concordia* this way might be found in Julian of Toledo's *Anticemenon*. Julian, in this dialogical text, responds to questions from an unnamed interlocutor regarding apparent contradictions in the text of Scripture. For instance, the first question asks how it was that God made night and day on the first day of Creation, but did not make the stars, which distinguish the two, until the fourth day.[70] Julian then offers a resolution to the problem. The *Anticemenon* has a certain similarity to Abelard's *Sic et non*, but it provides the answers that Abelard fails to.[71] The *Concordia* works in a similar fashion. A young monk may have asked Benedict how an abbot should be chosen; Benedict might then turn to the appropriate chapter in the *Concordia* and find the appropriate set of texts.[72] But all that done, what happens next? Just as the texts are in conversation, so might Benedict as well begin a discussion of what the various texts signify, and how they might be interpreted. In other words, the *Concordia* would not stand alone, but rather be a source book, the meaning of which could only be made clear through a conversation between students and teachers.[73] Like Julian's work, Benedict has gathered together problematic texts from the past; but, like Abelard, he offers no solutions in writing. Rather, faithful to the monastic tradition of education, the answer would arise through consultation, discussion, and conference. This, then, might offer us a very different view of Benedict of Aniane. Far from being the zealot as he is so often portrayed, the *Concordia regularum* offers us a picture of Benedict as a collaborator, as a leader of dialogue engaged in the constant struggle by Carolingian thinkers to make the past understandable, relevant, and useful.

Notes

I would like to offer my thanks to Steven Stofferahn and Cullen Chandler for inviting me to participate in the series of panels in John Contreni's honor; to the members of the Kalamazoo audience for their comments and suggestions on this paper; to Derek Anderson for his help in completing the text; and finally to John himself, for his friendship and help over the last many years.

1. The bibliography on Benedict and his reforms is long, but the best introduction remains Josef Semmler, "Benedictus II: Una Regula—Una Consuetudo," in *Benedictine Culture, 750–1050*, ed. W. Lourdaux and D. Verhelst, Mediaevalia Lovaniensia Series 1, Studia 11 (Leuven, 1983), 1–49. Philippe Depreux offers a more recent bibliography in *Prosopographie de l'entourage de Louis le Pieux (781–840)*, Instrumenta herausgegeben vom Deutschen Historischen Institut Paris 1 (Sigmaringen, 1997), 123–29. The problematic biography is by Ardo, *Vita Benedicti abbatis Anianensis*, ed. Georg Waitz, MGH SS 15.1, 198–220; trans. Allen Cabaniss, *The Emperor's Monk: A Contemporary Life of Benedict of Aniane by Ardo* (Elms Court, UK, 1979) (repr. in Thomas F. X. Noble and Thomas Head, *Soldiers of Christ: Saints and Saints' Lives from Late Antiquity and the Early Middle Ages* [University Park, PA, 1995], 215–54; and *Benedict of Aniane: The Emperor's Monk, Ardo's Life*, Cistercian Studies

Series 220 [Kalamazoo, MI, 2008]). The best recent work on Benedict's life in English is Felice Lifshitz, *The Name of the Saint: The Martyrology of Jerome and Access to the Sacred in Francia, 627–827*, Publications in Medieval Studies (Notre Dame, IN, 2006), 57–72.

2. Peter Godman, *Poetry of the Carolingian Renaissance* (Norman, OK, 1985), 124–25: "In te personuit quondam vox alma magistri, quae sacro sophiae tradidit ore libros."

3. Ibid., 122–23: "Sensibus et fuerant pervia cuncta tuis. Quicquid ab antiquo invenerunt tempore patres, nobile cuncta tibi pandit et ingenium."

4. C. H. Lawrence, *Medieval Monasticism: Forms of Religious Life in Western Europe in the Middle Ages* (New York, 1984), 69.

5. Ibid., 69–70.

6. Walter Horn and Ernest Born, *The Plan of St. Gall: A Study of the Architecture and Economy of and Life in a Paradigmatic Carolingian Monastery*, California Sudies in the History of Art 19 (Berkeley and Los Angeles, 1979), 21.

7. Lawrence, *Medieval Monasticism*, 70.

8. David Knowles, *The Monastic Order in England: A History of its Development from the Times of St Dunstan to the Fourth Lateran Council, 940–1216* (Cambridge, 1966), 28n2.

9. Benedict of Aniane, *Disputatio Benedicti levitae adversus Felicianum impietatem*, PL 103, cols. 1399–1411, which John C. Cavadini, *The Last Christology of the West: Adoptionism in Spain and Gaul, 785–820* (Philadelphia, 1993), 128, describes as "perhaps one of the most idiosyncratic of all the non-Hispanic anti-adoptionist works."

10. Jean Leclercq, ed., "Les 'Munimenta fidei' de saint Benoit d'Aniane," *Studia anselmiana philosophia theologica* 20, *Analecta monastica* 1 (1952): 21–74; Paolo Chiesa, "Benedetto di Aniane epitomatore di Gregorio Magno e commentatore dei Re?," *Revue bénédictine* 117 (2007): 294–338 (326–29), has recently called into question the authenticity of the attribution of this text to Benedict: see below, note 21.

11. Alcuin, ep. 56, in *Epistolae Karolini aevi II*, ed. Ernst Dümmler, MGH Epp. 4, 99–100, dated by the editor to 782–96. Elisabeth Magnou-Nortier, *La société laïque et l'église dans la province ecclésiastique de Narbonne (zone cispyrénéenne) de la fin du VIIIᵉ a la fin du XIᵉ siècle*, Publications de l'Université de Toulouse-Le Mirail Série A Tome 20 (Toulouse, 1974), 123, suggests that the Gellone Sacramentary, which seems to have been written in Cambrai, was given to Benedict by Alcuin.

12. Alcuin, ep. 56, MGH Epp. 4, 100: "aequalitatis animorum dulcedinem generare solet dilectionis." In ep. 57, ibid., 100–101, Alcuin says that he is writing hastily ("ad rememorandum amicitiae iocunditatem").

13. Alcuin, ep. 206, MGH Epp. 4, 342–43: "vos vero ambo laborate quasi boni pastores in grege Christi"; on the anti-Adoptionist "mission," see André Bonnery, "A propos du Concile de Francfort (794): L'action des moines de Septimanie dans la lutte contre l'Adoptionisme," in *Das Frankfurter Konzil von 794: Kristallisationspunkt karolingischer Kultur*, ed. Rainer Berndt, 2 vols. (Mainz, 1997), 2:767–86; Donald A. Bullough, *Alcuin: Achievement and Reputation*, Education and Society in the Middle Ages and Renaissance 16 (Leiden, 2004) 419–28; Cavadini, *Last Christology*; and Cullen Chandler, "Heresy and Empire: The Role of the Adoptionist Controversy in Charlemagne's Conquest of the Spanish March," *International History Review* 24 (2002): 505–27.

14. On Alcuin's "theology of friendship" and his belief in the necessity of spreading it widely, see C. Stephen Jaeger, "'Seed-Sowers of Peace': The Uses of Love and Friendship at Court and in the Kingdom of Charlemagne," in *The Making of Christian Communities in Late Antiquity and the Middle Ages*, ed. Mark Williams (London, 2005), 77–92.

15. Theodulf of Orléans, "Ad monachos sancti Benedicti," in *Poetae latini aevi Carolini I*, ed. Ernst Dümmler, MGH Poetae 1, 520–22.

16. Disputes regarding the authenticity of this copy seem to have died down to a considerable degree. On the text, see Ludwig Traube, *Textgeschichte der Regula S. Benedicti* (Munich, 1910); Rudolf Hanslik, ed., *Benedicti Regula*, CSEL 75, 2nd ed. (Vienna, 77); Paul Meyvaert, "Towards a History of the Textual Transmission of the *Regula S. Benedicti*," *Scriptorium* 17 (1963), 83–110; and J. Gilissen, "Observations codicologiques sur le codex Sangallensis 914," in *Miscellanea codologica F. Masai dictata*, ed. P. Cockshaw, M. C. Garand, and P. Jodogne (Ghent, 1979), 51–70.

17. *Epistolae Karolini aevi III*, ed. Ernst Dummler, MGH Epp. 5, no. 3, 301–2.

18. MGH Epp. 5, no. 5, 305–7: "quicquid morum honestorum in ordine regulari apud venerabilem illum abbatem."

19. Ibid., 305.

20. MGH Epp. 4, no. 40, 561–63. According to Dümmler (561), the letter is only transmitted in an eleventh or twelfth-century Paris manuscript (Paris, Bibliothèque nationale de France, MS 2390, Colbertinus 4310), the same manuscript that has our only copy of the *Munimenta fidei*.

21. Chiesa, "Benedetto di Aniane," 326–29, argues that the attribution to Benedict of both the *Munimenta* and the letter to Guarnarius is suspect. Regarding the letter, he draws particular attention to an attack on "moderni scholastici maxime apud Scotos," and suggests that this animosity is directed against Eriugena, who was writing some forty years after Benedict died; but he intimates that this part of the letter might have been a later interpolation. However, Mayke de Jong, "From Scolastici to Scioli: Alcuin and the Formation of an Intellectual Élite," in *Alcuin of York: Scholar at the Carolingian Court*, ed. L. A. J. R. Houwen and A. A. MacDonald, Germania latina 3, Mediaevalia Groningana 22 (Groningen, 1998) 45–57, suggests another way of identifying these "scholastici." To my mind, the prose style of most of the letter shows a remarkable similarity to other "authentic" works of Benedict. If at least most of the letter is indeed by Benedict, one wonders whether this is the same Guarnarius Dhuoda mentions in *Liber manualis*, 10.5; see Pierre Riché, Bernard de Vregille, and Claude Mondésert, eds., *Dhuoda: Manuel pour mon fils*, Sources chrétiennes 225, 2nd ed. (Paris, 1991), 354. A number of facts might support such a supposition. Geographically and socially, there were close ties between the family of Dhuoda's husband, Bernard of Septimania, and Aniane; and chronologically, the fact that Guarnarius seems to be recently dead when Dhuoda writes around 843 might indicate that he was alive during Benedict's lifetime. On the letter in general, see Chandler, "Heresy and Empire," 525–26.

22. Chandler, "Heresy and Empire," 561: "Fili mi exaudi oro vocem parentis post pergum pignoris exorantis, immo ut acceptes obsecro queetiam depromo."

23. Lifshitz, *Name of the Saint*, 65–68.

24. See Michael Holquist, "The Politics of Representation," in *Allegory and Representation*, ed. Stephen J. Greenblatt (Baltimore, 1981), 163–83 (169).

25. Prov. 21:20.

26. MGH Epp. 4, no. 40, 562.

27. Ibid., 562. The alliteration continues in the second half of the sentence, the whole reading being "uti sane exinde federe fidei federeris, formam fidei te exposcente decerpsi, qua te indeptum omnique erroris dempta deformitate, una nobiscum novando novale spiritu mentis tue, licet noster homo exterior corrumpatur, sed interior renovatur."

28. Ibid., 563: "Hac igitur doctus doctrina plurimorum ad iustitiam eruditor, fulgoratus hoc fulgore sacro in perpetuas aeternitates valeto."

29. Ibid., 563; see de Jong, "From Scolastici to Scioli," esp. 53–54.

30. Augustine, *On Christian Teaching*, 4.4–4.7, in *Sancti Aurelii Augustini De doctrina christiana*, ed. Joseph Martin, CCSL 34 (Turnhout, 1962), 119–31.

31. On the sort of bonds seen here between Benedict and Guarnarius, see John J. Contreni, "Education and Learning in the Early Middle Ages: New Perspectives and Old Problems," *International Journal of Social Education* 4 (1989): 9–25 (9). This letter might also offer an entrée to Benedict's "emotional community," by examining the "emotion words" that are used by him and those in his circle: see Barbara H. Rosenwein, *Emotional Communities in the Early Middle Ages* (Ithaca, 2006), esp. 23–29, for her definition of "emotional community," and 39–53 on "emotion words."

32. Due to considerations of length, I am unable here to discuss Benedict's short dialogue on his creed, and his interesting essay "De modis amiciciarum et vera amicicia," both included in the *Munimenta fidei*.

33. Ardo, *Vita Benedicti*, 38, MGH SS 15.1, 217.

34. The *Codex*, which survives only in one manuscript, Munich, Bayerische Staatsbibliothek, Clm 28.118, as a whole remains unedited and unpublished, although it is one of the primary transmitters of several rules, including the *Rule of the Master* and some of the Lérins rules. It is also one of the three earliest manuscripts that carry the pure text of *RB*. Pierre Bonnerue, ed., *Benedicti Anianensis Concordia regularum*, CCCM 168 (Turnhout, 1999), 71–84, has argued that the Munich manuscript is not the actual *Codex regularum* of Benedict, but rather a selection from it. For paleological and bibliographic details, see Bernhard Bischoff, *Katalog der festländischen Handschriften des neunten Jahrhunderts (mit Ausnahme der wisigotischen)*, pt. 2, *Laon—Paderborn* (Wiesbaden, 2004), 274–75, no. 3346.

35. Ardo, *Vita Benedicti*, ch. 38, MGH SS 15.1, 217: "ita ut prior beati Benedicti regula cunctis esset," meaning, perhaps, that the text from the *RB* should be read first?

36. Ibid.: "ex quo rursus ut ostenderet contentiosis nil frivola cassaque a beato Benedicto edita fore, set suam exaliorm fultam esse regulam."

37. On Benedict's method, see Pierre Bonnerue, "Benoît d'Aniane et la législation monastique," in François Bougard, *Le christianisme en occident du début du VIIᵉ siècle au milieu du XIᵉ siècle*, Regards sur l'histoire (Paris, 1997), 175–85 (177–79). Benedict was not alone in using this method—it was characteristic of many other Carolingian writers: see John J. Contreni, "Learning in the Early Middle Ages," in *Carolingian Learning, Masters, and Manuscripts* (Brookfield, VT, 1992), 1–21 (16).

38. *Concordia regularum*, prol. 1 and 2, ed. Bonnerue, 3–7.

39. Ibid., 3.

40. See Josef Fleckenstein, *Die Bildungsreform Karls des Grossen als Verwirklichung der Norma rectitudinis* (Freiburg i.B., 1953); Matthew Innes and Rosamond McKitterick, "The Writing of History," in *Carolingian Culture: Emulation and Innovation*, ed. Rosamond McKitterick (Cambridge, 1994), 193–220.

41. *Concordia regularum*, prol. 1, ed. Bonnerue, 3: "Dum communi utilitate consulens attentius quaererem, quomodo utilius possem cunctis prodesse."

42. Probably the most programmatic statement on *utilitas* is Charlemagne's letter *De litteris colendis*, which perhaps dates to 784–85: the MGH text (MGH Capit 1, no. 129) has been re-edited by T. Martin, "Bemerkungen zur 'Epistola de litteris colendis,'" *Archiv für Diplomatic* 31 (1985), 227–72 (231–35). On the importance of *utilitas* to the Carolingian

enterprise, see Réginald Gregoire, "L'Ordine ed il suo significato: 'utilitas' et 'caritas,'" in *Segni e riti nella chiesa altomedievale occidentale*, Settimane di studio del centro italiano di studi sull'alto medioevo 33 (Spoleto, 1987), 639–97 (660–65). For many, perhaps most, Carolingian writers, scholarship was not an end in and of itself, but rather a necessary step in determining the *norma* or *linea rectitudinis*; once determined, that became the basis for the necessary *correctio*: see Giles Brown, "Introduction: The Carolingian Renaissance," in *Carolingian Culture*, ed. McKitterick, 1–51 (26); M. A. Claussen, *The Reform of the Frankish Church: Chrodegang of Metz and the "Regula canonicorum" in the Eighth Century*, Cambridge Studies in Medieval Life and Thought (Cambridge, 2004), 3; Mayke de Jong, "Charlemagne's Church," in *Charlemagne: Empire and Society*, ed. Joanna Story (Manchester, 2005), 103–35 (104–5); Mayke de Jong, *The Penitential State: Authority and Atonement in the Age of Louis the Pious, 814–840* (Cambridge, 2009), 23; Fleckenstein, *Die Bildungsreform*; Matthew Innes, "'A Place of Discipline': Carolingian Courts and Aristocratic Youth," in *Court Culture in the Early Middle Ages: The Proceedings of the First Alcuin Conference*, ed. Catherine Cubitt, Studies in the Early Middle Ages 3 (Turnhout, 2003), pp. 59–76 (59–61); Rosamond McKitterick, *Charlemagne: The Formation of a European Identity* (Cambridge, 2008), 292–95 and 306–11; and, for later developments, Mary E. Summar, "Hincmar of Reims and the Canon Law of Episcopal Translation," *Catholic Historical Review* 88 (2002): 429–45.

43. *Concordia regularum*, prol. 1, ed. Bonnerue, 3: "beatum Benedictum suam a ceteris assumpsisse regulam, et veluti ex manipulis plurimis unum strenue contraxisse manipulum."

44. See David Knowles, *Great Historical Enterprises: Problems in Monastic History* (Edinburgh, 1964), 139–95, for a history of the controversy. It was renewed in the early 1990s by Marilyn Dunn, "Mastering Benedict: Monastic Rules and Their Authors in the Early Medieval West," *English Historical Review* 105 (1990): 567–94; Adalbert de Vogüé, "The Master and S. Benedict: A Reply to Marilyn Dunn," *English Historical Review* 107 (1992): 95–103; and finally, Marilyn Dunn, "The Master and St. Benedict: A Rejoinder," ibid., 104–11.

45. *Concordia regularum*, prol. 1, ed. Bonnerue, 4.

46. Ibid., prol. 2.1–3, ed. Bonnerue, 5: "Arbiter ut mundi tenebras depelleret omnes / sidus ab eo iussit consurgere, cuius / luce peropacae fugiunt ex orbe tenebrae."

47. Ibid., prol. 2.20–21, ed. Bonnerue, 5: "coetus apostolicus reboans per compita mundi / verba tonantis."

48. Ibid., prol. 2.22–23, ed. Bonnerue, 5: "roseo vestitus amictu / sanguine quippe so rutilans."

49. Ibid., prol. 2.34–36, ed. Bonnerue, 6: "Hic opere verbisque suis documenta salutis / demonstrauit ovans cunctis, qui regan polorum / scandere quantocius satagunt."

50. Ibid., prol. 2.42–43, ed. Bonnerue, 6: "Vir Benedictus et Ysidorus Basilius extant / eximii, quorum renitent sat dicta per orbem."

51. Ibid., prol. 2.52–53, ed. Bonnerue, 6: "una fides cunctos docuit et spiritus unus / una tenet patria, trames qua duxit."

52. Ibid., prol. 2.59–62, ed. Bonnerue, 7: "haec est vera via, porgit haec pocula vitae / pabula dulciflua melle quae dulcius extant / haec tribuit codex, tribuit sine fine beate / vivere cum Christo dignasque promere grates."

53. See above, note 42. I would like to thank the press's reader for calling attention to the similarity between Benedict's textual endeavor and Jerome's biblical translations; on the veneration the Carolingians had for Jerome, see Bernice M. Kaczynski, "Edition, Transla-

tion, and Exegesis: The Carolingians and the Bible," in *"The Gentle Voices of Teachers"*: *Aspects of Learning in the Carolingian Age*, ed. Richard E. Sullivan (Ohio, 1995), 171–85.

54. Karl Ferdinand Werner, "Hlodovicus Augustus: Gouverner l'empire chretién— Idées et réalités," in *Charlemagne's Heir: New Perspectives on the Reign of Louis the Pious (814–840)*, ed. Peter Godman and Roger Collins (Oxford, 1990), 3–123 (72). Of course, just how regular the Carolingians sought to make the cult is unclear: the orthodox position, that Pippin the Short and Charlemagne sought to bring the churches in Francia into some liturgical harmony, is outlined by Cyrille Vogel, *Medieval Liturgy: An Introduction to the Sources*, rev. and trans. W. G. Storey and N. K. Rasmussen (Washington, DC, 1986), 79–105, but this has been rather convincingly disputed by, among others, Yitzhak Hen, *The Royal Patronage of Liturgy in Frankish Gaul to the Death of Charles the Bald (877)* (London, 2001), esp. 42–95.

55. Contreni, "Education and Learning," 20–21; Albrecht Diem, "Rewriting Benedict: The *regula cuiusdam ad virgines* and Intertextuality as a Tool to Construct a Monastic Identity," *Journal of Medieval Latin* 17 (2007 [2009]): 313–28 (313–15).

56. John J. Contreni, "The Pursuit of Knowledge in Carolingian Europe," in *"Gentle Voices of Teachers,"* ed. Sullivan, 106–41 (110–11); and Contreni, "Learning in the Early Middle Ages," 15–20.

57. The classic study on monastic education is Jean Leclercq, *The Love of Learning and the Desire for God: A Study of Monastic Culture* (New York, 1972); and Jean Leclercq, "Pedagogie et formation spirituelle du VIᵉ au IXᵉ siècle," in *La scuola nell'occidente latino dell'alto medioevo*, Settimane di studio del centro italiano di studi sull'alto medioevo 19, 2 vols. (Spoleto, 1972), 1:255–90; more recently, see Albrecht Diem, "The Emergence of Monastic Schools: The Role of Alcuin," in *Alcuin of York: Scholar at the Carolingian Court*, ed. L. A. J. R. Houwen and A. A. MacDonald, Proceedings of the Third Germania Latina Conference, Germania latina 3 (Groningen, 1998), 27–44; Mayke de Jong, "Growing up in a Carolingian Monastery: Magister Hildemar and His Oblates," *Journal of Medieval History* 9 (1983): 99–128; George Ferzoco, "The Changing Face of Tradition: Monastic Education in the Middle Ages," in *Medieval Monastic Education*, ed. George Ferzoco and Carolyn Muessig (London, 2000), 1–6; Karl Suso Frank, "Vom Kloster als scola dominici servitii zum Kloster ad servitium imperii," *Studien und Mitteilungen zur Geschichte des Benediktiner Ordens und seiner Zweige* 91 (1980): 80–97; and Valerie L. Garver, "The Influence of Monastic Ideals upon Carolingian Conceptions of Childhood," in, *Childhood in the Middle Ages and the Renaissance: The Results of a Paradigm Shift in the History of Mentality*, ed. Albrecht Classen (Berlin, 2005), 67–85.

58. Leclercq, "Pedagogie et formation spirituelle," 255–59, offers a useful discussion of the various ends of monastic education, and the concomitant tension among them; see also de Jong, "Growing Up in a Carolingian Monastery," 114–16; and, more agnostically, Ferzoco, "Changing Face of Tradition," 1.

59. For the actual means of instruction, see Pierre Riché, *Education and Culture in the Barbarian West: From the Sixth through the Eighth Century*, trans. John J. Contreni (Columbia, SC, 1978), 458–66; Detlef Illmer, *Erziehung und Wissensvermittlung im frühen Mittelalter: Ein Beitrag zur Entstehungsgeschichte der Schule* (Kastellaun, 1979), 153–58; Mayke de Jong, "Growing Up in a Carolingian Monastery," 114–15; and de Jong, "From Scolastici to Scioli," 51–52.

60. Susan Boynton, "Training for the Liturgy as a Form of Monastic Education," in *Medieval Monastic Education*, ed. Ferzoco and Muessig, 11–16; and more expansively in

Boynton, *Shaping a Monastic Identity: Liturgy and History at the Imperial Abbey of Farfa, 1000–1125* (Ithaca, 2006), 65–88, which notes the importance and centrality of liturgical training to monastic education, especially how chanting the psalms, reading during meals, and listening to the lessons gave novices and young monks a deep exposure to the monastic tradition that went beyond learning to read and write; see also de Jong, "Charlemagne's Church," 119–22.

61. See for instance Contreni, "Education and Learning," 12–13; "Learning in the Early Middle Ages," 4–9; Kaczynski, "Edition, Translation, and Exegesis"; and Martin Irvine, *The Making of Textual Culture: "Grammatica" and Literary Theory, 350–1100* (Cambridge, 1994), 191–95. More generally, see Robert E. McNally, *The Bible in the Early Middle Ages* (Westminster, MD, 1957); and Beryl Smalley, *The Study of the Bible in the Middle Ages* (Oxford, 1984), 37–46.

62. *Benedicti Regula*, ed. Hanslik, 58.17. See Philibert Schmitz, "Conversatio (conversio) morum," *Dictionnaire de spiritualité: Ascétique et mystique, doctrine et histoire*, 17 vols. (Paris, 1932–95), 2:2206–12; Henricus Hoppenbrouwers, *Conversatio: Un étude sémasiologique*, Graecitas et latinitas christianorum primaeva (Nijmegen, 1964), 45–95; Jean Winandy, "Conversio (conversatio) morum," *Dizionario degli istituti de perfezione*, 10 vols. (Rome, 1974–2003), 3:106–10.

63. On this process, see de Jong, "Growing Up in a Carolingian Monastery."

64. See Claussen, *Reform of the Frankish Church*, 240–47; de Jong, "Growing Up in a Carolingian Monastery," 114–15.

65. *Rule of the Four Fathers*, prol., in *Les règles des saints pères*, ed. Adalbert de Vogüé, Sources chrétiennes 297 (Paris, 1982), 180: "Sedentibus nobis in unum, consilium saluberrimum conperti Dominum nostrum rogavimus ut nobis tribueret Spiritum Sanctum, qui nos instrueret qualiter fratrum conversationem vel regulam vitae ordinare possimus."

66. Despite the expressed belief of the various authors in Simon Goldhill, *The End of Dialogue in Antiquity* (Cambridge, 2008), dialogues between master and student, or between adversaries, remained a lively form of intellectual exchange in the Carolingian period: see especially ibid., "Introduction: Why Don't Christians Do Dialogue," 1–11 (5–8); and compare Kate Cooper and Matthew Dal Santo, "Boethius, Gregory the Great and the Christian 'Afterlife' of Classical Dialogue," 173–89 (175–76). The best known of the Carolingian dialogues is the riddle exchange between Alcuin and Charlemagne's son Pippin, the *Disputatio Pippini cum Albino*, in *Altercatio Hadriani Augusti et Epicteti philosophi*, ed. Lloyd W. Daly and Walther Suchier, Illinois Studies in Language and Literature 24, nos. 1–2 (Urbana, IL, 1939), 137–43. On dialogue as a form of Carolingian learning, see Chandler, "Heresy and Empire," 521–25; Chiesa, "Benedetto di Aniane," 321, citing Ardo, *Vita Benedicti*, 20; Contreni, "Education and Learning," 16–17; de Jong, "Charlemagne's Church," 104–05; and Magnou-Nortier, *La société laïque*, 92–93 and 122–23. Susan A. Keefe has shown, in *Water and the Word: Baptism and the Education of the Clergy in the Carolingian Empire* (Notre Dame IN, 2002), that many of the various Carolingian instructions about baptism are presented in dialogue form: see as well David Ganz, "Some Carolingian Questions from Charlemagne's Days," in *Frankland: The Franks and the World of the Early Middle Ages; Essays in Honour of Dame Jinty Nelson*, ed. Paul Fouracre and David Ganz (Manchester, 2008), 90–100.

67. Contreni, "Learning in the Early Middle Ages," 7; see also Contreni, "Education and Learning," 12–13.

68. Richard E. Sullivan, "The Context of Cultural Activity in the Carolingian Age," in *"Gentle Voices of Teachers,"* ed. Sullivan, 51–105 (59–63).

69. See G. R. Wieland, "The Glossed Manuscript: Classbook or Library Book?," *Anglo-Saxon England* 14 (1985): 153–73. I have examined three of the ten or so remaining manuscripts of the *Concordia*, but none of them show the features Wieland has described as typical for schoolbooks.

70. Julian of Toledo, *Anticemenon* 1, Interrogatio 1, PL 96, 595.

71. On Abelard's method here, see M. T. Clanchy, *Abelard: A Medieval Life* (Oxford, 1999), 34–37.

72. *Concordia regularum*, 4, ed. Bonnerue, 51–63.

73. Contreni, "Education and Learning," 20.

CHAPTER 6

Theodulf, Haimo, and Jewish Traditions of Biblical Learning: Exploring Carolingian Culture's Lost Spanish Heritage

JOHANNES HEIL

When Charlemagne, exhausted after years of struggle and painful defeats in Saxony and Spain, undertook a sharp turn in his policy shortly before 780 and, following the example of King Josiah, decided to combine the efforts for military and political expansion with a program for spiritual and ecclesiastical reform,[1] he initiated what modern scholars have called the "Carolingian Renaissance" (or, better, the "Carolingian Reform"), a period of impressive cultural productivity which contributed to the emergence of European medieval and modern culture. Yet there were almost no resources to mobilize from the midst of his empire for such an ambitious, unparalleled undertaking. Ecclesiastical structures existed in Gaul from the third century AD and in the Germanic lands east of the Rhine from the fifth century onwards. However, almost any written record of teaching and learning is lacking up to the eighth century, not only in the lands east of the Rhine, but in Gaul as well, with the notable exceptions of Lyon and few other western sites. Complaints about the poor state of cultural and cultic resources can still be heard in the ninth century, for example in a letter by Frechulf, bishop at Lisieux in about 820, to his friend and teacher Hraban Maur of Fulda. In this letter Frechulf requested biblical commentaries to be used for basic instruction, since—as he said—even a written Bible was missing in the cathedral of Lisieux when he arrived at his new position.[2] Naturally, some programmatic propaganda may have been at work here, but even so, this example reminds us that the driving force behind the Carolingian program for promoting learning was not an aspiration to sophisticated academic perfection, but the need of basic resources for liturgy and instruction. But what is also obvious is that the original intentions were soon overturned by the interior dynamics of school-building, discourse, and text-production. In order to achieve these very goals, Charlemagne attracted scholars from the peripheries of the empire, or even beyond its borders. Assistance came from three geographically distant areas: Italy, Spain, and Britain. However, the influx of men and texts from Italy remained rather weak. Though Charlemagne carefully cultivated good relations with Rome, there are only a few people and works meriting mention in this regard, such as the Lombard historiographer Paul the Deacon (d. ca. 799) or the grammarian Peter of Pisa (bishop of Pavia, d. ca. 795). And no example of an Italian installed in a see or abbey in the northern and western parts of the empire is known,[3] whereas Alcuin, a learned monk from England, could become abbot of the prestigious abbey of Tours,[4] and the Irishman Dungal (d. after 827) could in later years come to be the leading scholar at Bobbio.[5] The "Scots," as many of them were called (regardless of their various Irish, Scottish, or English origins), became legendary, especially in the minds of modern historiographers.[6] Not only did they provide treasures of spirituality and an understanding of biblical truth, but also furnished the keys for doing so: the *artes*, especially the classical works of grammar, rhetoric, and dialectic so necessary for appropriately understanding and teaching the Bible. Alcuin of York thus seems to have been the *spiritus rector* of all that the Frankish king and emperor initiated in terms of education and cultural productivity. He attracted pupils who became teachers in their own right and, later on, influential political figures as well, including Hraban Maur, Fridugis as abbot of Tours, and Leidrad of Lyons. To be sure, the impact the *peregrini* from Ireland and England had on the shape of Carolingian culture is beyond doubt and was certainly lasting. However, it was probably not nearly as pervasive or dominant as has been generally suggested.

The focus here, then, lies with a third group, Charlemagne's Spanish partisans, who were of considerable importance for the reform movement during his reign, but who astonishingly disappeared almost completely from the scene soon after his death. Indeed, one should be aware of the fact, overseen hitherto, that with the exception of Galindo-Prudentius of Troyes (d. 861), no Ibero-Frankish career can be detected during the second half of the ninth century. As far as we can see, the Spanish impact on Carolingian culture and politics ceased completely during the ninth century whereas the "Scoti" remained a reservoir of continuous immigration and inspiration well into the thirteenth century, to Germany and far beyond to the east, up to Kiev.[7]

Charlemagne had come into contact with Spanish theologians during his campaigns in southern France and northern Spain in the later 770s, and colonies of Spanish refugees had been formed even earlier in the century in the central and southern parts of France. Supported by the Frankish establishment, "orthodox" Spanish theologians had been leading the struggle against Spanish Adoptionism in the 790s. The course of these events shows that "Spanish" influence did not feature a uniform appearance easily determined. At least in its origin, Adoptionism had stemmed from an internal Spanish debate over the Trinity, theology, and policy. It was but the latest manifestation of ongoing tensions originating with Reccared's conversion from Arianism to Catholicism in 587, and Spanish resistance to the subordination of Spanish dioceses to the primacy of the Roman Church, increasingly dominated by the Franks in the ninth century.[8] Adoptionism itself, having been refuted by the synods of Regensburg (792) and Frankfurt (794), was, together with the other great issue of the time, the debate about images, a formative conflict for the Latin Church, by which it became clear that the centers of ecclesiastical and theological activity in the West were to move from south to north on the Continent—namely, Frankish metropols such as Lyon, Reims, Mainz, and Salzburg.[9]

While we may not have precise information about when Theodulf, the great Spanish scholar (ca. 760–ca. 821), joined the entourage of Charlemagne, it is clear that he played an active part in the fight against Adoptionism from the very beginning in the 790s. As the late Ann Freeman[10] has shown, in 792/93 he authored the official (though never officially published) Frankish response to Nicaenum II, the so-called *Libri Carolini*, which famously criticized the "errors" of the Greeks (and, unknowingly, those of the papal legates attending the meeting) with regard to the veneration of images. When a few years later Charlemagne initiated an adjustment of diverging text traditions of the Latin Bible, Theodulf transformed this task into a critical and philological undertaking trying to establish not simply an even text, but a thoroughly correct one. In clear contrast to Alcuin's more elegant version, only Theodulf's endeavor developed into what modern scholarship has for long suggested the whole undertaking to have been: a reformed version of the biblical text based on philological criticism.[11] In 798 Theodulf became abbot of Fleury and was elevated to the prestigious episcopal see of the former royal city of Orléans, and it was Christmas day 800—the day when Charlemagne gained the imperial title—that he received *ad personam* a *pallium* from the hands of the pope. After Alcuin's death in 804, Theodulf remained the dominant intellectual of the Frankish Empire, at least as regards theological issues. However, his access to the court remained limited, as did his political influence. Works such as *De processione spiritus sancti* and *De ordine baptismi* or his various steps to improve ecclesiastical life in his dioceses show that he undertook great efforts to put forward the program of reform.[12] Some of Theodulf's writings signal ongoing tensions between the scholars from the south and those from the north. Proof for this comes from Theodulf's satiric letter-poem to the Irish Andreas-Cadac,[13] but also from his heated debate with Alcuin in 802.[14] These debates were more likely a veritable conflict than a kind of academic ritual,[15] for soon after Charlemagne's death Theodulf's career came to an end. In 818 he was deposed from his episcopal see, and he died in a (comfortable) exile some years later—the result of having allegedly supported the uprising of Bernhard of Italy in 817/18.[16] And Theodulf was not the only Spaniard whose career came to an end during these years.[17] At first glance this happened for completely different reasons: Claudius of Turin was almost condemned as a heretic after readers discovered what they considered to be heretical opinions in his biblical commentaries (especially Corinthians, probably composed in 822/23). And Claudius resisted with derision the veneration of images and relics—an attitude which once had informed the Libri Carolini, but had become unpopular by the 820s.[18] Similarly, Archbishop Agobard clashed with the ecclesiastical and political establishment in 821 on the issue of ecclesiastical property in lay hands. In the 830s he was involved in the revolts of Louis the Pious's sons. He witnessed several comebacks until his death in 840 but in general he usually managed to play the wrong card.[19]

In political terms it seems that these bishops (and perhaps others), who once had endowed the Aquitanian court of Louis with its distinctive Iberian flavor, were, as Johannes Fried has pointed out, the price which Emperor Louis was ready to pay for an appeasement with the old partisans of his father, especially his cousins in the higher ecclesiastical echelons.[20] Regarding theology itself, the Spanish bishops represented an earlier stage of Frankish theology that had been continuously under revision since the failure of the Libri Carolini.

One might therefore come to the conclusion that the Spanish impact on Carolingian reform was marginal. What remains is the Libri Carolini, sent to the archives by order of Charlemagne immediately upon completion, and some further works by Theodulf, the biblical commentaries by Claudius of Turin (preserved in a few manuscripts only),[21] and the treatises against superstition, magic beliefs and practices, alleged Jewish misdeeds, liturgical "particularism" by Agobard.[22] What the Spanish had contributed to the emergence of Carolingian culture thus seems to have been momentarily spectacular, but poor in the long run.

This, however, is exactly the point requiring careful examination. I will argue that the Spanish influence on Carolingian and Western intellectual traditions did not end with the departure of the Spanish from the stage. On the contrary, Spanish traditions of teaching and approaches to understanding remained as important for the further development of Carolingian learned culture as those stemming from the British isles.[23] And while the Spanish factor no longer appeared explicitly after 825, it long continued to exercise important influence—albeit cryptically—from the bottom.

A good case in point is Claudius of Turin (d. 827). His commentaries on Genesis and Paul's letters were consulted heavily by both Haimo of Auxerre and Hraban Maur, one of Claudius's leading adversaries.[24] The ongoing influx of Spanish traditions continued in a kind of undercurrent, prompting an examination of what might be called the "Bermuda Triangle" of Carolingian culture—or rather the "Loire Triangle," since most of what has to be said happened not far east of Alcuin's Tours, in a triangle between Orléans, Auxerre, and Bourges/Nevers. Much can be said about it, but this essay will focus on two central aspects: the potential ties between Theodulf and Haimo of Auxerre, and the signficant role that Jewish learned traditions played in establishing these ties.[25]

Theodulf and Haimo

With regard to the sheer number of manuscipts that preserve his many biblical commentaries, Haimo of Auxerre was by far the most successful exegete of the ninth century. Anselm of Laon, Abelard, the Victorines, Peter Lombard, and even Jan Hus continued to quote from Haimo centuries and centuries later.[26] But we possess precious few details about Haimo's life. He gained little renown during his lifetime and remained an obscure figure long after his death. In ensuing ages he became Haimo of Halberstadt,[27] Haimo of Canterbury, Remigius, Remigius of Reims, and so on.[28] The first to identify the Haimo of this tradition (though on a hypothetical basis) with a heretofore unknown master at Saint-Germain, Auxerre was Eduard Riggenbach in 1907.[29] Almost sixty years later Riccardo Quadri studied the personal notes of the Auxerre scholar Heiric (841?–76)[30] in a manuscript from Melk/Austria, who mentioned a teacher at Auxerre named Haimo. Riggenbach's hypothesis thus turned into a well-founded theory. Much work has been done since then and Haimo, the phantom of the Carolingian reform, has slowly risen in stature, thanks especially to the careful efforts of John J. Contreni.[31] The list of works now definitvely attributed to Haimo has increased.[32] Indeed, it is now even possible to reconstruct at least an intellectual biography of this interesting figure.[33]

What is most remarkble about Haimo is his almost unique style. He was not a compiler like Alcuin, Hraban Maur, or other scholars of insular formation, who collected *florilegia* from the works of the Fathers in order to compose new commentaries with diligently arranged word-by-word quotations. Style for him was more than an issue of form. Already in the years of the Adoptionism controversy Alcuin had attacked the manner in which his Spanish colleagues defended orthodoxy, arguing that they had incorrectly quoted the Fathers in their writings against the Adoptionists: "You have not given names of books and the numbers of chapters."[34] The debate was not simply about form, but about how best to preserve the authentic voice of the Fathers, which for him really meant how best to preserve authorized truth.[35] Here is the demarcation line distinguishing the school of Alcuin from Theodulf's writings[36] and from exegetes like Claudius of Turin (who failed with the attempt to adopt the Alcuinian system for the composition of his commentaries),[37] but also from Haimo and—as I would argue—from the Spanish-Carolinigan tradition in general. This debate makes Haimo's strange noncareer, but also the brilliancy of his works, somewhat more understandable. In fact, we have to realize how aware someone like Haimo had to be about power and politics when writing biblical commentaries. Because of his nonconformist style he must always have been in fear of scrutiny or even condemnation from the Alcuinians,[38] and after Claudius the paths of the two schools did not cross until Hraban's pupil Walahfried (d. 849), who developed a rather independent style close to Haimo's and who informed Haimo's commentary on the "second law."[39] In the remoteness of Auxerre, Haimo combined an independent style with a sovereign acquaintance with patristic and early medieval text traditions.[40] Reading Haimo is a pleasure; his texts are well organized and written in an even, easy, and colorful Latin, informing for advanced readers and understandable for beginners as well.[41] Given this sharp contrast to the Alcuinians in terms of style and content, however, the question of Haimo's personal and scholarly formation suggests itself. Thanks to John J. Contreni and others we do have today some clear ideas about the man and the scholar. Yet the profile of the boy and pupil remains a mystery.

One clue as to Haimo's origin is provided by some early (and even some later) manuscripts of Haimo's commentary on Paul that indicate that this particular commentary originated from a homilary on the epistles (probably written by himself) later transformed into a commentary.[42] While some of the manuscripts lack whole sections of in-between exegesis (meaning sections between epistle-readings and their explanations),[43] other manuscripts do provide some of these parts.[44] (Other such "missing" parts were probably never written.)[45] This primitive homilary was based, as some longer and almost word-by-word quotations indicate, on an older anonymous homilary ("Ps.-Bede"), written sometime between 800 and 810, as the use of Alcuin's works and its own use by Smaragdus of St. Mihiel (mixed homilary, 810/12) indicate.[46] While on the one hand this older homilary is a witness for the strong interest in the Pauline letters at the time, on the other hand it is strange in its thoroughly ahistorical and deeply spiritualizing content, and especially in its restraint from making any anti-Jewish remarks. Even the homily for Good Friday has nothing to say about Jews. This work has been attributed to Bede and appeared in print in Cologne in 1535.[47] Seven manuscripts are preserved, all from the ninth/tenth century, showing a certain accumulation in southern Germany.[48] That Haimo made use of this text at Auxerre is not surprising, since at that time Auxerre had close relations with Bavaria and received much of its political personnel—for example, bishops, dukes—from there.[49] Somebody could have brought it from Bavaria to Auxerre, but it is also likely that it went the opposite way: from Auxerre to Bavaria, especially since by 800 no library east of the Rhine could provide as many different sources as those upon which the homilary is based.

The similarities in style between the Pseudo-Bedean homilary and Haimo's commentary are astonishing, which means that in the years when Theodulf was working at Orléans and Alcuin of Tours had just passed away, someone shaped Haimo's style and to a certain extent his thought—a teacher with a style clearly distinct from Alcuin's. Admittedly, though, up to here the threads between Theodulf, Pseudo-Bede, and Haimo remain merely extrinsic.

Yet there are further arguments to consider. Theodulf himself had mentioned students of his own and how he was supervising their progress. They were educated and working at the cathedral and/or at the abbey of Micy/St. Mesmin, one mile west of Orléans, most probably not at Fleury. And Theodulf appointed a certain Wulfinus as principal of the cathedral school, obviously a grammarian of Visigothic origin who in later years became bishop of Dié. The appointment of a principal indicates the existence of a veritable "academic" structure that would eventually attract students. While no names of students are known, it is obvious that Theodulf's many activities and his broad spectrum of writings required not only the contributions of scribes, but the collaboration of well-educated "student assistants" as well.[50] Basically Wulfinus's appearance at this stage helps to illustrate the Spanish orientation of Theodulf's school at Orléans. Furthermore, with the appointment of a grammarian, the instruction in theology must have remained the province of another teacher, presumably Theodulf himself.

Aside from the assumption that the Pseudo-Bedean homiliary (which Haimo had at hand) was written by Theodulf, is there any reason to believe that Haimo received his training at Orléans? Arguments come first from Haimo's biography, now long established. The "nationality" of Haimo had been a key issue already for Riggenbach in 1907 when challenging the identification of our Haimo with Hraban's pupil Haimo of Halberstadt, since an author who spoke so badly about the "Theutonici" can hardly have dwelled at Halberstadt or elsewhere in the Germanic lands. Haimo thus became a Frenchman. However, Riggenbach failed to realize that Haimo's remarks about the "Galli" were by no means any friendlier. Obviously our Haimo must have been a foreigner among the French.[51] Neither was he, as his style and manner of handling the tradition clearly indicate, a member of insular circles of learning. As with a divided echo, I have forwarded the idea elsewhere that Haimo must have been of Spanish extraction. Duly heeding the *contra* arguments articulated during the Auxerre meeting in 2005,[52] I will summarize the *pro* arguments here and will then rally further arguments in support of this contention.

First, in one of his few affirmative references throughout his commentary on Paul to Origen, Haimo spoke about the defeat of the "Germani." However, at the place in question, Origen had spoken about the "Gothi" and their defeat. Obviously, Haimo appreciated the argument, but not the manner in which it was made and therefore changed the names of the actors—perhaps for autobiographical reasons.[53] There are further hints in his exegetical works that likewise reveal a certain familiarity with Spain.[54]

Haimo furthermore shows acquaintance not only with the conventional Hispanic sources such as Isidore's *Etymologiae*, but also rather unique ones, for example the lost *Dialogue on the Nature of the Soul* by Julianus Pomerius,[55] the *Prognosticon* by Julian of Toledo,[56] and the so-called *Mythographus Vaticanus I*, a Spanish collection of fables that drew upon Isidore,[57] now known only through late medieval manuscripts and a reference by Remigius of Auxerre (ca. 841–908).[58] It is also interesting to see that Auxerre was a veritable center for the transmission of the repudiated Spanish exegete Claudius of Turin.[59] Finally, John J. Contreni has argued that Cessy-les-Bois, the tiny abbey where Haimo became abbot at the end of his life, had been populated by Spanish emigrants in the earlier eighth century and may have remained a Spanish center into the ninth century as well.[60]

Yet before establishing the link between Theodulf and Haimo, an argument to the contrary needs to be addressed. Some years ago Louis Holtz contended that Haimo had been raised at Auxerre by a certain Murethach/Muirdac in the 830s. No traces of theological works by this Irish grammarian are left,[61] which keeps open the question about Haimo's theological training. Nevertheless, according to Holtz's scheme Haimo must have been much younger, born by 810 or so. However, John J. Contreni has recently challenged Holtz's argument by noting that Murethach's remark about "Murethach et Aimo" does not necessarily refer to a teacher-student relationship; to the contrary, Murethach and Haimo may well have been colleagues as teachers at Auxerre, further undercutting the assumption that Haimo was of insular formation, especially in grammar.[62] In any event, the definitive biographical data for Haimo have not yet been established. Contreni has argued that by the time of Heiric's return to Auxerre (according to his personal notes in the Melk manuscript around 865), where he followed Haimo in the position of principal of the school, Haimo had not yet passed away (as Quadri had suggested), but had become abbot of the tiny abbey Cessy-les-Bois, working there until his death sometime between 870 and 875. It thus seems likely that Haimo must have already been at work by the 830s or 840s. Proof comes from a request to Count Conrad of Auxerre, relative of Empress Judith and lay abbot of Saint-Germain, to borrow or acquire Hraban's commentary on Ecclesiasticus in exchange for a copy of Quintus Rufus's *History of Alexander*.[63] This

must have been soon after the 830s, according to Hraban's dedication letter to
Ecclesiaticus.[64] And there are hints that Haimo made use of Hraban's commentary on Paul, itself completed by 842.[65] Assuming that Theodulf was born around
760 (or at least not much later, according to Dahlhaus-Berg),[66] he would have
been in his early thirties when he wrote the *Libri*, and about thirty-eight when
appointed to Orléans. From the *Libri* we thus then have a period of roughly fifty
years up to Haimo's most productive literary period (the 840s)—a distance still
permitting a teacher-student relationship. One should also recall that Alcuin (b.
ca. 730) would have been nearly seventy when he assumed the abbacy of Tours
and received Hraban as pupil. With Theodulf as archbishop at Orléans from 798
to 818, there is at least a good chance that Haimo met him personally and prof-
ited from his knowledge. But even without such an immediate personal relationship, a possibility remains at least that Haimo was raised in Spanish circles which
originated from Theodulf.

Theodulf's Hebraist and the "Latin *Midrashim*" of Auxerre

Astonishingly, the most potent argument to establish ties between Theodulf and Haimo comes from a rather unexpected field: the presence and the use
of learned Jewish traditions in Orléans and again in Auxerre. Hraban Maur and
Angelomus of Luxeuil consulted and reacted to it, respectively. This has been
documented elsewhere.[67] Yet Theodulf and the masters of Auxerre seem to have
enjoyed far more direct access to it.

The case of Theodulf and the marginal Latin notes on the basis of the
Hebrew text for his revision of the Bible has been broadly documented, especially by Elisabeth Dahlhaus-Berg[68] and Avrom Saltman.[69] According to Saltman, among the six authentic extant manuscripts of the "Theodulf-Bible," the
G-manuscript (Paris, Bibliothèque nationale de France [BnF], MS lat. 11937,
from Saint-Germain-des-Prés) resembles a kind of battlefield between the Greek
and the Hebrew, as it contains "physical attacks on the Septuagint" as a result
of the Hebrew annotator's attempt to establish an uncorrupted Latin text based
upon the Hebrew. For the books of Samuel alone, comments such as "h. non
habet" occur about eighty times in the margins. Saltman argued that this cor-
rector was a learned, though not a perfect, Hebraist, and that in some instances
his comments actually distorted the meaning of words. Saltman also assumed
that this was the same Hebraist who compiled the Pseudo-Jeromean *Quaestiones
hebraicae in libros Regum et Paralipomenon* (1–4 Kings and Chronicles),[70] an author
whom Hraban later quoted and called "a certain Jew of our times [*modernis temporibus*]."[71] Hraban's reason for consulting this rather unusual source was quite
simple: on Samuel/Kings, Chronicles or Lamentations[72] the Fathers had left no

comprehensive commentary, and on Maccabees no sources at all were at hand.[73] The skilled compiler solved the problem in part (with regard to the literal and historical sense of single verses) by drawing upon a Hebrew source. This source is mentioned already in the introductory letters to the commentaries in question, but to his audience the author remained a nameless Jew. One could well interpret such treatment as discrimination, but given the otherwise highly polemical tone with which Hraban attacked well-known Christian opponents as well as count-less others, the respectful anonymity he preserved in the case of the author of the *Quaestiones* surely did not constitute an expression of contempt. Rather, he sim-ply seems not to have known the name and never to have met with this curious author. He was almost certainly aware, however, that the author was a Jew, even if some modern scholars have felt the need to believe that an author writing in Latin with access to Hebrew sources must have been a faithful convert to Chris-tianity. Nonetheless, in the oldest surviving manuscript (Reims, Bibliothèque municipale, MS lat. 118) where the author again has no name, he clearly appears as a Jew (*ille Judaeus*) rather than a convert. Aside from a misleading addition by a much later hand attributing the text to Jerome, the original title itself even recommends a careful examination since the content subtly deviates from the teachings of the church.[74] Indeed: how could a serious convert have written a thoroughly "Jewish" commentary on Kings in Latin, meaning without any typo-logical reference to Christ and the church as the "true Israel"? This raises still more questions: given that the author was a Jew, how had his explanations come to be expressed in Latin? For which audience would such a Latin translation have been prepared? And what evidence is there to connect the author of the *Quaes-tiones* and Theodulf's assistant, other than the fact that there was a Jew, and here was a text? Admittedly, Saltman's identification has no solid basis, but even so, both attest to the very real impact Jewish learned traditions had on Carolingian exegesis which lasted—as we shall see—until the end of the ninth century.

Some years ago, Burton Van Name Edwards edited a commentary on Genesis from the school of Auxerre which he attributed to Remigius of Au-xerre ("Scriptoribus hebraeorum hic mos est"),[75] meaning to the third genera-tion of Auxerre scholars. His analysis shows that where the author says "dicunt Hebraei," the author not only used sources like the *Liber antiquitatum biblicarum* by Pseudo-Philo, but also traditions stemming from Midrash Rabba and the *Tar-gum* by Pseudo-Jonathan.[76] Yet a few problems remained unsolved, especially Haimo's acquaintance with the Hebrew acronym for "Bible," TaNa' Ch (*thora, newi'im, ktuwim*),[77] as well as several remarkable explanations that sound rather more "midrashic" than "patristic."

Some examples of the latter may prove illuminating. First, I will present a quotation from Haimo's commentary on the letters of Paul:

One shall ask, for which reason the Jews since they had an abundance of animals and cattle with them [in the desert] were seeking for meat, and why they did not consume the meat of [their] animals. What can be solved in the sense that they did not seek for meat of their cattle, but they desired the meat of birds which they had been accustomed to consume in Egypt. For the Nile is a river on whose banks and in whose fens nourishes many kinds of birds, even those that are not extant in the course of other rivers. Therefore let us flee all bad desires.

[Quaestio est, cum Judaei [i.e. in deserto] multitudinem animalium et pecorum secum haberent, quare desiderarent carnes, et quare non comederent carnes animalium? Quae hoc modo solvitur, quia non desiderabant illi carnes pecorum, sed carnes avium concupiebant, quibus soliti fuerant vesci in Aegypto. Nilus enim fluvius, in litoribus suis et palustribus locis multa genera avium habet, et talia qualia non habentur in circuitu aliorum fluminum. Fugiamus ergo concupiscentiam malam.][78]

None of Haimo's Christian precursors offered such a detailed record of menu preferences among the children of Israel in the desert. But the standard midrashic source on this, Exodus Rabba, also seems to be far removed from Haimo's version:

So persistent were the Israelites in their desire to return to Egypt, that Moses had to use force, after persuasive language had failed, to make them continue their journey. Their arguments were that God's object in bringing them out of Egypt was fivefold: (1) to give them the Egyptians' goods, to which they were entitled as wages for their work; (2) to lead them through the Red Sea; (3) to shelter them with his cloud of glory; (4) to avenge them on the Egyptians; (5) to enable them to sing hymns of praise to Him. Now that all these things were accomplished, the Egyptians drowned, and not sufficient left in Egypt to force them again to slavery, their best step would be, they thought, to return to a country where, free from slavery, they could enjoy life infinitely better than in the wilderness that faced them, where there was no bread and no water, not to mention the fish and the onions of Egypt. But Moses pointed out to them that there was a great debt which they had not yet discharged. "Ye shall serve God upon this mountain" (Exod. 3:12), which was, in fact, the token beforehand of God's being with Moses and his mission to Pharaoh.[79]

The one that comes closest to Haimo's explanation is Rashi, Salomon ben Isaak of Troyes (roughly a hundred miles from Auxerre), who, however, worked in the second half of the eleventh century at Troyes. Though he had built upon the older exegetical tradition available to him, this circumstance alone does not necessarily support any explicit conclusions about the existence and nature of potential common sources. Nevertheless, Rashi does give half of what Haimo had said: "For bread they [the children of Israel] asked properly for it is impossible for man [to live] without bread, but for meat they asked improperly, because they had an abundance of cattle. Furthermore they could get along without meat."[80]

It seems possible that Rashi had access to now-lost sources that Haimo had used before him. However, in detecting Jewish sources in Christian exegesis one must be very careful. Not every passage with a midrashic outlook necessarily indicates the access of Christian scholars to Jewish traditions, as borne out by the following example. In a section of a fragmentary commentary on Genesis in Migne (PL 131), which Van Name Edwards has convincingly attributed to Haimo (especially since it features characteristics in terms of form, argumentative procedure, and content consistent with a "true Haimo"),[81] Haimo writes:

> Then again Abraham took a wife, and her name was Keturah (Gen. 25:1), whose name shall be translated as "copulated" or "bound." Therefore the Hebrews convey her to be Agar, the mother of Ismael who was [Abraham's] concubine before, but [they assume that] after Sara's death she became legally married to Abraham. This they feign as Abraham's excuse so that the old, dying man does not appear to be inflamed by the desire for a new marriage.

> [Abraham vero duxit aliam uxorem Ceturam (Gen. 25.1). Quae [Ceturam] interpretatur *copulata* vel *conjuncta*. Unde tradunt Hebraei hanc esse Agar matrem Ismaelis quae prius concubina fuerat, sed post mortem Sarae Abrahae legitime copulabatur: quod ideo fingunt, ut excusent Abraham ne jam senex et depositus novis nuptiis videatur lascivisse.][82]

The argument is about the identity of Hagar and Cethura, which the author refutes with a remarkable sense for matters of daily life. Actually, he avoids explaining the true reason for his sharp refutation (*fingunt*) but it is fairly clear that this Jewish interpretation would de-emphasize the allegoric value of the Hagar/Sarah story in which Paul (Galat. 4:22–24) and the Fathers had discovered an archetype of sacred history in the Christian sense, meaning a pre-figuration of the "rejected" and the "true" Israel.[83] At first glance it seems that Haimo's version derives from Midrash Rabba on Genesis:

> "Abraham took another wife." R. Judah said: "His refers to Hagar." / Said to him R. Nehemiah: "And lo [hebr. = no], it is written 'Abraham took another wife.'" / [He said to him:] "This was on instruction on a statement from God . . . " etc. / [He said to him:] "But it is written 'and her name was Keturah'" [so how can you hold her name was Hagar?] / He said to him: "[It was the same person, but she was called Keturah], because she united [using the same letters as the name] the practice of doing religious duties with the work of doing good deeds."[84]

However, also the above-mentioned Latin *Quaestiones hebraicae in libros Regum et Paralipomenon* by the unknown Jewish author could have provided the orientation for this.[85] And in reading Jerome it becomes clear that Haimo's explanation was—unusually for him—almost a word-by-word quotation from the Church Father who himself was fairly acquainted with contemporary Jewish exegesis. In Jerome's *Quaestiones hebraicae* on Genesis we find:

> Cetura in the Hebrew language is translated as "copulated" or "bound." Therefore the Hebrews assumed that having changed her name she was the same Agar who after Sara's death from concubine turned to become his wife. And it appears as an excuse for the age of the matured Abraham, that one does not argue that the old man desired a new marriage. Setting aside what is uncertain, we say that the sons of Abraham are born from Cetura.

> [Cetura Hebraeo sermone *copulata* interpretatur, aut *juncta*.[86] Quam ob causam suspicantur Hebraei, mutato nomine, eamdem esse *Agar*, quae, Sara mortua, de concubina transierit in uxorem. Et videtur decrepiti jam Abrahae excusari aetas, ne senex post mortem uxoris suae vetulae, novis arguatur nuptiis lascivisse. Nos quod incertum est relinquentes, hoc dicimus, quod de Cetura nati filii Abraham.][87]

The only difference to Haimo is that Jerome gave some kind of report about Jewish interpretations and made assumptions about their motifs, whereas Haimo was expressively clear in his refutation.

Obviously Haimo's "tradunt Hebraei" may in many cases mean that he drew upon Jerome's *Quaestiones hebraicae* for Genesis. However there are a few other "suspicious" arguments in Haimo's commentary for which Jerome is clearly not the source, since the latter's *Quaestiones* do not provide any explanation for these verses. To take but one example:

> The Lord God made coats of skins, and clothed them (Gen. 3:21). In the soul for the sin of transgression; in the body, however, for the pain for sin. It is a stupid question if one tries to find out how or which way the animals were skinned. As God established everything from nothing, so also he does things in whatever way and manner he wishes.

> [Fecit Dominus Deus Adae et uxori ejus tunicas pelliceas (Gen. 3, 21). In anima quidem propter peccatum praevaricationis, in corpore vero propter poenam peccati. Stulta vero quaestio est, si quis velit requirere qualiter vel quo operante pelles ab animalibus subductae sint. Qui enim de nihilo condidit omnia Deus, hoc quoque quomodo vel qualiter voluit fecit.][88]

Since a thorough search yields no Hebrew source for this, it is likely that in this case Haimo is paraphrasing another text by Jerome, a part from his letter 51 to bishop John of Jerusalem.[89] Hence again, no Hebrew source. However, it is interesting to see that most of the Hebrew sources and also the *dubia* which Van Name Edwards discovered in Remigius's commentary on Genesis (CCCM 136) can also be detected in Haimo's commentary on the first book of the Bible (PL 131), although, as will be shown, with remarkable differences:

> *Haimo:* And God said, Let us make man in our image, after our likeness. . . . Let us make: While some people say that this refers to the angels, we nevertheless prefer it to refer to the holy trinity.
>
> [*Haimo:* Faciamus hominem ad imaginem et similitudinem nostram (Gen 1, 26) . . . : Faciamus. Quod, licet quidam ad angelos referendum dicant, melius tamen ad sanctam Trinitatem refertur.][90]

Haimo quoted a potential interpretation without specifying the author(s) (*quidam*), followed by a trinitarian interpretation which he obviously preferred. Two generations later, Remigius provided largely the same explanation, though with explicit reference to the interpretations of the "Hebraei" ("Loquens autem Deus, non ad angelos, ut Hebraei opinantur, dicit 'faciamus hominem', sed persona Patris introducitur Filium et Spiritum alloquentis"), which Van Name Edwards has deduced from traditions such as Pseudo-Jonathan, Targum, and the Midrash Rabba.[91]

Two further examples, however, show considerable differences in the versions by Haimo and Remigius:

> *Haimo:* And there he put the man (Gen. 2:8). And that the man is said to be placed in paradise leads one to understand that he was not formed there, but in our mortal world, since the divine prescience forsaw that he would sin and therefore be thrown from this holy earth into this vale of tears.
>
> [*Haimo:* In quo posuit hominem (Gen. 2,8). Ex quo, quod positus in paradisum homo dicitur, datur intelligi non ibi fuisse conditum, sed in hac nostra mortali terra, quia, divina praescientia, illum peccaturum et ob hoc ab illa sancta terra in hanc convallem miseriae propellendum.][92]

Haimo thus argued that Adam was created outside the paradise, providing this explanation: since God knew from the very beginning about the things to come, Adam's creation took place in the "mortal world." So far, this is consistent with Remigius's later explanation, but in that version this place in the "mortal world" came to have a name: Hebron, the city where Adam was also buried ("Aiunt namque Hebrei Adam in Hebron civitate, in qua sepulta est, fuisse formatum"). This, however, is exactly the localization which Targum Pseudo-Jonathan gives, whereas no Christian source can be named for this explanation. Remigius did not discard this version of Hebrews, and only pointed out that no one was compelled to accept such opinions ("quamvis huiuscemodi opinionibus nemo credere compellantur").[93]

Another example, again with obvious differences with regard to details, follows:

> *Haimo:* "A window shalt thou make to the ark (Gen. 6:16). Instantly the window was made on the top of the ark so that Noah would have access [and] through which he, as later he did, sent out the dove and the raven. This window the Hebrews convey to have been from crystal. In the mystical sense Noah, a just and perfect man by name and deed, typifies Christ.

> [*Haimo:* "Fenestram in arca facies (Gen. 6, 16). Ad hoc fenestra in arcae summitate facta est, ut haberet aditum Noe, per quam emitteret, sicut postea fecit emittens columbam et corvum. Quam fenestram tradunt Hebraei crystallinam fuisse. Mystice autem Noe, vir justus et perfectus nomine et actu, Christum significat.][94]

> *Remigius:* And the Hebrews say that this window was crystalline so that it would be not necessary to open it frequently, but standing inside and looking through this stone one might distinguish between day and night.

> [*Remigius:* Et ferunt Hebraei quod eadem fenestra cristallina fuerit ut non esset eam necesse crebram aperire, sed intus positi perspicuitate illius lapidis possent nosse discretionem inter diem et noctem.][95]

Remigius was interested in the literal sense only, even with regard to the technical details, and omitted Haimo's typological interpretation of Noah. Indeed, his approach is rather surprising, since Christian exegetes were normally interested foremost in the "higher" understanding of Scripture, and Haimo's works are an abundant source for typologies and allegories. Interest in the "literal" sense was thought of as typically "Jewish," but this is exactly what Remigius did.

In the next example, the situation becomes even more complicated:

> *Haimo:* "And Joseph brought unto his father their evil report (Gen. 37:2). Some believe that he charged them for having had intercourse with animals. Thus Alwinus in his Book of Questions. Others say that he charged him for the concubine of the father only, if so, by a synecdoche, which means that from the whole we must refer to the part. For he charged not all the brethren, but only one.

[*Haimo*: Accusavit fratres suos apud patrem crimine pessimo (Gen. 37, 2). Putant quidam quod accusaverit eos quia cum pecoribus commiscebantur. Sic Alwinus in Quaestionibus suis. Alii dicunt quod Ruben pro concubina patris solum accusaverit. Quod si ita est, per synecdochen, id est a toto partem debemus accipere. Non enim omnes fratres accusavit, sed unum solum.][96]

There is, however, no such explanation in Alcuin (Albinus, Alwinus),[97] and a further check of manuscripts would surely bring nothing of that kind to light, since this text was meant to be an instructive dialogue *ad usum scholarum* which most likely would not address the issue of sexual misbehavior so explicitly. Remigius does permit a similar version which he attributed to Jewish traditions, though the source has not yet been identified:

Remigius: The scripture remains silent about the crime for which he charged the brethren to the father. And it is the tradition of the Hebrews that it is for this reason that through illicit lust they had intercourse with males or with cattle.

[*Remigius:* Quo crimine fratres apud patrem accusaverit, scriptura tacet. Traditio tamen est Hebraeorum, quod ea de causa fratres suos filios ancillarum accusaverit, quia illicita voluptate vel masculis vel pecudibus se miscerent in coitu.][98]

Similarities in content and differences in detail are obvious here. Though the sources of Haimo's and Remigius's knowledge cannot be determined with certainty, it is clear that whatever material Haimo (erroneously or knowingly?) had falsely attributed to Alcuin was later attributed by Remigius to Jewish sources. Therefore it is clear that Remigius, writing at the end of the century, was copying Hebrew sources that Haimo may once have introduced into the study and text production cycles at Auxerre. Indeed, in many cases his paraphrases are closer to the original sources than Haimo's, which leads to the conclusion that fragments of post-biblical Jewish exegesis must have remained available at Auxerre and were studied throughout the ninth century.

In the end, we have a teacher without pupils and an outstanding pupil lacking a teacher—and curious Jewish sources written in Latin in between. So far the picture to be gained remains unclear, not only in the sense of being unable to determine the very character of ninth-century Jewish Latin sources with regard to provenance and audience. These aspects of the work of Theodulf and the exegetes also remain remarkably scattered. Haimo made use of this corpus when interpreting Genesis[99] and the letters of Paul. Other commentaries thought to provide further examples for "Latin *Midrashim*" were apparently written without having been influenced by Jewish sources: Haimo's commentary on the Song of Songs is in large part a rewriting of older Christian sources;[100] the same applies to his commentary on Isaiah,[101] as well as to most sections of the commentaries on the Minor Prophets attributed to Haimo. However, the Abdia commentary seems to be almost a "Jewish" commentary in Latin with only marginal Christological ingredients.[102] A closer look reveals that this commentary draws heavily upon Jerome, though omitting almost all of his allegorical and typological interpretations and providing a thoroughly literal-historical reading of the text. In fact, the Abdia commentary transmitted through the works of Haimo provides an almost completely de-Christianized reading of Jerome and other Fathers; it appears to be a *Hieronymus ad usum iudaeorum*. Again, little is known as to its author or audience. Is it possible to assume that Roman-Jewish scholars before 800 preferred to rewrite Jerome in a Jewish manner instead of consulting Hebrew sources? This requires further study and elaboration, but if so, this curious Abdia commentary may be a witness for a Roman-Jewish culture still flourishing in the western peripheries of the Mediterranean during the early Middle Ages not yet thoroughly absorbed by the expansion of rabbinic Hebrew culture and texts.[103]

The use of midrashic and other Jewish sources may someday emerge as a veritable key through which the works of the school of Auxerre may be distinguished from others of the Carolingian period. Obviously, the scholars at Saint-Germain, Auxerre, had access to collections of midrashic material on the Bible that must have been circulating in Spain and south-central Gaul. The extent and character of this material still needs to be determined, particularly relating to where this material came from and—more importantly—the form in which it came to Auxerre. Since this material remained available there until the end of the century (and perhaps beyond), it must have been brought at some point into a Latin form, more likely as collections of interpretations than as comprehensive commentaries, with the notable exception of texts such as the aforementioned Abdia commentary. What remains is the question of how, where, by whom, and for what audiences such translations were made. An answer requires further examination, especially with regard to whether usage in the commentaries from Auxerre followed distinct patterns or whether we are simply encountering occasional references based merely on a few *florilegia* of Jewish origin. If so, these *florilegia* may have been compiled at one place between Orléans and Auxerre to serve the needs of Christian exegetes. It seems possible that Theodulf had initiated the collection of such *florilegia* as a byproduct of his revision of the biblical text and in analogy to his encyclopedic collection of Latin *florilegia* to the Bible (as with Paris, BnF, MS lat. 15679).[104] Or had this material already been brought to Gaul in a Latin version by Jewish refugees from Spain? This is a potent possibility, although there is hitherto no textual evidence for such material being written for a non-Hebrew-speaking Jewish audience in eighth-century Spain or Gaul.

These suggestions, however, are not at all meant to subscribe to the naive or romantic conclusion that the Carolingians and especially their Spanish supporters were amicably inclined toward Jews and Judaism because of their traditional reservations toward images and because Charlemagne preferred to be compared to King David instead of Emperor Augustus.[105] Neither the fact that Theodulf decorated his oratory at Germigny with a picture of the Ark of the Covenant nor that Claudius of Turin ardently rejected the veneration of images and relics ultimately has very little to do with sympathy toward Judaism itself. Rather it shows esteem for the Torah—but in Christian hands. All this followed a thoroughly supersessionist or—more fashionably—colonial attitude which could even lead to a hostile perception of Jews and Judaism. The esteem given to ideal figures of the Old Testament in Visigothic-Catholic and again in Frankish-Carolingian ideology and self-perception supports this point. By declaring the Goths to be God's chosen people, Isidore of Seville in his *History of the Goths* left no place for the original holder of that position.[106] However, what we can observe in the years around 800 among theologians of Spanish origin is that following the dramatic downfall of Visigothic triumphalism and the exhaustion stemming from emigration, instability, and helplessness, they had developed a sense of pragmatism in which Jews and Jewish traditions could be acceptable, if in a strictly limited frame. They took the notion of *Hebraica veritas* serious in a way that went far beyond Jerome's understanding and a pure textual criticism of the biblical text.[107] Jewish exegetical traditions were thereby permitted to contribute to a Christian interpretation, though admittedly only in terms of literal and historical interpretations. Even so, this went considerably beyond Augustine's formula of Jewish servitude for the truth of Scripture and Gregory the Great's insistence, inspired by Roman juridical tradition, on the physical inviolability of Jews. This theology and its practice accepted—though on the lower level of interpretation only—Jewish traditions as veritable and valuable sources. More than a millennium before the *Nostra aetate* of Vatican II, one thus encountered a brief moment when the notorious *contra Judaeos* of years past and years to come was eclipsed by *cum Judaeos* instead.[108]

Notes

1. Kings 22–23:30, as pointed out in John J. Contreni, "'By Lions, Bishops Are Meant; by Wolves, Priests': History, Exegesis, and the Carolingian Church in Haimo of Auxerre's *Commentary on Ezechiel*," *Francia* 29 (2002): 29–56. For overviews, see Pierre Riché, *Écoles et enseignement dans le Haut Moyen Âge: Fin du Ve siècle-milieu du XIe siècle,*

2nd ed. (Paris, 1989); Rosamond McKitterick, *The Frankish Church and the Carolingian Reforms, 789–895* (London, 1977); Rosamond McKitterick, ed., *Carolingian Culture: Emulation and Innovation* (Cambridge, 1994); Ulrich Nonn, "Zur Vorgeschichte der Bildungsreform Karls des Großen," in *Karl der Grosse und sein Nachwirken: 1200 Jahre Kultur und Wissenschaft in Europa*, vol. 1, *Wissen und Weltbild*, ed. Paul Leo Butzer, Max Kerner, and Walter Oberschelp (Turnhout, 1997), 63–77; Mayke de Jong and Ian Wood, in *The Early Middle Ages*, ed. Rosamond McKitterick, Short Oxford History of Europe (Oxford, 2001), 131–33, 181–83.

2. Hrabanus Maurus, *Epistolae*, no. 7, ed. Ernst Dümmler, MGH Epp. 5, 391–93.

3. Dick Harrison, "The Lombards in the Early Carolingian Epoch," in *Wissen und Weltbild*, ed. Butzer, Kerner, and Oberschelp, 125–54; Dieter Schaller, "Karl der Grosse im Lichte zeitgenössischer politischer Dichtung," ibid., 193–219.

4. See Mary Garrison, "The English and the Irish at the Court of Charlemagne," in *Wissen und Weltbild*, ed. Butzer, Kerner, and Oberschelp, 97–123.

5. Bruce S. Eastwood, "The Astronomy of Macrobius in Carolingian Europe: Dungal's Letter of 811 to Charles the Great," *Early Medieval Europe* 3 (1994): 117–34.

6. Bernhard Bischoff, "Wendepunkte in der Geschichte der lateinischen Exegese im Frühmittelalter," in *Mittelalterliche Studien: Ausgewählte Aufsätze zur Schriftkunde und zur Literaturgeschichte*, ed. Bernhard Bischoff, 3 vols. (Stuttgart, 1966–81), 1:205–73. Recent works include Garrison, "English and the Irish"; Catherine Cubitt, ed., *Court Culture in the Early Middle Ages: Proceedings of the First Alcuin Conference*, Studies in the Early Middle Ages 3 (Turnhout, 2003); and Donald A. Bullough, *Alcuin, Achievement and Reputation* (Leiden, 2004).

7. Helmut Flachenecker, *Schottenklöster: Irische Benediktinerkonvente im hochmittelalterlichen Deutschland* (Paderborn, 1994).

8. See Roger Collins, *The Arab Conquest of Spain, 710–797* (Oxford, 1989), 214–15; Paul Freedman, "L'influence wisigothique sur l'eglise catalane," in *L'Europe héritière de l'Espagne wisigothique*, ed. Jacques Fontaine et al., Collection de la casa de Velázquez 35 (Madrid, 1992), 69–79, 75–76; José Orlandis, "Le royaume wisigothique et son unite religieuse," ibid., 9–16, 14; Peter Linehan, *History and the Historians of Medieval Spain* (Oxford, 1993), 17–19, 22–24, 28–29, 90–91; Roger Collins, *Early Medieval Spain: Unity in Diversity, 400–1000*, 2nd ed. (Houndmills, 1995), 259–60; Rachel L. Stocking, *Bishops, Councils, and Consensus in the Visigothic Kingdom, 589–633* (Ann Arbor, 2000), 174–91; Roger Collins, *Visigothic Spain (409–711)* (Oxford, 2004).

9. See John C. Cavadini, *The Last Christology of the West: Adoptionism in Spain and Gaul, 785–820* (Philadelphia, 1993); Abigail Firey, "Carolingian Ecclesiology and Heresy: A Southern Gallic Juridical Tract against Adoptionism," *Sacris erudiri* 39 (2000): 253–316.

10. Relevant articles appear in Ann Freeman, *Theodulf of Orléans, Charlemagne's Spokesman against the Second Council of Nicea*, Variorum Collected Studies Studies CS 772 (Aldershot, 2003).

11. See Bonifatius Fischer, "Bibeltext und Bibelreform unter Karl dem Großen," in *Karl der Große: Lebenswerk und Nachleben*, ed. Wolfgang Braunfels et al., vol. 2, *Das geistige Leben*, ed. Bernhard Bischoff, 2nd ed. (Düsseldorf, 1966), 156–216; Bonifatius Fischer, *Beiträge zur Geschichte der lateinischen Bibeltexte* (Freiburg i.B., 1986); Richard Gameson, ed., *The Early Medieval Bible: Its Production, Decoration and Use* (Cambridge, 1994); Johann B. Bauer, *Studien zu Bibeltext und Väterexegese* (Stuttgart, 1997); Roger Collins,

Charlemagne (Houndmills, 1998), 117–18, 135–36; Caroline Chevalier-Royet, "Les révisions de Theodulphe d'Orléans et la question de leur utilisation par l'exégèse carolingienne," in *Études d'exégèse carolingienne: Autour d'Haymon d'Auxerre*, ed. Sumi Shimahara, Collection Haut Moyen Âge 4 (Turnhout, 2007), 237–56.

12. Elisabeth Dahlhaus-Berg, *Nova antiquitas et antiqua novitas: Typologische Exegese und isidorianisches Geschichtsbild bei Theodulf von Orléans*, Kölner Historische Abhandlungen 23 (Cologne, 1975), 221–23; Collins, *Charlemagne*, 123.

13. Bernhard Bischoff, "Versus ad quendam Scottum nomine Andream," in *Mittelalterliche Studien*, ed. Bischoff, 2:21–23; Dieter Schaller, "Vortrags- und Zirkulardichtung am Hof Karls des Großen," in *Studien zur lateinischen Dichtung des Frühmittelalters*, ed. Dieter Schaller, Quellen und Untersuchungen zur lateinischen Philologie des Mittelalters 11 (Stuttgart, 1995), 90–102.

14. Alcuin, *Epp.* 245–46, 248–49; see Dieter Schaller, "Vortrags- und Zirkulardichtung," *Mittellateinisches Jahrbuch* 6 (1970): 14–36; Dieter Schaller, "Der junge 'Rabe' am Hof Karls des Großen (Theodulf.carm.27)," in *Festschrift Bernhard Bischoff*, ed. Johanne Autenrieth (Stuttgart, 1971), 123–41; Hélène Noizet, "Alcuin contre Théodulphe: Un conflit producteur de normes," *Annales de la Bretagne* 111 (2004): 113–32; Rob Meens, "Sanctuary, Penance, and Dispute Settlement under Charlemagne: The Conflict between Alcuin and Theodulf of Orléans over a Sinful Cleric," *Speculum* 82 (2007): 277–300.

15. Theodulf vs. Wibodus: *Poetae Latini aevi Carolini I*, ed. Ernst Dümmler, MGH Poetae 1, 489; see Janet Nelson, "Charles le Chauve et les utilisations du savoir," in *L'école carolingienne d'Auxerre de Murethach à Remi, 830–908*, ed. Dominique Iogna-Prat et al. (Paris, 1991), 44–45.

16. *Annales regni francorum*, s.a. 812–13, ed. Friedrich Kurze, MGH SS rer. Germ. 6, 136–38; Einhard, *Vita Karoli Magni*, ch. 19, ed. Georg Waitz, MGH SS rer. Germ. 25, 210; Regino of Prüm, *Chronicon*, s.a. 818, ed. Friedrich Kurze, MGH SS rer. Germ. 50, 73; Thegan, *Vita Hludowici imperatoris*, ch. 22, ed. E. Tremp, MGH SS rer. Germ. In usum school. 64, 211–12; also see Thomas F. X. Noble, "Some Observations on the Deposition of Archbishop Theodulf of Orléans in 817," *Journal of the Rocky Mountain Medieval and Renaissance Association* 2 (1981): 29–40.

17. See Johannes Fried, "Ludwig der Fromme, das Papsttum und die fränkische Kirche," in *Charlemagne's Heir: New Perspectives on the Reign of Louis the Pious (814–840)*, ed. Roger Collins and Peter Godman (Oxford, 1990), 231–73; see also Anna E. M. Pohlen, *Die südeuropäisch-spanisch-gotische Gruppe in den Auseinandersetzungen der Karolingerzeit* (Bonn, 1974).

18. For the date, see Johannes Heil, "Claudius von Turin: Eine Fallstudie zur Geschichte der Karolingerzeit," *Zeitschrift für Geschichtswissenschaft* 45 (1997): 389–412, esp. 397–98n45; see also Pierre Boucaud, "Claude de Turin († ca. 828) et Haymon d'Auxerre (fl. 850): Deux commentateurs d' 'I Corinthiens,'" in *Études d'exégèse carolingienne*, ed. Shimahara, 187–236.

19. Egon Boshof, *Erzbischof Agobard von Lyon: Leben und Werk* (Cologne, 1969); Johannes Heil, "Agobard, Amulo, das Kirchengut und die Juden von Lyon," *Francia* 25 (1998): 39–76; Jeremy Cohen, *Living Letters of the Law: Ideas of the Jew in Medieval Christianity* (Berkeley and Los Angeles, 1999), 123–45; see also Raffaele Savigni, "L'immagine dell'ebreo e dell'ebraismo in Agobardo di Lione e nella cultura carolingia," *Annali di storia dell'esegesi* 17 (2000): 417–61.

20. See Fried, "Ludwig der Fromme," 232–33, 252–66.

21. Heil, "Claudius von Turin"; see also Michael Gorman, "The Commentary on Genesis of Claudius of Turin and Biblical Studies under Louis the Pious," *Speculum* 72 (1997): 279–329, esp. 284–86.

22. Agobard of Lyon, *Opera omnia*, ed. L. van Acker, CCCM 52 (Turnhout, 1982).

23. Beyond the classic study by Beryl Smalley, *The Study of the Bible in the Middle Ages* (Oxford, 1984), see Silvia Cantelli, "L'esegesi al tempo di Ludovico il Pio e Carlo il Calvo," in *Giovanni Scoto nel suo tempo: L'organizzazione del sapere in età carolingia* (Spoleto, 1989), 261–336; *The Study of the Bible in the Carolingian Era*, ed. Celia Chazelle and Burton Van Name Edwards, Medieval Church Studies 3 (Turnhout, 2003); and Shimahara, *Études d'exgégèse carolingienne.*

24. See Heil, "Claudius von Turin."

25. This significance may be surprising, especially since Visigothic Spain had, with the conversion to Catholicism, become severely anti-Jewish. See Alexander P. Bronisch, *Die Judengesetzgebung im katholischen Westotenreich von Toledo*, Forschungen zur Geschichte der Juden A17 (Hannover, 2005); Wolfram Drews, *The Unknown Neighbour: The Jew in the Thought of Isidore of Seville* (Leiden, 2006).

26. See Johannes Heil, *Kompilation oder Konstruktion? Die Juden in den Pauluskommentaren des 9. Jahrhunderts*, Forschungen zur Geschichte der Juden A6 (Hannover, 1998), 289–90.

27. See "Haimo, Bischof von Halberstadt," in *Biographisch-bibliographisches Kirchenlexikon*, ed. Friedrich W. Bautz (Herzberg, 1999), 16:635.

28. Heil, *Kompilation*, 276.

29. Eduard Riggenbach, *Historische Studien zum Hebräerbrief*, vol. 1, *Die ältesten lateinischen Kommentare zum Hebräerbrief: Ein Beitrag zur Geschichte der Exegese und zur Literaturgeschichte des Mittelalters*, Forschungen zur Geschichte des neutestamentlichen Kanons und der altkirchlichen Literatur 8 (Leipzig, 1907).

30. Lupus studied with Hrabanus at Fulda from 829 to 836 and became abbot of Ferrières in 840. See Hubert Mordek, "Lupus," in *Lexikon des Mittelalters*, ed. Robert Auty et al., 9 vols. (Munich, 1977–99), 6:15–16.

31. See Riccardo Quadri, "Aimone di Auxerre alla luce dei *Collectanea* di Heiric di Auxerre," *Italia medievale e umanistica* 6 (1963): 1–48; Riccardo Quadri, *I Collectanea di Eirico di Auxerre*, Spicilegium Friburgense 11 (Fribourg, 1966); John J. Contreni, "The Career of Haimo of Auxerre (fl. 840–870) and a Leiden Manuscript (Leiden, Voss. lat. q. 60)," *The 2nd Saint Louis Conference on Manuscript Studies: Abstracts of Papers, Manuscripta* 20 (1976): 3–24; John J. Contreni, "The Biblical Glosses of Haimo of Auxerre and John Scottus Eriugena," *Speculum* 51 (1976): 411–34; John J. Contreni, "Haimo of Auxerre's Commentary on Ezechiel," in *L'école carolingienne d'Auxerre*, ed. Iogna-Prat, 229–42. See also Ermengildo Bertola, "Il Commentario paolino di Haimo di Halberstadt o di Auxerre e gli inizi del metodo scolastico," *Pier Lombardo* 5 (1961): 29–54; Ermengildo Bertola, "I precedenti storici del metodo *Sic et non* di Abelardo," *Rivista di filosofia neo-scolastica* 53 (1961): 255–80; Edmond Ortigues, "L'élaboration de la théorie des trois ordres chez Haymon d'Auxerre," *Francia* 14 (1986): 27–43; Dominique Iogna-Prat, "L'oeuvre de Haymo d'Auxerre: État de la question," in *L'école carolingienne d'Auxerre*, ed. Iogna-Prat, 157–79; Corinne Gabriel, "Commentaires inédites d'Haymon d'Auxerre sur Isaïe 5.1–6.1," *Sacris erudiri* 35 (1995): 89–114; Sumi Shimahara, "Introduction," in *Études d'exégèse carolingienne*, ed. Shimahara, 12–19.

32. John J. Contreni, "Haimo of Auxerre, Abbot of Sasceium (Cessy-les-Bois), and a

New Sermon on I John V, 4–10," *Revue bénédictine* 85 (1975): 303–30; Burton Van Name Edwards, "In Search of the Authentic Commentary on Genesis by Remigius d'Auxerre," in *L'ecole carolingienne d'Auxerre*, ed. Iogna-Part, 399–412; and an attribution to Haimo of a commentary on Matthew (but lacking any textual evidence) by Michael Gorman, "Manuscript Books at Monte Amiata," *Scriptorium* 56 (2002): 286–90.

33. See the works by Contreni noted above, particularly "'By Lions,'" 29–56; and Burton Van Name Edwards, "Deuteronomy in the Ninth Century: The Unpublished Commentaries of Walahfrid Strabo and Haimo of Auxerre," in *Study of the Bible*, ed. Edwards and Chazelle, 97–113.

34. Ann Freeman, introduction to *Opus Caroli regis contra synodum*, supp. 1 of *Concilia aevi Karolini*, MGH Conc. 2, 1–66 (repr. in Ann Freeman, *Theodulf of Orléans, Charlemagne's Spokesman against the Second Council of Nicea* [Aldershot, 2003], no. 13).

35. See Marc-Aeilko Aris, "'Nostrum est citare testes': Anmerkungen zum Wissenschaftsverständnis des Hrabanus Maurus," in *Kloster Fulda in der Welt der Karolinger und Ottonen*, ed. Gangolf Schrimpf, Fuldaer Studien 7 (Frankfurt a.M., 1996), 437–64.

36. See Dahlhaus-Berg, *Nova antiquitas*, 134–35.

37. Heil, "Claudius von Turin," 389–412.

38. Note that Bishop Jonas of Orléans (Theodulf's successor, d. 843) published in 840–44 a refutation of Claudius of Turin. The errant bishop had passed away many years earlier, but it appeared to Jonas that many of Claudius's disciples were still following his ideas. See Jonas of Orléans, *De cultu imaginum*, PL 106, col. 397A–B. This may refer to Auxerre as a center of dissemination of Claudius's manuscript, but there is no evidence for this assumption. On Jonas of Orléans, see "Jonas von Orléans," in *Biographisch-bibliographisches Kirchenlexikon*, ed. Bautz, 3:635; Franz Sedlmeier, *Die laienparänetischen Schriften der Karolingerzeit: Untersuchungen zu ausgewählten Texten des Paulinus von Aquileia, Alkuins, Jonas' von Orleans, Dhuodas und Hinkmars von Reims* (Neuried, 2000).

39. See Edwards, "Deuteronomy in the Ninth Century."

40. The issue of formation and different schools is also addressed by E. Ann Matter, "Haimo's Commentary on Song of Songs and the Tradition of the Carolingian Schools," in *Études d'exgégèse carolingienne*, ed. Shimahara, 91–96.

41. See only this on Gen. 42:29: "Quaeri autem potest cur sancti patriarchae tantum curam habuerint sepeliendorum corporum, cum scirent cadavera et in sarcophagis sepulta et sub nudo coelo aequaliter posse putrescere. Nam et poeta dicit: Coelo tegitur, qui non habet urnam" (PL 131, col. 123B). The quotation is from Marcus Annaeus Lucan, *Pharsalia*, 7.831.

42. The basic work on Carolingian homiliaries remains Henri Barré, *Les homéliaires carolingiens de l'école d'Auxerre: Authenticité, Inventaire, Tableaux comparatifs; Initia*, Studi e testi 225 (Vatican City, 1962); see also Réginald Grégoire, *Homéliaires liturgiques médiévaux: Analyse de manuscrits*, Bibliotheca degli studi medievali 12 (Spoleto, 1980); Raymond Étaix, "Les homéliaires carolingiens de l'école d'Auxerre," in *L'école carolingienne d'Auxerre*, ed. Iogna-Prat, 243–51.

43. For example, wide parts in Galatians and the whole exposition of Titus after Tit. 1:1–4 (which is a pericope mentioned in some Carolingian reading lists, such as the "Würzburg comes") in the PL edition and in most of the manuscripts I have been able to consult thus far.

44. Paris, BnF, MS lat. 14439/14440 (*s*.12), and Bale A. vi. 11 (*s*.15). Oxford, Bodleian Library, MS Bodley 863 (S.C. 2734, *s*.15), and Oxford, Magdalen College, MS 112 (*s*.15) offer still different versions and stages of achievement.

45. For the homiliary, see Iogna-Prat, "L'oeuvre d'Haymon," 160, who has argued that excerpts of Haimo's commentary were transferred into a homilary (not being identical with the PL 118 homilary and its reconstruction by Barré, *Les homéliaires carolingiens*). Textual evidence from the commentary, however, including a typical homily formular such as "Audite, fratres carissimi" or "In hac lectione vult . . . facere" (see Heil, *Kompilation*, 285–86) indicates that the process went the opposite way. Therefore one should assume that the codex Sangallensis 333 bears Haimo's original homilary, a version that laid the foundation for the commentary on Paul. For the commentary itself, it seems that for some parts even a fifteenth-century English manuscript may provide a text closer to the earliest witnesses (the Orléans, Bibl. Mun., MS lat. 88/85, *s*.9 from Fleury) than a tenth-century manuscript from central France.

46. See Heil, *Kompilation*, 208–14.

47. It remains a rare edition, for readers eventually realized that it was not a true Bede, but rather a Pseudo-Bede. Therefore the text dropped from circulation during the sixteenth century. One of the few copies is Herzog, August Bibliothek, MS Wolfenbüttel, Li Sammelband 49/14.

48. Manuscripts from St. Emmeram, Melk, Freising Cathedral, but also Mont-Saint-Michel, Trier, Cologne (a manuscript in which a later hand attributes the content to *haymo epsicopus*). See *Clavis patristica pseudoepigraphorum medii aevi*, ed. J. Machielsen, CCSL 1A–1B, 2 vols. (Turnhout, 1990), 2:571–605; Heil, *Kompilation*, 208; and Barré, *Les homéliaires*, 8.

49. See Josef Semmler, "Zu den bayerisch-westfränkischen Beziehungen in karolingischer Zeit," *Zeitschrift für bayerische Landesgeschichte* 29 (1966): 344–424; Joachim Wollasch, "Das Patrimonium Beati Germani in Auxerre: Ein Beitrag zur Frage der bayerisch-westfränkischen Beziehungen in der Karolingerzeit," in *Studien und Vorbereitungen zur Geschichte des großfränkischen und frühdeutschen Adels*, ed. Gerd Tellenbach (Freiburg i.B., 1957), 185–224; Yves Sassier, "Les carolingiens et Auxerre," in *L'école carolingienne d'Auxerre*, ed. Iogna-Prat, 21–36.

50. For the students, see *Theodulfi carmina*, MGH Poetae 1, nos. 30, 44, 65, 520–22, 542, 556. Micy was one of the oldest monasteries in the Loire area, but it had witnessed a decline during the eighth century; Theodulf's appointment as abbot was therefore a kind of re-foundation and re-formation. Fleury, to the contrary, pursued its own tradition (also in its own scriptorium) and in obvious distance to Theodulf, especially since the appointment of a bishop-abbot contradicted Fleury's former status as a royal (immediate) monastery. See Dahlhaus-Berg, *Nova antiquitas*, 61–66, nn. 9–11; for Theodulf's "associates" having written the *Libri Carolini*, see Celia Chazelle, "'Not in Painting but in Writing': Augustine and the Supremacy of the Word in the Libri Carolini," in *Reading and Wisdom: The "De Doctrina Christiana" of Augustine in the Middle Ages*, ed. Edward D. English (Notre Dame, IN, 1995), 1–22.

51. Heil, *Kompilation*, 279–82.

52. Johannes Heil, "Haimo's Commentary on Paul: Sources, Methods, and Theology," in *Études d'exégèse carolingienne*, ed. Shimahara, 103–21 (110), and Sumi Shimahara, "Synthèse de la discussion finale," ibid., 257–64 (263). See also Dominique Iogna-Prat, "Influences spirituelles et culturelles du monde wisigothique: Saint Germain d'Auxerre dans la seconde moitié du IXᵉ siècle," in *L'Europe héretière de l'Espagne wisigothique*, ed. Fontaine, 231–57.

53. Heil, *Kompilation*, 280.

54. See [Haimo], *Expositio* [. . .] *super breshit, id est super Genesim*, PL 131, cols. 51C–134C (col. 108B), commenting on Gen. 30:37–38: "Nec incredibile hoc videri debet cuiquam, cum hodieque in Hispania de equabus hoc idem fieri dicatur." This explanation is remarkable, since not required through the text and—as far as I can see—is without precedent in earlier commentaries on Genesis.

55. On 2 Cor. 12:3 see Haimo, *In divi Pauli epistolas*, PL 117, cols. 361C–938B (cols. 661A–B).

56. Ibid.

57. *Mythographi Vaticani*, ed. Péter Kulcsár, CCSL 91C (Turnhout, 1987), 1.189, and, for Haimo's source, 74. On 1 Cor. 9:24, see Haimo, PL 117, cols. 555B–556A.

58. See Jacques Fontaine, "Isidore de Seville. Pédagogue et theoricien de l'exégèse," in *Stimuli: Exegese und ihre Hermeneutik in Antike und Christentum; Festschrift für Ernst Dassmann*, ed. Georg Schöllgen et al., Jahrbuch für Antike und Christentum 23 (Münster, 1996), 423–34; Michael Baldzuhn, "Remigius von Auxerre (R. Autissiodorensis)," in *Biographisch-bibliographisches Kirchenlexikon*, ed. Bautz, 22:1146–49.

59. Claude Coupry, "Le groupe de manuscrits d'Heliseus," in *L'ecole carolingienne d'Auxerre*, ed. Iogna-Prat, 71–81. To the contrary, the only Italian manuscript of Claude's commentary on Paul (the portion on Hebrews) indicates no author (MS Monza, Biblioteca Capitolare c-2/62). The MS Monte Cassino 48 is an eleventh-century revision comparable to the revision promulgated under the names of Tietland (Einsiedeln) or Hatto of Vercelli.

60. Contreni, "Haimo of Auxerre, Abbot of Sasceium," 314–15; see also Shimahara, "Synthèse de la discussion finale," 263.

61. Louis Holtz, "Murethach et l'influence de la culture irlandaise à Auxerre," in Iogna-Prat, ed., *L'école carolingienne d'Auxerre*, ed. Iogna-Prat, 147–56. On Murethach, author of a commentary on Donatus's *Ars major*, see Bernhard Bischoff, "'Muridac doctissimus plebis,' ein irischer Grammatiker des IX. Jahrhunderts," *Celtica* 5 (1961): 40–44 (repr. in *Mittelalterliche Studien*, ed. Bischoff, 2:51–56).

62. Contreni, "'By Lions,'" 53–55.

63. According to the titulation of Paris, BnF, MS lat. 5716, fol. 1r; see Nelson, "Charles le Chauve," 45; Contreni, "'By Lions,'" 46.

64. Hraban Maur, *Eccl.*, PL 109, cols. 763–1126, written in the late 830s and dedicated to Archbishop Otgarius of Mainz (826–47); Hraban Maur, *Epistolae*, no. 21, MGH Epp. 5, 426–27. See also Contreni, "'By Lions,'" 46–47n62.

65. Heil, *Kompilation*, 325.

66. Dahlhaus-Berg, *Nova antiquitas*, 7.

67. In recent decades: Avrom Saltman, "Rabanus Maurus and the Pseudo-Hieronymian *Quaestiones Hebraicae in Libros Regum et Paralipomenon*," *Harvard Theological Review* 66 (1973): 43–75; Jean-Louis Verstrepen, "Raban Maur et le judaïsme dans son Commentaire sur les quatre *Livres des Rois*," *Revue Mabillon* 7 (1996): 23–55; Bat-Sheva Albert, "*Adversus Iudaeos* in the Carolingian Empire," in *Contra Iudaeos: Ancient and Medieval Polemics*, ed. Ora Limor et al., Texts and Studies in Medieval and Early Modern Judaism 10 (Tübingen, 1996), 119–42; Bat-Sheva Albert, "Anti-Jewish Exegesis in the Carolingian Period: The Commentaries on Lamentations of Hrabanus Maurus and Paschasius Radbertus," in *Biblical Studies in the Early Middle Ages*, ed. Claudio Leonardi (Florence, 2005), 175–92; Chevalier-Royet, "Les révisions de Theodulphe d'Orléans," 251–52.

68. Dahlhaus-Berg, *Nova antiquitas*.

69. Saltman, "Rabanus Maurus."

70. The identification of the author of the *Quaestiones* with Theodulf's assistant echoes earlier arguments by Martianay, Samuel Berger, Bonifatius Fischer, and others; see Avrom Saltman, ed., *Pseudo-Jerome, Quaestiones on the Book Samuel*, Studia post-biblica 26 (Leiden, 1975), 6–9.

71. Hrabanus Maurus, *Epistolae*, no. 18, MGH Epp. 5, 422–24, nn. 3–4; see Johann B. Hablitzel, "Der 'Hebraeus quidam' bei Paschasius Radbertus," *Historisches Jahrbuch* 47 (1927): 340–41.

72. PL 111, cols. 1181D–1272; cf. E. Ann Matter, "The Lamentations Commentaries of Hrabanus Maurus and Paschasius Radbertus," *Traditio* 38 (1982): 137–63, esp. 147–48.

73. Heil, *Kompilation*, 199.

74. Reims, Bibliothèque municipale, MS lat. 118, obviously from the cathedral church. The table of contents gives "B. Hieronymi Quaestiones in Io et IIo libris regum," etc.; fol 38: "In Dei nomine brevis Explanatio [Hieronymi] hystoriae primi libri Regum secundum judaicam traditionem incipit, sed curiosus lector, qui haec discere studet, consideret si ille Judaeus qui praefatum librum ita exposuit ab ecclesiastica doctrina in aliquibus discordat sententiis"; fol. 53: "Incipit expositio [Hieronymi] in Paralipomenon, secundum traditionem Judaeorum, ubi lector caute esse debet": cf. *Catalogue général des manuscrits des bibliothèques publiques de France*, vol. 38 (Paris, 1904), 109–12, ex dono "Hincmarus diaconus."

75. *Remigii Autissiodorensis Expositio super Genesim*, ed. Burton Van Name Edwards, CCCM 136 (Turnhout: Brepols, 1999). On the importance of Genesis commentaries, see also Michael Gorman, "The Encyclopedic Commentary on Genesis Prepared for Charlemagne," *Recherches augustiniennes* 17 (1982): 173–201; and Michael Gorman, "Wigbod, Charlemagne's Commentator: The 'Quaestiunculae super evangelium,'" *Revue bénédictine* 114 (2004): 5–74.

76. Van Name Edwards, *Remigii Autissiodorensis*, xil–l.

77. Heil, *Kompilation*, 199. Indeed, Haimo's acquaintance with the Latin version of the acronym TaNa' Ch—as in use up to our days—appears to be innovative in his time. There is only one instance in the whole pre-Carolingian literature that comes close to Haimo's version and may mirror its use among Jews in Milan or elsewhere in the Mediterranean in the fourth century: Ambrose of Milan, *De fide ad Gratianum Augustum*, PL 16, col. 447: "ut in lege accepimus et prophetis, scripturisque divinis caeteris." Hraban Maur in ch.7 of his *De institutione clericorum* (819, PL 107, col. 383C) speaks about the "triptartite order of the Hebrew canon," but has a different composition ("dividentes eos in tres ordines, legis scilicet, prophetarum et hagiographorum"), which is taken word by word from Isidore, *Etymologiae*, 6.1, and which derives from Jerome, *Praefatio in libros Samuel et Malachim*, PL 28, col. 554A ("veteris legis libri viginti duo; id est, Mosi quinque: Prophetarum octo: Hagiographorum novem").

78. Haimo, PL 117, cols. 560B–C. Likely inspired by Haimo was Bruno of Asti (ca. 1048–1123) in his *Com. in Exodus*, PL 164, cols. 233A–378A (268B), on Exod. 16:3: "Murmuravit populus exasperans et incredulus, et quamvis multa armenta bovum et greges ovium habeat, tamen sibi propter carnes mortem exoptat, desiderabat enim avium carnes, quibus in Aegypto uti solebat. Aves enim in Aegypto, et circa Nilum multum abundant."

79. Mordechai Margulies, ed., *Midrash ha-gadol Exodus* (Jerusalem, 1956).

80. *The Metsudah Chumach/Rashi*, vol. 2, *Shemos*, trans. Avrohom Davis (Hoboken, NJ, 1997), ch. Shemot–Beshalach 16:8–9, 205 (Mechilta, Yoma 75b); a forerunner is in

one of the oldest misdrashim, from tannaitic times, the so-called *Mekhilta de Rabbi Ishmael,* trans. Jacob Z. Lauterbach (Philadelphia, 1976), Tractate VaYassa II, 105: "From this we learn that the quail was given to Israel with a frowning countenance. The manna, however, which they were justified in asking, was given to them with a bright countenance"; see also *Talmud Babli,* Yoma, 75a–b. On Rashi and the problem of Jewish-Christian intellectual relations (and on problematic assumptions about it) see Hanna Liss, "Peshat-Auslegung und Erzähltheorie am Beispiel Raschbams," in *Rashi und sein Erbe,* ed. Daniel Krochmalnik et al., Schriften der Hochschule für Jüdische Studien Heidelberg 10 (Heidelberg, 2007), 101–24. A comprehensive study is likewise Hanna Liss, *Creating Fictional Worlds: Peshat-Exegesis and Narrativity in Rashbam's Commentary on the Torah,* Studies in Jewish History and Culture 25 (Leiden, 2011).

81. Van Name Edwards, "In Search of the Authentic Commentary"; see also Colette Jeudy, "Remigii autissiodorensis opera (*Clavis*)," in *L'école carolingienne d'Auxerre,* ed. Iogna-Prat, 457–500; Raffaele Savigni, "Esegesi medievale ed antropologia biblica: L'interpretazione di 'Genesi' 1–3 nei commentari carolingi ed i suoi fondamenti patristici," *Annali di storia dell'esegesi* 10 (1993): 571–614.

82. On Gen. 25:1 see [Haimo], *Expositio super Genesim,* PL 131, col. 100B; cf. col. 115B on Gen. 37:27. In his commentary on Galatians, Haimo combines this with the tradition (cf. Augustine et al.) that Cethura and her sons stand for those who have been in the faith, but rejected it; see PL 117, col. 688A.

83. See Haimo's explicit statement when commenting on Gen. 16:12, in *Expositio super Genesim,* PL 131, col. 87D: "Allegorice hae duae mulieres, exponente Apostolo, Synagogam et Ecclesiam significant. Agar quidem Synagogam quae in servitutem generat populum Judaeorum qui feri sunt et agrestes, jugum Domini leve et fidem ejus nolentes recipere, ideoque dispersi, et vagabundi sunt per totum orbem et omnibus maxime Christianis contrarii. Sara vero Ecclesiam quae primum sterilis et infecunda fuit, postea vero in libertatem fidei et gratiae plebem catholicam generavit." Hraban Maur was not aware of this problem and accepted the identification of Hagar with Cethura; see his *Com. in Paralipomenon,* PL 109, col. 310A: "Notandum autem quod Agar, unde Agarei exorti sunt, ipsa sit Cethura, quem post mortem Sarae Abraham duxit uxorem."

84. Genesis Rabbah [Midrash Genesis rabba, par. 61.4]; see Jacob Neusner, ed., *The Judaic Commentary to the Book of Genesis: A New American Translation,* vol. 2, *Parashiyyot Thirty-four through Sixty-seven on Genesis 8:15 to 28:9,* Brown Judaic Studies 105 (Atlanta: Scholars, 1985).

85. Jerome, *Quaestiones hebraicae,* ch. 1, v. 32: "CETHURA, ipsa est Agar: quod in psalmo manifestatur, cum dicitur: 'TABERNACULA IDUMAEORUM ET ISMAELITARUM MOAB ET AGARENI' (Vulg. Ps. LXXXII. 7). Ismaelitas vocans filios Ismael, qui utique Agar filius fuit: et Agarenos, Madianitas, et caeteras tribus, quas de Cethura procreatas, sacra Scriptura commemorat" (PL 23, col.1367A).

86. See also Jerome, *Liber interpretationis Hebraicorum nominum,* PL 23, col. 778 (cf. the edition by Paul de Lagarde, CCSL 72 [1959], 64); Adam Kamesar, *Jerome, Greek Scholarship, and the Hebrew Bible: A Study of the 'Quaestiones hebraicae in Genesim'* (Oxford, 1993).

87. Jerome, *Quaestiones hebraicae,* PL 23, col. 976A.

88. [Haimo], *Expositio super Genesim,* PL 131, cols. 123B and 67C.

89. This seems to be paraphrasing Jerome, *Epist.* 51, as in PL 22, col. 522A: "Praeterea frivolam ejus [Origenes] expositionem super tunicis pelliceis, quanto conatu, quantisque

egerit argumentis, ut tunicas pelliceas humana esse corpora crederemus. Qui inter multa ait: 'Nunquid coriarius aut sordiscarius [al. stortisarius] erat Deus, ut conficeret pelles animalium, et consueret ex eis tunicas pelliceas Adam et Evae?'" Hraban Maur, *In Genesim*, PL 107, col. 499B, from Bede, *In Genesim*, ed. Charles W. Jones, CCSL 118A (1967), 70, lines 2242–61, is certainly not the source for Haimo.

90. [Haimo], *Expositio super Genesim*, PL 131, cols. 56D–57A.

91. Remigius, *Expositio super Genesim*, CCCM 136, 27, lines 662–63; cf. Midrash Rabba ("the great/comprehensive Midrash") 1.8.8; and compare Pseudo-Jonathan, *Targum* ad loc., and Midrash Genesis Rabba, par 91.3.9, par 92.5.3. All references here and below are to Burton Van Name Edwards's introduction to CCCM 136, 79.

92. On Gen. 2:8, [Haimo], *Expositio super Genesim*, PL 131, col. 60C–D.

93. Remigius, *Expositio super Genesim*, CCCM 136, 39–40, lines 896–900.

94. On Gen. 6:16, [Haimo], *Expositio super Genesim*, PL 131, col. 75B.

95. On Gen, 6:16, Remigius, *Expositio super Genesim*, CCCM 136, 86, lines 1971–72.

96. On Gen. 37:2, [Haimo], *Expositio super Genesim*, PL 131, cols. 113D–114A.

97. Alcuin, *Interrogat. et Respons. in Genesi*, PL 100, cols. 553–54.

98. Remigius, *Expositio super Genesim*, CCCM 136, 170, lines 3880–84.

99. At least one further example for the Pentateuch is Deut. 23:3–4, as discussed by Burton Van Name Edwards, "Deuteronomy in the Ninth Century," 104–5n25. See also Gilbert Dahan, "Les interprétations juives dans les commentaires du Pentateuche de Pierre le Chantre," in *The Bible in the Medieval World: Essays in Memory of Beryl Smalley*, ed. Katherine Walsh and Diana Wood (Oxford, 1985), 131–55.

100. Haimo of Auxerre, *Commentarium in Cantica Canticorum*, PL 117, cols. 295–358; see Matter, "Haimo's Commentary on Song of Songs," 89–101.

101. Haimo of Auxerre, *Commentariorum in Isaiam libri tres*, PL 116, cols. 713–1086. On this commentary see Iogna-Prat, *Oeuvre de Haymo*, 163–64; Gabriel, *Commentaires d'Haymon sur Isaïe*, 89–114.

102. Haimo of Auxerre, *Enarratio in duodecim prophetas minores*, PL 117, cols. 9–294 (Abdia: cols. 119–28); see Iogna-Prat, "L'oeuvre de Haymo d'Auxerre," 166–70.

103. The cultural turn among Jews highlighted by the shift from Latin and Greek to Hebrew—a process still in need of a detailed examination—seems to have occurred at some point between the sixth and the late eighth century in the eastern parts of the Mediterranean (southern Italy in particular), as indicated by inscriptions from necropoles and tombstones. See David Noy, "Writing in Tongues: The Use of Greek, Latin and Hebrew in Jewish Inscriptions from Roman Italy," *Journal of Jewish Studies* 48 (1997): 300–311; David Noy, "Jews in Italy in the 1st–6th Centuries C.E.," in *The Jews of Italy: Memory and Identity*, ed. Bernard D. Cooperman and Barbara Garvin (Bethesda, MD, 2000), 45–64; Giancarlo Lacerenza, "Le antichità giudaiche di Venosa: Storia e documenti," *Archivio storico per le province napoletane* 116 (1998 [2000]): 293–418; and Cesare Colafemmina, "Le catacombe ebraiche nell'Italia meridionale e nell'area Sicula: Venosa, Siracusa, Noto, Lipari e Malta," in *I beni culturali ebraici in Italia: Situazione attuale, problemi, prospettive e progetti per il futuro*, ed. Mauro Perani (Ravenna, 2003), 119–46.

104. See Michael Gorman, "Theodulf of Orléans and the Exegetical Miscellany in Paris lat. 15679," *Revue bénédictine* 109 (1999): 278–323.

105. See Walter Mohr, "Christlich-alttestamentliches Gedankengut in der Entwicklung des karolingischen Kaisertums," in *Judentum im Mittelalter: Beiträge zum christlich-jüdischen Gespräch*, ed. Paul Wilpert and Willibald Paul Eckert, Miscellanea mediaevalia

4 (Berlin, 1966), 382–409; also Raymund Kottje, *Studien zum Einfluß des Alten Testaments auf Recht und Liturgie des frühen Mittelalters* (Bonn, 1964). For more nuanced studies, see Mary Garrison, "The Franks as the New Israel," in *Uses of the Past in Early Medieval Europe: Politics, Memory, and Identity*, ed. Yitzhak Hen and Matthew Innes (Cambridge, 2000), 114–61; Mayke de Jong, "Religion," in *The Early Middle Ages*, ed. McKitterick, 131–64 (183–41). See also Ivan G. Marcus, "A Jewish-Christian Symbiosis: The Culture of Early Ashkenaz," in *Cultures of the Jews: A New History*, ed. David Biale (New York, 2002), 449–516.

106. See Alexander P. Bronisch, *Reconquista und Heiliger Krieg: Die Deutung des Krieges im christlichen Spanien von den Westgoten bis ins frühe 12. Jh.* (Münster, 1998), 58–59, 66–68, 78; see also Joscelyn Hillgarth, "Historiography in Visigothic Spain," in *La storiografia altomedievale*, Settimane di studio dell Centro italiano di studi sull'alto medioevo 17, 2 vols. (Spoleto, 1970), 1:261–311 (273, 309); Bat-Sheva Albert, "Un nouvel examen de la politique anti-juive wisigothique," *Revue des études juives* 135 (1976): 3–29; Linehan, *History and Historians*, 64–67; Dahlhaus-Berg, *Nova antiquitas*, 195, 218–19; David F. Appleby, "Rudolf, Abbot Hrabanus and the Ark of the Covenant Reliquary," *American Benedictine Review* 46 (1995): 419–43, especially 420–21, 434–35, 439–40; and Thomas Renna, *Jerusalem in Medieval Thought* (Lewiston, ME, 2002), 105–8.

107. For a useful summary, see Gianfranco Miletto, "Die 'Hebraica veritas' in S. Hieronymus," in *Die Bibel in jüdischer und christlicher Tradition: Festschrift für Johann Maier zum 60. Geburtstag*, ed. Helmut Merklein (Frankfurt a.M., 1993), 56–65.

108. Albert, "*Adversus Iudaeos*"; and Cohen, *Living Letters in the Law*, also feature helpful summaries. For the notion of "word" in Spanish-Carolingian writing, see also Chazelle, "'Not in Painting but in Writing.'"

CHAPTER 7

Scotoma lexicographica: The Omission of Mathematical and Scientific Latin Terms from Classical and Medieval Latin Dictionaries

WESLEY STEVENS

Despite the supreme value of dictionaries of classical Latin for the understanding of Latin culture through interpretation of surviving documents, most are quite inadequate for expressions of mathematical and scientific usages. The same is true for lexicons of medieval Latin prior to AD 1200, the outer limit for this study. While all Latin dictionaries and lexicons are full of technical terms for grammar and rhetoric, as well as for terms expressing many other aspects of the lives of those who spoke and wrote Latin in its myriad forms, they often fail us for the terms in which geography, astronomy, and botany were normally used in all periods. These omissions have occurred for reading and interpreting the works of Cicero, Ovid, Quintillian, and other sources up to the years AD 180/200, as well as for the selected works of Tertullian and Augustine which were usually cited as sources for classical Latin. All lexicons of medieval Latin cite a few works written by Isidore of Seville, the Venerable Bede, Abbo of Fleury, and many other early Latin authors whose writings before AD 1200 have always been well known, but omissions of the mathematical and scientific terminology and usages of those authors are numerous. Often it seems as if such Latin terms did not exist.

There have been not only omissions but also overt errors by lexicographers in their definitions of terms which had been well known and actively used by both classical and early medieval writers to express their mathematical and scientific concepts and activities—an accumulation of modern errors which has obstructed the understanding of many Latin texts. Lexicography is a discipline from which all Latinists benefit, as improvements are made by successive scholars, as new texts are discovered, and as known texts are newly edited from time to time. We have all gained immeasurably from the progress that continues to be made by the labors and exceptional skills of many experts. Yet, with respect to significant aspects of Latin culture, even the finest contributors to lexicography may have underestimated the richness of their sources.

I

Amongst the best dictionaries of classical Latin are those by Ægidius Forcellini of Padua (1688–1768) and Wilhelm Freund of Vienna (1806–94). The first edition of the great *Lexicon totius latinitatis* by Forcellini was published posthumously in 1771 at Padua where he had worked as a teacher and had edited and studied the texts of many Latin writers.[1] Within a few years of its appearance, there was not only an *editio altera* of his *Lexicon* (Padua 1805–16), followed by several more editions,[2] but also a French translation,[3] another in German,[4] and three in English.[5] Each of these versions included new citations of sources for some terms, and there were additions of new lemmata with definitions and textual examples of their usages. There had been a number of dictionaries of classical Latin published north of the Alps, and this was stimulated especially with new works by Wilhelm Freund[6] in 1834–45 at Vienna in the south and in the north by Karl Ernst Georges[7] at Braunschweig in 1837/38; both were based upon the German translation in Austria of Forcellini. The work by Georges was republished by his family many times and is still recommended by some excellent German scholars for any Latin text whether classical, medieval, or Neo-Latin, without noticing that he had acknowledged his dependency not only upon Forcellini but also upon Freund.

The four volumes of the *Wörterbuch* by Wilhelm Freund were especially important for Latin lexicography, as they too were translated into French, Spanish, and English. Also significant was the two-volume edition of his *Gesammt-wörterbuch*,[8] the use of which was acknowledged by Georges, Riddle, Andrews, and others. The shorter version for home and school was translated into English by Joseph Edmond Riddle (1804–59) and by Ethan Allen Andrews (1787–1858) in what seems to have been a challenge-race of translators which was won by Riddle[9] with his edition of 1849. In the long run however, it was Andrews' translation[10] in 1851 which prevailed because it was absorbed into the *New Latin Dictionary* (1879) by Lewis and Short, who gave credit to Andrews before the title page was altered to emphasize the previous work of "William Freund."

Many Latinists still consider the *New Latin Dictionary* by Charleton T. Lewis and Charles Short to be the best for their reading of either classical or medieval texts. This practice may be convenient but cannot be sustained. Each reissue of Lewis and Short by Oxford University Press declares that it is new and has been revised; since 1879 however there have been no revisions, additions, or corrections.[11] Lewis and Short is found in every library and on most of our desks. It has been the basis for shortened versions by a succession of lexicographers published by the Cassells Publishing Company, upon which the current one-volume Harper's Latin dictionary is based.

In that series of dictionaries from Forcellini through Freund and Andrews to Lewis and Short, the quality of lexicographical expertise has been extremely high. Yet, they have left their users with a serious problem: all forms of addition and subtraction, multiplication and division receive little or no attention, or the terms themselves are simply omitted. In our heads and in our hearts we may know in general that those arithmetical functions were all actively pursued by a few Roman scholars, "though not very well," and we may project such functions upon the words to which we have become accustomed. Yet, to begin with the simplest example, if we are reading a text which requires an unexpected use of the verb *addo, -ere*, or of the substantive, *additio additionis*, and we find that their ordinary arithmetical usages for numerical addition are not given by the dictionaries on our desks, that puzzling Latin text at hand may seem to us confused. Many readers have had that experience, and many have inferred therefore that a Roman writer did not understand the mathematical disciplines, or that he must have been quite naive about them. Such inferences about one or another writer, enlarged into an image of an entire culture, appear often in lectures and books of the history of science and the history of mathematics, encouraged if not created by the neglect by all lexicographers of terms which were certainly and actively used in Latin cultures at all times.

Notice further that another verb for numerical addition is *supputo, -are*, the noun *ablatio* for subtraction; a verb for multiplication is *produco, -ere*; a verb for division is *partio, -ire*. *Quadrare* is used for squaring a number, *mediare* to halve any numerical amount, and *facere* or *colligere* or *habere* to reach and express the total result of any numerical operation. All such functions for those words were neglected by our dictionaries and lexicons, leaving the false impression that the acts they express were not present in Latin culture of the several periods. In that series of lexicographical aids which we have traced above, there is not only the apparent lack of arithmetical terms; there is also no definition of the common terms for geometry and very little for astronomy. That is not due to a lack of activity in those disciplines or to the lack of their terminology by Cicero, Ovid, Quintillian, Augustine, and other very good sources for Latin usage. Rather, it is due to the practices of the best Latin lexicographers from 1771 to the present in classical studies. Forcellini and Freund are now rarely available, largely due to massive destruction of European homes, schools, universities, and libraries during 1933–45. But for the understanding of Latin texts which use those terms and in order not to distort the culture in which they were produced therefore, one should avoid Georges, as well as Lewis and Short, and should be careful about using most other dictionaries available today which depend upon them.[12]

II

The same problem is found in most lexicons of medieval Latin, for which the pattern was set by the great work of Charles Dufresne, known as le Sieur Du Cange (1610–88), a century earlier than Forcellini. In the original three folio volumes of Du Cange's *Glossarium ad scriptores mediae et infimae latinitatis*, published in 1678 at Paris,[13] one will search in vain for any definition of *addo, subtraho, multiplico,* or *divido.* Although this scholar organized his work on the basis of substantives, he also included numerous verbal, adjectival, and adverbial forms under his primary lemmata, with many citations and quotations of their usages. Those volumes include "Addenda et Emendata" at the end of each volume, and his own large *Appendix* was published at Lyon in 1688, the year of his death.[14] At Frankfurt-am-Main in 1710, an edition of the *Glossarium latinitatis* was published with most of those additions from the *Appendix* and a few more additions which are unattributed.[15] Further contributions by a dozen or more lexicographers, especially those working out of the Benedictine monastery of St. Maur in Paris, were gathered by G. A. Louis Henschel[16] in seven volumes published at Paris during 1840 to 1850. In this Cangist tradition should also be mentioned a summary of Henschel in one volume by Maigne d'Arnis (1800–75), published at Paris in 1858 by J.-P. Migne.[17] The Henschel seven volumes were also reprinted in twelve during 1883 and 1887 in Niort (France) by Léopold Favre,[18] including his several lists of sources but did not take into account Du Cange's large 1688 *Appendix.* Favre also added his own contributions to French and Latin lexicography. That version was reprinted in large quarto under the seal of the Collège de France (Paris) in 1943 and again in regular quarto at Graz (Austria) in 1954, bearing the prominent name of Du Cange on the spine of each volume and on the title pages. The Favre edition (repr. 1954) and the Maigne manual (repr. 1868) are found today in most North American and European libraries. Rather than the seventeenth-century *Glossarium* in three volumes and *Appendix* by le Sieur Du Cange, however, it is the late nineteenth-century version which is usually cited erroneously as "Du Cange." The version edited by Henschel and reprinted by Favre will be cited here properly as "Henschel."

Lexicographers must build upon past work, in order to improve it by re-reading the sources, by adding new citations, and by including usages of words not recognized previously. That should have and has often benefited us all, step by step. In this case nevertheless, the results are disappointing. What Du Cange had to say or not to say about mathematical or scientific meanings of words in 1678 served to define some aspects of medieval culture for several centuries without significant change for many medieval scholars in modern times and especially for those scholars who labor outside of that field but consider it significant, positively or negatively. Latin texts from those early medieval centuries contained huge amounts of arithmetic, geometry, astronomy, the terms of which were usually omitted or given odd meanings by le Sieur Du Cange and later Cangists. Those terms and their meanings have often continued to be neglected by later lexicographers until quite recently.

It may be noted by those who have consulted Du Cange in any version that his index showed use of agrimensorial literature, and he did consult those texts far more diligently than most lexicographers. Yet, the basic terms for instruments of Roman and medieval surveying and building, *cardo* and *decumanus*, *decempeda* and *regula*, are missing from his lemmata, or they have been dealt with poorly by the later Cangists.[19] Thus,

cardo -inis (m.)

Du Cange[1]	N/A. Carduus, seu cardui strobilus, quo lanae carminatur. Vide *dccimanus*.
Du Cange[2]	Nil.
Du Cange[3]	N/A. Ditto Du Cange[1].
Henschel	N/A. Ditto.
Maigne	N/A. Ditto.

decimanus, decumanus -a -um (adj.)

Du Cange[1]	*Decimanus limes* – maximus limes inter agros, qui ab Oriente ad Occidentem per transversum dirigitur: qui quia × efficit, Decumanus est appellatus; ager divisus figuram denarii numeri efficit; nam cardo dicitur alius limes in agris qui à septrione directus est.
Du Cange[2]	Nil.
Du Cange[3]	Ditto Du Cange[1].
Henschel	*Decimanus limes*—maximus limes inter agros, qui ab Oriente ad Occidentem per transversum dirigitur; obnoxius decimae, qui decimas debet exsolvere; exactor decimarum vel publicanus.
Maigne	N/A. Obnoxius *decimae*, qui decimas debet exsolvere – celui qui doit la dîme; *decumani*—in Ecclesia Mediolanensi, canonicos vicarias.

decempeda -ae (f.)

Du Cange[1]	Nil.
Du Cange[2]	Nil.
Du Cange[3]	Nil.
Henschel	Nil.
Maigne	Nil.

One of the tools used by carpenters was the *regula* for measuring distances and spaces and for leveling the line of stones or bricks forming a wall. Those uses of *regula* as "ruler" for measure or leveling were not given by Du Cange. He did notice another usage of that word in computistical practice as a "rule" to be followed in calculation of dates in the current Bedan calendar, *regulares lunares* and *regulares solares*, though without definition; unfortunately, this citation was short-lived: his *regulares apud compotistae* were deleted by Henschel and by Maigne d'Arnis, which left *regula* as monastic and penitential rules but without any meaning in engineering or calendar texts. Thus, its definitions in Henschel and Maigne are denoted N/A:

regula -ae (f.)

Du Cange[1]	Canon, exactio, pensitatio; necrologio; canon poenitentialis; regularis, monasticae regulae addictus; regulares apud compotistae, seu computi ecclesiastici conditores, alii sunt solares, alii lunares.
Du Cange[2]	Nil.
Du Cange[3]	Ditto Du Cange[1].
Henschel	N/A. Ditto + principium, axioma vel argumentum seu hypothesis; oppidum vel vicus et ipsius loci commune; versus, versiculus; proclamatio, auctio; dele 'regulares apud compotistae, seu computi ecclesiastici conditores, alii sunt solares, alii lunares.'
Maigne	N/A. Ditto Du Cange[1]; dele 'regulares apud compotistae, seu computi ecclesiastici conditores, alii sunt solares, alii lunares.'

Two Latin terms that specified wide expanses of earth or sea or sky were *plaga* and *zona*. As well as in literary images for more general expressions of *regio*, either *plaga* or *zona* was used often for open or delineated spaces in astronomical and cosmological descriptions. The words were noticed by Du Cange, Henschel, or Maigne but without those meanings, thus N/A:

plaga -ae (f.)[20]

Du Cange[1]	N/A. Plaga legalis; plaga currit; *plagare*—plagas inferre, vulnerare.
Du Cange[2]	Nil.
Du Cange[3]	N/A. Ditto Du Cange[1].
Henschel	N/A. [*plagium*] regio.
Maigne	N/A. Regio—contrée, région olim plaie (s.xii); *plaga legalis*—blessure.

zona -ae (f.)[21]

Du Cange[1]	N/A. Cingulum, vestis sacerdotalis; ignis sacri species, quae medium hominum ambit.
Du Cange[2]	N/A. Adde cit.
Du Cange[3]	N/A. Ditto Du Cange[1].
Henschel	N/A. Ditto + circuitus, ambitus.
Maigne	N/A. Cingulum, vestis sacerdotalis—ceinture, particulièrement celles qui fait partie du costume ecclésiastique; corrigia, lorum—courroie, lanière; ignis sacri species, quae medium hominem ambit cingitque, erpes.

It is not only the names for the functions of Arithmetic or Astronomy or Engineering which are missing. Hundreds more Latin words for botanical, mathematical, geographical, mechanical, musical, and zoological knowledge are simply absent from Du Cange and are often left out of later lexicons dependent upon Du Cange.

A few more examples of lemmata from letter *a*, for which meanings are lacking in works of the Cangists, are abacus, abigo, abortio vel abortivus vel abortius, accentus, accessus, adiectio vel abiectio, addo, addispositio, adimo, adimplo, adinuentio, adluscino vel alluscino, administratio vel amministratio, adolescens vel adulescens, adviso, aequatio, aequator, aequidistans vel aequistans, aequilaterio vel aequilatatio, aequilaterus, aequinoctialis, aequinoctium, aequipendium, aequus vel aecus, aerius, aereus vel aeria, aes aeris, aestimo vel aestumo, aestus, africus, africanus, agrimensor, alligiditas, alteratio, amblygonius, amphicirtos vel amphicyrtos vel amphitricus, angulus, antarcticus, antecurro, antecurrens, antegradatio, anteverto vel antevertor vel antevorto, antichthon vel antichthones, antipodes vel antipodae, antiscii, apertura, apothema, aquatilis, arachne, arcticos vel arcticus, arctophylax, arctous, arcturus, argumentum, Aries, artus vel arctus, aspectus, astrologia, astronomia, astrum, athlum, atramentum, augmentor vel augmentum vel augumentum, auspex, australis, austrinus, austronotius vel austronotus, autochthones, aux, axioma, axis vel assis, axon. There is a myriad more lemmata of letter *a* alone which expressed mathematical or other scientific usages in Latin texts before AD 1200 but which seem to have been unknown to those lexicographers and thus to their learned readers.

New or improved definitions by the several Cangists collected by Henschel should be noticed for accipio, actualia vel actualis, adgregatio vel aggregatio, adminiculum, aequipes vel aequipedus, agna, agnua, alhidada vel alidada vel halhidada, altum vel altus, antelongior figura, apocatastasis, appono, arctos vel arctus, arcus vel arquus, arithmetica vel arithmetice, astrolapsus vel astrolabium, augmentatio, avena.[22]

For those who study these large aspects of medieval culture, this is a challenge. Efforts to read and interpret many Latin texts must often be made without the help of the lexicographical tools of the trade. That has been so frustrating for some scholars that they have been willing to throw in the towel and declare that, if a medieval Latin text cannot be clarified by reference to the best lexicographical aids, it was because the writers themselves must have been confused; or if those early writers did not chose the right words to express what we expect, they were probably just copying something without understanding the subject matter themselves. It is true that both Roman and medieval writers have sometimes "been treated as half-witted scribes who quite randomly had put together half-digested material in poor Latin," as Walter Pohl and others complained.[23] Quite often, none of those notions could be the case for texts requiring mathematical and scientific knowledge and language in context.

III

A good example of how a common term with ordinary cosmological meanings may be misconstrued is lemmata for the word *orbis*. In various contexts, *orbis* can have meanings which are two dimensional or three dimensional, a circle or a sphere. Forcellini gave priority to the use of *orbis* for things flat and distinguished this usage from *globus*, citing Cicero.[24] But he admits that his distinction does not fit all of the sources because *orbis* is often used for things round, like *globus*. Although his citations do not say so, he also believed that *orbis lunae* or *orbis solis* could mean a flat disk of the moon and a flat disk of the sun. Freund[1] narrowed these possibilities to "*orbis terrarum oder terrae*—der Erdkreis," explaining his interpretation, "da die Alten die Erde für eine Scheibe hielten." For this idea of "eine Scheibe" or "battle shield" or other planar disks to define *orbis*, he cited Cicero's notion of the great potency of the lands of the orb; and under his lemma for *amplexus*, "Umfassen, Umschlingen, Umgeben," Freund[2] could add an image of the horizon (*orbis finientes*) which he derives from Livy's Ocean embracing the lands of the orb (of Earth), even though Livy had not used that phrase.[25] To define the word *terra*, however, Cicero is quoted by Freund, "terra universa cernatur, locata in media sede mundi, solida et globosa." Thus, Cicero used *orbis* either as two-dimensional or as three-dimensional in different contexts, as acknowledged by Forcellini but not by Freund.

Lewis and Short promoted the idea that *orbis* was "anything of a circular shape: a ring, round surface, quoit or disk, hoop," or it could refer to "a circle (of men)" or "a cycle of thought." Both definitions are obviously correct in some contexts. With reference to the shape of Earth however, they followed Freund when they said that *orbis terrarum* or *orbis terrae* must have had only two dimensions, "since the ancients regarded the earth as a circular plane or disk." The sense of "rounding off, roundness, rotundity" referred to speech, they said, and not to a ball or a sphere. Unfortunately, neither of their citations describe the orb of earth or moon or sun to be anything remotely like a disc or shield.[26] They also eliminated Cicero's description of *terra universa* as *solida et globosa*. The definition of *orbis* given by Lewis and Short is a bit of fiction, to the detriment of their users.

For medieval usages, Du Cange and the Cangists did not agree that this word referred to the heavens or the earth at all; rather, they said that it could mean a two-dimensional wound on the skin, or the roundness of a three-dimensional ornament, especially one representing an empire:

orbis, orbs -is (m.)

Du Cange[1]	N/A. Imperium, regnum, dominatio; interdum pro pago, seu provincia; ornamentum contexuit, quod vocatur orbis terrarum, ille Caroli Calvi dissimillimum; orbus, orbare; ictus.
Du Cange[2]	N/A. Adde cit.
Du Cange[3]	N/A. Ditto Du Cange[1].
Henschel	N/A. Ditto.
Maigne	N/A. Regnum, imperium; provincia, regio; ictus latens—meurtrissure, coup, blessure qui ne saigne pas.

Tertullian (ca. AD 150–225) would not have agreed with them.[27] Nor would Macrobius or Martianus or their contemporary John Cassian (ca. AD 415). Nor later Gildas (fl. AD 540), Bede (AD 680–735), Frithegodus (ca. AD 950), Waltherus Spirensis (ca. AD 982–83), Egbertus (AD 1022–24), much less the *Geometria* anonymi (s. x–xi). Assuming another model of the spherical Earth, Paschasius Radbertus (AD 786–859) spoke "per totam quadratem orbem," as discussed below (pp. 130–31).

It may be noticed that either the disk shape of the cosmos or the tambourine-shape has been variously imputed to many pre-Socratic Greek scholars: Anaximenes, Anaxagoras, Archelaus, the atomists Leucippus and Democritus.[28] That the whole universe could take the shape of a sphere seems first to have occurred to the fifth-century Pythagoreans of Croton and their neighboring schools of Elea in southwestern Italy: Parmenides (ca. 512–450 BC), and of Acragas in Sicily: Empedocles (ca. 493–433). Furthermore, two of them from Syracuse may have supposed that Earth rotated on its own axis from West to East, and others proposed that Earth is a star moving in a great circle about a central fire. At least one member of the Academy in Athens agreed that Earth moved in a circle.[29]

Emphasis on circular rotation of heavenly bodies around a common central point (projected though not observed as a geometrical *polus*) may have prepared thinkers not only for a spherical model of the heavens but also for the analogous concept of Earth as a globe. Both ideas were promoted by Plato (ca. 427–347), in fragments of the works of Eudoxos (fl. 368–365), and by Aristoteles (ca. 384–322).[30] Thereafter Greek and Latin literature was replete with this idea of both cosmos and Earth as spheres, driving out all other concepts from the minds of Greeks and Romans, Hebrews and Christians alike.

Subsequent denial of three dimensions to Earth on the basis of limiting *orbis* to two dimensions of a planar surface in Latin texts by lexicographers during the period usually called the Enlightenment is simply mistaken, as has been well established by detailed review of those texts by Betten (1923), Jones (1934), and Stevens (1980).[31] But the "flat disk" idea attributed to Jews and especially to early and medieval Christians has had an amazingly strong influence in the history of cartography. It was expressed in 1883 for example by Bunbury, who said that from Homer to Hecataeus, the ancients "believed the earth to be a plane, of circular form, surrounded on all sides by the Ocean, which they conceived, not as a sea, but as a vast continuous stream, for ever flowing round and round the earth. The vault of heaven [has] a solid concave surface, like the 'firmament' of the Jews, . . . on all sides," concepts he would extend to the time of Herodotus. Warmington elaborated this idea in 1934: "In Homeric literature (c. 900) . . . the inhabited earth is a round plane with an ocean-river flowing round it, the sky being a concave vault resting on the edge like a lid; below the earth stretched dark Tartarus symmetrical with the heavens above."[32] Through René Taton, the idea of Earth as a disk found an honored place in the history of science generally, though for some historians the plane under a half bowl could shift into a cube.[33]

A similar way to attribute the flatness of Earth to darkened minds was to grant that the idea of sphericity of Earth was known by some but then to claim that it was resisted by Christians or somehow weakened. Beazley explained in 1897 that, during the first ten centuries after Christ, "The belief in a round or spherical world . . . was robbed of all practical value, in the few cases where it gained a hearing," though he cited no evidence for this assertion. In a Harvard thesis under the direction of Professor C. H. Haskins which was published immediately and became very influential for the history of science, J. K. Wright (1925) cited Beazley and agreed with him that Christians resisted the idea of spherical Earth, even suggesting that it could become grounds for the charge of heresy, but also without a shred of evidence.[34] Among the many examples of this *idée fixe* is a book by Marina Smyth (1996) which is otherwise excellent. The author was sure that "the early Irish scholars . . . were hampered by the nonavailability of more truly scientific models and by extremely limited technology." Apparently, she means that they would not have known Aristotle's arguments that the earth is a sphere, for she added that they "were most uncomfortable not only with the word *sphaera*, but with the concept." Smyth acknowledged that those same writers described Earth with the words *sphaera* and *globus*, but asserts that at the time (seventh century) the word *hemispera* [*sic*] "has nothing to do with half of some spherical object" and the word *globus* "referred to the bulk of an object, not with particular reference to its roundness." Rather, they compared the Firmament with the shell and the Earth with the yolk of *ovum*.[35] Yet, one may notice that, before it is broken into the pan and fried, an egg always has three dimensions, both the shape of its shell and the bulk of its yolk. True, the Irish would have benefited from classical sciences, but the Latin terms they used could not be applied to the Earth unless it were round like a ball: *pila* or an egg: *ovum*.

More careful was George H. T. Kimble (1938), who quoted the thoughtful discussion by Hrabanus Maurus (AD 780–856), whose *De natura rerum* or *De universo* is usually characterized as merely excerpts from Isidore of Seville and lacking originality or interest. Yet in section 12.2, "Orbis a rotunditate circuli dictus," Hraban discussed several descriptive figures of Earth, asking first how the two of them could be harmonized "when the figures themselves, as geometricians maintain, are different." From Psalm 71:18, he cited *orbis terrae* on the one hand and on the other Earth's expanse under four cardinal points in Psalm 106:3 and its "four corners" in Matthew 24:31: "a quatuor angulis terrae." Thus, said Hraban, "how the *demonstrativus quadratus* ought to be inscribed with the orb, Euclid clearly shows in the Fourth Book of the Elements." He went on to discuss the orb in two more figures with either three parts (Asia, Africa, Europa) or two parts (Oriens et Occidens). It appears that he was using several diagrams, including the *orbis quadratus* and the *rota terrarum*, by which the spherical Earth was usually depicted. For him there can be no doubt that *orbis terrae* is a sphere whose shape can be implied from several rhetorical figures of speech but also analyzed from the drawings of geometers. None of those diagrams are especially compelling, but each is worth considering: an effective teacher, as Kimble said.[36]

The flat Earth idea has been used repeatedly in modern biblical exegesis, having been expressed well in a 1941 essay by Rudolph Bultmann, significant for Form Criticism of the Synoptic Gospels. He begins by affirming that "[t]he world picture of the New Testament . . . is a three-story structure, with earth in the middle, heaven above it, and hell below it."[37] He thought that Gospel writers of the first Christian century presumed Earth to be flat. This was precisely the image of the cosmos supposed by Bunbury and Warmington for Greeks during Homeric times (s. 8 BC). They all three assumed that early Christian writers were ignorant of the several and diverse ideas about the shape of Earth, both popular and scientific, which had developed during eight centuries and surely would not be aware of the spherical concept proposed in the meantime by Pythagoreans and promoted by Platonists and Aristotelians.

Many biblical scholars today continue the same assumptions and repeat the three-tiered notion with a round but flat Earth, as expressed by several authors in the incredibly wide-ranging *Anchor Bible Dictionary* (1992). Although its section on "Cosmology in the NT" gives no description, R. A. Oden Jr. writes that "[t]he earth on which humanity dwells is seen as a round, solid object, perhaps a disk [Isaiah 40:22; cf. Proverbs 8:27], floating upon a limitless expanse of water. . . . The moon, sun, and other luminaries are assumed by these scholars to have been imagined as fixed in a curved structure which arches over the earth . . . . three-storied." W. Janzen says: "In most respects the NT shares the cosmology of the OT . . . a tripartite universe (heaven, earth, 'under the earth': Rev. 5:3, 13; Phil. 2:10)." Nevertheless, no term for the Earth as "disk" is found in the four texts cited by Oden and Janzen, nor any term for "a fixed" or "a curved structure" of the heavens, unless it be *orbis*. In his article on "Geography and the Bible," C. N. Raphael describes "O and T maps" in "[t]he Cottonian map, a 10th-century Anglo-Saxon predecessor to the traditional maps," which is anachronistic and mistaken in all details.[38] London, British Library, MS Cotton Tiberius B.v (s. xi ex) is a collection of materials of various dates: the Cottonian map on two facing folios, 28–29 (dated not earlier than AD 1050): it is centered on the Aegean Sea, placing Palestine and Jerusalem to the south of the Middle Sea, near the division between the continents of Asia and Africa. An earlier Cottonian map on folio 58 (ca. AD 1030) shows two walled cities with high towers south of the Mediterranean, but neither is named Jerusalem. It was only after British knights and clerics began returning from the Crusades that Jerusalem began to be moved nearer to or placed at the center of a few T-O maps. Raphael also cited "the *omphalos*, that is, the earth's navel," which he says portrayed Jerusalem "since ancient times," though without sources. Philip S. Alexander however noted that the meaning of Hebrew *abbúr* in Ezekiel 38:12 is disputed but was translated as Greek *omphalos* in the Septuagint, thus perhaps as "navel of the earth." He repeated the image of Earth "as a roughly circular disk . . . widespread in antiquity" (979), though he too lacked evidence for that generalization or term. However, Alexander differentiates a variety of other figurative references to the shape of Earth in OT, as does another author from references in NT who says: "the bipartite designation (heaven, earth) is dominant throughout." A more sophisticated methodology led to this wider range of images in NT:

> the earth's "four corners" (Rev. 7:1; 20:8),
> its "end" or "uttermost parts" (Acts 1:8; 13:14; cf. Isaiah 49:6),
> its "four ends" (Matthew 12:42 = Luke 11:31),
> or its face (Acts 17:26),
> the "four winds" (Mark 13:27 and Rev. 7:1).

The disparity of those rhetorical and poetical figures had not been taken into account by the prevailing Bunbury-Warmington-Bultmann schema. No citation from biblical literature provides Earth with a plane surface or uses a term for "disk" or describes a disklike shape of two dimensions. References to outer limits or to great distances were used in this literature, but no term for "corners" is found in Hebrew or Greek texts.[39] From this variety of images, no uniform, descriptive cosmology should be implied.

The notion that Earth was thought to have a plane or flat surface has also been a favorite of art historians. This depends not only upon errors by early historians or cartographers and the three-tiered model preferred heretofore by biblical scholars but also upon a strange but valuable Greek work from the sixth century which survives in a copy from the tenth century with rare illustrations. On that thin basis, encyclopedias of art and art history have often generalized broadly that early Christians believed that Earth was flat. Perhaps one of them did so. The author of that singular work was a Syrian merchant in maritime trade, a Nestorian Christian who may have been called Cosmas. His writings are heterodox, that is, not acceptable to the leaders of Christianity. Like any biblical fundamentalist, he selected certain texts from several books of the OT, placed strict interpretations upon certain words and phrases, and arrayed them into a picture of Earth and the stars, so that Earth would have a planar surface inside the walls of a tent under a two-tiered firmament.[40] The text, context, and illustrations do not justify assigning his cosmology or any aspect of it to any one else or to any other times. It was not a "Christian cosmology" and appears to have had no influence in medieval centuries in the Greek or Latin worlds.

The idea that not just crude peasants but even intelligent people back then (in the medieval period) thought that Earth was flat may have been expressed in print first around AD 1707, in a book found in the British Library by the historian of Tudor and Stuart geography, Eva Taylor. In that book of the early eighteenth century, a school teacher was inviting his students to see that world as Newton had opened it for them. In order to impress them with the new opportunities of science, he contrasted their own times with the medieval times when "they thought that the earth was flat." That idea continues to live today, especially in the minds of scientists, with the added fillip that Christianity is still opposing Science. It was repeated yet again by Nobel Prize–winner Steven Weinberg in his Phi Beta Kappa Oration at Harvard University (2008) and widely distributed: "Without God."[41] Natural scientists seem to grasp at the idea of the flat Earth today in the peculiar sort of dim past which they generate amongst themselves in order to emphasize bad times of the past by contrast to their own present good sense. The bad old days may be considered "too obscure or insignificant to merit serious study," as some might say, but appear quite valuable to them as a whipping post. Yet the real world is more complicated and its actual past more difficult to grasp than such generalizations allow.

IV

Lewis and Short were not the first to place a misleading definition upon the word *orbis*, plainly contrary to the texts that they cited. Rather, they were following the translations of earlier, more ambiguous definitions by Ægidius Forcellini, with modifications of Forcellini in the second and third editions by Funaletto and in the work of Wilhelm Freund. The effects may be seen in the use of *orbis* with other terms. Forcellini had defined *finiens* as "orizzonte" and quoted Cicero, *De divinatione*, 2.44.92: "Illi orbes, qui cælum quasi medium dividunt, & aspectum nostrum difiniunt, qui a Græcis 'ορίζοντες nominantur, a nobis finientes rectissime nominari possunt." Freund[1] mentioned *finiens* only under his lemma for *ficio* but did not define it; in his shorter work however Freund[2] added *orbis*, thus "finiens orbis—Horizont," and repeated the definition and citation from Forcellini. However, they both have also cited a text in astronomical use of *orbis* from L. Annaeus Seneca, *Quaestiones naturales*, 5.17: "finiens circulus." Could *orbis* and *circulus* be taken therefore as synonymus and as two dimensional? That was what Lewis and Short wanted to do in their definition: "*finiens orbis* or *circulus*—the horizon." The Oxford Latin Dictionary was also satisfied with only two dimensions.

However, *orbis* appears in the lemmata for other words which require it to have three dimensions in some contexts. For the meaning of *fascea* or *fascia*, Forcellini gave the zones of the sky which circle the orb of Earth, quoting Martianus Capella: "orbis terræ in quinque zonas, sive melius fascias dico, discernitur."[42] Freund cited the same text and translated *fascia* into German as "der Erdgürtel, die Zone." Either of his terms would require *orbis* to be *sphaera* or *globus*, around which circle the equator or zodiac or the *zonae* or *plagae* of the stars. Forcellini had been certain that *globus* applied not only to the heavens but to Earth: "non solum de sphæris cælestibus, & de terra, sed de omnibus rebus rotundis non concavis." It is remarkable that Freund[1], although he did not say so in his definition of *orbis*, affirmed in his definition of *globus* that it applied to "Der kugelrunder Körper jeder Art, die Kugel: globus terrae." This definition was expanded by Freund[2]: "globus terrae, stellarum globus, in coelo animadversi globi." In each of these definitions, Earth is a three-dimensional ball. Forcellini had also given a simile for the adjective *globosa*, "quæ *rotunda* simul & solida, ut lusoria pila," while Freund[2] explained *globosus* as "kugelförmig, kugelrund: *mundus, stella, terra.*" Likewise contrary to their definition of *orbis terrae* as flat, Lewis and Short would define *globus* as "[a] round body, a ball, sphere, globe" and *globosus* as "round as a ball, spherical, globose: *mundus, terra.*" Oxford is of two minds: it also knew *globus* as "the sphere of a heavenly body" but not terrestrial, whereas *globosus* described "stellae, terra universa, luna."[43]

In medieval Latin, Du Cange's definition of *globosus* was applied to the sphere of Earth, though not to a sphere of the heavens; that distinction was repeated by Henschel, while Maigne was silent about the shape of both the heavens and Earth. It is no wonder that readers of Latin texts have had difficulty with the shape of Earth if their best dictionaries and lexicons were so erratic and inconsistent.

A common classical model for speaking of *mundus* or of *terra* was *orbis quadratus* or *orbis quadrifarius*.[44] Freund had quoted Augustine and others about four parts of the heavens and four parts of Earth, but he did not name the model as *orbis quadratus*. Other writers in that period such as Lactantius and Julius Honorius assumed four parts of heaven and Earth and were quoted by lexicographers but also without using the term *orbis quadratus* directly. That term is also not found in Du Cange under either *orbis* or *quadratum*, though his language sometimes assumes that model. Henschel included *quadratum* as a lemma but did not define it; rather, he gave a kind of periphrastic rendering by citing examples of its use: *quadratura, quadratus lapis, quadrificium orbem*; he also named *quadratus orbis* and defined that phrase "in quatuor partes divisus." To Du Cange's definitions of *quadrificium* or *quadrificum* or *quadrifidus*, Henschel added *orbem quadrificum*, but only to refer back to *quadratus orbis* without definition. Maigne retained Henschel's list of usages for these forms of *quadratus* also without definition. None of the Cangists however mentioned *quadratus orbis* as a use of *orbis*.[45]

The texts used by Du Cange and the Cangists however include the *Commentary on Matthew* by Paschasius Radbertus of Corbie who used the phrase *per totum quadratum orbem*. This text was cited by Albert Blaise (1967) for the meaning of the adjective *quadratus* in medieval Latin. His translation of that phrase as "divisé en 4 parties" was correct and could be understood as referring to the *quadratus orbis* model of Earth. But Blaise explained that "4 parties" meant "aux quatre coins du monde" or "Équarrie." Blaise's "monde médiévale" with "quatre coins" is the image of a planar surface or an area with angular corners, not the image of a sphere or ball or apple which is divided into four equal parts, as not only this but also each of his sources intended.[46] One result is that readers of classical and medieval texts today may refer to the cartographic model of *orbis tripartitus terrarum* from Cicero and Macrobius[47] ⊕, oriented to the east, but usually do not know *orbis quadratus* ⊕, oriented to the north. Both models were used by the same writers in classical and medieval literature.[48] The *rota terrae* is often called T-*rota* by cartographers today because two lines representing waters dividing the three continents within the *rota* are often simplified to intersect in the shape of T within a circle drawn upon a manuscript page. The term was also applied to the sun, *rota solis*, for which Forcellini supplied many alternatives of either two or three dimensions: "ipsum solis corpus, discus, orbis, rotundus globus." From these, Freund selected only "die Sonnenscheibe," and he was followed by Lewis and Short with "disk" or "shield," to the exclusion of "orbis, rotundus globus." For cartographers, this narrowed the meaning of the figurative *rota* to that of a physical *discus*. The term *rota terrarum tripartita*, referring to the whole Earth as discus rather than as one-quarter of the *globus*, is thus modern and did not occur in medieval Latin; rather, *rota = discus* to describe the shape of Earth was an invention of nineteenth-century lexicographers and cartographers. There is much misleading literature about this *rota* as a T-O model, without recognizing that it represents one quarter of Earth, within which are three continents, while the other three quarters of *orbis quadratus* are not shown.

Another related term is *orbiculus* or *parvus orbis*, which according to Forcellini and *Thesaurus linguae latinae* could apply "ad figuram circuli, gyri; ad formam globi." An example of the latter is *lapidus rotundi*. No other classical dictionaries give this alternative, though their sources do so. Lacking *forma globi*, they turned to *circulus*, *rotula*, or "kleine Scheibe, Rolle, Nabe" (Freund). Lewis and Short translated this from German as "a small disc; a sheave, roller, pulley." Their "nave of a wheel" was expressed by *Thesaurus* more broadly as "de parte machina" and by Oxford as "a revolving drum." For the editors of the *Thesaurus* however, that *machina* could be "de horologio aquario," a meaning for *orbiculus* unknown to all other classical dictionaries. Du Cange did not give the terms at all, and the Cangists knew *orbiculus* only as "Ludi species; jeu du palet."

V

One may search further for the meaning of *orbis* among terms which describe similar actions or concepts, such as *gyrus*, *motus coeli*, *mundus*, and the adjectival forms based upon *mundus*. Thus, *gyrus* (m.), transliterated from Greek into Latin, could mean "circumversio in orbem," according to Forcellini, with synonyms, "ambitus, circuitus, circulus," and examples, "grues, apes, piscis, serpens." Freund and most lexicographers took *gyrus* to mean "to turn, move in a circle, revolve," with a variety of usages, such as the movement of a horse in a ring. Some of them found *gyrus* used in texts of astronomy: "the orbit of a heavenly body, one of the imaginary circles in the heavens," such as the tropics, equatorial or equinoctial circle, or the Zodiac, which imply a three-dimensional orb of Earth around which they turn. From this background, Lewis and Short offered also "a circuit, career, course (of times: mensis, annus, dies)" but not revolution of an orb or a circle about an orb. For medieval Latin Du Cange did not know the word *gyrus* at all, but Henschel could add the form *gyramen*, restricted to the meaning "gyrus, circuitus, orbis" without distinction; this was repeated by Maigne with the French translation "rond, tour, circuit" without clarification of dimensions. Nevertheless, *Thesaurus linguae latinae* recognized *gyrus* "de ipsa caeli vel terrae rotundu forma (vergit ad notionem globi)." And from his sources AD 200–600, Alexander Souter defined the word not only as others had done, "circumference, round about, in a circle round; chain (of stars); spiral staircase," but also *gyrus* in "globular form (of heaven or earth)." Another adjective which implies curvature is *convexus*, used to modify *coelum*, *firmamentum*, *mundus*, and *orbis*, as well as *luna* and *terra*.

Forcellini did not know either *motus coeli* or *motus terrae*, used by Boethius and Cassiodorus. But Freund[1] defined *motus* as "Die Bewegung: *orbes*, *caelum*, *terra*," citing both Cicero, *Republic*, 6.17 ("orbes, qui versantur contrario motu") and Virgil, *Aenid*, 4.297 ("motus crebri terrae"). However, Freund[2] replaced his motions of "orbes, caelum" with "motus astrorum, terrae." Motion of Earth was given again from early Latin by *Thesaurus*: "movere de orbis terrae." For those lexicographers, it seemed that their classical Latin texts had meant to say that Earth could move either around itself or around another body. Those ideas had been bruited about in Hellenistic astronomers but were not accepted by Hipparchus or by Ptolemy, whose notions of a central, immobile Earth eventually prevailed from the late second century forward, supported to some extent by advanced mathematical formulae if not always by the best observations. It should be recognized however that earlier Latin texts may reveal that some writers could assume or assert that Earth moved either by revolving upon its own axis or by following its own orbit about another focus in the heavens, probably around the sun.

Such terms were not given by Lewis and Short or by Oxford, but both cited Virgil: *motus crebri terrae*, the shaking of Earth by an earthquake. They, along with Freund, gave other usages of *motus*, for example "movere de corporis: Gestikulation, Tanz," "cursu temporis," "an activity (of the senses)," "an operation (of the mind)," but not simply *motus terrae* or *motus caeli*. In medieval Latin, Du Cange, Henschel, and Maigne did not know the word at all, so that one could not discover from them any *motus* of the body, of Earth, of the orb of Earth, or of the orb of heavens.

Further sense of *orbis* ought to be found in lemmata for *mundus*, translating Greek κόσμος. Forcellini's lemma for *mundus* began with *munditia*, explained as "universitas rerum, corpus cælo terraque," but ended with "instrumentum ornatus muliebris." Freund reversed this order, giving priority to "Der Schmuck, Putz (der Frauen)" and added "das Geräth, Werkzeug." Lewis and Short kept both meanings in play and retained the universe with heavenly bodies and Earth with its inhabitants; but they also defined *mundus* as "the infernal regions; this world (of sin and death, as opp. to the church or Christ's kingdom)," thus secular as opposed to spiritual. For medieval Latin *mundus*, Du Cange substituted "*saeculum*—le siècle," explaining that "κόσμος usurpatur pro eo quod saeculum Latini Patres vocant." And he was followed by Henschel who added "*mundanalis*—laicus; *mundiales*—homines; muliebris supellectilis; multitudo." Maigne repeated and elaborated these additions. There is confusion in the adjectives *mundanus*, *mundanalis*, and *mundialis*, omitted by Du Cange but defined by the Cangists. Henschel introduced "mundalis, saecularis—mondain"; and Maigne excluded their origin in *mundus* with its meaning of Greek κόσμος, the whole universe, in order to emphasize them all as less than spiritual "*mundanalis*, saecularis—du monde, de siècle," or English mundane.

Nevertheless, that was contrary to all related Latin terms in those same dictionaries and to all the citations accompanying them in Forcellini and Freund, and it was even contrary to the texts cited by Lewis and Short themselves. Indeed, it was contrary to all of the surviving Latin literature and cosmological diagrams. Without being more specific, Du Cange and his successors referred *orbis* only to "Imperium, regnum, dominatio" and to an illustration of Charles the Bald holding an "ornamentum dissimillimum," assuming that his readers would know the Vivian Bible in the royal library.[49] That ornament is not simply decorative as he seemed to have imagined. Rather, it is the *orbis terrarum*, the globe of Earth in three dimensions. Many other uses of the term *orbis* in medieval cosmology and geography were simply ignored by le Sieur Du Cange and his followers. That lexicographical tradition made it easy for Washington Irving to make up the fiction of sailors fearing to fall off the outer edge of a flat earth when their captain, the brilliant Christopher Columbus, set out bravely to discover America. Didn't Columbus prove that Earth was really round and that those stupid sailors and peasants and kings were just so ignorant? Irving's narrative promotes progress, ingenuity, freedom, making it clear that scholars and all Europeans lacked such good sense. Americans loved it and still do, even if the story were totally false, right down to the last detail.[50]

VI

If we may broaden our scope a bit, let us survey ten dictionaries of classical Latin and eighteen lexicons of medieval Latin.[51] A few examples may clarify the patterns of lexicography which continue to infest scholars like a plague. Most lexicographers find in their sources *abacus*. How was it handled?

abacus -i (m.)
Forcellini[1]   [ἄβαξ, ἄβακος] mensa, tabula, in qua aliquid deponitur ad usum, vel ad pompam—banco, credenza, mensa, tavola; tabula, in qua Arithmetici numeros ducunt subinde delendos, & Geometræ

	figuras designant; alveolus aleatorius—scacchiere; crustæ, tabulæve quadratæ e marmore, vitro, quae parietum ornamenta erant; in architectura est quadrata planities in summis columnarum capitulis—abbaco, tagliere, dado. [*Appendix*[1]] adde cit.
Forcellini[2]	Ditto.
Freund[1]	Das Rechenbrett; jedes in Felder abgetheiltes Spielbrett; Schenktisch, Kredentisch; ein mit Musivarbeit kunstvoll verzierten Tischen als Untersatz für Vasen; (arch.) bunte Tafelchen zur Bekleidung der Wände in Prunkzimmern; die obere Platte auf den Kapitälern der Säulen; ein Teller.
Freund[2]	[ἄβαξ] Bank, Platte, Tafel; ein mit Musivarbeit verziertes Tischen, als Untersatz für Vasen und sonstige Kunstgeräthe, Putztisch; Schenktisch, Kredenztisch; ein in Felderabgetheiltes Spiel- oder Rechenbrett; (arch.) die obere Platte auf den Säulenkapitalern.
Georges	[ἄβαξ] der Abecetisch, d.h. das nach dem dekadischen Ziffersystem in viereckige Felder abgetheilte Spielbrett; jedes in Felder abgetheilte Spielbrett; ein, zur Aufstellung der mit einem spitzigen Fuße versehen Weinkrüge; Kredenztisch; (arch.) das Getäfel.
L & S	[ἄβαξ] square tablet, marble sideboard for display; a counting board, divided into compartments for playing dice; counting table covered with sand or dust for arithmetical computation.
Cassell[2]	Counting board; gaming-board divided into compartments; side board; mosaic paneling; (arch.) square slab on the top of a column.
Cassell[4]	Ditto + a square board; painted ceiling panel.
Thesaurus	Mensa simplex, mensa pretiosa; tabula lusoria et aleatoria, alias alveus (alveolus); tabula geometrica, astronomica, geographica falso explicant stilum vel virgam geometricalem.
Oxford	[ἄβαξ] a slab-topped table, sideboard; ornamental panel on a wall or top of a column; counting-board or sand table; board for playing games on.
Du Cange[1]	N/A. Mensa in qua vasa et pocula ad coenam reponuntur.
Du Cange[2]	Nil.
Du Cange[3]	Abacus, Arithmetica: nam Arithmetici, in abaco, vel mensa pulvere conspersa numerorum notas delineabant.
Henschel	Arithmetica vel mensa pulvere.

Maigne	Praetor notos significatus (comptoir, damier, buffet de service, table carrée servant, dans les festins, à déposer les pots et les verres, table de Pythagore), sumitur etiam pro *arithmetica* ipsa, quia arithmetici in abaco, vel mensa pulvere conspersa numerorum notas delinabant. Hinc *libri signati per abacum* sunt codices notis numericis per singulas paginas signati.
Souter	Nil.
Blaise[1]	Nil.
Blaise[2]	N/A. Calcul (méton.); table d'autel; vide *credentia, oblationarium*—crédence (placée du coté de l'épitre).
Niermeyer[1]	N/A. Arithmétique.
Niermeyer[2]	N/A. Ditto.
Wörterbuch	[*ἄβαξ*] tabula calculatoria—Rechenbrett (math.); de partibus vel rationibus abaci (angulus, divisio, figura, finis, linea, meta, norma, numerus, pars, ratio, regula, tabula); Staubtafel; Kolumnenabakus; tabula lusoria ad rhythmimachiam apta—Spielbrett für die Rythmimachie; rechende Hand; Kunst des Abakusrechnens; Abhandlung über das Abakusrechnen; Abdeckungsplatte des Kapitelles; Rückstand von Honig, Wabe.
Iugoslav	Nil.
British	[*ἄβαξ*] reckoning-board, abacus; 'cupboard,' clothes-press or sideboard; (in wordplay) soulless calculator.
Nederland	N/A. [*abactus, abax*] credenstafel; credentia.
Italica[1]	N/A. Abaque, vide *uva.*
Italica[2]	Nil. Vide *abacu*—perper.
Italica[3]	Nil.
Eire	Nil.

The Greek and Roman *abacus*, as an instrument for reckoning with numbers, was well known to lexicographers of classical Latin but apparently not to those of medieval Latin. A simple definition was added in the 1710 edition of Du Cange[3] only after his death. The word was not reported by Souter from sources for AD 180 to 600, nor by Albert Blaise (1954) in his sources for early Christian usage "jusqu'á la fin de la période mérovingienne." Henschel mentioned the word briefly; and Maigne elaborated on several meanings of the word and enlarged upon its use in arithmetical functions. It does not appear in the Lexicon Iugoslav, leaving the impression that people from several nations of that region did not count, surely not the case. The word is improperly defined as equivalent with Arithmetic in the second dictionary by Blaise, those of Nederland and Italia, but it does not appear in the latter two lexica Italicae, nor in Eire, though certainly the *abacus* was used in all of those areas. It is only with the *Mittellateinisches Wörterbuch* that useful information was provided when its first fascicle appeared in 1967.

But very much more is known about the *abacus*, in both classical and medieval usages. It was a mathematical instrument in form of a flat, smooth surface dusted with fine sand, upon which were placed geometrical counters to be manipulated. This surface could be a board, table, or sandy soil. Its uses were often described to be geometrical, as noted especially by the *Thesaurus*.[52] Counters could be unmarked stones or chips (*tesserae, apices, caracteres, contorniates*) placed in order and position right to left to indicate units, sixes, or twelves; alternately, units, fives, tens, or twenties. The counters could also be marked with Hebrew, Arabic, or Greek letters representing numerals, or with Roman figures I, V, X, or even intervening numerals; and coins could be used for the purpose.[53] During both periods, *abacus* took several forms for the purpose of numerical reckoning: one type was divided by a horizontal line, so that addition or subtraction above the line could have results placed below and retained; a second type was divided by both a horizontal and a vertical line, so that more complicated transactions could be handled, left and right, including multiplication and division.

A new form of *abacus* was found by Gerbert of Aurillac in Catalonia and introduced to his students at Reims in AD 983. This was described during AD 991–98 by Richer,[54] as a flat, smooth board but with twenty-seven columns in groups of three for integers 1 to 9; within the ninth group his followers could add an extra symbol, *sipos* in form of a triangle, circle, or cursive letter *a*, perhaps representing an empty space. An early form of this abacus also added three columns for fractions. Each group of three columns for integers was headed by initials C (*centenum*), D (*decenum*), M (*mille*), and S (*singulare*). Each group received a Hindi-Arabic form of numeral with a "Western Arabic" name.[55] The sign ± within a circle ⊕ or a small letter Ⓐ within a circle was the sign of a special marker which could be placed anywhere in this system to ensure proper position of other numerals in units, tens, hundreds, and thousands. As a counting board does not need a numeral to show that a column is empty or null, *sipos* may not yet have served as equivalent with the numeral later called "Arabic zero."[56] These nine "Western Arabic" names appeared only briefly from about AD 1025 to the early twelfth century and did not reappear after the influence of Gerbert waned, but the forms of numerals which accompanied them continued to be used; the circular figure for marker *sipos* or *zepher* came to be called "zero" during the thirteenth to fifteenth centuries, especially in Latin translations of technical writings of arithmetic, geometry, and astronomy.[57]

Lexicographers need not have taken that interesting episode into account. Yet, many other Latin *abacus* texts had been edited and published during the nineteenth century, notably those of Herigerus of Laubach (fl. 970–1007); Abbo of Fleury (ca. 945–1004); Bernelinus of Paris (fl. 1000); Gerlandus compotista (d. ca. 1081/84); Thurkill vel Turchillus compotista (fl. 1115); Adelard of Bath (d. 1150); and Radulphus Laudunensis (d. 1131), as well as the anonymous *Geometria* II, Pseudo-Boethii (s.xi²). No lexicon of medieval Latin referred to any of them in any way before 1967.

The simplest terms of basic astronomy may present even greater difficulties in Latin lexicography. Illustrations of the global heavens are found in hundreds of manuscripts with various terminology to name the wide bands of *klimata* or *plagae* or *zonae*: what we might call "regions of latitude," represented by the lines themselves rather than spaces between lines. Those broad bands of latitude were often projected also from the heavens onto the global Earth. Extreme regions were described in Latin as *frigida* or distinguished as *arcticus* and *antarcticus*. The latter terms have been transliterated into English *arctic* and *antarctic*, of course, so that the reader would never have to look them up. But if you did so, what would you find?

arcticos, arcticus –a –um (adj.)

Forcellini[1]	[ἀρκτικός] settentrionale; ad arctum, hoc est ursam pertiens, quod est signum cæleste, in septentrionali plaga situm; *circulus arcticus* est ad polum septentrionis—il circolo arctico: cui opp. *antarcticus*; vertex antarcticus, antarcticæ terræ.
Freund[1]	[ἀρκτικός] zum Bärgestirn gehörend, nördlich: *arcticus circulus.*
Freund[2]	Ditto; dele 'arcticus circulus.'
Georges	[ἀρκτικός] nördlich.
L & S	[ἀρκτικός] (pertaining to the constellation of the Bear, ἀρκτικός), hence northern, arctic: *circulus.*
Cassell[2]	Nil. Vide *arctos.*
Cassell[4]	Nil. Ditto.
Thesaurus	[ἀρκτικός] circulus, finis, orbis, polus, apex, vertex, septentrionalis.
Oxford	[ἀρκτικός] arctic.
Du Cange[1]	Nil.
Du Cange[2]	Nil.
Du Cange[3]	Nil.
Henschel	Nil.
Maigne	Nil.
Souter	Nil.
Blaise[1]	Nil.
Blaise[2]	Nil.
Niermeyer[1]	Nil.
Niermeyer[2]	Nil.
Wörterbuch	[ἀρκτικός] septentrionalis, aquilonalis—nördlich.

Iugoslav	Nil.
British	[ἀρκτικός] arctic, northern.
Nederland	N/A. [s.xv]
Italica[1]	Nil.
Italica[2]	Nil.
Italica[3]	Nil.
Eire	[articus, arcticus] finis; region, territory.

If your understanding of the heavens and the earth in the texts were dependent upon the definitions provided by our lexicographers, you would have to be careful about which ones you used. When these adjectives were used, were northerly regions or directions specified? Yes, for six classical dictionaries and for two medieval; but no, for the other eighteen which did not define the term at all, including Oxford, which gave only a transliteration, undefined. Related to *arcticos* is *antarcticos*:

antarcticus -a -um (adj.)

Forcellini[1]	[arcticus: ἀνταρκτικός] il circolo antartico, positus in polo meridionali; vertex antarcticus; antarcticæ terrae.
Freund[1]	[ἀνταρκτικός] südlich.
Freund[2]	Ditto.
Georges	Ditto.
L & S	[ἀνταρκτικός] southern.
Cassell[2]	Nil.
Cassell[4]	Nil.
Thesaurus	[ἀνταρκτικός] vertex immobilis.
Oxford	[ἀνταρκτικός] antarctic, southern: polus, circulus.
Du Cange[1]	Nil.
Du Cange[2]	Nil.
Du Cange[3]	Nil.
Henschel	Nil.
Maigne	Nil.
Souter	Nil.
Blaise[1]	Nil.
Blaise[2]	Nil.
Niermeyer[1]	Nil.
Niermeyer[2]	Nil.
Wörterbuch	[ἀνταρκτικός] australis—südlich.
Iugoslav	Nil.
British	[ἀνταρκτικός] antarctic.
Nederland	N/A. [s.xv]
Italica[1]	Nil.
Italica[2]	Nil.
Italica[3]	Nil.
Eire	Nil.

Are southerly regions or directions given for *antarcticus*? Yes. Forcellini[1] is rather good for defining a circular band of latitude of the sky and on Earth, with its *vertex*. That would have scientific use in understanding the descriptive cosmology of classical texts. *Thesaurus* retains the *vertex immobilis*, without a *circulus* in heavens or on Earth. Oxford is better, for it names the southern *circulus* and its *polus*. If, however, you work at your desk with Lewis and Short or the Cassells (or Harper's) which were derived from it, you may continue to assume that *antarcticus* only gives a vague direction and nothing more specific: the simple but necessary terms relative to descriptive cosmology, *circulus* and *polus*, are not there.

Drawings of the five or more circles of latitude for the heavens are included in thousands of medieval Latin manuscripts, corresponding with the texts which explain them—texts and diagrams which have often been published during the eighteenth to twentieth centuries. But was there an arctic circle in the heavens or on Earth? No, for medieval Latin lexicography. Sixteen do not recognize the word *antarcticus* at all. One will turn you towards the south. One transliterates the term without definition. But none of the lexicographers in medieval Latin will tell you that *antarcticus* may modify *circulus* in a descriptive schema of five or more *climata caeli*, or in divisions of the *mundus*, or that this schema is often projected onto *terra* in the prevailing medieval cosmology of every century and every land where there were schools. Nor will they tell you that the *circulus antarcticus* may be envisioned upon that *orbis* with *polus* or *vertex* and was so described in many texts accompanying those diagrams.[58] Something is wrong about this.

VII

The results of this survey of Latin lexicography may be summarized briefly. The evidence is large and inclusive. Thus far, about fifteen hundred Latin nouns, verbs, adjectives, and adverbs which appear in mathematical and scientific texts written before AD 1200 have been recorded, and the definitions of those terms given by twenty-nine dictionaries and lexicons have been compared. Another seven hundred such terms are known, and the number creeps up. In addition, several more medieval lexicons are important and should be included, such as those of Catalonia, where there was significant new mathematics and astronomy in the eleventh and twelfth centuries. Usually for the additional terms, results are similar to what has already been recorded. Many of those terms however were more difficult than the words *arcticus* and *antarcticus*, whose meanings may seem obvious but were in doubt for so many excellent lexicographers. There is some good and some bad in all of this.

The bad news of *scotoma lexicographica* is a record of neglect which extends far beyond Freund and Du Cange. For mathematical and scientific language, the first work by Albert Blaise on early Christian Latin in 1954 for example does define some appropriate terms used in the period before AD 750 but not others, without rhyme or reason. Yet, his second and larger work in 1967 on early medieval Latin deleted the correct definitions of terms that he had found in 1954, terms which continued to be used with scientific meanings throughout his longer period. The work by J. F. Niermeyer (1954–58, 1964, 1976) is strong for language of feudalism and law, as has often been recognized, but it is just hopeless for the Latin scientific culture which was blossoming in the eleventh and twelfth centuries; in this respect the new edition by J. W. J. Burgers (2002) is no improvement. Sources for *Lexica Iugoslavia* (1973–78) and *Lexica Nederlandica* (1970–2005) were restricted to those texts created originally within their regions. The editors interpreted their terms of reference narrowly, so that most early literature which was surely used in their schools and libraries before 1200 in the regions now designated "The Netherlands" are not cited, such as Isidore's *De natura rerum* and Bede's *De temporibus ratione*. Fascicles of *Lexica Italica* have always been published in issues of the *Archivum latinum medii aevi* before being printed as separate books. Its first two versions (1953–2001) are very strange and inconsistent about mathematical and scientific terms, and Editio altera became a word list often without definitions. But the third version now in progress (2002 et seq.) is rather more valuable. The *Dictionary of Medieval Latin from Celtic Sources* has the same limitations as Iugoslav and Nederlandica, but it further excludes lemmata of Latin words used in Eire if they were also classical, that is, if they are known in the *Oxford Latin Dictionary*—a strange requirement which may have been imposed by the funding agency in Ireland.

Such varying parameters for lexicons of medieval Latin are rather parochial. They create very high hurdles for scholars whose standards are of the quality to require their use, for one must have the entire array of lexicons available in order to decipher a text for which the definitions and usages in context are uncertain. It is a rare library in which that is possible.

However, there have been some positive gains in Latin lexicography for scientific terminology. While the *Thesaurus linguae latinae* appears to have excluded mathematical and scientific terms systematically for letters *a* through *m*, its definitions and citation of sources for lemmata beginning with letter *o* have improved, and those for words beginning with letter *p* are quite excellent. One may usually depend upon lemmata of the second half of *Oxford Latin Dictionary*, beginning with letter *m*, though even for that fascicle, there are significant *scotomae* (as explained above for the term, *orbis*). No other dictionaries of classical Latin may be recommended.

For Latin in the early Middle Ages, *Mittellateinisches Wörterbuch* has defined some terms commencing with letters *a*, *b*, *c*, *d*, and *e* with scientific meanings rather well but not others, arbitrarily. Fascicle 19 begins in the middle of the word *comprovincialis*; from that point forward the *Wörterbuch* became more inclusive of scientific terminology and has remained so to the present time, well into lemmata for words beginning with letter *e*. Usually not reliable for letters *a* through *l* is the *Dictionary of Medieval Latin from British Sources*; but there was a change with letter *m*, and since then it has become more dependable. In order to make up for delays in other medieval lexicons, the *Novum glossarium* commenced with letter *l* and has completed letter *o* with some uncertainties and inconsistencies about the language of mathematics and the sciences; but with letter *p*, those aspects of Latin culture are accounted for more fully.[59]

New and critical editions of Latin texts and the analyses of them in many publications have contributed greatly to modern lexicography. Many of those scholars might be called lexicographers professionally who have contributed to a better knowledge of the Latin language. For mathematical and scientific terminology, so long neglected, lexicography began to improve during the 1960s and has flourished especially since the 1980s. Classicists and medievalists however still have to be careful about what they find in dictionaries and lexicons available locally, in order to enjoy the richness of Latin cultures.

Notes

1. *Lexicon totius latinitatis*, consilio et cura Jacobi Facciolati, opera et studio Ægidio Forcellini alumni seminarii Patavini lucubratum, Praefatio a Gaetano Cognolato, 4 vols. (Padua, 1771); hereafter cited as Forcellini[1]. Facciolati (1682–1769) was first the master and then colleague of the younger Forcellini; they conceived of the work together, but evidently he contributed little thereafter. *Addenda et corrigenda* were issued by Joseph Furlanetto (1775–1850) in four parts, the last in 1816, the year of the second edition of Forcellini.

Note that there are changes in definitions of lemmata in second and third editions of some lexicons. In order to distinguish those editions from each other, I have enumerated and cited them separately. Such distinctions have not always been observed by library cataloguers, whose dates, selections of information from titles, and translations into English have often been misleading. Thus, it is necessary to identify some lexicons here with more bibliographical detail than usual.

2. *Lexicon totius latinitatis*, ab Ægidio Forcellini seminarii Patavini alumno lucubratum, Praefatio a Gaetano Cognolato; cura Joseph Furlanetto, 4 vols. (Padua, 1805–16); hereafter cited below as Forcellini[2]. This second edition included occasional revisions by the editor Furlanetto but did not acknowledge Forcellini's *Addenda et corrigenda* to the first edition. Further Italian editions were edited by Francisco Corradini, Joseph Perin, and Vincentius De Vit.

3. François Joseph Michel Noël, *Dictionarium Latino-Gallicum*, composé sur le plan de l'ouvrage intitulé Magnum totius Latinitatis Lexicon, de Facciolati. Nouvelle édition (Paris, 1822).

4. F. G. W. Härtel, A. Voigtländer, C. Lehmann, *Totius latinitatis lexicon . . .*, secundum tertiam editionem, cuius curam gessit J. Furlanetto, correctum et auctum labore variorum, 4 vols. (1831–35). The first two volumes were published by Schumann in Schneeberg

(Austria) and the second two in Leipzig by Hahn. The four volumes were reprinted together in 1839 by Hahn, and in 1913 and 1920 by Schumann.

5. James Bailey, *Totius latinitatis lexicon*, concillio et cura Jacobi Facciolati, opera et studio Ægidio Forcellini . . . edidit, Anglicam interpretationem in locum italicae substituit (London, 1826); there was a new edition enlarged by Bailey (London, 1828). Joseph Edmond Riddle, *Totius latinitatis lexicon: A Dictionary of the Latin language* . . . , revised and translated into English (Oxford, 1835). Frederick Percival Leverett, *A New and Copious Lexicon of the Latin Language*, compiled chiefly from the Magnum Totius Latinitatis Lexicon of Facciolati and Forcellini, and the German works of Scheller and Lünemann (London, 1837). Scheller and Lünemann are mentioned below in note 7.

6. *Wörterbuch der lateinischen Sprache*, nach historisch-genetischen Principien, bearbeitet von Dr. Wilhelm Freund, 4 vols. (Leipzig 1834–45); hereafter cited as Freund[1]. He was the rector of the Hebrew Academy in Vienna and was prominent in social and political affairs.

7. K. E. Georges, *Lateinisch-Deutches Handwörterbuch*, nach Jmm. Joh. Gerh. Scheller und Georg Heinr. Lünemann, Achte vielfach verbesserte und vermehrte Auflage, vol. 1, A–J, vol. 2, L–Z (Leipzig, 1837, 1838). Although the title also said: "neu bearbeitet von Dr. Karl Ernst Georges," he informed the users that he was reworking the seventh edition by Lünemann on the basis of Freund but had only reached lemmata for letters *a–e* and a few articles for letter *f* before the publisher required him to publish. That process may not have been complete for the eighth edition (1839) before his death. But K. E. Georges was said to be responsible for the "Neunte, gänzlich umgearbeitete Auflage des Scheller-Lünemannischen Handwörterbuches" (Leipzig, 1843); that was reaffirmed by his grandson, Heinrich, when the *Lateinisch-Deutches Handwörterbuch* was reissued in 1913 by Hahn Verlag in Leipzig.

8. *Gesammtwörterbuch der lateinischen Sprache*, zum Schul- und Privat-Gebrauch, von Wilhelm Freund, 2 vols. (Breslau, 1844–45)—a shorter version hereafter cited as Freund[2].

9. J. E. Riddle, *A Copious and Critical Latin-English Lexicon*, founded on the German-Latin dictionaries of Dr. William Freund (London, 1849). This was revised and reissued in the same year by Charles Anthon for the first American edition (1849) and reissued in England both by Thomas Kerchener Arnold (1859, 1860) and by John Tabourdin White (1862, 1869).

10. E. A. Andrews, *A Copious and Critical Latin-English Lexicon*, founded on the larger Latin-German lexicon of Dr. William Freund; with additions and corrections from the Lexicons of Gesner, Facciolati, Scheller, Georges, etc. (New York, 1851). There were new editions in New York by Harper (1852, 1854, 1855, 1865) and in London by Sampson Low (1853). Thereafter Harper also controlled the sales in England.

11. Digital versions of Lewis and Short (L & S) are now offered by two sources: the first is available without charge from http://archimedes.fas.harvard.edu/pollux/, though its use is often interrupted by malfunction of the site; the second is available by subscription to the Database of Latin Dictionaries, Corpus Christianorum and brepolis@brepols .net. James Dobreff (Classics, University of Massachusetts, Boston) has brought it to my attention that there may have been a few corrections to later digital versions of L & S, for example, in the lemma for *orbis*.

12. Major improvements in recent lexicography since the mid-1960s are cited below.

13. *Glossarium ad scriptores mediae et infimae latinitatis*, auctore Carolo du Fresne Domino Du Cange, 3 vols. (Paris, 1678); hereafter cited as Du Cange[1].

14. *Appendix ad glossarium mediae et infimae latinitatis*, in *Glossarium ad scriptores mediae et infimae Graecitatis* (Lyon, 1688), vol. 2, pt. 13, cols. 1–244; hereafter cited as Du Cange[2]. The *Appendix* cites additional sources (usually later than our period) and was not intended to serve as an independent glossary. Nevertheless, it includes usages of some terms not found in the 1678 *Glossarium* of Du Cange. We have used the first edition (1678) and the *Appendix* (1688) in print.

15. *Glossarium ad scriptores mediae et infimae latinitatis*, auctore Carolo du Fresne Domino Du Cange, 3 vols. (Frankfurt a.M., 1710); hereafter cited as Du Cange[3]. The 1710 edition is accessible online from http://www.uni-mannheim.de/mateo/camenaref/ducange.html.

16. *Glossarium mediae et infimae latinitatis*, conditum a Carolo Du Fresne Domino Du Cange auctum a monachis ordinis s. Benedicti cum supplementis integris D. P. Carpenterii, Adelungii, aliorum, suisque digesset G. A. L. Henschel, 7 vols. (Paris, 1840–50); hereafter cited as Henschel. This was reprinted without change at Paris: Librairie des Sciences et des Arts, 1937.

17. *Lexicon manuale ad scriptores mediae et infimae latinitatis*, par W.-H. Maigne d'Arnis (publié par M. l'Abbé Migne, Paris, 1858; repr., 1866); hereafter cited as Maigne.

18. *Glossarium mediae et infimae latinitatis*, conditum a Carolo Du Fresne Domino Du Cange auctum a monachis ordinis s. Benedicti cum supplementis integris D. P. Carpenterii, Adelungii, aliorum, suisque digesset G. A. L. Henschel sequuntur Glossarium Gallicum, Tabulae, Indices auctorum et rerum, Dissertationis. Editio Nova aucta pluribus verbis aliorum scriptorum a Léopold Favre, 12 vols. (Niort, 1883–87), including Du Cange's long essays on numismatics and on Constantinople. The Favre version is compacted into fewer bindings and smaller fonts in subsequent reprints. Neither Du Cange (1678) nor Henschel (1850) is found online. Rather, it is the later edition (1887) which is in the Database of Latin Dictionaries, part of *Brepolis Latin*, offered by subscription at brepolis@brepols.net. The huge *Brepolis Latin* gives online access to all series of Latin texts published in print by Corpus Christianorum and much else, but it is not enumerated as an item of CC.

19. In the following records, Nil means that the term is not a lemma in a lexicon and has not been located within definitions of other words. N/A means that the term is present as a lemma but without the mathematical or scientific meaning found in Latin sources prior to AD 1200. A Greek word from which the Latin term is derived or a variant form of the term is given in square brackets if provided by that dictionary. Ditto refers to repetition of the definition in the preceding lexicon or in the one named, either in whole or in part. Ditto + means that a previous definition has been repeated with additions. Dele means that the text following in 'single quotation marks' has been deleted from the previous definition being used by the lexicographer.

20. Cf. Oxford "[πέλαγος, πλάξ] an open expanse (of land, sea, or sky), tract; a territory, region; a climatic region, zone." *Mittellateinisches Wörterbuch* has not reached letter *p* for *plaga* but, as one definition of the word *clima*, it gives "plaga caeli—Weltgegend, Himmelsrichtung."

21. Cf. Oxford "[ζώνη] any of the imagined bands encircling the earth, a celestial zone; (medical) shingles." The *Oxford Latin Dictionary* also found additional usages for *zona*: "an encircling band or marking; (as used by a man) a girdle to hold up the tunic, esp. incorporating a pouch to hold money; (as worn by a woman) by unmarried girls, hence its removal signifying loss of virginity."

22. It should be noticed that in 1710 the term *apocatastasis* was added to lemmata of

Du Cange[3], and in 1887 *arcus vel arquus* was added to the Favre edition with definitions recognizing scientific usages.

23. Walter Pohl, "History in Fragments," *Early Medieval Europe* 10 (2001): 343–74, esp. "Some methodolical remarks," concerning tension between "realities of the mind" and the fact that "things really happened in the past" (345).

24. Forcellini: "*orbis*—circulo, cerchio, sfera, ruota, giro—circulus, sphæra, globus; proprie differt a globo: *orbis* enim de plano corpore circulari dicitur, *globus* de solido rotundo." Cicero, *De natura deorum*, 2.18: "cum duae formae praesantes sind, ex solidis globus (sic enim σφαῖραν interpretari placet) ex planis autem circulus, aut orbis, qui κύκλος Graece dicitur."

25. Titus Livius (59 BC–AD 17), *Ab urbe condita libri CXLII*: "Oceanus, qui orbem terrarum amplexu finit," repeated by Lucanus and Macrobius, though the latter adapts it to the four-part spherical Earth in *Commentari*, 2.9. Cicero, *De lege agraria*, 2.13: "permittitur infinita potestas orbis terrarum."

26. Mary Gratia Ennis, *Vocabulary of the Institutiones of Cassiodorus* (Washington, DC, 1939), 60: the Latin word for a warrior's shield is *clypeus*, for which *orbis* is not used.

27. For the explanation of Earth divided into four parts by equatorial and meridonal streams of Ocean which collide at the poles, see Ambrosii Theodosii Macrobii, *Commentarii in Somnium Scipionis*, ed. J. Willis (Leipzig, 1963), 2.9; cf. 1.14: "novem tibi orvilus vel potius globi convexa sunt omnia"; 168.15; 224.12; 274.2. Martianus Minneus Felix Capella, *De nuptiis Philologiae et Mercurii libri IX*, ed. J. Willis (Leipzig, 1983); ed. A. Dick (Leipzig, 1925), book 6 (p. 196). Explanations of the spherical Earth by Macrobius and Martianus are summarized by W. H. Stahl in the introduction to his translation of *Macrobius, Commentary on the Dream of Scipio* (New York, 1952), 16–17 and 48–49. See also Tertullianus, *Apologeticus*, 16: "orbis terrae"; Cassianus, *Collationes*, 19.1.2; Gildas, *De excidio et conquestu Britanniae*, 8; Bede, *In Proverbia*, 1029; Frithegodus, *Vita metrica s.Wilfridi*, 34; Egbertus, *Fecunda ratis*, 1.355: "equos a puncto formabit circinus orges"; Waltherus Spirensis, *Vita Christophori*, 1.206: "quinque parallelos Urania complicate orbes"; *Geometria* II anonymi: "nam CCLII milia stadiorum circuitum universi terreni orbis esse pronuntiavit" (ed. N. M. Bubnov, *Gerberti Opera mathematica* [Berlin, 1889; repr. Ann Arbor, 2005], p. 363).

28. Extant fragments of authentic writing and the notions of later commentators from a hundred to a thousand years later have often been accepted at equal value by historians of science. A more discriminating evaluation of cosmological ideas of the pre-Socratic/Greeks is by D. R. Dicks, *Early Greek Astronomy to Aristotle* (London, 1970); see especially 39–42 on method.

29. At various levels of reliability, the evidence for ideas of Philolaus in southern Italy (fifth and fourth centuries BC), Hicetas and Ecphantus of Syracuse (ca. 400 BC), and Heraclides of Pontus (ca. 390–310 BC) is carefully assessed by Dicks, *Early Greek Astronomy to Aristotle*, 65–66, 73–74, 132–37.

30. Plato, *Timaeus*, 63a; Aristotle, *De caelo*, 2.14.298a; Eudoxos: see Claude Nicolet, *Space, Geography, and Politics in the Early Roman Empire* (Ann Arbor, 1991), 59 and notes.

31. F. S. Betten, "Knowledge of the Sphericity of the Earth during the Earlier Middle Ages," *Catholic Historical Review*, n.s., 3 (1923): 74–90; C. W. Jones, "The Flat Earth," *Thought* 9 (1934): 296–307; W. M. Stevens, "The Figure of the Earth in Isidore's *De natura rerum*," *ISIS* 71 (1980): 268–77 (repr. in *Cycles of Time and Scientific Learning in Medieval Europe*, Collected Studies of Wesley M. Stevens [Aldershot, 1995]), item 3; Ste-

vens, "Cosmology and the Earth," cols. 143a–145b, and "Earth, Models of (before 1600)," cols. 182b–88a, in *The History of the Geosciences: An Encyclopedia*, ed. Gregory A. Good (New York, 1995); Stevens, "Rappresentazione della Terra," in *Storia della Scienza*, vol. 4, *Medioevo, Rinascimento* (Rome, 2001), pt. 1, cols. 179–83.

32. E. H. Bunbury, *A History of Ancient Geography*, 2nd ed., 2 vols. (1883; repr. New York, 1959), 1:33–36 and 75; E. H. Warmington, *Greek Geography* (1934; repr. New York, 1973), xiii–xvi: "The new ways of thinking . . . that the earth is not a planet, but the stationary centre of a 'kosmos' . . . or 'universe'"; J. O. Thomson, *History of Ancient Geography* (Cambridge, 1948), 94–95: "The Earth-Disk . . . a flat (or at best a tilted or concave) disk."

33. René Taton, "Phénice et Israël," ch. 3 in *La science antique et médiévale*, vol. 1 of *Histoire Générale des Sciences*, 2nd rev. ed. (Paris, 1966), 141: "la Terre, le continent, est comme un disque émergeant sur cet Océan cosmique." Thomas Africa, *Science and the State in Greece and Rome* (New York, 1968), 88, imagined that Earth was supposed to take the shape of a box, though sources are lacking.

34. C. Raymond Beazley, *The Dawn of Modern Geography* (1897; repr. New York, 1949), 44–45; J. K. Wright, "Early Christian Belief in a Flat Earth," in Wright, *Geographical Lore of the Time of the Crusades* (1925; repr. New York, 1965), 53–54 and 384n48.

35. Marina Smyth, *Understanding the Universe in Seventh-Century Ireland* (Rochester, NY, 1996), 81, 108–9, 113.

36. G. H. T. Kimble, *Geography in the Middle Ages* (London, 1938), 31. Maria Rissel, *Rezeption antiker und patristischer Wissenschaft bei Hrabanus Maurus* (Bern, 1976), reviewed two of Hraban's teaching manuals, *De computo* and *Excerpta Prisciani*, as well as his reflections upon teaching, *De institutione clericorum*, from which she concludes that Hraban was unsure about the rotundity of Earth. She based this judgment upon his use of Bedae *De temporum ratione*, but omission of chs. 32 to 34, in which Bede's evidence and arguments for the sphericity of Earth are excellent. Rissel however seems to have overlooked *De rerum naturis*, 12.2. See a review of her interesting study by Stevens in *Speculum* 55 (1980): 829–31.

37. Rudolf Bultmann, *New Testament and Mythology*, trans. Shubert M. Ogden (Philadelphia, 1984), 1.

38. *The Anchor Bible Dictionary*, ed. David Noel Freedman et al. (New York, 1992). This multivolume dictionary was reissued by Yale University Press (2005).

39. R. A. Oden Jr., "Cosmology in the NT," in *Anchor Bible Dictionary*, 1:1167b–68a; W. Janzen, "Earth in the NT," ibid., 2:247a–b; Raphael, ibid. 2:964a–b; Alexander, ibid., 3:979. Those were not Jewish or early Christian concepts. See Anna-Dorothea von den Brincken, *Fines Terrae. Die Enden der Erde und der vierte Kontinent auf mittelalterlichen Weltkarten*, MGH Schriften (Hannover, 1992), 36, 60–62, evidently revising her earlier views published from 1973 to 1976.

40. Wanda Wolska, *La topographie chrétienne de Cosmas Indicopleustes* (Paris, 1962); Marshall Clagett, *Greek Science in Antiquity*, 2nd ed. (New York, 1963), 169, 175–76, 179, 207–17.

41. Eva G. R. Taylor, "Some Notes on Early Ideas on the Form and Size of the Earth," *Geographical Journal* 85 (1935): 64–68; G. R. Taylor, *Ideas on the Shape, Size and Movements of the Earth*, Historical Association Pamphlet 126 (London, 1943). Steven Weinberg, "Without God," a talk given on June 3, 2008, and published in *New York Review of Books*, September 25, 2008, 73–76.

42. Martianus Capella, *De nuptiis* (see n. 27, above).

43. In the meantime, Ennis, *Vocabulary of the Institutiones*, 45, had cited the sources used by those lexicographers: Plautus, Cato, Varro, Cicero, Lucretius, Sallustius, Nepos, Vergilius et alii, to mean "a ball, sphere, celestial body," though not to describe Earth, as most of those writers did. She was more interested in Cassiodor's use of *globus* for eye, eyeball in his *Institutio*, 2.22.26, citing also Chalcidius and Paulus or Paulinus Nolanus.

44. Crates of Mallos and Pergamum described "orbis quadrifariam duplici discretus oceano" in some detail; he is known through fragments, for which see Hans J. Mette, *Sphairopoiia: Untersuchungen zur Kosmologie des Krates von Pergamon* (Munich, 1936). Thomson, *History of Ancient Geography*, 202–3, held this image up for ridicule, but it is found in many Greek and Latin texts. Ennis, *Vocabulary of the Institutiones*, 17, cited some of the following uses of *quadrifarius* or *quadratus* with reference to *orbis*, *mundus*, or *terra*: Arnobius Afer (fl. 295), Hieronymus Stridonensis (ca. AD 347–420), Aurelius Augustinus (AD 354–430); Cassiodorus Senator (d. ca. 570), *Institutio* 1.22.8: "quadrivaria divisione"; *Variae*, 1.45.5; 3.51.5; proem. 86. In addition, notice Ambrosius Mediolanensis (AD 339–397), *De Abraham*, 2.7.37: "oriens enim et occidens et septentrio det meridies . . . totus orbis . . . ," that is, God's promise to Abraham included the whole world with its four parts, extending in four directions "to the North and to Africa, and to the East and to the sea" (Genesis 13:14), ed. C. Schenkl, CSEL 32.1 (Vienna, 1897), 498–638. Augustinus, *In Joannis Evangeliuim*, 24, referred to four quarters of the earth, cited by Henry P. Smith, *Essays in Biblical Interpretation* (London, 1921), 335; that the earth is a sphere was asserted: *De Genesi ad litteram*, 1.10, ed. J. Zycha, CSEL 28.1 (Vienna, 1894), 15.6; *Quaestiones evangelicarum*, 2.14, PL 35, col. 1339; *De civitate dei libri*, 16.9–17, ed. Bernard Dombart, Alphons Kalb, 4th ed., 2 vols. (Leipzig, 1878–79) (repr. CCSL 47–48 [Turnhout, 1955]). Notice that lack of evidence for people called *antipodae* does not imply rejection of the globe or its parts. Aldhelm (ca. AD 650–709/10), *Aenigmata*, ed. Rudolf Ehwald, MGH Auct. ant. 15, no. 58 (Vesper Sidus), 2: "occidua mundi complector cardine partes" (cardinal parts of the globe are four, located in regions indicated by directions). *Liber de ordine creaturarum*, 11.2, "orbis quadratus," ed. Manuel C. Díaz y Díaz (Santiago de Compostela, 1972), 168, often attributed to Isidore or called Pseudo-Isidore. (For this citation, I am grateful to John Carey, Harvard, who also pointed out references for the five zones and the three parts of *oikumenê* in Irish evidence.) Beda Venerabilis (ca. AD 680–735), *Expositio actuum apostolorum et retractatio*, ed. Max L. W. Laistner (Cambridge, MA, 1939): "quia per quattuor partes orbis terrarum mysterium Sanctae Trinitatis a duodecim apostolis praedicandum erat."

45. For his definition of *quadrificus*—quadripartite, Niermeyer later found *per orbem quadrificum*, citing a text from AD 873 in *Gallia christiana in provincias ecclesiasticas distributa*, 2nd ed., 16 vols. (Paris 1715–1865), vol. 4, col. 226. Like other lexicographers, he neglected this usage in his *lemma* for *orbis*.

46. Paschasius Radbertus, *Commentarium in Mattheum*, 9 pr., PL, 120, col. 646. This was cited by Albert Blaise, *Dictionnaire Latin-Français des auteurs du moyen-âge: Lexicon latinitatis medii aevi, praesertim ad res ecclesiasicas investigandas pertinens*, CCCM (Turnhout, 1975). Another example of medieval usage is one page from Oxford, Bodleian Library, MS Douce 180, called the Douce Apocalypse, which included the phrase *super quatuor partes terre*. The image of the *mundus* or *kosmos* on that page was projected onto Earth in four parts, quite common in early Latin literature, both classical and early medieval.

47. Cicero (106–43 BC), *Oratio pro Sesto*, 61.129: "qui tripartitus orbis terrarum oras atque regionas notarit"; Macrobius (fl. AD 400), *Commentarium in Somnium Scipionis libri*

duo, ed. J. Willis (Leipzig, 1970): 168.15; 224.12; 274.2: "orbis tripartitus or tripertitus."
They both referred to two, three, or four parts of the globe, but in these quotations they
seem to have meant three regions of the northeast quarter of *orbis quadratus,* elsewhere
called Asia, Africa, Europa. Macrobius was also edited by Franz Eyssenhardt (2nd ed.
[Leipzig, 1893]).

For the common classical references to the globe of earth in two parts of *orbis quadratus: occidens* ① *oriens,* see Árpád Szabo, "Roma quadrata," *Rheinisches Museum* 87 (1938):
160–69, and Szabo, "Roma quadrata," *Maia* (1956): 243–74.

48. *Orbis quadratus* was also omitted in three articles "prepared from materials supplied by Germaine Aujac" for *The History of Cartography,* ed. J. B. Harley and David
Woodward (Chicago, 1987): "The Foundations of Theoretical Cartography in Archaic
and Classical Greece" (130–47), "The Growth of an Empirical Cartography in Hellenistic
Greece," (148–60), "Greek Cartography in the Early Roman World" (161–76). Among
others who continue this oversight was Natalia Lozovsky, *The Earth Is Our Book: Geographical Knowledge in the Latin West ca.400–1000* (Ann Arbor, 2000), 41–45.

49. Paris, Bibliothèque nationale de France, MS lat.1, with numerous and lavish illu-
minations, presented by Count Vivien or Vivian, lay abbot of St. Martin's, Tours, when
the king visited that abbey in AD 846. The figure is printed often, e.g., Ingo F. Walther and
Norbert Wolf, *Codices illustres: The World's More Famous Illuminated Manuscripts, 400 to
1600* (Cologne, 2005).

50. Washington Irving, *The Life and Voyages of Christopher Columbus* (London, 1828).
A good account of this wishful thinking was given by Jeffrey B. Russell, *Inventing the Flat
Earth: Columbus and Modern Historians* (Westport, CT, 1991), with a foreword by David
Noble.

51. In addition to information about them in footnotes above, these dictionaries and
lexicons have been described by Stevens in his "Numerus in se facere," *Archivum latinitatis
medii aevi* 65 (Paris 2007): 117–64, esp. 124; and earlier articles there cited. Notice that
Du Cange[2] cites his *Appendix* (1688), which is intended only to be a supplement for citations omitted from the *Glossarium* (1678). Nevertheless, it sometimes adds new meanings
to the previous definitions.

52. Cited from London, BL, MS Harley 3376, ed. *Archiv* 1 (1884) 150. Additional
sources for *abacus* are Persius, Apuleius, Vitruvius, Hieronymus, and others.

53. Elizabeth Alföldi-Rosenbaum, "The Finger Calculus in Antiquity and in the
Middle Ages," *Frühmittelalterliche Studien* 5 (1971): 1–9.

54. *Historiae,* 3.43 and 54 = Richerus Remensis, *Historiarum libri IV,* ed. Robert
Latouche (Paris, 1930–37); a new edition by Hartmut Hoffmann, MGH SS 38 (2000),
35–309, 310–11.

55. Menso Folkerts, "Frühe westliche Benennungen der indisch-arabishen Ziffern
und ihr Vorkommen," in *"Sic itur ad astra": Studien zur Geschichte der Mathematik und
Natur wissenschaften; Festschrift für den Arabisten Paul Kunitzsch zum 70. Geburtstag,* ed.
Menso Folkerts and Andreas Kühne (Wiesbaden, 2000), 216–33.

56. Gillian A. Evans, "Difficillima et Ardua: Theory and Practice in Treatises on the
Abacus, 950–1150," *Journal of Medieval History* 3 (1977): 21–38.

57. Further discussion of these numerals is by Folkerts, "Frühe westliche Benennungen"; Richard Lorch, "Greek-Arabic-Latin: The Transmission of Mathematical Texts in
the Middle Ages," *Science in Context* 14 (2001): 313–31; Paul Kunitzsch, *Zur Geschichte
der 'arabischen' Ziffern,* Sitzungsberichte der Bayerische Akademie der Wissenschaften,

Philosophisch-historische Klasse 3 (Munich, 2005); Wesley M. Stevens, "Addo et Sub-traho: Medieval Glosses to Modern Lexicography," in *"Inquiriens subtilia diversa": Dietrich Lohrmann zum 65. Geburtstag,* ed. Horst Kranz and Ludwig Falkenstein (Aachen, 2002), 237–59; and several essays by Charles Burnett in his *Collected Studies: Numerals and Arithmetic in the Middle Ages* (Farnham: Ashgate Variorum, 2010).

58. *Apex* was used as a synonym for *polus* or *vertex* in mathematical contexts, but that usage has not been found in classical or medieval texts of descriptive cosmology.

59. Funding for *British Sources* was briefly suspended by the British Academy, then renewed when the Hewlett Packard Foundation (USA) began to support *British Sources*. The situation was similar for the *Novum glossarium*, first published in Copenhagen; after funds were withheld by the Danish Research Institute, it was supported by the French and German national research systems and is now based in Paris. This international support continues fruitfully, though it is sufficient for only a single member of staff—a restriction which is absurd. Given the high quality of its published fascicles, the *Novum glossarum* is often referred to as "The New Du Cange."

CHAPTER 8

Renovatio Abroad:
The Politics of Education in Carolingian Italy

STEVEN A. STOFFERAHN

In the spring of 825, the young king Lothar (795–855) was a troubled man. Though titularly equal to his father, he found himself relegated to overseeing imperial affairs in the Carolingian subkingdom of Italy, an assignment he must have understood as a kind of banishment from the northern Frankish heartlands, where from his perspective most things of any real importance happened. Almost three years had passed since Louis the Pious had sent him away, and there looked to be no immediate end to this tenure in sight. This was especially unsettling, given the birth in 823 of his new stepbrother, Charles the Bald, whose mother was doing her level best to secure his future, largely at Lothar's expense. With that threat on the horizon, along with the potential troubles posed by Louis's other partial heirs, Lothar must have found his own position in Italy rather galling.[1] He was, in theory, the chief representative there of Carolingian authority; yet the reality of that title proved elusive, since his father sought to maintain his own grip on imperial power. As long as this debilitating situation persisted, Lothar knew that his own future viability as emperor lay open to assault. Something clearly had to be done. So it was that he used one of his earliest independent capitularies to make a subtle but effective power play. Subtle, because it adopted the ingenious appearance of educational reform so familiar to the successors of Charlemagne; and effective, since the plan fit perfectly into the broader continuum of the Carolingian *renovatio*. Indeed, it fit so well that not only did it draw upon earlier reform plans but even influenced subsequent efforts. By considering, then, a key chapter of Lothar's 825 Olona capitulary in its immediate political and cultural context, one may push an analysis of it past either educational reform or political maneuverings, and toward a more pragmatic fusion of the two.

The story of Carolingian Italy began, of course, long before Lothar's rule there did. After Pippin III's initial forays against the Lombards in support of the papacy, Charlemagne established Frankish control in earnest over the northern and central parts of the peninsula through his victory over King Desiderius in 774. While the Lombards were allowed to retain many of their traditional rights and practices, the ensuing decades nevertheless witnessed the integration of successive waves of Franks, Alemans, and Bavarians into the administrative structure of the new realm.[2] Only in 781 did Charlemagne's son, Pippin, assume direct command of the province as subking. At Pippin's death in 813, rule in turn passed to his son, Bernard. No real problems arose between the new Italian ruler and his uncle, Emperor Louis the Pious, until the latter issued the famous *Ordinatio Imperii* in 817, a blueprint for imperial succession and division of territories whose provisions conspicuously excluded Bernard.[3] Failing in his quest to gain confirmation of his authority, a rebellious Bernard was captured in the fall of 817 and died on April 17, 818, two days after having his eyes gouged out.[4] Louis left Italy in the hands of his intendants for the next five years, although his trust in their abilities began to falter after the revolt of the Croat prince Ljutewit in the early 820s. The time was therefore ripe for a change in policy concerning the administration of far-flung territories. Immediately following the dramatic proceedings of the imperial assembly at Attigny in August 822, Louis dispatched sons as subkings for two of the empire's most important provinces: Pippin to Aquitaine and Lothar to Italy.

Studies on Lothar have traditionally focused on his role in the revolts of the 830s and civil wars of the early 840s. If any attention has been given to his time in Italy, it has usually centered on his sojourn there from 834 until his reconciliation with Louis in 839.[5] It is in these latter years—often viewed through the lens of intensifying Frankish cultural influence in Italy, and hence the shaping of a *regnum Italiae* in place of the former *regnum Langobardorum*—that Lothar has been seen as free at last to pursue his own goals according to his own wishes. Yet his early tenure in Italy merits special notice as well, particularly with regard to the development of his authority. While the appellation "Hlotarius augustus invictissimi domni imperatoris Hludowici filius" featured in several early charters hardly indicates a state of independence, this should not preclude serious consideration of Lothar's own rule there. In terms of residency, he seems to have been active in Italy between September 822 and May 823, then again from August 824 to June 825, before returning to Francia to be officially named as co-emperor at Aachen and to rule the empire jointly with his father until their break in 829. While in Italy, he spent most of his time at the royal courts of Aureola and

Olona, both in the northwestern part of the realm. His activity was far from limited to these centers, however—a fact well illustrated by two important trips to Rome. The *Annales regni francorum* records that on his way back to Francia in the spring of 823, Lothar was summoned by Paschal to the papal see where on Easter Sunday he received the title of emperor—an arrangement calculated, it seems, to emphasize his precedence over his younger brothers. Then, in the fall of 824, Louis dispatched Lothar to Rome to impose upon the papacy the so-called Roman Constitution, a tool whereby the Carolingians could keep closer tabs on papal affairs. Jörg Jarnut has made a strong case for viewing the 824 Roman Constitution as the royal son's first earnest expression of his own political authority.[6] But while this act may well have introduced Lothar into the realm of early medieval *Weltpolitik*, one must also remember that he was, after all, on an errand for his father—the constitution having already been set forth by Louis (although Lothar does seem to have taken some liberties in its application). One is thus left to search for an even clearer expression of Lothar's coming of age—a transition that can more properly be identified with the promulgation in May 825 of an innovative reform plan for the Italian kingdom's educational system. It was through this action that the young Carolingian articulated not just his vision for school reform but his own nascent sense of political independence as well.[7]

Addressing himself primarily to the bishops of his new realm, Lothar used the sixth chapter of the *Capitulare Olonnense ecclesiasticum primum* to set forth his plan for improving the quality of education in the *regnum Italiae*. Its goals were ambitious, its strategy meticulously crafted:

> Concerning learning, which because of the great negligence and laziness of certain *praepositi* is everywhere totally extinguished, it would please us that everyone observe what we have ordered, namely that those whom we have arranged to teach others in specified places do so with the greatest zeal so that the students entrusted to them might progress and pursue learning as present times require. For the convenience of everyone, we have provided handsomely for suitable places in this endeavor so that no one might be excused because of the difficulty of great distance and poverty. Therefore, first let them come to Dungal in Pavia from Milan, Brescia, Lodi, Bergamo, Novare, Vercelli, Tortona, Acqui, Genoa, Asti, Como; in Ivrea let the bishop be in charge; in Turin let them come from Ventimiglia, Albenga, Vado, Alba; in Cremona, they will teach [those students] from Reggio, Piacenza, Parma, Modena; from Tuscany, they will look to Florence; they will come from [the duchy of] Spoleto to Fermo; to Verona from Mantua and Trent; to Vicenza from Padua, Treviso, Feltre, Ceneda, Asolo; and from the remaining cities they will come to the school in Cividale del Friuli.[8] [See Fig. 1.]

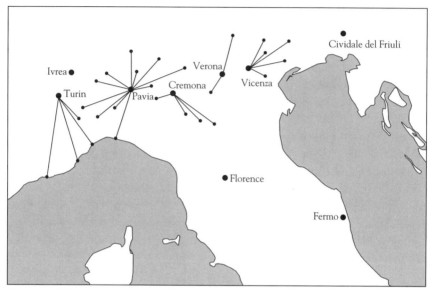

Figure 1. Educational Centers Envisioned in Lothar's Olona Plan of 825

Key aspects of this series of directives have attracted the attention of generations of historians. Not least debated among them has been Lothar's sweeping claim that learning itself was "everywhere totally extinguished" in Italy by the early ninth century. A century ago, Georg Hörle argued that the sophistication of early medieval Italian literary culture abruptly disintegrated as a direct result of the Lombards' lost independence. Arrigo Solmi concurred that the splendor of Lombard education in the eighth century gave way to decadence in the early ninth, in sad and surprising contrast to the "vivace florimento degli studi in Francia."[9] Subsequent studies, however, have since ameliorated such stark assessments. Ugo Gualazzini, for one, acknowledged that while early ninth-century Italian scholars may have lagged behind the achievements of their Frankish and Irish contemporaries, Lothar's claim was almost certainly an exaggeration.[10] In his overview of the history of Italian schooling, Giuseppe Manacorda likewise noted evident survivals of educational activity well after the defeat of the Lombards and before Lothar's decree of 825, especially at the cathedral schools of Milan and Verona and the palace school at Pavia. He also drew attention to Bishop Podone of Piacenza (808–39), whose epitaph celebrated his excellent education, steeped as it was in the works of Virgil, Ovid, and Venantius Fortunatus.[11] The fact that even Piacenza, a town not deemed worthy of serving as a gathering point for scholars according to the 825 plan, could feature such an erudite scholar would seem to undercut Lothar's condemnation of the kingdom's universal ignorance. True, the state of learning probably had declined to some degree, but several centers clearly continued to attract worthy students and teachers.

Another point of contention has revolved around the type of school Lothar had in mind for the object of his reforms and patronage. In contrast to earlier arguments that the centers enumerated in the Olona project were to be ecclesiastical schools dedicated to the preparation of the clergy (because the king had issued his order in a *capitulare ecclesiasticum* and had referred to *doctrina* rather than *studia litterarum* or *studia liberalium artium*), Hörle and Solmi contended that the plan in fact envisioned the revival of schools for the laity, or perhaps "mixed" schools for both clergy and laity emphasizing the trivium and quadrivium. The meaning of *doctrina* was not, they believed, limited to Christian doctrine, but rather embodied learning of all kinds, including reading, grammar, computus, music, theology, and even philosophy.[12] In this view, Lothar was seen as working with and through his bishops to hold up the school at Pavia as a model for other centers, with the ultimate goal of forming "un nuovo ordinamento scolastico" based on the liberal arts.[13]

Finally, the scheme's organizational structure has itself inspired intense speculation. Gualazzini believed it to be a mere matter of practicality. Since it was not feasible to sponsor schools in all the important bishoprics and towns of Carolingian Italy, the best alternative was simply to consolidate students and teachers in a few major centers.[14] Giuseppe Salvioli, however, maintained (like so many other Italian scholars before and since) that the plan of 825 did not necessarily indicate a wholly new development, but rather a revitalization of the earlier Lombard educational system.[15] Most generally convincing, however, is Solmi's conclusion that topography and geography must have played the most formative role in constructing the Olona strategy. The working idea in Lothar's mind, he argued, was that the schools ought to lie in cities that were both easily accessible and, if possible, traditional administrative centers. Pavia, for example, was the realm's capital, but also possessed an honored reputation for its schools, especially for rhetoric and philosophy. The presence there of Dungal, the Irish monk renowned for his astronomical expertise and enviable book collection, testified to that. Keeping track of important subsidiary regions also affected the manner in which Lothar set up his system, as seen in the choices of Florence for Tuscany (administratively unimportant, but far more accessible than Lucca), Fermo for Spoleto (of great strategic consequence to the Carolingian hold on central Italy and Rome), and Cividale del Friuli (a crucial bastion on the eastern frontier). Solmi also addressed the exclusion of several apparently key cities by noting that such centers as Grado, Venice, Bologna, Ravenna, Rimini, Ancona, and all of Benevento simply lay outside the Italian kingdom and thus outside Lothar's jurisdiction.[16]

Educational altruism notwithstanding, political gain is presumably always on the mind of an enterprising ruler. In conjunction with enhancing his own reputation as a reformer vis-à-vis his famous forebears, Lothar was almost certainly seeking more tangible benefits as well. But in order to serve that purpose, the Olona proposal needed to resonate clearly within the context of earlier reforming endeavors. This it did so well, in fact, that not only did it draw strength from earlier exemplars, it even went on to transmit the vibrancy thus gained to later actions. To begin with, the plan's basic educational goals found clear inspiration in earlier Carolingian policies, beginning with Charlemagne's own *Admonitio generalis* (789), whose provisions for improving the training of boys provided the foundation for subsequent directives. In his detailed study of Carolingian synods, Wilfried Hartmann has pointed out how the five major reforming councils of 813 actually aired few complaints about any outright ignorance of the clergy, and likewise contained few specific recommendations regarding clerical training—hence illustrating the real successes stemming from the initial phase of the *renovatio*.[17] Chapter 45 of the Council of Mainz (813) in some ways reflected this progress by directing all Christians to send their children to schools (either monastic or parish), where they would learn the *credo* and the *pater noster*. Similarly, the Council of Châlons (813) referred to Charlemagne's patronage of more and more schools to spread correct doctrine among increasing numbers of believers—the people who should, after all, be "the salt of the earth."[18] Louis the Pious certainly continued this tradition of patronage, as witnessed at Attigny in August 822. Most famous for Louis's dramatic public penance, this assembly also featured significant gestures of support for education, including a pronounced concern for proper episcopal oversight of area schools and parishes (particularly with regard to the training of clergy, so as to wipe out the ignorance of parish priests), as well as promises (reiterated later on) to build additional schools to accommodate more and more pupils. According to the council's proceedings, all prospective clerics would be required to visit schools which were to have been built in every see; when a diocese became too big, there might be two or even three schools. Parents or lords were also to provide for the students they sent there.[19]

In addition to echoing preceding patterns of Carolingian patronage, Lothar's efforts may also have affected succeeding educational policy, particularly as embodied in post-825 conciliar decrees. The most striking example is the Council of Rome called in November 826 by Pope Eugenius II, who happened to owe his papal election to Lothar's close advisor, Wala. Many of the council's thirty-eight decisions certainly echoed earlier traditions, whether from capitularies or council proceedings. Of particular importance were those canons dealing with the education of priests: no *ineruditi* or *illiterati* were to be allowed to enter the priesthood under any circumstances.[20] Far more noteworthy, however, was

the canon instructing bishops to arrange for teaching laypeople their letters, doctrine, and liberal arts.[21] Of the sixty-two bishops in attendance, three hailed from
dioceses touched by Lothar's Olona plan of the year before: Lupus of Fermo, Ali-
prand of Florence, and Sebastian of Pavia.[22] The degree to which their attendance
could account for some of the carryover from capitulary to council is difficult to
measure, but the fact that each of them came from a bishopric which was to serve
as one of the gathering points in Lothar's plan could well indicate such an influence. Hörle believed that the 826 council did in fact amount to an attempt by
several northern Italian bishops to emulate the 825 capitulary, adopting similar
goals under the auspices of a Roman council.[23] He drew particular attention to
the great lengths to which the attendees were willing to go to appropriate the
idea as their own. The fact that this plan was to apply *in universis episcopiis* testified, he believed, to their desire to surpass Lothar. Evaluating the 826 council
in the broader context of papal history, Thomas F. X. Noble has argued that the
driving force behind this bold action was Pope Eugenius II himself, motivated by
his fervent desire "to take over the leadership of the church reform initiated so
long before and nurtured so carefully by the Carolingians."[24] And, Noble added,
the rather less honorable motive of revenge may have been in the air as well,
since the papacy still burned in humiliation from the imposition of the Roman
Constitution two years before.

 Yet the influence of Lothar's 825 plan was even longer lasting than the
pope expected. The ideals enunciated so clearly in the Olona capitulary continued to echo throughout the rest of the century, not only in Lothar's own territories but also, significantly, in northern councils. The Council of Paris (829),
for instance, issued a canon calling for Emperor Louis the Pious to establish
public schools in at least three designated sites in the empire.[25] In fact, even
twenty-eight years after the plan's promulgation, some of its key elements were
still surfacing in church councils. The Council of Rome (853), summoned by
Pope Leo IV, simply recapitulated many of the same directives, though this time
around it had become even more practical-minded, the sole emphasis now being
on scripture.[26] Drawing a parallel to an earlier observation, three of the fifty-nine
attending bishops hailed from original Olona centers: Joseph of Ivrea, Noting of
Brescia, and Peter of Spoleto—the first two as imperial *missi* sent there by Lothar
himself. His use of them could very well indicate his reliance on their expertise in education policy, in view of the prominence of their dioceses in his plan
years before. Further potential influence is likewise seen in the proceedings of
the Councils of Valence (855) and Langres (859), which continued to voice support for establishing *scolae publicae* dedicated to both secular and religious education.[27] Of course, considering this erstwhile influence's circumstantial nature, one
may well question the reality of the Olona plan's effect on so many subsequent

councils, and might also suggest, as has John Contreni, that the need to repeat the same recommendations in 853 that had been brought forth so many years before illustrates the difficulties inherent in carrying out meaningful and lasting educational reforms in the early Middle Ages.[28] Yet the fact that the very idea of reform, as it had been transformed by Lothar's plan, still circulated among the leading intellectuals of the day also testifies to the continuing currency of that Carolingian ideal.

How Lothar managed to fuse a widely accepted reformist ethos with traditional goals of power seeking is a testament to his political savvy. It is also well worth noting steps he had taken in this regard even before issuing his edict at Olona. Looking back for a moment to the 824 visit to Rome, one of Lothar's seemingly spontaneous additions to the Roman Constitution certainly merits attention. In the midst of all the rest of that document's provisions, this Carolingian scion seems to have inserted an order for all those in Rome who possessed legal skills to register with certain authorities, and then make themselves known at his court, so that he might draw upon their services in his administration in the future.[29] This was clearly a move intended to prepare for some future time when he would be much freer to administer his own territories (in this case, Italy). The added fact that it so clearly presages the very methodical manner in which he would spell out his plan for school reform the next year further supports the idea of a king-not-yet, but in the immediate making.

Of far greater significance, however, was Lothar's acknowledgment that the only way for him to exercise any real power over the *regnum Italiae* was to gain control (or at least the goodwill) of the Italian bishops. Chris Wickham, for one, has noted that bishops were almost always the most important men in early medieval Italian towns and cities, unless challenged by an exceptional count.[30] It was also a uniquely Frankish innovation to incorporate the episcopate into the formal governmental apparatus in Italy. As Eduard Hlawitschka's seminal work has made clear, right from the start the Carolingians made it a priority to establish hegemony over the church in their Italian domains. Many of Charlemagne's loyal vassals were installed as bishops, most prominently in Pavia, Spoleto, Verona, Vicenza, Vercelli, and Milan—all centers later incorporated into the Olona plan.[31] The strength of Lothar's approach was to combine this trusted strategy (already put to good use by his predecessors) with a more palatable partnership emphasizing royal patronage of important local efforts to bolster schools. When looking through the sources of Lothar's reign, one sees a clear pattern of alliance between him and the episcopal leaders of these particular centers.[32]

With this in mind, it is no surprise that the specific relationship between Lothar's 825 plan and the Italian episcopate has likewise garnered a good deal of attention, particularly on the question of who would provide for the

Table 1. Bishops in Office at the Promulgation of the Olona Plan of 825[33]

Bishop	See	Dates in Office	Olona Destination
Sebastian	Pavia	814–29	Pavia
Angilbertus II	Milan	824–60	Pavia
Rampert	Brescia	815–44	Pavia
Tachimpaldus	Bergamo	797–828	Pavia
Albinus II	Vercelli	c.800–826	Pavia
Agatho	Acqui	821–?	Pavia
Willelmus	Genoa	821–?	Pavia
Roserius	Asti	<827–?	Pavia
Claudius	Turin	815–30	Turin
(Sigifredus)	Alba	?–829	Turin
Atto	Cremona	818–23	Cremona
Simpert	Cremona	823–27	Cremona
Nodebert (Norbert)	Reggio	814–35	Cremona
Podo	Piacenza	808–38	Cremona
Diodat (Deusdedit)	Modena	813–40	Cremona
Aliprand	Florence	<826–33	Florence
Lupus	Fermo	<826–?	Fermo
Ratholdus (Ratold)	Verona	799–840	Verona
Erfulf	Mantua	823–27	Verona
Daniel	Trent	<814–27	Verona
Heimbertus	Trent	827–?	Verona
Franco(nius, -arius)	Vicenza	<826–?	Vicenza
Dominicus	Padua	<827–?	Vicenza
Lupus (Lupone)	Treviso	813–?	Vicenza
Ama(ura)tus	Feltre	<827–?	Vicenza
Artemius	Asolo	<827–?	Vicenza

education stipulated by the capitulary. Here one must return to the decree's precise terminology: Who were the "negligent and lazy" *praepositi* so roundly chastised in the capitulary? Although Niermeyer's *Mediae latinitatis lexicon minus* features no fewer than fifteen possible definitions for the term itself, scholars have generally come to agree with good reason that Lothar was clearly laying the blame for the calamitous state of Italian education squarely at episcopal feet.[34] But who exactly were these bishops? (See table 1.) It would be impossible to re-create exactly the intricate web of political interests that tied together—and split asunder—the Carolingian empire; this is certainly no less true for the Italian realm. But in at least a few cases, tantalizing clues exist that may shed some light on the Olona plan's logic. Of those included in the roster of bishops in office around 825 for the sees listed in the proclamation, two figures stand out in particular. First, reflecting upon the odd fact that students from the archdiocese of Milan were consigned to go to school in the lesser diocese of Pavia, Heinz Löwe noted that the latter had not only served as the capital for both the Lombards and now for the Carolingians but that Lothar himself spent a good deal of time there (or at least at the royal estate at Olona just a few miles distant). Far more significant, though, was Milan's continued stubborn adherence to its Ambrosian liturgy. The city's refusal to adopt the "standardized" practices encouraged by Carolingian reformers likely ruled out the possibility of taking advantage of Milan's strong educational tradition, Löwe argued, since it posed a threat to the quest for uniformity.[35] The king's new proposal could therefore be seen as an attempt to pressure the clergy of Milan to conform to Carolingian wishes in these matters, since the loss of its students by designating Milan subordinate to Pavia would surely have constituted a blow to its prestige and even viability. In bringing such pressure to bear, Lothar seems to have been positioning himself as his grandfather's truest heir.

Another case, however, may be even more revealing. Wearing the pallium from 799 to 840, Bishop Ratold of Verona is thought to have exercised a great deal of influence in the Italian episcopate, and not just because of his longevity. As one of Louis the Pious's staunchest supporters, Ratold had been rewarded on June 13, 820, for example, with a confirmation of rights (ensured by the emperor's personal guarantee of protection) for the school he was to run in Verona.[36] It is also well established that Lothar and Ratold were at loggerheads in the struggles of the 830s, eventually resulting in Ratold's inability to return to Verona. If one adds to this Hlawitschka's conclusion that Ratold was an Aleman, it is not unreasonable to posit a "history" of sorts between these two men. For Judith, too, hailed from Alemannia, and eventually went to great lengths to wrest that particular province away from Lothar for her son Charles. Of course, Lothar still decreed Verona to be one of the educational centers of the realm. Given its school's reputation and its productive scriptorium—Bernhard Bischoff identified at least twenty-seven manuscripts as originating in Verona in the ninth century[37]—how could he have done otherwise? Yet it is tempting all the same to consider the possibility that Lothar may have been aiming his accusation at one *praepositus* in particular.

With such background in tow, by what standards should then the 825 Olona plan be judged? Should it be deemed a success or a failure? From a long-term educational standpoint, it would be difficult to argue with John Contreni's own passing comment that while Lothar's plan was certainly ambitious, it was not exactly what one would call successful in terms of systematically fostering new schools and scholars. Dungal, for one, retired in short order to the monastery of Bobbio, and Lothar himself (mostly absent between 825 and 829 in any case) plunged into the disastrous revolts of the early 830s, leaving, it seems, precious little time to supervise the progress of his educational program. Under these circumstances, the plan would indeed appear to have been, in Contreni's term, "stillborn."[38] Yet a historical consideration might nevertheless be well served by shifting the focus away from tangible results and rather to the unique character of the attempt itself, emblematic as it was of the intimately related concerns for *renovatio* and concrete political authority. In using the one to effect the other, Lothar's 825 capitulary significantly advanced the creative Carolingian fusion between reformist theory and political reality. Despite the antagonistic scenario posited above between Lothar and Ratold of Verona, it is clear that no Carolingian ruler could have hoped to succeed in Italy (or anywhere else, for that matter) without the support and talents of the episcopate. The documentary record is unfortunately not strong enough, even in Hlawitschka's hands, to illustrate clearly how Lothar rewarded his supporters in Italy. It is evident, however, that he was particularly busy in confirming the rights and privileges previously granted to the important bishoprics of Cremona, Milan, Novara, Brescia, Piacenza, Padua, Como, and Verona by his grandfather and father.[39] These actions, in combination with the steady efforts to consolidate influence via educational reforms, solidified Lothar's control over Italy to the extent that when, in the late 840s, Louis II ordered his bishops to investigate ecclesiastical and secular abuses in the Italian kingdom, he could still rely on the help of such trusted advisors as Angilbert II of Milan, Joseph of Ivrea, and Noting of Brescia to help him address the problems— a clear legacy of his father's determined efforts to achieve a sense of independence so early in his own reign.[40]

Supposedly ensconced in their ivory towers, many academics have long imagined themselves to be above the fray of ordinary power politics. Ever-scarcer state resources for today's universities, however, may well be fomenting ever-increasing awareness of the close relationship between patronage and education. While best known, perhaps, for having so richly illuminated the life of the Carolingian mind over the past four decades (and many more, we trust), the scholar honored in this present collection has always exhibited the enviable knack of keeping his scholarship well grounded in the realities of the early Middle Ages. Following that lead, it would be all the wiser to remember that when a Carolingian ruler like Lothar devised an enterprising scholastic reform program, he need not have been thinking solely of education or of politics alone. Rather, in a world where ideals and practicalities often danced together on the edge of a sword, he was probably thinking of both.

Notes

1. Considering the complexity of Frankish dynastic relations, it is all the more fitting that the ensuing episode transpired amid the profoundly ambiguous "pluralità di poteri" of early medieval Italy, as described by Giuseppe Albertoni, *L'Italia carolingia* (Rome, 1997), 103.

2. The most encompassing study of this process remains Eduard Hlawitschka, *Franken, Alemannen, Bayern und Burgunder in Oberitalien, 774–962* (Freiburg, 1960).

3. *Ordinatio imperii* (817), MGH Capit. 1, 270–73 (273).

4. Jörg Jarnut, "Ludwig der Fromme, Lothar I. und das *Regnum Italiae*," in *Charlemagne's Heir: New Perspectives on the Reign of Louis the Pious (814–840)*, ed. Peter Godman and Roger Collins (Oxford, 1991), 349–62 (349–50).

5. Ibid., 358–60. In Jarnut's view, Lothar was loathe to give himself completely over to Italian affairs, since doing so would be to abandon his greater designs on the wider empire. For a contrasting view, see Paolo Delogu, "Lombard and Carolingian Italy," in *The New Cambridge Medieval History*, vol. 2, *c. 700–c. 900*, ed. Rosamond McKitterick (Cambridge, 1995), 290–319. For a view of Lothar's stay in Italy as tantamount to exile, see Steven A. Stofferahn, "Banished Worlds: The Political Culture of Carolingian Exile, 750–900" (Ph.D. dissertation, Purdue University, 2003), 198–203.

6. Jarnut, "Ludwig der Fromme," 354–55. He also notes, however, the significance of the fact that Louis deemed it necessary to crown Lothar as co-emperor himself at Aachen in 825, thereby putting his own stamp, as it were, on the rogue actions taken two years earlier in Rome. As for 824 itself, it may be more accurate to view Lothar's time in Rome in 824 as a formative period during which he began to consider how best to go about declaring his independence. As Paolo Delogu presents it, Lothar decisively marched into Rome to pacify the "violent internal conflicts" there, compelling the pope to sign his father's document and swear an oath of loyalty to the emperor. He also provided for future imperial control over papal elections, administration, and political activities, and likewise arranged for a permanent imperial *missus* to reside in Rome. See Delogu, "Lombard and Carolingian Italy," 311.

7. It could also be that having the brash royal advisor Wala with him during the early years in Italy further emboldened Lothar to undertake such bold actions. On Wala's particular efforts to rein in the power of local counts, see Lorenz Weinrich, *Wala: Graf, Mönch, Rebell: Die Biographie eines Karolingers* (Lübeck, 1963), 47.

8. MGH Capit. 1, 326–27: "De doctrina vero, quae ob nimiam incuriam atque ignaviam quorundam praepositorum cunctis in locis est funditus extincta, placuit ut sicut a nobis constitutum est ita ab omnibus observetur. Videlicet ut ab his qui nostra dispositione ad docendos alios per loca denominata sunt constituti maximum detur studium, qualiter sibi commissi scolastici proficiant atque doctrinae insistant, sicut praesens exposcit necessitas. Propter oportunitatem tamen omnium apta loca distincte ad hoc exercitium providimus, ut difficultas locorum longe positorum ac paupertas nulli foret excusatio. Id sunt: primum in Papia conveniant ad Dungalum de Mediolano, de Brixia, de Laude, de Bergamo, de Novaria, de Vercellis, de Tertona, de Aquis, de Ianua, de Aste, de Cuma; in Eporegia ipse episcopus hoc per se faciat; in Taurinis conveniant de Vintimilio, de Albingano, de Vadis, de Alba; in Cremona discant de Regia, de Placentia, de Parma, de Mutina; in Florentia de Tuscia respiciant; in Firmo de Spoletinis civitatibus conveniant; in Verona de Mantua, de Triento; in Vincentia de Patavis, de Tarvisio, de Feltris, de Ceneda, de Asylo; reliquae civitates Forum Iulii ad scolam conveniant."

9. Georg H. Hörle, *Frühmittelalterliche Mönchs- und Klerikerbildung in Italien* (Freiburg i.Br., 1914), 68; Arrigo Solmi, "Sul capitolare di Lotario dell'anno 825 relativo all'ordinamento scolastico in Italia," in *Contributi alla storia del diritto commune*, ed. Arrigo Solmi (Rome, 1937), 271–81 (273). For one testimonial of the Lombards' cultural greatness, see Giovanni Battista Pighi, *Verona nell' ottavo secolo* (Verona, 1963), 15, who used a combination of documentary and archaeological evidence to illustrate the sophisticated environment of early eighth-century Verona.

10. Ugo Gualazzini, *Richerche sulle scuole preuniversitarie del medioevo: Contributo di indagini sul sorgere delle università* (Milan, 1943), 2.

11. Giuseppe Manacorda, *Storia della scuola in Italia*, 2 vols. (Palermo, 1916), 2:306, 314–16, 335.

12. See Wilhelm Giesebrecht, *De litterarum studiis apud Italos primis medii aevi saeculis* (Berlin, 1845), 10; and Hörle, *Frühmittelalterliche Mönchs- und Klerikerbildung*, 71. Solmi maintained that Giesebrecht's reading was too myopic, ignoring as it did the difficulty one often encounters in distinguishing between ecclesiastical and mundane interests in Carolingian legislation. See Solmi, "Sul capitolare di Lotario," 278–79.

13. Solmi, "Sul capitolare di Lotario," 280. For similar ruminations on this revival of the liberal arts–based *scolae publicae*, see Pierre Riché, *Écoles et enseignement dans le Haut Moyen Âge: Fin du Ve siècle-milieu du X^{ie} siècle*, 2nd ed. (Paris, 1989), 76–98, 354. Ugo Gualazzini's study adopted the hybrid perspective that the reform plan did seem to have clerical education in mind, but that such a system was designed to serve the "state's" interest above all else. Noting his book's 1943 publication date, one is forced to wonder about the potential influence of fascist rhetoric. See Gualazzini, *Richerche*, 5.

14. Gualazzini, *Richerche*, 2.

15. Giuseppe Salvioli, *L'istruzioni in Italia prima del mille* (Florence, 1912), 20.

16. Solmi, "Sul capitolare di Lotario," 274–77.

17. Wilfried Hartmann, *Die Synoden der Karolingerzeit im Frankenreich und in Italien* (Paderborn, 1989), 430.

18. MGH Conc. 2, 274–75. "Oportet etiam, ut, sicut domnus imperator Karolus, vir singularis mansuetudinis, fortitudinis, prudentiae, iusticiae et temperantiae, praecepit, scolas constituant, in quibus et litteraria sollertia disciplinae et sacrae scripturae documenta discantur, et tales ibi erudiantur, quibus merito dicatur a Domino: Vos estis sal terrae, et qui condimentum plebibus esse valeant, et quorum doctrina non solum diversis heresibus, verum etiam antichristi monitis et ipsi antichristi resistatur, ut merito de illis in laude ecclesiae dicatur: Mille clypei pendent ex ea, omnis armatura fortium."

19. MGH Capit. 1, 357. "Scolas autem, de quibus hactenus minus studiosi fuimus quam debueramus, omnino studiosissime emendare cupimus, qualiter omnis homo sive maioris sive minoris aetatis, qui ad hoc nutritor ut in aliquo gradu in ecclesia promoeatur, locum denomit natum et magistrum congruum habeat. Parentes tamen vel domini singulorum de victu vel substantia corporali unde subsistant providere studeant, qualiter solacium habeant, ut propter rerum inopiam doctrinae studio non recedant. Si vero necessitas fuerit propter amplitudinem parroechiae, eo quod in uno loco collegi non possunt propter administrationem quam eis procuratores eorum providere debent, fiat locis duobus aut tribus vel etiam ut necessitas et ratio dictaverit."

20. MGH Conc. 2, 568.

21. Ibid., 581: "De scolis reparandis pro studio litterarum. De quibusdam locis ad nos referatur non magistros neque curam inveniri pro studio litterarum. Idcirco in universis

episcopiis subiectisque plebibus et aliis locis, in quibus necessitas occurrerit, omnino cura et diligentia habeatur, ut magistri et doctores constituentur, qui, studia litterarum liberaliumque artium ac sancta habentes dogmata, assiduae doceant, quia in his maximae divina manifestantur atque declarantur mandata."

22. Hartmann, *Die Synoden der Karolingerzeit*, 174. Their approximate dates of office are featured in table 1 below.

23. Hörle, *Frühmittelalterliche Mönchs- und Klerikerbildung*, 64.

24. Thomas F. X. Noble, "The Place in Papal History of the Roman Synod of 826," *Church History* 45 (1976): 1–16 (10).

25. Hartmann, *Die Synoden der Karolingerzeit*, 186; MGH Conc. 2, 675.

26. Hartmann, *Die Synoden der Karolingerzeit*, 236; MGH Conc. 3, 327–28.

27. Hartmann, *Die Synoden der Karolingerzeit*, 268, 270; MGH Conc. 3, 362, 478.

28. John J. Contreni, "The Carolingian Renaissance: Education and Literary Culture," in *The New Cambridge Medieval History*, vol. 2, *c. 700–c. 900*, ed. McKitterick, 709–57 (724).

29. MGH Capit. 1, 323: "Placuit nobis, ut cuncti iudices sive hi qui cunctis praeesse debent, per quos iudicaria potestas in hac urbe Roma agi debent, in praesentia nostra veniant; volentes numerum et nomina eorum scire et singulos de ministerio sibi credito admonitionem facere."

30. Chris Wickham, *Early Medieval Italy: Central Power and Local Society, 400–1000* (Ann Arbor, 1981), 56.

31. Hlawitschka, *Franken*, 30–32. Paolo Delogu has added that special attention (including actual jurisdictional authority) was lavished on the episcopate, since it could constitute a ready network of support for the king or emperor throughout the realm. It is not surprising, then, that most Italian bishops soon became intimately aligned with the Carolingian rulers—a connection Lothar would readily exploit. He has also illustrated the increasingly close bond that developed between the bishops' political aims and their cities' interests in expansion. See Delogu, "Lombard and Carolingian Italy," 307–10. Pierre Riché, *The Carolingians: A Family Who Forged Europe*, trans. Michael Idomir Allen (Philadelphia, 1993), 285–87, also features a helpful discussion of the Carolingian reorganization of the system of metropolitan provinces, several Italian heads of which were listed in Charlemagne's last will (e.g., Rome, Ravenna, Milan, Cividale del Friuli, and Grado).

32. For example, Joseph, abbot of Novalese and bishop of Ivrea, was a crony of Lothar for many years and later the archchaplain under Louis II. Similarly, bishops Ratold of Verona and Angilbert of Milan were also close associates of the Italian Carolingians. See Wilhelm Wattenbach and Wilhelm Levison, *Deutschlands Geschichtsquellen im Mittelalter: Vorzeit und Karolinger*, vol. 4, *Die Karolinger vom Vertrag von Verdun bis zum Herrschaftsantritt der Herrscher aus dem Sächsischen Hause: Italien und das Papsttum*, ed. Heinz Löwe (Weimar, 1963), 401.

33. Compiled from Fedele Savio, *Gli antichi vescovi d'Italia dalle origini al 1300 descriti per regioni: La Lombardia* (Bergamo, 1932) and Pius Bonifatius Gams, *Series episcoporum Ecclesiae Catholicae* (Graz, 1957). Note that in a few cases, bishops have been included whose dates only approximately correspond with the capitulary's promulgation. To add a further word of caution, Donald A. Bullough has discussed the difficulty (and often impossibility) of delimiting early medieval diocesan boundaries in "The Counties of the *Regnum Italiae* in the Carolingian Period," *Papers of the British School of Rome* 23 (1955): 148–68 (153).

34. Solmi was the first modern scholar to identify the *praepositi* as Italian bishops. Gualazzini took this conclusion further, noting that with the singular exception of Pavia, only the bishops would have been in a position to administer Lothar's plan. It was absurd, he argued, to conclude (as Manacorda had) that just because the capitulary's text dwelled specifically on the bishop of Ivrea's duty in this matter, the schools in other places had nothing to do with the bishops. Ivrea's exceptionality lay rather in the unified identification between school and diocesan districts, rather than in some unique proxy for the bishop there to teach the laity. He went on to argue for a clear identification of the Olona-plan centers at Cremona, Verona, Ivrea, Turin, and Fermo as cathedral schools; he could not with any certainty, however, say the same for Vicenza, Firenza, or Cividale del Friuli. Pavia, of course, featured a palace school headed by Dungal. It was, then, almost certainly the bishops who were most active in Lothar's proposed educational system, regardless of its character, since earlier studies' assumptions of Ivrea's exceptionality had been founded on a distinctly different issue altogether. See Solmi, "Sul capitolare di Lotario," 272; and Gualazzini, *Richerche*, 6–7, 18.

35. Löwe, *Die Karolinger*, 407–8.

36. J. F. Böhmer, *Die Regesten des Kaiserreichs unter den Karolingern, 751–918*, ed. Engelbert Mühlbacher (Hildesheim, 1966), 722. This is the same school, presumably, that had been overseen earlier by the famous archdeacon Pacificus of Verona until he ran afoul of Louis and Ratold in the affair surrounding King Bernard. See Cristina la Rocca, "A Man for All Seasons: Pacificus of Verona and the Creation of a Local Carolingian Past," in *The Uses of the Past in the Early Middle Ages*, ed. Yitzhak Hen and Matthew Innes (Cambridge, 2000), 250–79 (250).

37. Bernhard Bischoff, *Katalog der festländischen Handschriften des neunten Jahrhunderts (mit Ausnahme der wisigotischen)*, 2 vols. (Wiesbaden, 1998–2004), referring to entries 117, 325, 379, 409, 410, 416, 433, 435, 437, 686, 900, 906, 1143, 1149, 1221, 1587, 1783, 1851, 2269, 2333, 2396, 2564a, 3073, 3077, 3315, 3492, and 3766.

38. Contreni, "Carolingian Renaissance," 721–24.

39. Böhmer, *Die Regesten des Kaiserreichs*, 839, 844–45, 862, 863–64, 868.

40. Wickham, *Early Medieval Italy*, 61.

PART 3

Context and Connections

CHAPTER 9

Theodulf's Mosaic at Germigny, the Sancta Sanctorum, and Jerusalem

LAWRENCE NEES

This essay is in honor of a great scholar of the Carolingian period, John J. Contreni, from whose work I have learned so much, and whose gracious friendship I have much valued over the years. The last time we shared a program at Kalamazoo prior to the sessions at which this paper was first presented was in the millennium year 2000, when he was kind enough to comment on two papers devoted to the *Visio Baronti* manuscripts, presented by myself and by Michelle Lucey-Roper. John's commentary was so learned and sensitive that in revised form it eventually appeared as a splendid article in *Speculum*, which greatly advanced the scholarly discussion on that fascinating text in particular, and on Carolingian thought and politics more generally.[1] This paper dealing with learned Carolingian people and issues, is, I hope, an acceptable tribute to John, but it builds more directly on the work of another great scholar of the period who deserves remembrance, Ann Freeman. Ann died on February 28, 2008, after a long illness, and given my subject I must say a word about Ann. She proved that sweetness of temperament and human kindness were by no means incompatible with a scholarship that was profound, tenacious, and indeed sometimes combative. It is a lesson that has long inspired me, even though I surely fail to meet that high standard. How lucky we who study Carolingian culture are to have such wonderful colleagues as Ann and John!

Ann's last article, co-authored with her husband and the friend of so many, Paul Meyvaert, was published in 2001 in *Gesta*,[2] and it brought important insights to bear on the famous and often-studied mosaic at Germigny-des-Prés (see fig. 1).

Figure 1. Mosaic with Ark of the Covenant and Cherubim, from Theodulf's oratory at Germigny-des-Prés (photo: J. Feuillie/© C.N.M., Paris).

That mosaic had figured prominently in Ann's first article, the great study of 1957 demonstrating that the treatise then already well known as the *Libri Carolini* was authored by Theodulf,[3] and again in her monumental and indispensable edition of that remarkable text in 1998, which suggested that the treatise should better be known as the *Opus Caroli regis contra synodum*.[4] I shall henceforth refer to it as the *Opus Caroli*. That great edition has stimulated other scholars to deal more deeply with the very intriguing text, including a recent article by Karl Morrison,[5] and a recent book by Thomas Noble, both of which have taught me much.[6] After completing her edition of the *Opus Caroli*, Ann and Paul were clearly not yet finished with Theodulf and his mosaic, for their 2001 article made many new observations and contributions, especially by suggesting connections with Rome not previously noted.

Freeman and Meyvaert were the first to consider in depth the implications for the Germigny mosaic of the evidence that Theodulf had accompanied Charlemagne to Rome in 800—evidence which seems persuasive, including Theodulf's own statement in a late poem that he had received a pallium from the pope's hands, and a letter of 801 from Alcuin to Theodulf.[7] In Freeman and Meyvaert's view, Theodulf's visits to the ancient churches of Rome played a large role in stimulating Theodulf to undertake a mosaic in his own chapel and may well have inspired some specific features of that mosaic. My own favorite among the observations by Freeman and Meyvaert has to do with the four groups of three little humps, two at each side of the mosaic near its lower edge. These humps had been all but ignored by earlier scholars, not surprising given the concentration upon the central motif of the Ark of the Covenant with two small cherubim upon it (following the description of the ark made for Moses's tabernacle in Exodus), and two much larger cherubim at the sides (following the description of Solomon's Temple in 1 Kings). Freeman and Meyvaert used an old drawing,[8] and some new digital skills, to produce a computer-enhanced version of the mosaic that shows the twelve stones more clearly, and they read these humps as a reference to the twelve stones mentioned in Joshua, taken from the Jordan River after the miraculous parting of waters that allowed the Ark of the Covenant to pass across, and set up in Galgala as a memorial. They pointed out that Theodulf had discussed these twelve stones at length in the *Opus Caroli* and obviously had given them much thought. What he saw in Rome resonated with what he had said in the *Opus Caroli* eight years earlier and contributed to the iconographic program of the mosaic he erected at Germigny six or so years later.

For this motif, Freeman and Meyvaert especially saw links with earlier mosaics then, and still, visible in Rome, the fifth-century mosaics at S. Maria Maggiore and the sixth-century mosaics at SS. Cosma e Damiano, whose significance to Theodulf they explained largely through the *Opus Caroli* text. At S. Maria Maggiore the fifth-century mosaics on the lateral nave walls include an image of the ark carried across the Jordan, but the twelve stones are not shown. The ark actually is represented three times in the fifth-century mosaics on the nave walls, in each case as a rectangular box carried by four men, that in the Jordan crossing having the closest resemblance to what is represented at Germigny, taking the form of a flat rectangular box. In one of the scenes only, the ark being carried around Jericho, the ark has a prominent circular boss or medallion on one side,[9] a strange motif that does not occur in Theodulf's mosaic, and is thus understandably not discussed by Freeman and Meyvaert. I think that that little detail is worth notice and discussion, and brings new material and new perspectives that might shed light on what Theodulf had in mind in making his mosaic.

In the same year that saw Freeman and Meyvaert's article published (2001), a major exhibition was devoted to Charlemagne and Rome,[10] and its catalogue included the wooden chest in the Sancta Sanctorum chapel, in the papal palace at the Lateran, in a decent color reproduction (see fig. 2). Prior to that time the object was little known to scholars, having been presented in an engraving in Hartmann Grisar's 1907 book on the Sancta Sanctorum and its

Figure 2. *Arca Cipressina* reliquary chest of Pope Leo III, Sancta Sanctorum Chapel, Lateran Palace, Rome (photo: Roma, ICCD, Fototeca Nazionale, E 59948).

treasures,[11] and in a 1991 publication devoted to the Lateran Palace.[12] The 2001 exhibition catalogue added little to these studies. The chest is made of cypress wood, and it is now encased in a marble altar provided with bronze doors, a work commissioned by Pope Innocent III in the early thirteenth century, which effectively hid the chest from view and from modern scholarship. The chest, which since the eleventh century has been known, at least on some occasions (and henceforth in this discussion), as the Arca Cipressina, has two compartments one above the other, each with double doors, each one of which is decorated with a

prominent circular medallion. The inscription along the top reads "LEO INDIG-
NUS TERTIUS EPISCOPUS D(e)I FAMULUS FECIT" in large capital letters; at
the top center on a small plaque interrupting Leo's inscription is a later smaller
plaque inscribed "SCA SCO RV." That later plaque probably dates from the time
of the Arca Cipressina's installation by Innocent IIII (1198–1214) in the newly
constructed altar of marble, behind heavy bronze grille, or more likely that altar's
installation in the newly dedicated Sancta Sanctorum chapel constructed by
Pope Nicholas III (1277–80), where it remains today. To my knowledge no one
has questioned that the large inscription is original, nor do I see any reason to
doubt on paleographical, historical, or textual grounds that it was created for and
refers to Pope Leo III (796–816). Even the unusual formula "DEI FAMULUS" is
attested in other closely related texts from the end of the eighth and early ninth
centuries, one of which is a dedication.[13]

The first study that probed the significance of the Arca Cipressina was
published in 2002 by Erik Thunø, in an important book devoted specifically to
early medieval Rome, indeed concentrating on the Carolingian period and particularly on the formation and significance of the reliquary collection that came
to be located in the Arca Cipressina, especially the objects associated with Pope
Paschal I (817–24). Thunø lamented that the object "has received almost no
scholarly attention despite its connection to the most holy chapel of the city
of Rome," and then dealt sensitively with the issue of reconstructing just who
thought what when about the Arca Cipressina, always difficult for historians and
particularly so in regards to Rome, where on principle nothing is ever new.[14] The
name Sancta Sanctorum (Holy of Holies) for the great papal reliquary chapel at
the Lateran does not demonstrably predate the late thirteenth century, when its
present decoration was largely executed (see fig. 3), but it is manifestly not altogether new; indeed, it is filled with earlier objects and references.[15] For example,
busts of Peter and Paul in the thirteenth-century mosaics not only depend upon
but refer to two small likely eighth-century encaustic images that were preserved
in the chapel.[16]

There are tantalizing early medieval references to the Sancta Sanctorum
at the Lateran, both splendidly problematic, discussed by Thunø and others,
notably Raymond Davis, including mentions in the Liber pontificalis for Benedict
III (855–58)[17] and perhaps an allusion for Gregory IV (828–44).[18] Before that
time, the most important chapel at the Lateran seems to have been dedicated
to St. Lawrence, and appears already in the Liber pontificalis entry for Stephen III
in the second half of the eighth century.[19] It is not known when that chapel was
established or where it was located.[20] Early in his pontificate Leo III was involved
in major donations to existing churches and new building campaigns, including his council chamber and triclinium,[21] which Manfred Luchterhandt recently

NON·EST·IN·TOTO·SANCTIOR·ORBE·LOCVS

Figure 3. *Sancta Sanctorum* Chapel, interior view with reliquary altar and *acheropita* image (photo: Roma, ICCD, Fototeca Nazionale, E 111107).

termed "the most significant secular structures of post-antique medieval Rome."[22] The *Liber pontificalis* calls the new *triclinium* at the Lateran "greater than all other such, adorned on a wondrous scale," and dates its construction to 797–98.[23] Apparently the *triclinium* was sufficiently completed to have served in 799–800 as the place in which Leo's Roman accusers were questioned by a group of Frankish bishops led by Hildebald of Cologne and Arn of Salzburg, with Theodulf not being listed.[24] We have a good idea of the rather remarkably large and ostentatious form, and location, of these Leonine constructions, still visible and in use in the late medieval period. Among his extensive donations to many Roman churches listed by the *Liber pontificalis*, there is, alas, no mention of the Arca Cipressina; obviously the lists are not complete.

In the Sancta Sanctorum chapel today (fig. 3), above the Arca Cipressina in its altar case stands the famous Christ image known as the *acheropita*, from the Greek ʾαχειροποίητον, the image "not made by human hands,"[25] which is first mentioned in the *Liber pontificalis* account of Pope Stephen II (752–57), which describes the pope carrying the image on his shoulder into S. Maria Maggiore in a ceremony aimed at seeking divine defense against the "pestilential threats to the Romans by the king of the Lombards."[26] The current image is late medieval, but beneath it and its metalwork cover are the remains of an early medieval image now almost entirely disappeared. A probably twelfth-century painting now in Tivoli may give an approximate idea of the early medieval form of the image, which presented Christ enthroned.[27] The *Liber pontificalis* text does not say whence the procession stemmed, or indicate where the *acheropita* was normally kept at that time, but in a recent study Serena Romana suggests that the image may have been in the St. Lawrence chapel at the Lateran as early as the later sixth century.[28] Eventually everything came together in the Sancta Sanctorum, but was Leo III's Arca Cipressina already associated with the historical and ideological conception of the Sancta Sanctorum, if not necessarily with a chapel bearing that name? As already noticed by Grisar in the early twentieth century, however, the existence of nail holes from an earlier plaque combined with the way it interrupts the dedication inscription suggests that the current plaque replaces an earlier one, whose inscription is unrecoverable. In Thunø's view, "it cannot be excluded that Leo's chest also originally bore the title Sancta Sanctorum."[29]

Space does not permit even a summary relisting of the evidence for the complex web of associations between the Arca Cipressina in the Sancta Sanctorum, and of both with the wooden altar termed "St. Peter's altar" of the Lateran basilica, and the Ark of the Covenant, so I shall here merely quote Erik Thunø's conclusion that "during Leo's pontificate at the latest, the Lateran high altar was understood as a hybrid of St. Peter's altar and the Ark of the Covenant,"[30] and that in turn "the idea of a hybrid of the Ark of the Covenant and the altar of St. Peter—directly inspired by the Lateran high altar—remains the most compelling way of understanding Leo's chest,"[31] the Arca Cipressina. Clearly that work had significant impact at an early date, for the famous mid-ninth-century golden reliquary altar of S. Ambrogio in Milan providing access to the relics through double doors, each with two large medallions, is unusual and likely inspired by the Arca Cipressia in the Lateran.[32]

The medallion motif connects the Arca Cipressina not only with later, but with some earlier works in a surprising way, and thereby strengthens the likelihood that it was designed from the beginning (that is, when commissioned by Leo III) to be connected with the Ark of the Covenant and the Sancta Sanctorum. Why the circles? As mentioned, there is one circle on one of the three images of the ark in the mosaics of S. Maria Maggiore, but otherwise the motif is rare on the numerous images of the Ark of the Covenant and/or the Sancta Sanctorum, whether in earlier manuscripts like the Ashburnham Pentateuch,[33] or Carolingian manuscripts like the Bible made for Charles the Bald now in Rome,[34] or in the many representations of the ark and/or Sancta Sanctorum in numerous works of Jewish art of the fourth to sixth centuries such as mosaics

Figure 4. Gold-glass fragments, from Rome, with Ark of the Covenant/Torah shrine. New York, Metropolitan Museum of Art, Rogers Fund 18.145 a and b (photo: The Metropolitan Museum of Art, Rogers Fund, 1918 (18.145.1a, b), Image © The Metropolitan Museum of Art).

from Palestinian synagogues at Hammath Tiberias B, Beth Alpha, or Beth Shean A.[35] In these latter cases it seems likely that the representation of the ark is in some manner merged with the appearance and representation of Torah shrines in contemporary synagogues, making the point of the sacredness of Scripture as the word of God and the holiness of the synagogue as in some manner the successor and continuation of the Temple and its cult.[36] The medallion motif seems to be rare everywhere, except in and around the city of Rome. Rome has a significant group of images dating from the fourth-century Jewish synagogues and catacombs that prominently feature circles at the center of the ark/shrine, where in some cases, such as the image of the Torah Shrine in the fourth-century Villa Torlonia catacomb in Rome, the open doors reveal circles indicating the ends of rolls given a strongly circular form.[37] This is a form that recurs on several fragmentary bits of the distinctively Roman gold glasses (fig. 4),[38] while in some reliefs such

Figure 5. Tomb slab from the Monteverde catacomb, with Ark of the Covenant/Torah shrine. Naples, Museo archeologico Nazionale no. 4521 (photo: Soprintendenza archeologica Napoli e Pompeii).

as two from the Monteverde catacomb (fig. 5) the central ark/Torah shrine is indicated by abstract circles alone,[39] making an image that strongly recalls Leo III's Arca Cipressina (fig. 2).[40]

The late eleventh-century *Descriptio Lateranensis ecclesiae* locates the Arca Cipressina, as it terms it, in the St. Lawrence chapel.[41] By that time it already housed Paschal I's and many other reliquaries, notably the small box datable to roughly the seventh century containing a collection of stones from the Holy Land inscribed in Greek with their places of origin, as well as painted images on the inside of the lid showing events associated with those places.[42] The same text also makes the remarkable claim that the wooden altar in the Lateran basilica contained the Ark of the Covenant from the Temple in Jerusalem. That claim is less odd than it at first seems,[43] for the Arch of Titus famously depicts the booty from the sack of the Jerusalem Temple being brought to Rome, in a relief that, unlike many other ancient works, was always visible through the medieval period. The great menorah is clearly shown, so why not think that the ark, too, was brought to the city? If so, where would it be but in the Lateran, the Basilica Constantiniana, preeminent imperial gift?[44] The papal liturgy for Maundy Thursday celebrated in the Lateran Basilica includes a citation of Hebrews 9:7: "But the second tent is entered by the high priest alone, and that only once a year." Discussed at length by Sible de Blaauw some years ago, the most complete presentation is in an *Ordo in cena domini* compiled from older elements in a pontifical for Innocent III.[45] At the Lateran, and in no other church, the pope entered the sanctuary alone, celebrated alone at the altar, and communicated alone—thus deliberately casting himself as the successor to the high priest of the Old Testament invoking God in what is explicitly denominated the Sancta Sanctorum.[46]

De Blaauw has traced this liturgy to "early roots" from the early ninth century and even before, and has described "the complex interweaving of linguistic and allegorical associations and confusions" among all the various wooden boxes referred to with the Latin term *arca*.[47] He even suggests that what he terms the "unique" use of the word *renovabit* in the *Liber pontificalis* to describe Leo III's addition of silver panels to the wooden altar in the Lateran basilica should be taken as evidence that the wooden altar linked with the Sancta Sanctorum of the Temple was already in existence and regarded as of particular importance.[48] What I would like to do here is return to Theodulf and his mosaic, and his experiences in Rome, starting with the citation of Hebrews 9:7 in the papal liturgy at the Lateran for Maudy Thursday. At the end of Hebrews 7 is written that "the high priests appointed by the law are men in all their weakness, but the priest appointed by the words of the oath which supersedes the law is the Son, who has been made perfect for ever." At the beginning of chapter 8: "My main point is: this is the kind of high priest we have, and he has taken his seat at the right hand of the throne of Majesty in heaven and is minister in the real sanctuary, the tent set up by the Lord, not by man." In the following chapter (9:11) is written: "But Christ, being come an high priest of the good things to come, by a greater and more perfect tabernacle not made with hand, that is, not of this creation."

Theodulf does not cite these particular passages from Hebrews 7 and 8 in the *Opus Caroli*, according to Ann Freeman's magnificent edition, which I have cited to give a sense of the larger context in which the passage from Hebrews 9:7 occurs. Theodulf does, however, cite Hebrews 9:11, and does so in a most interesting context. In book 1, chapter 29 when rejecting the citation of Psalm 25(26):8's "I have loved, O Lord, the beauty of thy house" (Domine dilexi decorem domus tuae) as a justification for the use of images to decorate churches, he answers that the beauty meant is spiritual, not sensual,[49] and immediately after mentioning the ark and cherubim (to which he refers his reader to the extended discussion in 1.15)[50] he quotes Paul the Apostle on the "more perfect tabernacle not made with hand [*non manufactum*] ... not of this creation."[51] There is nothing novel in Frankish thinking of the second half of the eighth century in the insistence that it is Christ who is now the true ark and Mercy Seat, which is a theme first presented in the Gundohinus Gospels miniature of Christ enthroned between cherubim from 754, and apparently also in a lost monumental apse decoration at Gorze described in 765.[52]

How then would Theodulf have reacted to seeing the pope deliberately casting himself through the liturgy on Maundy Thursday as the high priest in the Jerusalem Temple, in effect re-enacting the pre-Christian rite? My own view is that Theodulf, very likely along with Charlemange, would have witnessed, or at least under the circumstances would have known about, such a performance. According to the *Royal Frankish Annals*, Charlemagne stayed in Rome through Easter in 801, leaving for Spoleto only on April 25, three weeks after Easter, which fell on April 4 in 801.[53] We cannot be certain whether Theodulf stayed with the king or not, and here I must disagree with the supposition by Freeman and Meyvaert that he did not.[54] If he did see Pope Leo performing such a ceremony, Theodulf left no explicit comment about his reaction, so his reaction cannot be known for certain. On the basis of extensive study of his writings and involvement with artistic issues of many kinds, it seems to me that he would have been aghast at what he saw. One may remember that Leo III had a very low reputation at the Frankish court and only a year before had fled Rome to seek assistance from Charlemagne, who was now in Rome to adjudicate the charges brought against Leo.[55] More than ten years ago I published a book arguing *in extenso* that Theodulf was by no means a supporter of a "Roman imperial" policy for Charlemagne, and in a long poem of 798 made a subtle but impassioned argument against picking up the imperial mantle.[56] I think it is fair to say that not all scholars were entirely convinced by my arguments, but surely the broad tenor of Theodulf's works—at least his major ones—is full of criticism of Roman practices. I find it hard to dismiss as mere coincidence Theodulf's use of the phrase *non manufactum* (not made with hand)[57] in conjunction with the spiritual tabernacle and the phrase *acheropita* (not made with hand) in use in Rome already several decades earlier to refer to a painted likeness of Christ credited with miraculous powers, which happens to stand today atop Leo III's Arca Cipressina in the Sancta Sanctorum (fig. 3), as it may have done already when Theodulf and Charlemagne visited Rome in 800.

The inscription on Theodulf's mosaic at Germigny, usually thought to date from around 806, was cogently discussed, and translated, by Freeman and Meyvaert as follows:[58]

ORACLUM SCM ET CERUBIN HIC ASPICE SPECTANS
ET TESTAMENTI EN MICAT ARCA DEI /
HAEC CERNENS PRECIBUSBQUE STUDENS PULSARE
TONANTEM THEODULFUM VOTIS IUNGITO QUAESO TUIS

[As you gaze upon the holy propitiatorium and Cherubim, beholder
[*or* As you gaze upon this inner sanctuary with the Cherubim, beholder,]

And see the shimmering of the Ark of God's covenant,
Perceiving these things, and prepared to beset the Thunderer with prayers,
Add, I beg you, Theodulf's name to your invocations.][59]

Freeman and Meyvaert point out that the opening word *oraclum* surely refers to Jerusalem, not to Rome, for this is the term used in connection with the Ark of the Covenant when its making is first described in Exodus 37:6, while in *De templo* "Bede sometimes uses *oraculum* to mean the holy of holies, the place within the Temple where the ark was kept."[60] Of course, it is obvious that Theodulf is thinking of the Old Testament here in some sense—either the ark or the Sancta Sanctorum in which it was kept, or both. The problematic issue is to discern and articulate what Theodulf had in mind or wanted to communicate through the inscription. Is he in some manner proposing that the Ark of the Covenant depicted in his mosaic is worthy of veneration? He granted that in the Old Testament veneration of this manufactured object was authorized by god, who directed the object to be made, but his fundamental point is that such veneration should not be extended to manufactured images, which were not specifically authorized by holy Scripture, as was the ark. He says nothing positive about the propriety of venerating an *image* of the ark, such as he created at Germigny, as noted below. There is a ninth-century image of the ark and cherubim that seems to indicate that some believed that the Old Testament passage refuted those who doubted the propriety of venerating images, but it is in a Greek Psalter manuscript vilifying the iconoclasts;[61] this was precisely the position that in the *Opus Caroli* Theodulf was at pains to reject. To be sure, the mosaic and oratory are likely a decade or more later, and he might have changed his views, although I know no evidence in support of such a change. Here it may be that the translation offered by Freeman and Meyvaert, in rendering the Latin text, overspecifies; Theodulf's *haec* at the beginning of the third line has no associated noun, and Englishing it with an unspecified "these" is awkward. Freeman and Meyvaert add "things," "these things," but one could instead read "images," especially as the first line ends with *aspice spectans*, highlighting that the beholder's experience here is visual.

In my view, then, the mosaic (fig. 1) is not advocating a return to the Old Testament, or to Temple cult, but is precisely noting that understanding of the Old Testament accounts of the Sancta Sanctorum and its contents must be through the lens of the Christian message and tradition. Theodulf's inscription, and the mosaic that it accompanies, is not "antiquarian" but spiritual, and perhaps ultimately eschatological in thrust, focused not on the past but the future. Indeed, Theodulf's own words seem to support this proposed interpretation of the mosaic as images not suitable for veneration, not a revival of Old Testament patterns of thought or behavior, but as images of "future mysteries." In his *Opus Caroli* Theodulf writes in book 1, chapter 15, of the ark in this wise:

> The holy Moses is said to have made, at God's command, a propitia-tory—the ark of the Testament—and also to have hewn two tablets of stone: yet he never gave any command to worship these things; nor did he make them as memorials of the past as a most sacred pre-figuration of future mysteries. . . . These things—the ark, propitiatory, and cherubim— . . . we seek not to see in painted tablets or walls, but to behold with the eye of the mind in the hidden shrine of the heart.[62]

> [Fecisse sanctus Moyses praecipiente Domino propitiatorium et ar-cam testamenti et duos cherubim aureos nec non et excidisse tabulas lapideas legitur, non tamen adorare iussisse; nec ea ob praeteritarum quarundam rerum memoriam, sed ob futurorum mysteriorum sacratis-simam praefigurationem creditur condidisse.[63]. . . Haec igitur insignia, arca videlicet et quae in ea sunt, propitiatorium sive cherubim, semper a nobis spiritali intuit cernantur et tota mentis intentione quaerantur. Nec ea in depictis tabulis sive parietibus quaeramus, sed in penetra-bilibus nostri cordis mentis oculo aspiciamus].[64]

To be sure, these statements are firmly datable to 792–93, approximately ten years before the Germigny mosaic was commissioned, but it seems to me that the burden of proof rests with one who would claim that during the intervening decade Theodulf had fundamentally changed his attitude toward the ark and its significance. Indeed, it is striking that the choice of words is very much the same: the inscription uses *aspice* and *cernens*, this *Opus Caroli* passage *aspiciamus* and *cernantur*.

Theodulf may have been always something of an outsider at the court of Charlemagne, and I would not claim his views as "typical" of contemporary thinking. Charlemagne as David, Hildebald of Cologne as Aaron,[65] the ques-tion of the Franks as the "new Israel,"[66] putting the breastplate of an Old Testa-ment high priest on the chest of Christ in a miniature closely associated with Alcuin and Charlemagne and datable to around 800; these and many other phe-nomena point toward a powerful interest in the Old Testament on many lev-els, including as a source of inspiration and a kind of model, with the Frankish king urged to emulate David and Solomon and Josiah rather than Constantine, much less Augustus.[67] I can no more than point out that the intense interest in Jerusalem and its Temple around 800[68] is also witnessed wherever the Book of Kells was produced—most think at Iona, for it has very few narrative miniatures but does present the Temptation in the Temple, highlighted with a rare full-page initial facing it.[69] For Theodulf, however, the Old Testament was also a negative exemplum and admonition, and like the Roman imperial heritage needed at the very least to be reinterpreted and corrected in Christian terms. In neither of these regards is he really so peculiar. Take the citation of the Old Testament as a negative exemplum, specifically the sentiment that I believe is expressed in the Germigny mosaic (fig. 1) that, following Paul, since the coming of Christ Old Testament ideas and practices had been superseded and should not be followed. Recently Steven Fine called attention to John Chrysostom's condemnation of the practice of Christians attending the synagogue on Rosh ha-Shanah, Yom Kippur, and Sukkot, in which he contrasts the synagogue with the Temple, the latter (unlike the former) full of holy things, but entirely lost: "What sort of ark [kibotos] is it that the Jews now have, where we find no propitiatory, no tablets of the law, no Holy of Holies, no veil, no high priests, no incense, no holocaust, no sacrifice, none of the things that made the ark of old holy and august?"[70] This is a sentiment with which Theodulf would have been fully in agreement, in my view, and it is sharply at variance with the papal liturgy that he would have seen in Rome, which implied revival or continuity. Theodulf understood the Ark of the Covenant and Sancta Sanctorum and high priest of the Old Testament as historical and allegorical, in line with Hebrews and Chrysostom, not something that can or should be emulated or revived in the manner that seems to have been expressed by Pope Leo III through his artistic patronage, and as we have seen very likely through his liturgical practices.

Notes

For John, and also for Ann and Paul.

1. John J. Contreni, "'Building Mansions in Heaven': The *Visio Baronti*, Archangel Raphael, and a Carolingian King," *Speculum* 78 (2003): 673–706. My own article, already in press when I presented a condensed version at Kalamazoo, which prevented me from taking his wonderful comments into account, confusingly only appeared after John's contribution, as Lawrence Nees, "The Illustrated Manuscript of the *Visio Baronti* [*Revelatio Baronti*] in St. Petersburg (Russian National Library, cod. lat. Oct. V. I. 5)," in *Court Culture in the Early Middle Ages: The Proceedings of the First Alcuin Conference*, ed. Catherine Cubitt, Studies in the Early Middle Ages 3 (Turnhout, 2003), 91–128. Although, unfortunately, not included in the exhibition, the St. Petersburg manuscript was recently published in Melanie Holcomb, ed., *Pen and Parchment: The Art of Drawing in the Middle Ages* (New York, 2009), no. 3, 42–43.

2. Ann Freeman and Paul Meyvaert, "The Meaning of Theodulf's Apse Mosaic at Germigny-des-Prés," *Gesta* 40 (2001): 125–39.

3. Ann Freeman, "Theodulf of Orléans and the Libri Carolini," *Speculum* 32 (1957): 663–705.

4. Ann Freeman [with Paul Meyvaert], ed., *Opus Caroli regis contra synodum* (*Libri Carolini*), MGH Conc. 2, Supp. 1, esp. 29–30 and fig. 16 on the Germigny mosaic.

5. Karl Morrison, "Anthropology and the Use of Religious Images in the *Opus Caroli*

regis (*Libri Carolini*), in *The Mind's Eye: Art and Theological Argument in the Middle Ages*, ed. Jeffrey F. Hamburger and Anne-Marie Bouché (Princeton, 2006), 32–45.

6. Thomas F. X. Noble, *Images, Iconoclasm, and the Carolingians* (Philadelphia, 2009).

7. Freeman and Meyvaert, "Meaning," 126, drawing on Theodulf's Poem 72, ed. Ernst Dümmler, *Poetae latini aevi Carolini I*, MGH Poetae 1, 565, line 66: "Solius illud opus Romani praesulis extat, Cuius ego accepi pallia sancta manu"; and Alcuin's letter 225, ed. Ernst Dümmler, *Epistolae Karolini aevi II*, MGH Epp. 4, 368–69.

8. For discussion of the current state of the mosaic and the evidence for earlier conservation and restoration see Anne-Orange Poilpré, "Le décor de l'oratoire de Germigny-des-Prés: L'authentique et le restauré," *Cahiers de civilisation médiévale* 41 (1998): 281–98; nineteenth-century restorations were extensive, but probably did not significantly alter the iconography of the mosaic, and although the inscription is now probably entirely composed of nineteenth-century *tesseare*, but the text had already been recorded prior to the restoration, and was not altered.

9. Joseph Wilpert and Walter N. Schumacher, *Die römischen Mosaiken der kirchlichen Bauten von IV.–XIII. Jahrhundert*, rev. ed. (Freiburg, 1976), pl. 47.

10. *Carlo Magno a Roma* (Rome, 2001), 186–89, and color plate of the front with doors and inscription on 187.

11. Hartmann Grisar, *Il Sancta Sanctorum ed il suo Tesoro sacro: Scoperti e studii dell'autore* (Rome, 1907), 68–71 on the "scrigno" of Leo III (engraving fig. 21).

12. Giovanni Morello, "Il Tesoro del Sancta Sanctorum," in *Il Palazzo Apostolico Lateranense*, ed. Carlo Pietrangeli (Florence, 1991), 91–105.

13. For example, in the Godescalc Evangelistary, Paris, Bibliothèque nationale de France, MS n.a. lat. 1203, fols. 126v–127r, datable 781–83: "ultimus hoc famulus studuit complere Godescalc." See Marie-Pierre Lafffitte, Charlotte Denoël, and Patricia Roger, eds., *L'évangéliaire de Charlemagne*, Art de l'enluminure 20 (Paris, 2007), 4–8, with the entire text of the colophon reproduced in color and translated into French. For the Latin text see Dümmler, *Poetae latini*, 94–95, conveniently reproduced with a German translation in Bruno Reudenbach, *Das Godescalc-Evangelistar* (Frankfurt a.M., 1998), 98–101.

14. Erik Thunø, *Image and Relic: Mediating the Sacred in Early Medieval Rome*, Analecta romana instituti danici supplementum 32 (Rome, 2002), 160–66 (160).

15. See *Sancta Sanctorum* (Milan, 1997). For important evidence on the history of the *Sancta Sanctorum* and its collection see Bruno Galland, *Les authentiques de reliques du Sancta Sanctorum*, Studi e testi 421 (Vatican City, 2004), a reference for which I am grateful to Julia M. H. Smith. This catalogue of 130 surviving identifying labels for relics from the *Sancta Sanctorum* concludes (87–90) that by far the largest number are found to date, on palaeographical grounds, from the late seventh to the ninth century, with some added later, into the thirteenth century. Roughly half of the early labels are palaeographically not linked with others in the collection as now constituted; the collection was a composite, in other words, bringing together objects already labeled at their place of origin or previous collection, not after arrival at the St. Lawrence chapel. Some of the relics were already in the chapel before the major renovation and construction of the Arca Cipressina under Leo III.

16. For those panels see color reproductions in Leonard von Matt, Georg Daltrop, and Adriano Prandi, *Art Treasures of the Vatican Library* (New York, [1970]), fig. 65.

17. Thunø, *Image and Relic*, 166n462, citing Louis Duchesne, ed., *Le Liber pontificalis*, 2 vols. (1886–92), 2:142 (2nd ed., ed. Cyrille Vogel [Paris, 1955]). For translation and

discussion of this passage see Raymond Davis, *The Lives of the Ninth-Century Popes (Liber Pontificalis): The Ancient Biographies of Ten Popes from* A.D. *817–891*, Translated Texts for Historians 20 (Liverpool, 1995), 173 and n. 31, arguing that the phrase words *Sancta Sanctorum* in the texts as a place where a large crowd assembled must be metaphorical and not a reference to the St. Lawrence chapel. I have not yet been able to consult Judson J. Emerick, "Altars Personified: The Cult of the Saints and the Chapel System in Pope Paschal I's S. Prassede (817–819)," in *Archaeology in Architecture: Studies in Honor of Cecil L. Striker*, ed. Judson Emerick and Deborah Deliyannis (Mainz, 2005), 43–63.

18. Thunø. *Image and Relic*, 166 and n. 462. The Gregory IV reference is especially interesting, having to do with the statement that the oratory of St. Lawrence was entered by the pope alone, analogous to the high priest entering the Holy of Holies in the Jerusalem Temple alone; for this he cites Duchesne, *Liber pontificalis*, 2:81, but I find there no explicit support for the statement.

19. Duchesne, *Liber pontificalis*, 1:469; trans. Davis, *Lives of the Eighth-Century Popes*, no. 6, 89. The editor's note that the reference to the oratory or St. Lawrence in the Lateran where Stephen II was ("against the holy canons") consecrated in 768 is "the earliest mention of the Sancta Sanctorum at the top of the *Scala Santa* is to say the least not helpful to scholars" and deeply anachronistic, although not necessarily incorrect.

20. According to the *Liber pontificalis*, Leo III established at the Lateran a chapel dedicated to the archangel Michael, which he built from the ground up. The text suggests a date of 810–11 for it, and says that it was richly decorated with mosaics, picture, and colored marbles. See Davis, *Lives of the Eighth-Century Popes*, 223.

21. See Charles McClendon, *The Origins of Medieval Architecture: Building in Europe*, A.D. *600–900* (New Haven, CT, 2005), 123–27, for discussion and literature, rightly locating these works in Rome immediately between Aachen and Germigny.

22. Manfred Luchterhandt, "Päpstlicher Palastbau und höfisches Zeremoniell unter Leo III.," in *799, Kunst und Kultur der Karolingerzeit: Karl der Grosse und Papst Leo III. in Paderborn; Beiträge zum Katalog der Ausstellung Paderborn 1999*, ed. Christoph Stiegemann and Matthias Wemhoff (Mainz, 1999), 109–22 (116).

23. Davis, *Lives of the Eighth-Century Popes*, 183; Luchterhandt, "Papstlicher Plastbau," 116.

24. Davis, *Lives of the Eighth-Century Popes*, 189.

25. On this image see Serena Romano, "L'acheropita lateranense: storia e funzione," in *Il volto di Cristo*, ed. Giovanni Morello and Gerhard Wolf (Milan, 2000), 36–45. One way of explaining the absence of a claim that the acheropita image was already in the Sancta Sanctorum chapel from Leo III's time is that it was not there, and we must imagine another location for it. Another way of explaining the absence would be reluctance to highlight something that had turned out to be highly controversial. Theodulf's mosaic may well be an early indication of that controversy and indirectly might be taken as evidence for the presence of the *acheropita* image in Leo's Sancta Sanctorum chapel.

26. Davis, *Lives of the Eighth-Century Popes*, 57.

27. See Hans Belting, *Likeness and Presence: A History of the Image before the Era of Art*, trans. Edmund Jephcott (Chicago, 1994), 64–68 and 323–25, and fig. 192.

28. Romano, "L'acheropita," 39, with references. See also for a recent discussion Sible de Blauuw, "Il Patriarcho, la Basilica Lateranense e la liturgia," *Mélanges de l'École française de Rome, Antiquité* 116 (2004): 161–71, a reference kindly brought to my attention by Kirstin Noreen.

29. Thunø, *Image and Relic*, 161n438.

30. Ibid., 165.

31. Ibid., 166.

32. For the Milan altar see Carlo Capponi, *L'altare d'oro di Sant' Ambrogio* (Milan, 1996). It is my impression that the impressive Archangel Michael chapel of Leo III dropped from sight, for I have found no mention of it in later sections of the *Liber pontificalis*.

33. For a recent discussion see Dorothy Verkerk, *Early Medieval Bible Illumination and the Ashburnham Pentateuch* (Cambridge, 2004), with an argument that the manuscript might have been made in Rome. For a color illustration see Herbert L. Kessler, "The Word Made Flesh in Early Decorated Bibles," in *Picturing the Bible: The Earliest Christian Art*, ed. Jeffrey Spier (New Haven, CT, 2007), 140–68, and fig. 117.

34. For the manuscript, Rome, Abbazia de S. Paolo fuori le mura, s.n. fol. 32v, the frontispiece to Leviticus, see now Joachim Gaehde, "La decorazione: Le miniature," in *Commentario storico, paleografico, artistico, critico della Bibbia di San Paolo fuori le mura (codex membrananceus saeculi IX)*, ed. Girolamo Arnaldi (Rome, 1993), 235–328 (239–40), and for a convenient color illustration of the miniature depicting the ark see André Grabar and Carl Nordenfalk, *Early Medieval Painting* (Geneva, 1957), 153.

35. See illustrations in Steven Fine, ed., *Sacred Realm: The Emergence of the Synagogue in the Ancient World* (New York, 1996), pls. 30, 32, and 36 respectively.

36. For discussion see, inter alia, Steven Fine, "From Meeting House to Sacred Realm: Holiness and the Ancient Synagogue," in *Sacred Realm*, ed. Fine, 21–47. For a large catalogue of the representations with discussion see Elisabeth Revel-Neher, *L'arche d'alliance dans l'art juif et chrétien du second au dixième siècles: Le signe de la rencontre* (Paris, 1984).

37. Fine, *Sacred Realm*, pl. 20. The same publication provides a drawing reconstructing a fourth-century Torah shrine from Ostia, which has doors opening to reveal ends of the rolls, and which perhaps gives a plausible idea of how the object represented in the catacomb painting would have appeared (42, fig. 2.17).

38. Ibid., pl. 18a and pl. 18b, no. 14.

39. Ibid., figs. 3.7c and 3.12, the former on a fourth-century tomb slab with funerary inscription for a woman named Besula, with an image of a Torah shrine with circles indicating rolls flanked by two menorahs, and the latter, here illustrated, with the Greek inscription "EULOGIA" (blessing).

40. It is interesting that although there are a large number of images of Torah shrines and/or the Ark of the Covenant in synagogue mosaics from Palestine, they do not have this circular motif as far as I have seen. Revel-Neher, *L'arche d'alliance*, figs. 41 and 42, presents two stone reliefs that do have a single prominent circle represented in what is likely meant as a Torah shrine or Ark of the Covenant. For the latter see also Fine, *Sacred Realm*, pl. 31 and no. 40, who suggests that although the provenance is unknown, it was likely from the Palestinian region and has been dated to the fifth or sixth century. It can now be found in the Hebrew University Institute of Archaeology, no. 2473.

41. Dominicus Giorgi, ed., *Descriptio lateranensis Ecclesiae*, in Giorgi, *De liturgia romani pontificis in solemni celebratione missarum liber quartus*, vol. 3, *Liber quartus* (Rome, 1744), 542–55; also in R. Valentini and G. Zucchetti, eds., *Codice topographico della città di Roma*, 4 vols. (Rome, 1940–53), 3:310–73.

42. Anton Legner, ed., *Ornamenta ecclesiae: Kunst und Künstler der Romanik*, 3 vols. (Cologne, 1985), 3:80–81, no. H8. See von Matt, *Art Treasures of the Vatican Library*, fig. 66, for a color plate of both cover and contents.

43. On the connection between the Lateran specifically and Jerusalem (the Holy Sepulchre, not the Temple) note that these two seem likely, on the basis of surviving evidence, to have shared many elements in the apse decoration, especially the focus on a large cross probably with a bust of Christ. See discussion in Christa Ihm, *Die Programme der christlichen Apsismalerei von vierten Jahrhundert bis zur Mitte des achten Jarhhunderts* (Wiesbaden, 1960), 83–85. The numerous ampullae produced in Palestine for pilgrims, and surviving now chiefly in Monza and Bobbio, may preserve something of this iconography; for these see André Grabar, *Les ampoules de la Terre Sainte* (Paris, 1958).

44. The *Liber pontificalis* text refers, in the *Life of Leo III*, to what we call the Lateran basilica as the *Basilica Salvatoris Constantiniana*.

45. Sible de Blaauw, "The Solitary Celebration of the Supreme Pontiff: The Lateran Basilica as the New Temple in the Medieval Liturgy of Maundy Thursday," in *Omnes Circumadstantes: Contributions towards a History of the Role of the People in the Liturgy; Presented to Herman Wegman on the Occasion of His Retirement from the Chair of History of Liturgy and Theology in the Katholieke Theologische Universiteit Utrecht*, ed. Charles Caspers and Marc Schneiders (Kampen, 1990), 120–43. For the ceremony he describes, he cites *Pontificale romanum saec. XIII*, in Michel Andrieu, *Le pontifical romain au Moyen Âge*, vol. 2, *Le pontifical romain de la Curie romaine au XIIe siècle*, Studi e testi 87 (Vatican City, 1940), 2:439–61. Although he says that the Hebrews text "is cited again and again in the liturgical books describing the papal liturgy of Maundy Thursday" (120), he gives no specific citation. He erroneously identifies the passage from Hebrews as 8:7, when in fact it is 9:7.

46. De Blaauw, "Solitary Celebration," 120–21 and n. 4 at no. 17: "That means what is written in the Old Testament that the pontifex alone once a year entered the Holy of Holies" (Tunc pontifex ad sacrificandum intrat solus infra arcam, ut signifecetur quod in veteri testamento scriptus est quia solus pontifex intrabat semel in anno in Sancta Sanctorum).

47. De Blaauw, "Solitary Celebration," 140 and 135, respectively.

48. Ibid., 132.

49. *Opus Caroli*, 1.29, p. 225 (lines 3–6).

50. *Opus Caroli*, 1.15 and 1.19–20, on the Ark of the Covenant and the cherubim, and 2.26 again on the ark. These are prominently cited again in the fragmentary surviving epistolae of Pope Paschal to Emperor Leo V (between 817 and 824), for which see Giovanni Mercati, "La lettera di Pasquale I a Leone V sul culto delle sacre imagini," in Mercati, *Note di letterature biblica e Cristiana antica*, Studi e testi 5 (Rome, 1901), 227–35, summarized by Noble, *Images, Iconoclasm, and the Carolingians*, 189.

51. *Opus Caroli*, 1.29, pp. 227 (line 25)–28 (line 5).

52. The image seems to have depicted a *Maiestas domini* image of Christ while referring to the ark and cherubim, and using the word "thunderer" (*tonantis*) that is so notable in Theodulf's dedication. The inscription at Gorze read "Hac sedet arce dues iudex, genitoris imago. Hic seraphim fulgent, domini sub amore calentes. Hoc inter cherubim volitant arcane tonantis." See André Grabar, "Les mosaïques de Germigny-des-Prés," *Cahiers archéologiques* 7 (1954): 171–83, discussed by Elisabeth Revel-Neher, "*Antiquus populus, novus populus*: Jerusalem and the People of God in the Germigny-des-Prés Carolingian Mosaic," in *The Real and Ideal Jerusalem in Jewish, Christian and Islamic Art: Studies in Honor of Bezalel Narkiss on the Occasion of his Seventieth Birthday*, ed. Bianca Kühnel, Jewish Art 23–24 (Jerusalem, 1998), 54–66 (57).

53. Georg H. Pertz and Friedrich Kurze, eds., *Annales regni francorum*, MGH SS rer. Germ. 6, 114; trans. Bernhard Walter Scholz, *Carolingian Chronicles* (Ann Arbor, 1970), 81.

54. Freeman and Meyvaert, "Meaning," 26, argued that Theodulf likely returned to Francia with Candidus probably in February: "It would seem from Alcuin's allusions that Candidus was in fact Theodulf's companion during his stay in Rome and that they probably traveled back to Gaul together." Although this might have been the case, our only evidence, Alcuin's letter, does not persuade me that this was necessary or even likely. Freeman and Meyvaert's translation implies too much by rendering *famulus* as "companion" here. The Latin text reads "Maxime, quia filius noster Candidus, vester fidelis famulus." *Famulus* is difficult to translate, but as noted above, it is the term that Godescalc used to describe his relationship to Charlemagne (*ultimus famulus*) in a context that involves having probably journeyed together to and from Rome in 781–82; however, it is not that term that persuades scholars that they traveled together. Indeed, it is the very word used by Pope Leo III in the inscription on the reliquary chest in the Sancta Sanctorum, where he calls himself "indignus episcopus . . . dei famulus." The term implies a close subordinate relationship, no more, and certainly not a traveling companion. Furthermore, Alcuin's letter describes only Candidus's reports of Theodulf's activities while in Rome.

55. See among others, discussion in Thomas F. X. Noble, *The Republic of St. Peter: The Birth of the Papal State, 680–823* (Philadelphia, 1984), 256–308.

56. Lawrence Nees, *A Tainted Mantle: Hercules and the Classical Tradition at the Carolingian Court* (Philadelphia, 1991), 47–146.

57. I owe to Thomas Noble the wise suggestion that I should look at other occurrences of *manufactum* in the *Opus Caroli*. The term appears twenty times in association with the noun *imago*, but perhaps the most interesting occurrence is the unique occurrence with *vultum* (i.e., face). The term occurs three times in rapid succession in 1.24 (*Opus Caroli*, 213), in which Theodulf argues that Psalm 44:13 ("vultum tuum deprecabuntur omnes divites plebis") should not be related to a *manufacto vultu*. The third and last of the occurrences of the term rejects the claim by saying that it implies that if, as "they" (i.e., the Acta of 787) claim, images made by hand are to be petitioned, those images are able to favor the petitioners. This usage sounds very much like the procession and liturgy of the *acheropita* in Rome!

58. Freeman and Meyvaert, "Meaning," 125.

59. Note that the inscription at Germigny is in gold against a blue background, the same scheme used in the Dome of the Rock in Jerusalem. Literary sources tell us that dedicatory inscriptions in gold against blue were placed in the three great mosques, in Damascus, Medina, and Jerusalem, built by Caliph al Walid (I) b. 'Add al-Malik in the early eighth century, and another in this technique was recently discovered in the Umayyad market place in Bet Shean. See Elias Khamis, "Two Wall Mosaic Inscriptions from the Umayyad Market Place in Bet Shean/Bays n," *Bulletin of the School of Oriental and African Studies, University of London* 64 (2001): 159–76, with discussion of the group, limited to the Islamic examples. For and extended study of this scheme, including its Jerusalemic and Solomonic overtones, see Lawrence Nees, "Blue behind Gold: The Inscription of the Dome of the Rock and Its Relatives," in *"And Diverse Are Their Hues": Color in Islamic Art and Culture*, ed. Jonathan Bloom and Sheila Blair (New Haven, CT, 2011), 152–73.

60. Freeman and Meyvaert, "Meaning," 135n3.

61. Athos, Pantokrator, cod. 61, fol. 165r, with David, Bezaleel, and probably the iconoclastic patriarch John the Grammarian before the ark in the tabernacle, for which see Suzy Dufrenne, *L'illustration des psautiers grecs du Moyen Âge: Pantocrator 61, Paris grec 20, British Museum 40731*, Bibliothèque des cahiers archéologiques 1 (Paris, 1966), 34–35

and pl. 26. Stanley Ferber, "The Temple of Solomon in Early Christian and Byzantine Art," in *The Temple of Solomon: Archaeological Fact and Medieval Tradition in Christian, Islamic and Jewish Art*, ed. Joseph Gutmann (Missoula, MT, 1976), 21–44 (33–35 and fig. 14), also pointed out that this image is presented in a manner that makes the ark an endorsement of venerating images.

62. The translation is from John Mendham, *The Seventh general Council, the Second of Nicaea, in which the worship of images was established, with copious notes from the "Caroline books" compiled by order of Charlemagne for its confutation* (London, 1850), 163.

63. Freeman, *Opus Caroli regis*, 169. This phrase was cited by Noble, *Images, Iconoclasm, and the Carolingians*, 189.

64. Freeman, *Opus Caroli regis*, 175.

65. Mary Garrison, "The Social World of Alcuin: Nicknames at York and at the Carolingian Court," in *Alcuin of York*, ed. L. A. J. R. Houwen and A. A. MacDonald, Germania latina 3 (Groningen, 1998), 59–79. Note that Aaron is also the name, as presented in Carolingian sources, of the contemporary Caliph Harun al-Rashid, who had important relations with Charlemagne involving Jerusalem at just this period. See recently Anne Latowsky, "Foreign Embassies and Roman Universality in Einhard's Life of Charlemagne," *Florilegium* 22 (2005): 25–57, and Lawrence Nees, "Charlemagne's Elephant" [in Spanish translation as "El Elefante de Carlomagno"], *Quintana: Revista do Departamento de historia da arte, Universidade de Santiago de Compostela* 5 (2006): 13–49.

66. Mary Garrison, "The Franks as the New Israel?," in *The Uses of the Past in the Early Middle Ages*, ed. Yitzhak Hen and Matthew Innes (Cambridge, 2000), 114–61, and Mayke de Jong, "Charlemagne's Church," in *Charlemagne: Empire and Society*, ed. Joanna Story (Manchester, 2005), 103–35 (113–14).

67. Trier, Stadtbibliothek, cod. 23(I), fol. 28v, for which see Lawrence Nees, *The Gundohinus Gospels* (Cambridge, MA, 1987), fig. 52. For the most recent discussion of the book, see Isabelle Lachat, *Medieval Mastery: Book Illumination from Charlemagne to Charles the Bold, 800–1475* (Louvain, 2002), no. 4, with earlier references.

68. Of course, such interest is not limited to that period, nor is interest in the ark and in recreating it in some form. For a fascinating example of later date see Julie Harris, "Redating the Arca Santa of Oviedo," *Art Bulletin* 77 (1995): 82–93.

69. For a detailed discussion of this miniature see Carol Farr, *The Book of Kells: Its Function and Audience* (London, 1997), 51–103.

70. Fine, "From Meeting House to Sacred Realm," 40–42 (42). He cites as his source *Adversus Iudaeos.* 6.7, PG 48, col. 913.

CHAPTER 10

A New View of a Catalonian *Gesta contra Iudaeos*: Ripoll 106 and the Jews of the Spanish March

CULLEN J. CHANDLER

Ripoll 106 is one of the oldest manuscripts in the Archive of the Crown of Aragon (Arxiu de la Corona d'Aragó, or ACA) in Barcelona, one that deserves to be more widely known than it is. While the later medieval Crown of Aragon, which consisted of Catalonia and surrounding regions, is known for its wealth of documentary evidence, Anglophone scholars have just recently begun to explore the archive's possibilities for earlier ages. The region possessed a religious diversity that is by now well known.[1] In the last ten years studies in English have moved the chronological horizon back to the tenth century, and even the ninth, but still focus on the mundane matters recorded in charters.[2] Manuscript evidence of the learned culture of monastic and cathedral schools is still relatively unknown to the readers of this recent literature, despite what it has to reveal about relationships between Christians and Jews in the ninth-century Spanish March. Ripoll 106 provides valuable clues about exactly this issue, the religious diversity of the March and what Christian educators thought about it.

From the time the doctrinal controversy over Spanish Adoptionism settled down early in the ninth century, it seems the Carolingian Spanish March lay dormant from the standpoint of cultural activity.[3] But throughout the century, monasticism thrived. Documentary evidence shows that several houses were founded, often at comital initiative, while many others received royal immunities and protection.[4] Smaller houses may have lost their independence, but they continued to function as subordinates of larger, more powerful foundations.[5] During and after the conquest of the Spanish March, the Carolingians established their religious institutions in Catalonia, encouraged the use of Benedict's *Rule*, and vigorously opposed the Adoptionist heresy perceived to be plaguing their Gothic provinces.[6] Those sent to reform the March brought with them important texts, including monastic regulations.[7] It is easy to imagine that other texts necessary for the monastic vocation, including schools, made the journey south as well. The cultural context of the Spanish March makes it interesting and important to study. Frankish and Visigothic warriors wrested the land from the hands of its Muslim rulers in the late eighth and early ninth centuries.[8] The military aspect of this story is important, yet it is only one part. To understand the complexity of the conquest and the region's integration into the Carolingian kingdom, what is needed is a history of the politics of culture. Besides the problems cultural differences between Goths and Franks sometimes posed, such as the Adoptionist controversy, the diversity of the Spanish March is noteworthy for at least one other prominent reason. It was an area where Christians lived near Muslims and Jews lived among Christians.

As John Contreni has noted, we lack any comprehensive study of Jews in the Carolingian world.[9] The limited nature of available sources bears significantly on this lapse. Certainly the contributions and deeds of a few Jewish individuals are recounted in contemporary records, including Isaac, who traveled from Aachen to Baghdad and back, and Bodo, who converted to Judaism, took the name Eleazar, and moved to Spain.[10] And there is obviously the work of Agobard of Lyon, famously illustrating negative clerical attitudes toward Jews.[11] Jewish sources for the Carolingian period are hard to come by, so historians must rely on theological and polemical texts to develop a picture of the place of Jews in the larger society. Agobard and Claudius of Turin, both immigrants from Spain, have attracted attention in the last decade or so.[12]

Historians have long recognized the presence of a powerful Jewish community in Catalonia, even from its days as part of the Visigothic kingdom of Toledo.[13] As Bernard Bachrach has shown, this community was prominent enough to influence royal policy, as some kings would court Septimanian Jews while others would act against them to gain popularity with other groups elsewhere in the kingdom.[14] Some evidence from the late eighth century highlights the importance of Jews in the establishment of the Carolingian Spanish March, in addition to the Goths and Franks, whose military actions factor prominently in relevant sources. Earlier, in consolidating his control of Septimania, Pippin III recognized the historical clout of the Jewish population there and favored them with legal freedoms they did not always enjoy under Visigothic kings.[15] Charlemagne followed Pippin's example.[16] As Bachrach has further pointed out, all holders of allods in this part of the Visigothic kingdom were obliged to render military service under the command of the counts, an obligation that continued

under Frankish rule. The campaign for Barcelona included levies from Aquitaine, Burgundy, Gascony, and Septimania, which was home to many Jews—
some of whom, according to Bachrach, were allod holders. Thus Jews likely
formed part of the army that took Barcelona, serving as campaigning soldiers,
garrison troops, and march settlers, although they must have been relatively few
in number. However small the contribution of Jews was, it must be acknowledged
as part of the "Frankish" conquest of the Spanish March.[17] Positions of power,
however, were the preserve of the Frankish and Visigothic aristocrats who participated directly in the conquest or came from families of note in the Frankish
realms. These magnates and their successors controlled the Spanish March as a
province of the Carolingian Empire for generations, until a local family became
de facto sovereigns in the face of weakening and distant royal authority around
the turn of the tenth century.[18]

Surviving evidence thus hints at the presence of a Jewish community in
the Spanish March since its establishment under Charlemagne. Unfortunately,
evidence for the status, roles, and activities of the Jewish population of the Spanish March during the ninth century is quite scarce. While it is well known that
Jews constituted a minority, of indefinable number, and were a socially marginal-
ized group, more precision is difficult to come by because the documentary and
annalistic sources are scant and clarify little in terms of what might pass for sociological data.[19] In fact, research has turned up no documents related to the Jews
of the March from the first half of the ninth century. The earliest surviving reference comes from the entry for 852 in the *Annals of St-Bertin*. David Romano, who
has studied the Jews of early medieval Catalonia as much as anyone, has called
this very short note hard to interpret. Key to his problem is the supposed lack of
context and mulitfaceted meaning of the word *prodentibus*. The most plausible
reading for the passage in question, though, is the annalist's blaming of the Jews
for a victorious Muslim siege and pillaging of the city.[20] There is also a more
generic reference to a Jewish community in Barcelona in correspondence by the
gaon Amram of Sura in Iraq, sent to the master of a rabbinic academy from 869
to 887 in the city.[21] The earliest certain evidence for wider political activity is a
document recording an individual's name in Barcelona in 876–77, although it is
not certain whether he was from Barcelona or a traveler only temporarily in the
city. The notice, preserved as a parchment original and a copy in the *Liber anti-
quitatem* of the Cathedral of Barcelona, is a royal diploma addressed to Barcelona
residents by Charles the Bald, and it mentions the activity of one Jew, named
Judas. The original carries no dating clause but must date to the period 875–77,
since Charles used the title "imperator augustus." But since Judas appears to be
serving as a go-between for the king and his *peculiares* in Barcelona, some have
been reluctant to claim that he lived permanently in Barcelona.[22] Despite this

hesitance, the conclusion does seem reasonable, because Judas came to Charles to report on the loyalty of the emperor's men in Barcelona. Another document, from the late tenth century and preserved in an eighteenth-century copy, mentions a place called *Iudaicas in termino Coscolio*, in the county of Besalú. Some Jews lived there, on an allod that they bought from Count Dela of Girona, who had established Jews in the city of Girona much earlier. This record, if trustworthy, is significant for two pieces of information. First, that Jews were established in Girona, one of the first cities to come under Carolingian rule south of the Pyrenees; and second, that they acquired the allod from the count, making them landowners.[23] Finally, there is information on the political activity of certain Jews in the early tenth century. An individual named Menahem ben Saruq served as ambassador from Córdoba to the court of Count Sunyer I of Barcelona to conclude a peace treaty. More importantly for assessing the presence of Jews who lived in the March is the case of another ambassador, sent to Córdoba from Barcelona, who had in his service a Jew named Bernat.[24] As is clear from this brief overview of the surviving evidence related to the Jews of the Spanish March, any new light that different evidence can shed is badly needed.

To this lingering uncertainty and relative dearth of sources, however, one might well add a consideration of another kind of source made ubiquitous in the wake of Carolingian educational reforms: monastic school manuscripts. In particular, the close study of a late ninth-century codex from the Spanish March holds promise for illuminating Christian attitudes toward Jews as well as other aspects of learned culture in the Spanish March. The manuscript, Barcelona, ACA, Monacals, Ripoll 106, has long been identified as a monastic schoolbook and contains many interesting texts such as the fifth-century Sedulius's *Carmen paschale* and parts of Isidore of Seville's *Etymologiae*. But while these contents certainly shed additional light on early medieval pedagogical culture, it is the manuscript's added inclusion of a text titled *Gesta graecorum de passione Domini contra iudaeos* that merits special interest here, hinting as it does at the significant presence of Jews in Carolingian Catalonia. Only a few scholars concerned with the transmission of a certain ancient work seem to know the true identity of this intriguing text.

Elsewhere in the Carolingian empire, scholars propounded negative attitudes toward Jews—Agobard arguably the most vehement. While scholars' comments often used "theoretical Jews" as a rhetorical device,[25] there is every indication that any Catalonian concern about Jews would be based on the presence of a Jewish population in the region. Despite this promising context, the *Gesta graecorum* text itself gives no outright indication of anti-Judaic sentiment among the clerics of the March. In other words, the text is not a narrative of hostile acts on the part of any Greeks against Jewish communities or individuals. There is, however, another way to understand the presence of this text in the manuscript. Consider that the rubric "Gesta graecorum contra Iudaeos" does not indicate an account of historical "Deeds of the Greeks," but rather the transmission of certain literary "Works of the Greeks," now translated into Latin. That is the more likely case, since the text is really a very early copy of the *Gospel of Nicodemus*, an apocryphal account of Jesus's trial before Pontius Pilate, his crucifixion and resurrection, and most intriguingly, his descent into hell. The themes of the *Gospel* first appeared in Greek and in the late antique context of Christian efforts to confront Jews. In the context of the ninth-century Spanish March, the text's appearance in a schoolbook of the Ripoll monastery suggests its appropriateness for young monks as they familiarized themselves with the story of Christ's redeeming power and victory over death, while also perhaps indicating a desire to stabilize local society by strengthening Christians in their own faith and even urging Jews to convert to Christianity.

The text's title as given in Ripoll 106 indicates some connection to earlier Greek writing, if not action, against Jews. Byzantine anti-Jewish texts have been relatively well studied, and may give some context for the cultural themes prevalent in the Ripoll *Gesta graecorum/Gospel of Nicodemus* and even its dialogue structure. Greek dialogues written in seventh-century Syria and Palestine featured figurative Christians and Jews in debate. Most of these texts, though, were responses to Christian self-doubt brought on by military defeats, intended to convince Christians not to apostacize. One exception, which was intended for conversion, featured as its protagonist a converted Jew with a record of anti-Christian behavior.[26] The *Gospel of Nicodemus*, being the account of a believing Jew allegedly recorded in Hebrew by a witness to its events, likewise can be seen to carry some authority in attempts to convert early medieval Jews. If the heading *Gesta graecorum* indeed indicates that the work was translated into Latin from Greek, these conversion texts provide the late antique context for its production. The eighth-century military Muslim victory over Christians in Iberia and the presence there of Jews—embarrassing reminders of Christianity's ancient triumph over an old religion in the face of defeat at the hands of a new one—nicely parallels the seventh-century Byzantine situation and forms the perfect backdrop to the copying of the *Gospel of Nicodemus* in Spain.[27] A later copyist would add the text to the monastic library of Ripoll.

Surviving evidence, scant though it is, does suggests that there was a Jewish community of some size and importance in the Spanish March around the time of the founding and flourishing of the Ripoll monastery. Ripoll 106 is one of the most important surviving manuscripts for understanding the literary and scientific culture of the Spanish March. Ripoll itself was founded in the late ninth century by Wifred the Hairy and his wife Winidilda, count and countess of Barcelona and other areas in the March. Situated in uplands south of the main spine of the Pyrenees, it was part of Wifred's settlement effort and established networks with both the comital family and lesser laypeople in the decades around 900. It housed the largest monastic library of Old Catalonia and, according to some, drew to its environs Gerbert of Aurillac in his quest for mathematical and scientific learning in the 960s.[28] The script of Ripoll 106 is of the same type as that of many manuscripts from Frankish centers and thus illustrates the spread of Carolingian miniscule as well as the texts it carried.

The manuscript itself consists of 140 folios and measures approximately 225 × 265 mm. The first eight folios are twelfth-century additions, and folio 26 is another later and smaller insertion from when the codex was bound into its current format. Fortunately, the manuscript benefits from the thorough studies of Lucio Toneatto, who remarked that it contained "miscellaneous" texts on scientific and religious themes; his main interest was the Ars gromatica Gisemundi, a surveying text of Catalonian origin.[29] The other texts of the manuscript include a medicinal recipe, many moral and spiritual texts, and other instructional pieces. The last few folios contain an inventory note and hymn. (See table 1.) Toneatto discovered, through investigation of the physical construction of the codex, that folios 9 through 92 comprised a coherent unit.[30] That means the school at Ripoll used most of the existing codex for texts on the trivium and quadrivium, as well as practical scientific topics. The last forty-eight folios therefore originally constituted another book, or even two; it is here that modern readers will find the Gesta graecorum/Gospel of Nicodemus.

Wifred and Winidilda founded Ripoll in the early phase of what has been termed a resettlement of that area of the March. The monastery, along with its sister house Sant-Joan de les Abadesses, served as an anchor point in the land-holding networks in the plain of Vic, which had been lost in a military uprising in the 820s.[31] This immediate setting, in addition to the cultural heritage and parallel to the seventh-century Byzantine anti-Jewish literature, provides the context for the copying of the Gospel of Nicodemus in late ninth-century Ripoll. The Gospel narrates the events surrounding Christ's trial before Pontius Pilate, the Crucifixion, Resurrection, and Ascension, and the rising of other righteous souls to heaven. In most surviving copies, the Gospel of Nicodemus also features the Descensus, depicting the descent of Christ into hell and his confrontation with Satan. The descent episode, unlike the Trial and the Passion, is clearly not based on the canonical Gospels, but may well be an expansion of a reference to such an event in the Apostle's Creed.[32] The text, as it became known in the Middle Ages, consisted of what seem to have been two separate items, the Acts of Pilate (including the Descensus) and a Letter of Pilate (addressed to a Roman emperor, alternatively Claudius or Tiberius in different versions). These texts are basically pious forgeries of what would have been considered historical documents, the kind of writing usually designed to defend the faith.[33] However, in the case of the

Table 1. Table of Contents, MS Ripoll 106

fols. 1–8	Later additions not considered here
fol. 9r	Medicinal recipe
fols. 9v–25v	Bede, *De arte metrica et de schematibus et tropis libri ii*
fol. 25v	Computus fragment
fol. 26v	Music fragment (later addition)
fol. 27r	Leporius, *Libellus emendationis siue satisfactionis*
fols. 27r–50r	Augustine, *Soliloquia*
fols. 50r–50rc	*Disticha Catonis*
fols. 53rc–58v	Prosper of Aquitaine, *Epigrammatum liber* fragments
fols. 58v–74v	Sedulius Scottus, *Paschale Carmen*
fols. 74v–75v	Sedulius Scottus, Hymn 1
fol. 75v	Computus table, called "Quadratica"
fols. 76r–86v	Gisemundus, *Ars gromatica* (out of original chapter order)
fols. 86v–89r	Isidore, *Etymologiae* excerpts
fol. 89r	Computus fragment
fol. 90r	Fragment "De generibus numerorum"
fol. 90r	Bede, *De natura rerum* excerpts
fols. 90v–92r	"De localibus ubi est magnum intellectum ad fidei nutrimentum"
fol. 92v	Music fragment
fols. 93r–95r	Computus fragment
fols. 95r–96r	"De obedencia"
fols. 96r–101r	Dionysius Exiguus, translation of Gregory of Nyssa, *De opificio hominis*
fols. 101r–102v	Letter of Hieronimi Presbiteri
fols. 102v–114v	Boethius to deacon John on Trinity
fol. 114v	Music fragment
fols. 114v–117r	Script changes, becomes messy . . . calendar?
fols. 117r–121v	"Liber Methodii"
fols. 121v–122r	Jerome on Daniel
fols. 122r–139v	"Gesta graecorum contra Iudaeos"
fol. 140r	Inventory note
fol. 140v	Hymn

Nicodemus author—like that of the Byzantine "Jacob the Newly Baptized"—certain texts were almost certainly intended to convert Jews.[34]

    Although experts in biblical and apocryphal studies date the themes treated in the *Gospel of Nicodemus* to the second century, the oldest surviving Latin copy is the fifth-century palimpsest in Vienna, Österreichische Nationalbibliothek, MS

563.[35] Latin versions of the text survive along with Greek, Coptic, Syriac, Armenian, and later medieval Old Slavonic and Western vernaculars.[36] Judging from accusations levied against Jesus in the Acts of Pilate portion of the text, the ideas carried in the text must be relatively old, as it holds that the Jews claimed Jesus's birth had resulted from Mary's act of fornication rather than later medieval notions of her alleged adultery. Surviving copies of the Acts of Pilate may well be augmented compared to the putative lost original; they are further adapted from those texts used by Epiphanius in the first verifiable reference to the existence of the apocryphon.[37] Since the Vienna palimpsest appears in a ninth-century manuscript, the question of the apocryphal work's age was a matter of debate, but the weight of scholarship supports the earlier, fifth-century date.[38] Biblical scholars have for more than a century used the printed edition of Constantine Tischendorf, but he worked with a limited number of manuscripts and did not know Ripoll 106.[39]

The manuscript context of the Gospel of Nicodemus at Ripoll is worth considering. Teachers in the ninth century did not waste the precious resources that went into bookmaking by randomly assembling unrelated texts together between two covers.[40] Several texts of the group that were originally kept at Ripoll with the Gospel of Nicodemus were clearly meant for religious instruction. Ripoll 106 contains part of an anonymous commentary on Kings and Dionysius Exiguus's translation of Gregory of Nyssa's De opificio hominis.[41] Following that are two works of St. Jerome and Boethius's treatise on the Trinity. Among these is a computus table.

Taking the manuscript in its current form, it provides us with what would have been at least two separate codices among the first to be held at the Ripoll monastery. Concerning the trivium, the school possessed texts dedicated to verse. The current binding preserves, for example, one of a handful of local copies of Bede's De arte metrica. Ripoll's students received moral instruction through the versified Disticha Catonis, a common elementary schoolbook, since students were expected to internalize ethical precepts as they learned Latin.[42] Other late antique moral and spiritual texts in this rich codex, such as Augustine's Soliloquiae and works by the fifth-century African bishop Leporius and Prosper of Aquitaine, suggest that the monks of Carolingian Catalonia worked within a very old tradition of spiritual instruction throughout the ninth and tenth centuries, using what they wanted to address specific questions.[43]

Quadrivium texts large and small serve as windows into the scientific classrooms of Carolingian Catalonia. Several anonymous tracts pop up amongst the larger texts of Ripoll 106. Amidst the tracts on grammar, verse, and morality, computus tables and rules for the calculation of the calendar surface intermittently. Geometry and surveying held a special place in the Spanish March as settlement expanded into desert areas. Indeed, the most important intellectual contributions of Catalonia came in these fields. A table of constellations precedes

the text of Gisemundus, a text significant for its transmission of classical surveying works, but is also important for the context of the manuscript and the *Gesta
graecorum/Gospel of Nicodemus*. Ripoll itself loomed large in the settlement of its
locality, and it is easy to imagine the difficulties terrain and uncertain ownership
posed to the initiative.[44] Gisemundus did his neighbors a considerable service
by compiling his tract. Even more significant, the settlers from the mountains
of Cerdanya, to the north of Ripoll, may not have been moving into completely
empty land. While surviving documentation makes no mention of any previous inhabitants, events of the earlier ninth century give reason to postulate the
presence of Muslim or even Jewish villagers in the Ter River valley before Christians moved in. The region occupied by the abbeys of Ripoll and St-Joan de
les Abadesses and by the bishopric of Vic in the late ninth century had been
lost in an armed rebellion involving both Christian and Muslim locals in the
820s. Conceivably the colonization Count Wifred sponsored in the 880s entailed
apportioning the lands vacated by the earlier settlers (both Christian and non-
Christian), drawing up new property lines, and even assimilating some remaining
Jews and Muslims.[45] In this sort of environment, a narrative like the *Gospel of
Nicodemus* could be employed both to shore up the faith and to convert those
who did not yet share it.

This, the final text in Ripoll 106, sheds further light on the religious
context of intellectual activity at the monastery.[46] Although it is given the title
Gesta graecorum de passione Domini contra iudaeos, the text directly addresses
neither actions taken by Greeks against real Jews, nor the situation of Jews
in the Spanish March; likewise it omits discussion of the errors in belief early
medieval Jews held. Instead, it offers readers a narrative of the events surrounding the crucifixion of Jesus Christ, from the accusations levied against him by
leaders of the Jewish community to the Resurrection. This apocryphal Gospel
omits the Last Supper, Judas's betrayal, and Peter's denials, but gives more detail
on the figures' conversations than any of the canonical Gospels, employing
dialogue almost exclusively to convey its story. For example, in recounting a
detailed dialogue between Pontius Pilate and the *principes Iudaeorum*, the text
includes the charges against Jesus that the Jewish leaders brought before Pilate:
namely, that he cured the lame, deaf, paralyzed, blind, leprous, and those possessed by demons on the Sabbath in violation of the law not to work on that
day. Whereas the story in Matthew, Mark, and Luke continues with a very
brief exchange between Jesus and Pilate, the *Gospel of Nicodemus* follows John
18:33–38 in recounting a much more involved scene extending well beyond
Pilate's question. It follows Luke and John in their detailed narrative of Pilate's
remarks to the Jewish people that there is no solid case against Jesus, and so he
should merely be flogged and released.

The Ripoll 106 text thus combines the differing accounts of the four evangelists into a useful digest, going so far as to include some of Jesus's most famous exhortations: "Why have you forsaken me?"; "Forgive them; they know not what they do"; and "Into your hands I commend my spirit."[47] Likewise, it includes not only the Roman soldiers' mocking of Jesus, but also his conversation with the thieves crucified along with him. From Luke 23:39–43 the *Gospel of Nicodemus* has one criminal taunting Jesus, as did the soldiers and passersby (who are not in Luke, but in Matthew and Mark), drawing a rebuke from the other. Jesus tells the second thief, "In truth I tell you, today you will be with me in paradise." Following this exchange, Jesus breathes his last mortal breath, the sky darkens and the earth shakes, and those present admit that he is the Son of God. The apocryphal Gospel thus follows the canonical accounts but does not deliver on the salacious events the scribe had promised in its title. Instead, it offers an instructional synthesis for Christian readers. In its narrative elements, there are no Greeks performing actions against the Jews. The given title, though, more likely refers to the original language of the text, indicating that the manuscript features a translation from Greek. The noncanonical story would have benefited from the added authority antiquity of tongue bestowed.

The text begins to deviate more markedly from the canonical Gospels on folios 129r–133v of the Ripoll manuscript. After Roman soldiers inform the Jewish leaders that Jesus's body is not in the tomb, and after certain Jews bribe them to tell Pilate that the disciples have stolen the body, the Jewish high priests Annas and Cayphas [*sic*] come to believe in Jesus and tell "omnes principes [Iudaeorum]" of the miracle of Christ's resurrection. Nicodemus then enters the narrative and gives his witness to the miracle, in almost exactly the same language in which it was previously related to the reader. Almost as if in awe, the Jews reiterate Nicodemus's testimony. The high priests repent and decide to fetch Joseph from Aramathea, who had removed Christ's body from the Cross and placed it in his tomb. Annas and Cayphas send Joseph a written apology for imprisoning him to show their good faith and to encourage him to share what he saw with them. Joseph then gives his story to Annas, Cayphas, and Nicodemus, telling them that after he had buried Jesus, angels appeared, and Jesus himself ordered him to go to Galilee. Joseph adds that others besides Jesus had risen from the dead as well. Joseph tells these authorities that a man named Simeon had two sons, Leucius and Charinus, who had actually participated in this great resurrection. Hastening along, the party finds these two brothers adoring wood fashioned into the sign of the cross. Annas, Cayphas, Nicodemus, and Joseph ask them to explain such adoration, to which the brothers answer that they had died and had personally witnessed Jesus's sojourn in hell.

Here the text moves into the so-called Descensus, narratively ushering the audience down into hell. Satan appears, engaged in a dialogue with the Prince of Death (also styled the Prince of Hades), complaining about Jesus's talents as a teacher and healer, and debating who possessed more power over human affairs. Satan is upset about Jesus's authority and his penchant for overturning all evil. The audience learns of Satan's plot to arrange for Jesus to die and descend to hell, thus ending Satan's problems and giving him ultimate power over the human race. Jesus does indeed enter the world of the dead, but instead of falling victim to the enemy's power, consigns Satan to hell. Those righteous souls in hell—including many figures familiar from the Old Testament—call to Jesus *magna voce* for redemption as the law requires and the prophets foretold. He saved the living with his cross, and so must also save the dead with his own death. "The king of glory" (rex gloriae) then extends his hand and announces that those who follow him can overcome damnation by the wood of the Cross, just as he did. Jesus makes the sign of the cross over Adam and "over all his saints" (super omnes sanctos suos), and they all ascend out of hell to their rightful place in heaven. And so, having witnessed such a miracle and having been raised from the dead themselves, Leucius and Charinus began to worship wood arrayed in the form of a cross, as they were when the others found them.

The depiction of Leucius and Charinus adoring a cross holds potential for understanding the presence of the *Gospel of Nicodemus* in the Ripoll codex. Ripoll 106 is one of only seven manuscripts that include the representation of the Cross in this particular respect, the others dating to the later Middle Ages. One additional, relatively old manuscript, Paris, Bibliothèque nationale de France (BnF), MS n.a. lat. 2171, also originated in Spain as is evident from its Visigothic script.[48] Spain was thus a key area for the early medieval transmission of the text. In this context, the rationale for maintaining the narrative of cross adoration in copies of the *Gospel of Nicodemus* may be the presence of a sizeable Jewish minority in Spain and the controversy over religious images. Regarding the seventh-century Byzantine anti-Jewish dialogues and their environment—that shared much in terms of political and religious situations with ninth-century Spain—Averil Cameron has noted the parallel of their prevalence with the "rise to prominence of the whole question of religious images."[49] The controversy over images, of course, persisted into the eighth and ninth centuries in both the Greek and the Latin Christian worlds. In the West, the most outspoken critics of images were *hispani* like Theodulf of Orléans and Claudius of Turin.[50] In Spain, where Muslims and Jews adhered to a more stringent form of monotheism and followed more strictly the prohibition against worshipping images, Christians had to formulate responses. Either they could adopt rigid positions against images, or develop apologetic arguments to the contrary. In emphasizing the Cross as a symbol of salvation, the *Gospel of Nicodemus* thus served to support the use of a material object in worship. The wood that Leucius and Charinus adored was arrayed into the form of a cross, but depicted no humans, saints, or angels; it did not even carry an image of Christ as God. The text therefore effectively defended the Christian practice of worshipping before a cross in the face of antagonism from other monotheistic groups, and perhaps even extreme Christian icono-clasts.[51] On this point, Christian thought toward a representation of the Cross in the Spanish March did not oppose Theodulf's strict image-wary ideals, for indeed, even Theodulf recognized the Cross as a *res sacrata*.[52]

Ripoll 106 is not the only manuscript in the Carolingian period to include the *Gospel of Nicodemus*. As many as eleven others date to the ninth century, among them two of uncertain date which may belong to the tenth. Another six are certainly tenth-century productions.[53] One of these early manuscripts indicates that the *Gospel of Nicodemus* was known at the school of perhaps the most famous teacher of the late Carolingian age, Martianus Hiberniensis, who is known to have personally owned Laon, Bibliothèque municipale, MS 265. The copy of the *Gospel of Nicodemus* in Laon 265 is in Martianus's own hand.[54] These copies, plus a well-known Austrian manuscript, however, do not include the episode of Leucius and Charinus adoring the Cross.[55] Only those manuscripts originating in Spain do, which may indicate that the presence of Jewish and Muslim communities was a factor in the story's transmission.

Fewer than twenty Carolingian-era manuscripts contain the *Gospel of Nicodemus*, but that is not the only ninth-century text to treat the soteriologi-cally significant Descensus theme. In the decades before Ripoll 106 was created, well-known Carolingian poets dealt with Christ's journey into hell. Audradus of Sens, near the middle of the ninth century, composed a poem known as *De fonte vitae*, a verse narrative of biblical history and the events up to Jesus's death on the Cross plus miraculous happenings thereafter.[56] John Scottus treated the same idea in his poetry, especially a short work now known as "Descensus ad inferos et resurrectio."[57] As in the Ripoll 106 version of *Nicodemus*, the Cross figures into the verse treatments of Audradus and John Scottus. Despite these similarities in subject matter, any connection of contemporary poetry to the *Gospel of Nicode-mus* remains indemonstrable.[58] Clearly its major themes had become part of the mainstream educated Christian culture—and its preoccupation with the place of Jews in the world—during the ninth century.[59]

Given the somewhat broad geographic and chronological distribution of texts on similar themes, it is as yet unclear how exactly the *Gospel of Nicodemus* text originally found its way to Ripoll. Zbigniew Izydorczyk, who has studied the manuscript transmission of various versions of the text through six centuries, has concluded that the Ripoll 106 copy is one of the two oldest surviving examples of its family, the Iberian-based C version. The other also originated from Spain and was owned by the monastery of Santo Domingo at Silos. Five other manuscripts contain the reading "et ante eos erat lignum in signum crucis" (part of the text is rubbed off and illegible in one of these), so Izydorczyk considers it one of the characteristic readings of the C group.[60] Without older copies of the same version of the text to study in relation to Ripoll 106, it will be difficult indeed to explain the transmission of the *Gospel of Nicodemus* to Ripoll beyond Izydorczyk's hypothesis of an older Iberian copy. Regardless of the details of who copied it, where, and when, it remains clear that the monks of ninth-century Ripoll wanted the apocryphal Gospel in their library along with other useful texts. The apparent Spanish origins of the C family of *Gospel of Nicodemus* manuscripts—the only versions containing the reference to "wood in the sign of the cross"—certainly lends credence to the idea of monastic concern with Jewish culture and the controversy over religious images. The parallels between the seventh-century Byzantine and eighth-century Spanish contexts serve only to strengthen the idea further. The Visigothic kingdom had long been home to a significant Jewish population, especially in the northeastern corner, and had undergone Muslim and Frankish conquests in the century and a half before the foundation of Ripoll. During that interval, the presence of Jews in the Spanish March seems not to have diminished, while the political and religious concerns of Christian lords like Wifred and Winidilda certainly provided a backdrop for the intellectual activities of local monks.

The *Gesta graecorum de passio Domini nostri contra Iudaeos* text in Ripoll 106 does not mention Greeks at all, much less their deeds against any Jews. Its tone, moreover, does not so much denounce Jews as emphasize the Christian doctrine of Redemption through the Crucifixion. Yet the religious content of its story certainly held great value for the instruction of young monks in terms of their learning about the Passion and the Resurrection. Through this text, pupils at the monastic school of Ripoll would have learned—or relearned—to blame the Jews for Christ's death; they also would have learned about the power of the Cross as a symbol of redemption. The fact that the text is actually a copy of the least common version of the *Gospel of Nicodemus* shows that the Ripoll monks were participating in a long tradition of teaching Christ's victory over death and evil by using an apocryphal text. The version of *Nicodemus* in Ripoll 106 seems to have originated in Spain and belongs to the only one of the three surviving manuscript families of the text to mention the image of the Cross. It claims to be a translation of a now lost Greek version. Seen in the context of earlier apocryphal and anti-Jewish literature as well as the politico-religious history of eighth- and ninth-century Catalonia, the *Gospel of Nicodemus* would indeed have been a valuable text for the monks of Ripoll. It could serve them in several ways. Masters found it useful to instruct their pupils on the topic of Christian salvation, and the monks could use it to shore up the faith in their lay neighbors in an area once lost to Christianity. The text and its heading bear subtle witness to a significant Jewish presence in the Spanish March, hinting that the monks defended their religious practices against Jewish neighbors, and perhaps even saw in the *Gospel of Nicodemus* the means to convert Jews to the true faith.

Notes

1. On Jews in the late medieval period, see David Nirenberg, *Communities of Violence: Persecution of Minorities in the Middle Ages* (Princeton, 1996), and for Muslims in Crown territories, Brian Catlos, *The Victors and the Vanquished: Christians and Muslims of Catalonia and Aragon, 1050–1300* (Cambridge, 2004). See also Jonathan M. Elukin, *Living Together, Living Apart: Rethinking Jewish-Christian Relations in the Middle Ages* (Princeton, 2007).

2. Three very good examples of this trend are Adam J. Kosto, *Making Agreements in Medieval Catalonia: Power, Order, and the Written Word, 1000–1200* (Cambridge, 2001); Jeffrey A. Bowman, *Shifting Landmarks: Property, Proof, and Dispute in Catalonia around the Year 1000* (Ithaca, 2004); and Jonathan Jarrett, *Rulers and Ruled in Frontier Catalonia, 880–1010* (Woodbridge, 2010).

3. Many scholars have continued to uphold this idea, even in recent years. See Ramon Abadal i de Vinyals, *La batalla del adopcionismo en la desintegración de la iglesia visigoda* (Barcelona, 1949); Jesus Alturo, "Manuscrits i documents llatins d'origen català del segle ix," in *Symposium Internacional sobre els orígens de Catalunya* (Barcelona, 1991), 273–80.

4. For the establishment of the important female house of Sant Joan de les Abadesses, see Federico Udina Martorell, ed., *El Archivo Condal de Barcelona en los siglos IX–X* (Barcelona, 1951), no. 3, which, while not authentic, is probably an attempt to restore the written record after the sack of Barcelona in 985. Its contents are validated by the consecration, ibid., no. 4. One example of royal protection: ibid., no. 1.

5. As was the case with Sant Pere d'Albanyà, a small monastery that became dependent on Santa Maria d'Arles in Vallespir. See *Catalunya carolingia*, vol. 2, *Els diplomes carolingis a Catalunya*, ed. Ramón d'Abadal i de Vinyals (Barcelona, 1926), 6–8 and 30–32. Ibid., 219–21, for Sant Julià del Mont, which ended up dependent on Banyoles.

6. Cullen J. Chandler, "Heresy and Empire: The Role of the Adoptionist Controversy in Charlemagne's Conquest of the Spanish March," *International History Review* 24 (2002): 505–27.

7. For the texts, including the *De institutione canonicorum*, *De institutione sanctimonialium*, and *Capitulare monasticum*, see MGH Conc. 2, 312–421 and 422–56; and MGH Capit. 1, 343–49.

8. The classic studies are Ramon d'Abadal i de Vinyals, *Dels visigots als catalans*, ed. Jaume Sobrequés i Callicó, 2nd ed., 2 vols. (Barcelona, 1974); Archibald Lewis, *The Development of Southern French and Catalan Society, 718–1050* (Austin, 1965); and Josep María Salrach, *El procés de formació nacional de Catalunya (segles VIII–IX)*, 2 vols. (Barcelona, 1978).

9. John J. Contreni, "Charlemagne and the Carolingians: The View from North America," *Cheiron* 37 (2002): 111–54.

10. For Bodo/Eleazar, see Frank Reiss, "From Aachen to al-Andalus: The Journey of Deacon Bodo (823–76)," *Early Medieval Europe* 13 (2005): 131–57.

11. Agobard, *Opera omnia*, ed. L. Van Acker, CCCM 52 (Turnhout, 1981), 113–17 (*De baptismo mancipiorum iudaeorum*), 183–88 (*Contra praeceptum impium de baptismo iudaiorum mancipiorum*), 189–95 (*De insolentia iudaeorum*), and 229–34 (*De cauendo et conuictu societate iudaica*).

12. Johannes Heil, "Agobard, Amolo, das Kirchengut und die Juden von Lyon," *Francia* 25 (1998 [1999]): 39–76, as well as his "Claudius von Turin–Eine Fallstudie zur Geschichte der Karolingerzeit," *Zeitschrift für Geschichtswissenschaft* 45 (1997): 389–412, and "Nos nescientes de hoc velle manere—'We wish to remain ignorant about this': Timeless End, or Approaches to Reconceptualizing Eschatology after AD 800 (AM 6000)," *Traditio* 55 (2000): 73–103.

13. For this point see discussions throughout E. A. Thompson, *The Goths in Spain* (Oxford, 1969); Lewis, *Development*, 12.

14. See especially Bernard S. Bachrach, "A Reassessment of Visigothic Jewish Policy," *American Historical Review* 78 (1973): 11–34.

15. *Annales d'Aniane*, in *Histoire générale de Languedoc*, ed. Claude de Vic, and Joseph Vaissète, 16 vols. (Toulouse, 1872–1905), vol. 2, cols. 1–12; *Chronicon Moissiacense*, ed. Georg H. Pertz, MGH SS 1, 280–313. This event forms part of the basis of the highly problematic thesis of Arthur J. Zuckerman, *A Jewish Princedom in Feudal France, 768–900* (New York, 1972). Zuckerman argues for a collective grant of vast lands to the Jews of Septimania and the appointment of a sub-king to rule them. This stretches the evidence, to say the least, and I will not follow it here, preferring simply to point out the existence of an important, yet minority, Jewish population in the region.

16. Walter Kienast, "La pervivencia del derecho godo en el sur de Francia y Cataluña," *Boletín de la Real Academia de Buenas Letras de Barcelona* 35 (1973–74): 265–85; Josep M. Salrach, "Práctica judiciales, transformación social y acción política en Cataluña (siglos IX–XIII)," *Hispania* 47 (1997): 1009–48; Michel Zimmermann, "L'usage du droit wisigothique en Catalogne du IXe au XIIe siècle," *Mélanges de la Casa de Velázquez* 9 (1973): 233–81; Roger Collins, "Visigothic Law and Regional Custom in Disputes in Early Medieval Spain," in *The Settlement of Disputes in Early Medieval Europe*, ed. Wendy Davies and Paul Fouracre (Cambridge, 1986), 85–104; Marie A. Kelleher, "Boundaries of Law: Code and Custom in Early Medieval Catalonia," *Comitatus* 30 (1999): 1–10.

17. Bernard S. Bachrach, "On the Role of the Jews in the Establishment of the Spanish March (768–814)," in *Hispanica Judaica: Studies in the History, Language and Literature of the Jews in the Hispanic World*, ed. Josep María Sola-Solé (Barcelona, 1980), 11–19.

18. Ramon d'Abadal i de Vinyals, *Els primers comtes catalans* (Barcelona, 1958), esp. 53–72 and 327–44.

19. David Romano, "Els jueus de Barcelona i Girona fins a la mort de Ramon Borrell (1018)," in *Symposium internacional sobre els orígens de Catalunya (Segles VIII–XI)*, 2 vols. (Barcelona, 1991–92), 2:124.

20. Romano, "Els jueus de Barcelona i Girona," 125; *The Annals of St-Bertin*, ed. Janet L. Nelson (Manchester, 1991), 74; *Annales de Saint-Bertin*, ed. Félix Grat, Janne Vielliard, and Suzanne Clémencet (Paris, 1964), 64. The difficult passage: "Mauri Barcinonam, judaeis prodentibus, capiunt; interfectisque pene omnibus christianis et urbe vastata impune redeunt." My reading concurs with that of Nelson, who translates it as Jewish betrayal of the city.

21. Romano, "Els jueus de Barcelona i Girona," 126n5; David Romano, "Notes sobre l'activitat dels jueus a Catalunya l'any mil," in *Actes del Congrés internacional*

Gerbert d'Orlhac i el seu Temps: Catalunya i Europa a la fi del Ir milleni, ed. Imma Ollich i Castanyer (Vic, 1999), 697. In his earlier work, Romano expressed uncertainty on the grounds that the academy's location is not concretely provable. Unfortunately, the nature of his published work on the question, deriving from symposium proceedings, appears to have prevented Romano from citing the relevant evidence in either of these papers. His sources have been quite difficult to track down. See also Michael McCormick, *Origins of the European Economy* (Cambridge, 2001), 931 (appendix 4, no. 526).

22. D'Abadal i de Vinyals, *Els diplomes carolingis*, 66–70; see also McCormick, *Origins of the European Economy*, 677.

23. Romano, "Els jueus de Barcelona i Girona," 125–26.

24. Romano, "Notes sobre l'activitat," 697–98.

25. David M. Olster, *Roman Defeat, Christian Response, and the Literary Construction of the Jew* (Philadelphia, 1994).

26. Olster, *Roman Defeat*, 116–79. The exceptional text is known as the *Doctrine of Jacob the Newly Baptized*. See also Averil Cameron, "Byzantines and Jews: Some Recent Work on Early Byzantium," *Byzantine and Modern Greek Studies* 20 (1996): 249–74. While Cameron points out some weaknesses in Olster's argument, there is agreement about the text's intent to convert Jews (ibid., 258–65).

27. The text in Ripoll 106 represents the least common of three manuscript types, the so-called C type; it is one of the two oldest C type manuscripts, both of which date to the ninth century and originated in Spain. Zbigniew Izydorczyk, "The *Evangelium Nicodemi* in the Latin Middle Ages," in *The Medieval Gospel of Nicodemus: Texts, Intertexts, and Contexts in Western Europe*, ed. Zbigniew Izydorczyk (Tempe, AZ, 1997), 43–101 (51–52).

28. The location of Gerbert's study is the subject of recent debate. See Ramon Ordeig, "Ató de Vic, mestre de Gerbert d'Orlhac," in *Actes del Congrés internacional Gerbert d'Orlhac*, ed. Ollich i Castanyer, 593–620, and Pierre Riché, "Gerbert d'Aurillac en Catalogne," in *Catalunya i França meridional a l'entorn de l'any Mil*, ed. Xaier Barral i Altet et al. (Barcelona, 1991), 374–77.

29. Lucio Toneatto, "Manoscrito dell'ars Gromatica Gisemundi," in *Codices artis mensoriae: I manoscriti degli antichi opusculi latini d'agrimensura (V–XIX Sec.)*, vol. 3, *Tradizione indiretta, appendici, bibliografia, indici* (Spoleto, 1995), 997–1012; Lucio Toneatto, "Note sulla tradizione del *Corpus agrimensorum romanorum*," *Mélanges de l'Ecole française de Rome* 94 (1982): 191–313.

30. Toneatto, "Manoscrito dell'ars Gromatica Gisemundi," 999.

31. Abadal i de Vinyals, "La Catalogne sous l'Empire de Louis le Pieux," *Études roussillonnaises* 6 (1957): 147–77; Roger Collins, "Pippin I and the Kingdom of Aquitaine," in *Charlemagne's Heir: New Perspectives on the Reign of Louis the Pious (814–840)*, ed. Peter Godman and Roger Collins (Oxford, 1990), 373–80.

32. Zbigniew Izydorczyk and Jean-Daniel Dubois, "Introduction," in *Medieval Gospel of Nicodemus*, ed. Izydorczyk, 17. Josef Kroll, *Gott und Hölle: Der Mythos vom Descensuskampfe* (Leipzig, 1932), 83.

33. Wolfgang Speyer, "Neue Pilatus-Apokryphen," *Vigilae Christiana* 32 (1978): 53–59.

34. See Olster, *Roman Defeat*, which refers to the *Doctrine of Jacob the Newly Baptized*.

35. Guy Philippart, "Fragments palimpsestes latins du Vindobonensis 563 (Ve Siècle)," *Analecta Bollandiana* 90 (1972): 391–411.

36. Felix Scheidweiler, "The Gospel of Nicodemus: Acts of Pilate and Christ's

Descent into Hell," in *New Testament Apocrypha*, ed. Wilhelm Schneemelcher, trans. R. McLachlan Wilson, rev. ed., vol. 1, *Gospels and Related Writings* (Louisville, KY, 1991), 501–03; Izydorczyk and Dubois, "Introduction," 3. I thank my colleague Steven R. Johnson of the Lycoming College Department of Religion for the reference to Scheidweiler's essay.

37. Scheidweiler, "Gospel of Nicodemus," 501–3; Izydorczyk, "*Evangelium Nicodemi* in the Latin Middle Ages," 44–45.

38. G. C. O'Ceallaigh, "Dating the Commentaries of Nicodemus," *Harvard Theological Review* 56 (1963): 21–58; Philippart, "Fragments palimpsestes latins," 391–411; Zbigniew Izydorczyk, *Manuscripts of the "Evangelium Nicodemi": A Census* (Toronto, 1993); Zbigniew Izydorczyk and Jean-Daniel Dubois, "Nicodemus's Gospel before and beyond the Medieval West," in *Medieval Gospel of Nicodemus*, ed. Izydorczyk, 21–41. Support for Philippart can be found in Izydorczyk, "*Evangelium Nicodemi* in the Latin Middle Ages," 44–45.

39. Constantin von Tischendorf, *Evangelia Apocrypha: Adhibitis plurimis codicibus Graecis et Latinis maximam partem nunc primum consultis atque ineditorum copia insignibus* (Leipzig, 1876), liv–lxxviii, for introductory remarks, 333–434 for an edition of the Latin texts contained in Ripoll 106. Maurice Geerard, ed., *Clavis apocryphorum Novi Testamenti* (Turnhout, 1992), 43–46, refers to Tischendorf's and later editions as well as leading scholarship on versions of the *Gospel of Nicodemus* in a variety of its late antique and medieval linguistic variations.

40. Ernst P. Goldschmidt, *Medieval Texts and Their First Appearance in Print* (London, 1943), 93–95, points out that manuscript compendia were often created based on the similar size of various pieces of parchment, rather than solely on the similarity of their content. But see above on the current state of Ripoll 106 being formed of two late ninth-century sections pieced together with other, later parchment of uneven size; Godschmidt's observations in any case do not deny that texts would be grouped by content.

41. The text headed *Imago Dei* has been identified as a part of Gregory of Nyssa's work: PL 67, cols. 370B–377C.

42. Tomás González Rolán, "La tradición de los Dicta Catonis y el Ripollensis 106," *Habis* 5 (1974): 93–106.

43. Toneatto, "Manoscrito dell'ars Gromatica Gisemundi," 1001; Alfred Cordoliani, "Los manuscritos de cómputo eclesiástico en las bibliotecas de Barcelona," *Analecta sacra Tarraconensia* 23 (1950): 103–29.

44. For a brief outline of the settlement program, see Michel Zimmermann, "Origines et formation d'un état catalan (801–1137)," in *Histoire de la Catalogne*, ed. Joaquim Nadal i Farreras and Philippe Wolff (Barcelona, 1982), 237–55 (244–45).

45. Salrach, *El procés de formació nacional*, 2:107–8, gives some details of the settlement initiative. As far as I know, no one yet has studied the text of Gisemundus sufficiently to ascertain its significance in this context.

46. Romano, "Notes sobre l'activitat," 697–700; M. Isabel Miró Montoliu, "Els jueus i l'ensenyament de les primeres lletres," in *Actes del congrés internacional Gerbert d'Orlhac*, ed. Ollich i Castanyer, 701–11.

47. Matthew 27:46, Luke 23:34 and 23:46.

48. Izydorczyk, *Manuscripts of the "Evangelium Nicodemi,"* 150.

49. Averil Cameron, "Byzantines and Jews: Some Recent Work on Early Byzantium," *Byzantine and Modern Greek Studies* 20 (1996): 249–74; Charles Barber, "The

Truth in Painting: Iconoclasm and Identity in Early Medieval Art," *Speculum* 72 (1997): 1019–36.

50. Theodulf's famous work against the adoration of images is the *Opus Caroli regis contra synodum (Libri Carolini)*, ed. Ann Freeman and Paul Meyvaert, MGH Conc. 2, Supp. 1. See also David Ganz, "Theology and the Organization of Thought," in *The New Cambridge Medieval History*, ed. Rosamond McKitterick, vol. 2, c. 700–c. 900 (Cambridge, 1995), 758–85. See now Thomas F. X. Noble, *Images, Iconoclasm, and the Carolingians* (Philadelphia, 2009) for a full treatment of the controversy over religious images.

51. Ganz, "Theology and the Organization of Thought," 775, on Claudius removing even crosses from churches in Turin. Noble, *Images*, 287–313, on Claudius, his teaching, his activity, and responses to him.

52. Theodulf, *Opus Caroli regis*, 2.26–20. For Carolingian thoughts on the Crucifixion more generally, see Celia Chazelle, *The Crucified God in the Carolingian Era: Theology and Art of Christ's Passion* (Cambridge, 2001), esp. 39–52, for Theodulf and the *Opus Caroli regis* in particular. Noble, *Images*, 158–206, treats the *Opus* in detail.

53. Izydorczyk, *Manuscripts of the "Evangelium Nicodemi,"* 234. The manuscripts are, from the ninth century: Kassel, Landesbibliothek und Murhardsche Bibliothek der Stadt Kassel, MS 2°, theol. 271; Laon, Bibliothèque municipale, MS 265; Munich, Bayerische Staatsbibliothek, clm 29275; Saint-Omer, Bibliothèque municipale, MS 202; Munich, Universitätsbibliothek, MS 2°, cod. 87a; Ripoll 106; Berlin, Staatsbibliothek Preussischer Kulturbesitz, MS theol. lat. oct. 157; Bern, Bürgerbibliothek, MS 582; London, British Library, MS Royal 5 E. xiii; Paris, BnF, MS n.a. lat. 1605. Of uncertain date (s. ix/x): Copenhagen, Kongelige Bibliotek, MS Gl. kgl, S. 1335, 4°; Orléans, Bibliothèque municipale, MS 341 (289), which also might be of eleventh-century origin. Tenth century: Einsiedeln, Stiftsbibliothek, MS 169; Einsiedeln, Stiftsbibliothek, MS 326; Munich, Bayerische Staatsbibliothek, clm 19105; Paris, BnF, MS lat. 2825; Paris, BnF, MS lat. 5327; and Chartres, Bibliothèque municipale, MS 34 (109), which was destroyed in 1944.

54. On this manuscript, see John J. Contreni, *The Cathedral School of Laon from 850 to 930: Its Manuscripts and Masters* (Munich, 1978), 37–38, 95–96, 130–34, and appendix A on the contents of manuscripts.

55. H. C. Kim, ed., *The Gospel of Nicodemus: Gesta Salvatoris; Edited from the Codex Einsiedlensis, Einsiedeln Stiftsbibliothek, MS 326* (Toronto, 1973).

56. Audradus of Sens, *Il fonte della vita*, ed. Francesco Stella (Florence, 1991), 47–49, and for the Descensus, 112 and thereafter; Kroll, *Gott und Hölle*, 134–35.

57. MGH Poetae 3, 536 (poem 6). Kroll, *Gott und Hölle*, 135–36. See also a different poem, MGH Poetae 3, 543.

58. Kroll, *Gott und Hölle*, 137.

59. See Johannes Heil, "Labourers in the Lord's Quarry: Carolingian Exegesis, Patristic Authority, and Theological Innovation; A Case Study in the Representation of Jews in Commentaries on Paul," in *The Study of the Bible in the Carolingian Era*, ed. Celia Chazelle and Burton Van Name Edwards, Medieval Church Studies 3 (Turnhout, 2003), 75–95.

60. Zbigniew Izydorczyk, personal communication, July 22, 2008.

CHAPTER 11

The Reception of Visitors
in Early Medieval Rome

THOMAS F. X. NOBLE

To study the early Middle Ages is frequently to encounter people who went to Rome. Why people went there is reasonably clear. They sometimes went as the diplomatic or political agents of a northern court, most often the Carolingian court, to the papacy. More often, one supposes, they were pilgrims who wished to visit the threshold of the apostles or the many shrines to saints and martyrs located within and without the city. There is evidence that official visitors sometimes did a little "private" touring. One interesting question concerning all these visitors is this: How were they accommodated in Rome? The following pages attempt to offer some details and interpretations on this interesting and important topic.

One need not be a specialist in the history of the early Middle Ages to be able to bring quickly to mind the names of many prominent visitors to Rome: Wilfrid and Benedict Biscop, Willibrord and Boniface, Charlemagne and Charles the Bald. But a nonspecialist might well assume that the thick and constant flood of visitors to Rome would have left behind a dense documentation. Nothing could be further from the truth. The sources are few in number and lacking in detail. It would actually be easier to talk at length about all that we do not know than to elaborate what we do know. Were I theoretically clever, I could spin a tale about the history of absence or the articulateness of silence. Instead I shall simply admit the absence of history and try to fill in a few gaps and blanks.

Why does the subject matter? The place of Rome in the medieval mind is a vast, important, and understudied subject.[1] Knowledge about Rome's visitors is

one path into that subject. The dissemination of Roman relics and the dedica-
tions of churches in the names of Roman saints, Peter most obviously but many
others too, is one gauge of Roman ecclesiastical power and influence.[2] Papal
privileges for monasteries generally had to be obtained in person, so the issu-
ance of such privileges is another sign of papal authority.[3] Rome's art, liturgy,
and music were long and deeply influential. In crucial respects, such influences
were direct products of visitors to Rome. In the eighth and ninth centuries Rome
suddenly became a vastly more prosperous place than it had been since the fifth,
maybe since the fourth, century. I have attributed this newfound wealth to the
Carolingian *pax Italiae* and to corresponding gains in the productivity of central
Italian agriculture.[4] But Paolo Delogu—and others—attribute Rome's wealth to
pilgrims' offerings.[5] In short, knowing something about Rome's visitors is a way of
knowing many things about the history of the early Middle Ages. My focus here
will rest on Rome itself and on the visitors attracted to and accommodated by the
city, its people, and its institutions.

Who went to Rome? There were first of all the grand visitors like Emperor
Constans II; the Anglo-Saxon kings Oswiu of Northumbria, Caedwalla of Wessex, Cenred of Mercia, Offa of Essex, Ine of Wessex, and Offa of Mercia; Carloman, the brother of Pippin III; and the Carolingian rulers Charlemagne, Lothair,
Louis II, and Charles the Bald. Various motives impelled their steps, and we'll
come back to some of them.[6] There were numerous envoys, often from the Carolingian world, who consulted with popes on political or theological issues. One
thinks of Chrodegang, Angilbert, and Adalhard, for example. Some came seeking relics or books. In many cases, these visitors also spent some time touring the
city's churches and frequenting the tombs of the martyrs. That is, they were in
some sense also pilgrims. Pilgrims as such were surely the largest number of visitors.[7] They came from many lands, spent varying periods of time in and around
Rome, and then returned home. There were also what might be termed perpetual
pilgrims: persons who went to Rome intending to spend the rest of their lives
near the *loca sancta*. Such people eventually made up the resident populations
of the *scholae*—to which we shall return. There were persons who fled the early
Arab conquests and the two phases of Byzantine iconoclasm. Such persons were
perhaps less pilgrims than refugees. Finally, there were the Romans themselves
who never ceased to stream outside the city to the tombs and catacombs that
flanked virtually every major road and who paraded through the city in the stational and penitential processions.

It is not possible to construct even a vague sociology of the visitors. How
many of them were there? Nicholas I, in a letter to Emperor Michael III, boasted
of "so many thousands of pilgrims" who come to Rome daily (*cotidie*).[8] This is
not helpful. But it is no less unhelpful than, say, the conflicting reports we have

for the Jubilee year of 1300 which range between 600,000 and 2.5 million. One scholar says, cautiously, "it was probably somewhere between one and two million."[9] One would need fewer than the normal complement of fingers to count the women pilgrims named by the sources. I suspect that, notwithstanding Boniface's solicitude for the virtue of English women pilgrims,[10] many more men did in fact make the journey. But I cannot prove this. The rich and the potent make a splash in the sources when they showed up with impressive entourages, but kings and emperors must have been outnumbered by prominent clerics and laymen of whose continuous presence we have fragmentary records. I think that ordinary people must have been the most numerous of all but the sources speak of them only in general terms. Catacombs and churches are full of graffiti. To my knowledge, Jean Guyon's enumeration of the names in Saints Marcellinus and Peter—11.1 percent are demonstrably northern—is the only one of its kind.[11] May we conclude anything from it? Anna Esposito suggests that northern pilgrims clustered most densely in the two to three centuries immediately following the conversion of a region or people.[12] As an inference, this seems plausible. As a fact, it cannot be credited. We are reduced to concluding that there were always numerous pilgrims of differing degrees of wealth and prominence who spent varying periods in and around the city.

Pilgrim destinations can be tracked with some certainty. Several guides for pilgrims were prepared in the seventh century. Almost certainly these were prepared locally for local use and then came to the attention of northern visitors who made copies of or extracts from them. The most important of these, the *Notitia ecclesiarum urbis Romae*, was compiled during the pontificate of Honorius I (625–38). It was expanded late in the eighth century with a list of some holy places in Milan and a description of St. Peter's. It exists today in Vienna in a late eighth-century manuscript where it nestles between two letters of Alcuin.[13] The guide has an engagingly personal quality in that it is written in the second person singular and provides frequent indications of direction. The opening of the text will serve to illustrate its character. It begins, inexplicably, at Saints John and Paul on the Caelian Hill and then continues in a narration that focuses exclusively on the suburbs:

> From there you will travel through the city to the north and then you
> will arrive at the Porta Flaminia where St. Valentine the martyr rests
> in a huge basilica on the Via Flaminia. Honorius repaired it. There are
> other martyrs beneath the ground in the field to the north. From there
> you go to the east and you will come to the church of John the Martyr
> in the Via Salaria where Diogenes the Martyr rests and in another
> little chamber under the ground Boniface the Martyr and Fistus the
> Martyr, and Blastus the Martyr, then John the Martyr, and after that

Longinus the Martyr. From there you go to the south along the Via
Salaria and you will come to St. Ermete. There one stops in the first
place at the basilica of Basilla the virgin and martyr, and otherwise
Maximus the Martyr and St. Ermete the Martyr, far under the ground.
In another cave Protus the Martyr and Hyacinth, and then the martyr
Victor. Subsequently by the same route you will come to the martyr
St. Pampulus, twenty-four steps beneath the earth.[14]

The guide carries on in this fashion, in a clockwise direction, right around the city.

Another fairly comprehensive text is entitled *De locis sanctis martyrum
quae sunt foris civitate Romae*. This exists today in a late eighth-century Vienna
manuscript as well as in tenth-century manuscripts from Vienna and Würzburg.
Lacking the personal tone and many of the directional pointers of the *Notitia*,
this text begins at St. Peter's and proceeds counterclockwise around the city.
Although space does not permit a detailed investigation here, I think this text
betrays itself as a copy of the *Notitia*. After the text reaches the Via Flaminia, it
contains an incomplete list—beginning with the Constantinian basilica, that is
the later St. John Lateran—of the basilicas in the city. I concur with those who
believe that this list must have been added later.

There are also some fragmentary guides. A catalogue of Rome's cemeteries,
preserved today in five manuscripts ranging from the twelfth to the fifteenth centuries, begins on the Via Salaria and proceeds clockwise but is woefully incomplete both as to the streets and regions covered and the tombs mentioned.[15]
William of Malmesbury transmits another text that he almost certainly copied
from a guide compiled between 648 and the middle of the eighth century.[16] It
also proceeds clockwise and begins with St. Peter's. Its organizational principle,
however, focuses on the gates in the Aurelian walls and not on the roads leading
out of Rome. It is generally less detailed than the *Notitia* but does contain a few
details not found in the latter.

Internal evidence dates these texts, at least their original portions, to the
period between about 640 and 760. The texts themselves permit two inferences.
First, in the seventh and early eighth centuries, visitors to Rome who came as
pilgrims concentrated their attention on the regions outside the city. Second, it
would have taken pilgrims many days, probably weeks, to follow up any one of
these itineraries. It is unlikely that prominent visitors who came on political or
ecclesiastical missions would have had the time to devote weeks to a circuit of
Rome. To my knowledge, we have only one reasonably detailed account of an
early medieval visitor's perambulations. Sigeric, recently elected archbishop of
Canterbury, went to Rome in 990 to obtain his pallium. Apparently he managed
to visit twenty-three churches in two days. His itinerary is interesting, too. He
departed from St. Peter's, crossed the Tiber and went to San Lorenzo in Lucina,

then left the city by the Porta Flaminia and moved, clockwise and selectively, around to San Paolo fuori le Mura, re-entered the city at the Porta Ostiense and worked his way to Santa Maria in Cosmedin before crossing to Trastevere and ending up outside the walls at San Pancrazio.[17] Leaving aside the elite and those who went to Rome to spend the rest of their lives there, we are probably dealing most of the time with ordinary people of modest means. These people would have required accommodation in ways that the rich and powerful would not have. They will engage us again.

A manuscript that is today in Einsiedeln, but that was probably composed at Reichenau, contains three texts that shed considerable light on visitors to Rome.[18] One text mentions San Silvestro in Capite but does not mention Santa Maria Nova. This appears to date it after 750 and before 847. The most famous text in the collection is the so-called Einsiedeln Itinerary. It differs sharply from all the seventh-century itineraries in that it concentrates exclusively on the churches inside the city. The document provides ten different itineraries through the city, arranged street by street with indications of what is to be found on the right-hand side and what is on the left. In addition to mentioning the churches in Rome, the itineraries also point out secular monuments, although by no means all of them, and never by way of detouring the pilgrim from Rome's religious sites. This attention to Rome's both holy and profane is interesting, but I would particularly call attention to the dramatic shift to the city itself. The explanation for this must be the massive project of translating suburban relics into the city beginning with Paul I in the 750s and 760s and continuing well into the ninth century.[19] Rome's ever-developing urban liturgy may also have played a role in focusing attention on the churches of the city itself.[20] As far as visitors are concerned, the point is obvious: down to about 750 they traveled about outside the city and after that they were to be found within the walls.[21]

That Einsiedeln codex contains two other texts that confirm and expand this point. First there is a remarkably detailed description of the Aurelian walls. Second, there is a lengthy set of inscriptions copied down from Roman buildings both sacred and secular. To the latter collection we may add similar ones of about the same date that are connected with Tours, St-Riquier, Lorsch, and Würzburg.[22] While the copying of inscriptions suggests people who were literate, not to say elite, their collection from so many different kinds of buildings and monuments points to a wide array of visitors' interests. Rome of the saints never lost its pull, but Rome of the caesars seems to have had a magnetism in the eighth and ninth centuries that it did not have in the seventh. Perhaps this is an unexpected consequence of the so-called Carolingian Renaissance and the restoration of a Western empire.

The itineraries, therefore, provide insights into the destinations of Rome's visitors and also some hints about local solicitude for visitors. Let us now turn directly to the accommodation of visitors. Of crowned visitors little can be said. The imperial palace on the Palatine still had a *custos* in the early eighth century— the father of Pope John VII.[23] But among Rome's Byzantine rulers only Constans II visited Rome, in 663. He stayed twelve days in the city and may have used the Palatine palace.[24] It seems that Charlemagne renovated a "palace" on the south side of St. Peter's during his stay in the city in 781. This may well have served him, those of his successors who visited Rome, and at least some of the Carolingian offi- cials dispatched to the city as a residence. An Ottonian palace is better attested.[25] I suspect we are dealing with comfortable quarters for the Carolingian elite. Ordi- nary soldiers, such as those who came to Rome with Charlemagne more than once, probably lodged in tents in the Campus Neronis. Charlemagne entered the city on several occasions but no source relates that he ever spent the night there. It is easy to think of churchmen, let us say, Wilfred, Boniface, Chrodegang, Fulrad, Arn, Hartbert, Hatto, who had consultations with the pope at the Lateran. It is not far-fetched to suggest that the papal household would have accommodated some of these important visitors, but no source states this explicitly. The strongest hint that I know is found in the vita of Leo III in the *Liber pontificalis*. The impres- sive entourage—seven bishops and three counts are named—that accompanied Leo back to Rome in 799 held public inquiries for a week or more in Leo's new *triclinium* at the Lateran.[26] Might they have slept nearby?

The sources do provide a few hints about the lodgings secured by some visitors. A letter of Sidonius Apollinaris to his friend Heronius may serve to open the discussion. "Rome burst upon my sight. . . . But before allowing myself to set foot even on the outer boundary of the city I sank on my knees at the triumphal threshold of the apostles . . . after which proof of heavenly protection I found quarters in a hired lodging [*devorsorii parte susceptus*]."[27] Cummian resided in an *ospitium* where his fellow guests were an Egyptian, a Jew, a Greek, and a Scyth- ian.[28] His letter *On the Easter Controversy*, not the tidiest of texts, says he returned to the north after three years. Did he spend all that time in Rome? In any case, he seems to have found lodgings in an international boarding house! Thomas of Farfa found rooms "with a certain consecrated virgin" and a bit later some others who were looking for Thomas stayed there too.[29] It seems reasonable to suppose that people in Rome opened their homes to pilgrims, but the evidence is scanty. Eigil tells us that Sturm spent a year visiting Roman monasteries.[30] Einhard's relic-hunting envoys stayed "for some time" with the larcenous deacon Deusdona in his house near San Pietro in Vincoli.[31] A bit later Waltpert spent fourteen days with a prior.[32] Again, it is not hard to imagine "professional courtesy" accorded by Roman clergy to their northern counterparts. But it is hard to document it.

Around 500 Pope Symmachus erected *pauperibus habitacula* near St. Peter's, St. Paul's, and St. Laurence Outside-the-Walls. At St. Peter's, moreover, he put a fountain outside the atrium and built a public lavatory. He also installed a fountain outside the nearby church of St. Andrea. Likewise at St. Paul's he attended to the water supply and built a bath.[33] This could be no more than the leading edge of the urban caritative services that the papacy gradually took over from the vanishing Roman government. But Symmachus's action evokes two comments. First, as Peter Brown has recently argued, patronage of the poor in ecclesiastical circles in late antiquity need not be taken narrowly as meaning the provision of material needs to the destitute. As a way of defining and perhaps expanding their pastoral mandate, bishops tended to regard virtually their whole flocks as "poor."[34] Second the location of these little dwellings near three of Rome's major extra-urban basilicas brings to mind those seventh-century itineraries, and this in two respects. Many visitors would have approached Rome along the roads leading past one of those basilicas, and pilgrims in those days tended to pay their respects outside the city. The *Life* of Amandus says that he spent his days visiting the churches of the city and at night he "returned to St. Peter's."[35] I don't know what that means but I wonder if he stayed in the sort of place that Symmachus had instituted; and I did not mention above that Symmachus also covered the atrium of St. Peter's, thereby perhaps providing a more commodious shelter. On one of his rampages the Lombard king Aistulf destroyed houses and indeed the northern suburbs near St. Peter's.[36] Could these have been Symmachus's *habitacula*? Might Aistulf have been trying consciously to disrupt pilgrims?

Let us suppose that pilgrims did figure somehow in Symmachus's thinking. His successors continued to take thought for Rome's poor, whoever they were, and unquestionably looked after pilgrims. More than a dozen popes, as the *Liber pontificalis* amply testifies, built or refurbished *xenodochia*; Stephen II alone restored four inside the city and constructed a new one there and built two additional new ones near St. Peter's.[37] The meaning of this word is ambiguous in the extreme. Its lexical range runs from poor-house, to hostel, to hospital.[38] Gregory I attempted to preserve the endowments for a *xenodochium* for pilgrims at St. Peter's.[39] Cummian and his diverse companions stayed in an *ospitium* in the same region. Just outside the portico of St. Peter's stood the *hospitale* of St. Gregory.[40] Are these words synonyms? Leo III built an *hospitalis* at Naumachia, a few hundred meters from the Via Triumphalis. This he did to support "the poor, strangers, and pilgrims." To ensure that support, he endowed it with rural estates.[41] Closer to St. Peter's, on the north side of the basilica, Leo "built from the foundations a house beautifully decorated on a wondrous scale, and placed in it dining couches." Was this for the poor and pilgrims too, or perhaps for more elite visitors? Nearby he built a bath for the poor and pilgrims.[42] Constructing a bath in this location was facilitated by the branch of the Aqua Sabbatina that Hadrian had extended to the south side of the basilica. He did this "for the basilica's atria and bath and for the needs of pilgrims and those who serve there."[43] Might one or another of these establishments, if not the portico itself, be the sort of place to which Amandus "returned every night"? Before his election as pope, Paschal I was abbot at St. Stephen's monastery located right behind St. Peter's apse. The *Liber pontificalis* says that he was assiduous in providing hospitality to pilgrims.[44] Over the eighth and ninth centuries, as noted already, popes were no less solicitous of the *xenodochia* inside the city. It is worth noting that most of these laid right along Rome's main streets and were mentioned in the Einsiedeln Itinerary during the very period when, as we saw, the attention of visitors of all kinds reoriented itself to the city proper. Hints abound, in other words, that the local authorities made impressive efforts to provide pilgrims and other visitors with places to spend the night.

Leo's grand hall at St. Peter's with its dining couches was probably intended for the affluent and important. Where did ordinary visitors get a meal? Pope Zachary (741–52) instituted a new kind of rural estate, the *domusculta*.[45] He created four of these. One of them, the *domusculta* of St. Cecilia, located five miles outside Rome on the Via Tiburtina, was placed under the ownership of St. Peter's and its proceeds were restricted to the pope's own use and added to the *ratio dominica*, the papal household budget. Zachary's vita goes on to say that he commanded that "on frequent days" food should be provided to the poor and pilgrims who were to be found in the vicinity of St. Peter's.[46] It does not seem adventurous to connect at least the *domusculta* of St. Cecilia and the papal budget to the feeding of pilgrims at St. Peter's. Our best hints on the feeding of pilgrims are supplied by the deaconries.[47] Rome's oldest deaconry is mentioned under Benedict II in the late seventh century. Consensus holds that it is older, however. Across the eighth century popes built or refurbished deaconries. Hadrian erected three in the vicinity of St. Peter's and Leo III added two more. They numbered twenty-three by 816 when Leo died. Hadrian endowed some of them with rich rural estates. In principle deaconries were places where people gathered on Thursday or Friday mornings for a procession with psalm-singing, a visit to the baths, and a distribution of food. As a rule, the deaconries provided food to the urban populace, but scholars agree that pilgrims and other visitors may well have availed themselves of the food distributions.[48] In this regard, it is striking that twenty-one of them appear on just two of the Einsiedeln Itinierary's ten pathways through the city: Number 9 on the streets from the Porta Aurelia to the Porta Praenestina and Number 12 on the streets running from St. Peter's to St. Paul's.[49] This prompts a guess wrapped up in a quip. I am inclined to think of the Einsiedeln Itinerary as the forerunner of the Baedeker or Michelin guides—"just across the street from the church of St. So-and-So there is a lovely place to eat." Lest one think that people in Rome ate only once a week, it is worth recalling that late antique Rome's 256 public bakeries made weekly distributions of bread and that meat was also charged against the *annona* on a weekly basis.[50]

Gregory I once provided that revenues from the patrimonies in southern Gaul be dedicated to supplying clothing for the poor.[51] I know of no other reference like this one. Might pilgrims have qualified as "poor"? Given that the poor and pilgrims are regularly coupled in papal sources, might we suppose that the papal administration provided some distributions of clothing to pilgrims?

There were also residential quarters for the persons who settled in Rome more or less permanently: the *scholae*. Of these there were eventually five. The area extending south and west from the Palatine, centering on the deaconry of Santa Maria in Cosmedin, was the heart of the Schola Graecorum. Not much is known about it. Sansterre believes that it was created around 774 and continued developing until about 835.[52] More widely noticed by historians, but not necessarily by the sources, are the four *scholae* that were in existence around St. Peter's by 799 at the latest: their members greeted Leo III when he returned from Francia in that year.[53] The Schola Frisonum is first mentioned in 799. Little is known about it. Its tenth-century tower is still standing just to the east of St. Peter's. The Schola Francorum was created in the last decades of the eighth century but we cannot say just when with confidence.[54] Charlemagne granted it the church of San Salvatore in Territorio. The *schola* was located south and east of St. Peter's— were it still there it would flank Bernini's left-hand colonnade. The Schola Langobardorum was founded by Ansa, the wife of the Lombard king Desiderius, in about 770. It was situated slightly north of St. Peter's, perhaps roughly where the Vatican Library is now. The Schola Saxonum is shrouded in legends. It may go back to Ine of Wessex or it may owe its foundation and financial endowment to Offa of Mercia. It was located east of St. Peter's near the Tiber bank just south of the porticus. Its church of Santa Maria "in Sassia" was restored by Pope Leo IV (847–55), so it was older than his time but the date of its foundation cannot be ascertained precisely. Today's hospital of Santo Spirito in Sassia sits on the site of the medieval *schola*. Each *schola* provided housing, a church, and a cemetery. Clerics called *scholenses*, apparently twelve in number, served in the churches, supervised the cemeteries, and provided tours of the city's shrines. The *scholae* must have been relatively humble entities. The Schola Saxonum burned down in 817 and the Schola Langobardorum went up in flames in 847. Residents of the *scholae* were recruited to fight the Saracens in 846.

Construction of one more kind gives evidence for yet another way in which Rome provided for its visitors. Beginning in the late sixth century, large cemeterial basilicas were erected at some of the most frequently visited sites, such as San Lorenzo and Sant'Agnese. At St. Peter's and St. Paul's the sanctuaries were rearranged to achieve two goals at once: to celebrate Mass directly over the saint's body and to permit the installation of an annular crypt so that pilgrims could continually visit the saint's tomb without disturbing the more regular uses of the basilica. Such reconstruction to improve traffic flow was also introduced in, at least, San Pancrazio, San Valentino, San Crisogono, Santa Susanna, Santa Prassede, Santa Cecilia, San Marco, Santi Quattro Coronati, Santo Stefano degli Abissini, San Martino ai Monti, Santa Maria Nova, and perhaps Santa Maria in Domnica.[55] All of this rebuilding represented a considerable expenditure of funds on behalf of pilgrims and perhaps a concern for their physical and spiritual well-being.[56]

Let me conclude with two anecdotes that together illustrate the frustrations felt by the student of Rome and her visitors. When Boniface IV rededicated the Pantheon as the church of St. Mary and all the Martyrs, he instituted the feast of All Saints on May 13. Gregory III dedicated a chapel in St. Peter's to "All Saints" on November 1 and henceforth All Saints' Day was celebrated on that day in Rome. In about 835 Gregory IV then made the feast universal for the Frankish Empire, ostensibly because this was a good time for pilgrims to visit Rome.[57] This is a good example of the kinds of hints we have about the presence of pilgrims in Rome and papal solicitude for them without concrete details. When Zachary was elected pope in 741, Boniface wrote him a long letter full of questions and one startling set of complaints and criticisms. Some "common people" had been to Rome and they reported seeing in the neighborhood of St. Peter's Church "bands of singers parading the streets in pagan fashion, shouting and singing sacrilegious songs and loading tables with food day and night. . . . They also say that they have seen women with amulets and bracelets of heathen fashion on their arms and legs, offering them for sale to willing buyers."[58] May we take this as a hint that not all of Rome's visitors were totally engaged in seeking out the tombs of the martyrs and that not all of their accommodation was edifying.

Notes

1. Astonishingly, the only monograph dedicated to this topic was published more than eighty years ago: Fedor Schneider, *Rom und Romgedanke im Mittelalter* (1925; repr. Darmstadt, 1959).

2. A huge subject: For an introduction and good bibliography see Julia M. H. Smith, "Old Saints, New Cults: Roman Relics in Carolingian Francia," in *Early Medieval Rome and the Christian West: Essays in Honour of Donald A. Bullough*, ed. Julia M. H. Smith (Leiden, 2000), 317–49.

3. Hans Hubert Anton, *Studien zu den Klosterprivilegien der Päpste im frühen Mittelalter* (Berlin, 1975).

4. Thomas F. X. Noble, "Paradoxes and Possibilities in the Sources for Roman Society in the Early Middle Ages," in *Early Medieval Rome*, ed. Smith, 55–83, esp. 79–83.

5. Paolo Delogu, "The Rebirth of Rome in the Eighth and Ninth Centuries," in

The Rebirth of Towns in the West, A.D. *700–1050*, ed. Richard Hodges and B. Hobley, CBA Research Report 68 (London, 1988), 33–42; Paolo Delogu, "Oro e argento in Roma tra il VII e il IX secolo," in *Cultura e societé nell'Italia medievale: Studi per Paolo Brezzi*, Istituto storico italiano, Studi storici 184–87 (Rome, 1988), 273–93; Paolo Delogu, "La storia economica di Roma nell'alto medioevo: Introduzione al seminario," in *La storia economica di Roma nell'alto medioevo alla luce dei recenti scavi archeologici*, ed. Delogu (Florence, 1993), 11–29. See also Richard Hodges, "The Riddle of St. Peter's Republic," ibid., 353–66.

6. To avoid bloating the notes I shall not provide a reference for each of these visitors. None is controversial.

7. For a good start see Debra Birch, *Pilgrimage to Rome in the Middle Ages* (Woodbridge, 1998). Birch's bibliography is excellent down to its date of publication.

8. Nicholas I, ep. 88, ed. Ernst Perels, MGH, Epp. 6, 477: "tanta milia hominum . . . cotidie."

9. Paul Hetherington, *Medieval Rome: A Portrait of the City and Its Life* (New York, 1994), 78.

10. *Die Briefe des heiligen Bonifatius und Lullus*, ed. Michael Tangl, MGH, Epp. sel. 1, no. 78, 169.

11. Jean Guyon, *Le cimetière aux deux Lauriers: Recherches sur les catacombes romains*, Bibliothèque des écoles françaises d'Athènes et de Rome 264 (Rome, 1987), 472.

12. Anna Esposito, "Pellegrini, stranieri, curiali ed Ebrei," in *Roma medievale*, ed. André Vauchez (Rome, 2001), 214.

13. *Notitia ecclesiarum urbis Romae*, in *Codice topografico della città di Roma*, ed. Roberto Valentini and Giuseppe Zuchetti, Fonti per la storia d'Italia 81, 88, 90, 91, 4 vols. (Rome, 1940–53), 2:72–99 (with introductory comments, 67–71); also in *Itineraria et alia geographica*, CCSL 175 (Turnhout, 1965), 305–28.

14. *Notitia ecclesiarum urbis Romae*, 73–75.

15. *Cymiteria Totius Romanae Urbis*, in *Codice Topografico*, ed. Valentini and Zuchetti, 2:60–66 (introductory material, 49–59).

16. William of Malmesbury, *Gesta Regum Anglorum: The History of the English Kings*, ed. and trans. R. A. B. Mynors, R. M. Thomson, and M. Winterbottom (Oxford, 1998), 4.352, 614–20; see also Bauer, "Pellegrinagio," 70.

17. William Stubbs, ed., *Memorials of St. Dunstan, Archbishop of Canterbury*, Rolls Series 63 (London, 1874), 391–95. See also Birch, *Pilgrimage*, 98; Veronica Ortenberg, "Archbishop Sigeric's Journey to Rome in 990," *Anglo-Saxon England* 19 (1990): 197–246.

18. Gerold Walser, ed., *Die einsiedler Inschriftensammlung und der Pilgerführer durch Rom (Codex Einsidlensis 326): Facsmimle, Umschrift, Übersetzung und Kommentar*, Historia Einzelschriften 53 (Stuttgart, 1987). The Einsiedeln Itinerary is also in *Itineraria et alia geographica*, 331–43, as is the *Silloge epigraphica*, 163–207.

19. The fullest study to date is old: F. Grossi Gondi, *Principi e problemi di critica agiografica: Atti e spoglie dei martiri* (Rome, 1919). Caroline Goodson is preparing a survey of relic translations into Rome.

20. John F. Baldovin, *The Urban Character of Christian Worship: The Origins, Development, and Meaning of Stational Liturgy*, Orientalia Christiana Analecta 228 (Rome, 1987), 105–66.

21. Birch, *Pilgrimage to Rome*, 97–99, thinks that the city only became the prime focus in the late tenth century.

22. Bauer, "Pellegrinagio," 70–71. Such collections were actually fairly common in

the early Middle Ages. See Mark Handley, "Epitaphs, Models, and Texts: A Carolingian Collection of Late Antique Inscriptions from Burgundy," in *The Afterlife of Inscriptions: Reusing, Rediscovering, Reinventing & Revitalizing Ancient Inscriptions*, ed. Alison E. Cooley, Bulletin of the Institute of Classical Studies, Supplement 75 (London, 2000), 47–56, esp. 47–48.

23. John's father, Plato, is known from an inscription that was preserved in the church of St. Anastasius until the fifteenth century. It has been published several times. See Louis Duchesne, ed., *Le Liber pontificalis*, 2nd ed., 2 vols. (Paris, 1955), 1:386 (hereafter *LP*).

24. *LP*, 1:343 (*Life of Vitalian*).

25. Alain J. Stoclet, "Les établissements francs à Rome au VIIIᵉ siècle," in *Haut Moyen-Âge: Culture, éducation et société; Études offertes à Pierre Riché*, ed. Claude Lepelley et al., La Garenne-Colombes: Éditions européennes Erasme (Paris, 1990), 232–33; Louis Reekmans, "Le développement topographique de la région du Vatican à la fin de l'antiquité et au début du Moyen Âge," in *Mélanges d'archéologie et d'histoire de l'art offerts au Professeur Jacques Lavalleye*, Université de Louvain recueil de travaux d'histoire et de philologie, 4th ser., 45 (Louvain, 1970), 222–23; Carlrichard Brühl, "Die Kaiserpfalz bei St. Peter und die Pfalz Ottos III," *Quellen und Forschungen aus italienischen Archiven und Bibliotheken* 34 (1954): 1–30; Carlrichard Brühl, "Neues zur Kaiserpfalz bei St. Peter," ibid., 18 (1958): 266–68.

26. *LP*, 2:6–7.

27. Sidonius, ep. 1.5.9, in *Sidonius: Poems and Letters*, ed. W. B. Anderson (Cambridge, MA, 1936), 358–60.

28. *Cummian's Letter De controversia Paschali*, ed. Maura Walsh and Dáibhí Ó Cróinín, Studies and Texts 86 (Toronto, 1988), 92–94.

29. *Constructio monasterii farfensis*, ed. Ugo Balzani, Fonti per la storia d'Italia 33 (Rome, 1903), 11–12.

30. *Vita Sturmi*, ch. 14, ed. Georg H. Pertz, MGH, SS 2, 371.

31. Einhard, *Translatio et miracula sanctorum Marcellini et Petri*, ch. 3, ed. Georg Waitz, MGH SS 15.1, 241.

32. Rudolf and Meginhard, *Translatio sancti Alexandri*, ch. 5, ed. G. H. Pertz, MGH SS 2, 678.

33. *LP*, 1:262–63.

34. Peter Brown, *Poverty and Leadership in the Later Roman Empire*, Menahem Stern Jerusalem Lectures (Hanover, NH, 2002).

35. *Vita Amandi*, chs. 6–7, ed. Bruno Krusch, MGH SS rer. Germ. 5, 434.

36. *LP*, 1:451–52, for his rampages. For the houses, *The Fourth Book of the Chronicle of Fredegar, with Its Continuations*, ed. J. M. Wallace-Hadrill (London, 1960), *Continuationes*, ch. 38, 107.

37. *LP*, 1:440–41.

38. J. F. Niermeyer, *Mediae latinitatis lexicon minus* (Leiden, 1984), s.v. "xenodochium," 1137–38. The key study remains W. Schönfeld, "Die Xenodochien in Italien und Frankreich im früheren Mittelalter," *Zeitschrift der Savigny-Stiftung für Rechtsgeschichte, kanonistische Abteilung* 12 (1922): 1–54; also Egon Boshof, "Armenfürsorge im früheren Mittelalter: Xenodochium, Matricula, Hospitale pauperum," *Vierteljahrschrift für Sozial- und Wirtschaftsgeschichte* 71 (1984): 153–74.

39. Gregory I, *Registrum epistularum: Libri VIII–XIV*, ed. Dag Norberg, CCSL 140A (Turnhout, 1982), 9.63, 131 (619–20, 681–82).

40. *LP*, 1:506.

41. *LP*, 2:28.

42. *LP*, 2:27–28.

43. *LP*, 1:503–4, 510.

44. *LP*, 2:52.

45. Thomas F. X. Noble, *The Republic of St. Peter: The Birth of the Papal State, 680–825* (Philadelphia, 1984), 246–49.

46. *LP*, 1:434–35 (*Vita Zacharii*, chs. 25–27).

47. Noble, *Republic of St. Peter*, 231–34, with the older literature.

48. For instance, Richard Krautheimer, *Rome: Profile of a City, 312–1308* (Princeton, 1980), 80–81.

49. "Das Itinerar der einsiedler Handschrift," in Walser, *Die einsiedler Inschriftensammlung und der Pilgerführer durch Rom*, 196–200, 205–11.

50. Bertrand Lançon, *Rome in Late Antiquity: Everyday Life and Urban Change*, AD *312–609*, trans. Antonia Nevill (New York, 2001), 76–80.

51. Gregory I, *Registrum epistularum: Libri I–VII*, ed. Dag Norberg, CCSL 140 (Turnhout, 1982), 6.10 (378–79).

52. Jean-Marie Sansterre, *Les moines grecs et orientaux à Rome aux époques byzantine et carolingienne*, Académie royale de Belgique, Mémoires de la classe des lettres, 2nd ser. 66, 2 vols. (Brussels, 1982), 102–4n388.

53. M. Perraymond, "Le scholae peregrinorum nel borgo di San Pietro," *Romanobarbarica* 4 (1979): 183–200; L. Casanelli, "Gli insediamenti nordici in Borgo: 'Le scolae peregrinorum,'" in *Rome e l'eta carolingia* (Rome, 1976), 217–22; Reekmans, "Le développement topographique," 215–28; W. J. Moore, *The Saxon Pilgrims to Rome and the Schola Saxonum* (Fribourg, 1937).

54. Stoclet, "Les établissements francs."

55. Birch, *Pilgrimage to Rome*, 91–97. The transformations of individual churches may be tracked conveniently in Matilda Webb, *The Churches and Catacombs of Early Christian Rome* (Brighton, UK, 2001).

56. Bryan Ward-Perkins thinks this small-scale modification of churches points to a lack of cash: *From Classical Antiquity to the Middle Ages: Urban Public Building in Northern and Central Italy*, AD *300–850* (Oxford, 1984). In light of what I have called a "building boom" in Rome between about 750 and 850, I am inclined to disagree and to insist that accommodations were being made for local residents and numerous visitors: Noble, "Paradoxes and Possibilities"; Thomas F. X. Noble, "Topography, Celebration, and Power: The Making of a Papal Rome in the Eighth and Ninth Centuries," in *Topographies of Power in the Early Middle Ages*, ed. Mayke de Jong and Frans Theuws, Transformation of the Roman World 6 (Leiden, 2001), 49–56.

57. F. L. Cross, ed., *Oxford Dictionary of the Christian Church*, 3rd ed., rev. by E. A. Livingstone (Oxford, 2005), 42; Ludwig Eisenhofer and Joseph Lechner, *The Liturgy of the Roman Rite*, trans. A. J. Peeler and E. F. Peeler (Edinburgh, 1961), 237.

58. *Die Briefe*, ed. Tangl, no. 50, 84–85.

CHAPTER 12

Les trois XIe siècles

PIERRE RICHÉ

C'est avec un grand plaisir que j'ai accepté de contribuer aux "Mélanges John J. Contreni", un collègue que je connais depuis longtemps et dont j'apprécie beaucoup les travaux. En effet, John J. Contreni était venu me trouver à l'Université de Paris X–Nanterre, où j'enseignais le Haut Moyen Âge depuis 1967. Il était en quête d'une thèse et il trouva dans les manuscrits de la bibliothèque de Laon de quoi le satisfaire. D'où son beau livre sur "l'École cathédrale de Laon au IXe et au Xe siècle". En 1976, il accepta de traduire ma thèse de doctorat en américain avec une préface de son maître Richard E. Sullivan. Depuis, nous nous sommes revus quelquefois en France ou aux États-Unis et je n'ai pas cessé de me tenir au courant de ses études sur les temps carolingiens.

Pour célébrer John J. Contreni, je ne veux pas tout à fait quitter l'époque carolingienne, mais je voudrais montrer que le XIe siècle est une période qui prolonge l'époque carolingienne et qui annonce le XIIe siècle. Un siècle qui comme beaucoup d'autres n'a pas d'unité mais présente différents visages.

Jusqu'au milieu du XIe siècle, nous sommes encore dans la période post-carolingienne, puis vers 1030, avec l'arrivée d'une nouvelle génération de gouvernants, s'ouvre en Occident une crise qui se produit dans beaucoup de domaines, en particulier ceux de la croyance religieuse et de la culture. Mais ceci n'est rien à côté des bouleversements que connaît le milieu du XIe siècle. Alors, peu à peu, de nouvelles structures sociales et religieuses se mettent en place qui annoncent déjà le siècle suivant.

Par certains côtés, le XIe siècle peut être comparé à notre XXe siècle. En effet, jusqu'aux années 30, c'est-à-dire jusqu'à la grande crise économique, le XIXᵉ siècle se prolongeait. Puis s'ouvre alors une période nouvelle avec l'époque stalinienne en URSS et la domination hitlérienne en Allemagne, et peu à peu l'annonce des conflits qui ne se terminent qu'en 1945. Alors, au milieu du siècle, les événements se précipitent en quelques décennies. La bombe atomique, le rideau de fer en Europe, la décolonisation, le Spoutnik lancé par les Russes en 1957 et dix ans après, les premiers hommes sur la Lune, une première esquisse de l'Europe, le concile Vatican II et vers 64 les premières émeutes étudiantes dans le monde. Et il faudrait parler des innovations nouvelles: généralisation de la pénicilline, des ordinateurs, des méthodes contraceptives, etc. Nous étions alors déjà dans le XXIᵉ siècle.

Présentons donc ces trois périodes du XIᵉ siècle en insistant sur l'accélération de l'histoire au milieu du siècle. Mais revenons au début du XIᵉ siècle. Il est admis maintenant, heureusement, que l'an mille n'a pas été une coupure dans l'histoire médiévale, que la "mutation de l'an mille" est un mythe, que les temps carolingiens se poursuivent jusque vers les années trente.[1]

1

Regardons une carte de l'époque. Au centre de l'Occident s'étend l'Empire restauré par Otton I et qui va du Danemark à l'Italie du centre. À l'ouest, limité toujours par les frontières du Traité de Verdun, le royaume de France et celui de Bourgogne. Au nord, les royaumes anglo-saxon se sont unifiés et bientôt vont être rattachés à l'Empire anglo-danois de Knut le Grand (995–1035). Au sud, les petits royaumes chrétiens du nord de l'Espagne résistent comme ils peuvent au califat arabe de Cordoue.

Le christianisme a gagné tout, ou presque tout, l'Occident. Les deux états, entrés dernièrement dans l'Église romaine sont le royaume de Hongrie et le principat de Pologne. Leurs frontières orientales séparent jusqu'à nos jours les Églises d'Occident et d'Orient.

Les royaumes restent fidèles aux institutions carolingiennes. En France, la nouvelle dynastie capétienne reprend la tradition de leurs prédécesseurs, comme Lemarignier l'avait bien démontré autrefois.[2] Dans l'Empire, l'empereur Otton III a fait en l'an mille son pèlerinage au tombeau de Charlemagne et avec son ancien maître, le pape Sylvestre II, qui représente type du lettré carolingien, il a pendant de trop courtes années réalisé la *Renovatio imperii* avec Rome comme capitale. La société, comme le dit Adalbéron de Laon, un évêque qui fit beaucoup parlé de lui à cette époque, est divisée en trois groupes.[3] D'abord ceux qui prient, clercs et moines, puis ceux qui combattent, enfin ceux qui travaillent.

Comme à l'époque carolingienne, les évêques sont des princes issus de familles aristocratiques.[4] Ils sont en général cultivés, ils sont riches et peuvent être de grands constructeurs et des mécènes, ils mènent une vie mondaine et paraissent de vrais seigneurs avec des grandes propriétés—quelquefois maîtres de tout un comté—avec des châteaux, avec des vassaux. Certains évêques, en Germanie, interviennent dans la vie économique, recevant des souverains les diplômes leur permettant d'ouvrir des marchés, de lever des tonlieux et de frapper monnaie. Ainsi, par exemple, l'évêché de Liège est une principauté et le restera pendant longtemps.

Mais ces évêques-prince sont soumis aux rois et empereurs. Ils sont nommés par les souverains, en sont les vassaux, leurs doivent le *consilium* et l'*auxilium*. Nous sommes encore dans les temps carolingiens. Avec les autres grands vassaux, ils assistent aux assemblées et s'il le faut, ils envoient leurs troupes pour aider leur souverain. On se souviendra encore des hauts faits militaires du légendaire archevêque de Reims, Turpin, l'ami de Charlemagne. Dans une lettre (n° 14), Fulbert, évêque de Chartres, déplore l'existence de ces évêques "occupés aux affaires de la guerre, ayant à leur côté une importante escorte de soldats", et il les considère comme des "tyrans".

En principe, depuis le concile de Chalcedoine, les monastères dépendent des évêques. Mais déjà, certains abbés cherchent à se libérer. Abbon de Fleury-sur-Loire obtient l'exemption romaine en 997.[5] En 1025, l'abbé de Cluny, Odilon, réussit à échapper lui aussi à l'autorité de son évêque. Il est vrai que Cluny est une grande puissance depuis la fin du xe siècle. Odilon (1015–1048) est lui aussi un grand seigneur. Plus de 70 monastères sont rattachés à l'abbaye bourguignonne. L'abbaye de Cluny II, dont la construction a commencée à la fin du xe siècle, est trois fois plus grande que Saint-Pierre de Rome. Odilon est un véritable roi, comme l'appel alors Adalbéron de Laon, qui reproche à Robert le Pieux, d'être trop influencé par l'abbé et ses "guerriers". Cette toute puissance du clergé, qui en principe doit "prier", compromet la vie religieuse de l'Occident, comme elle l'avait fait à l'époque carolingienne.

Ceux qui combattent: sont les souverains et les grands féodaux. Ils ont, comme je l'ai dit, hérité de la tradition carolingienne. Ils réunissent de grandes assemblées, telle que celle de 1027, lorsque Robert le Pieux décida de faire couronner son fils Henri. Comme disait déjà Abbon de Fleury: "Le roi ne peut pas suffire seul à l'utilité de tout le royaume". L'idée de la puissance publique et de l'État est toujours affirmée. L'expression *respublica* est continuellement employée.[6] Les grandes familles aristocratiques qui sont fières d'avoir parmi leurs ancêtres des Carolingiens ou des fidèles de ces derniers ont des principautés territoriales dans lesquelles ils veulent faire régner leur autorité. Guillaume le Grand, duc d'Aquitaine, est un des meilleurs représentants de ces grandes familles.[7] Sans doute, ils ont tendance, du moins en France plus qu'en Germanie, à avoir leur autonomie et ils n'hésitent pas, comme le roi le fait dans le Nord, à nommer les évêques. Mais déjà apparaissent les *milites*, gardiens des châteaux de plus en plus nombreux; le comte d'Anjou, Foulque Nerra (987–1040) en a fait construire une trentaine. Ils sont au service des comtes et de la grande aristocratie mais, nous le verrons, après les années 1030, ils iront à la conquête de leur indépendance.

Reste le troisième ordre, celui de ceux qui travaillent et qui forment la grande majorité de la population. Certains sont des artisans au service des grands qui bâtissent églises et châteaux, mais la plus part sont des paysans qui vivent dans la misère. Adalbéron de Laon écrit même:

> Cette race accablée ne peut rien acquérir sans douleur. Qui pourrait reconstituer en comptant les signes sur l'abaque, l'effort des serfs, le cours de leur vie et leurs travaux innombrables? Fournir à tous la richesse, le vêtement: voilà la pâture du serf. Car aucun homme libre ne peut vivre sans serf. Quand un travail se présente et qu'ils désirent en faire la dépense, le roi comme les évêques semblent se mettre sous la dépendance de leurs serfs. Le seigneur est nourri par le serf qu'il suppose nourrir. Il n'y a pas de fin à la plainte et aux larmes des serfs.[8]

Un autre caractère de cette époque est relatif à la vie culturelle. J'ai même pu parler ailleurs de "Troisième renaissance carolingienne".[9] En effet, après la grande crise qui suivit la destruction de l'Empire carolingien, la culture intellectuelle et artistique reprenant les critères que l'on avait connus dans les deux premières "Renaissances", celles du VIIIe et du IXe siècles, s'expriment à nouveau dans les lettres, les sciences et les arts. Les bibliothèques des monastères sont réorganisées, des grands princes tels Guillaume d'Aquitaine ou l'empereur Henri II sont amateurs de livres. Ce dernier donne au nouvel évêché de Bamberg une quantité de livres d'auteurs antiques, mais aussi de modernes. La bibliothèque de Gerbert d'Aurillac, que ce dernier avait donné à Otton III, s'y retrouve et même le manuscrit autographe de Richer de Saint-Remi de Reims.

J'ai étudié ailleurs la floraison des écoles monastiques et épiscopales de tout l'Occident, et les moyens et méthodes de l'acquisition du savoir.[10] Mais j'aimerai, de nouveau, insister sur l'étude des arts libéraux *trivium* et *quadrivium*. Des manuscrits d'Horace et de Virgile portent des notes de musique, ce qui permet de mieux retenir les poèmes. Ceux du vieux grammairien Priscien sont toujours recherchés. Un évêque catalan, en 1044, vend sa maison pour acquérir deux exemplaires et Fulbert de Chartres (1006–1028) fait même envoyer à un évêque hongrois un exemplaire du même Priscien. Fulbert connaît aussi bien que Gerbert, dont contrairement à la légende il n'a pas été l'élève, les arts du *trivium* et du *quadrivium*.[11] Le manuscrit 100 de la bibliothèque de Chartres, malheureusement brûlé en 1944, contenait non seulement des poèmes de Fulbert, mais l'*Isagogue* de Porphyre, les *Categories* d'Aristote, le *Perihermeneias*, les *Topiques* de Cicéron, les nouveaux traités de Boèce étudiés par Abbon de Fleury et même le traité sur "Le raisonnable et l'usage de la raison" offert par Gerbert d'Aurillac à l'empereur Otton III. Ce n'est pas sans raison qu'Adelman, élève de Fulbert, rappelle à un de ses condisciples, que nous reverrons bientôt: "Notre vie commune très douce et agréable que nous avons vécue ensemble à l'Académie de Chartres sous notre vénérable Socrate".

Les arts du *quadrivium* sont en grande estime dans les écoles du début du XIᵉ siècle. Les chiffres arabes, peut-être déjà connus de Gerbert, on en discute, le sont de Fulbert.[12] Les disciples de Fulbert à Liège s'intéressent à la géométrie et à l'astrolabe, cet instrument venu d'Espagne. Francon de Liège cherche la "quadrature du cercle". Une nouvelle géométrie attribuée à Boèce est écrite en Lorraine.[13] L'enseignement de la science musicale est, comme à l'époque carolingienne, enseigné dans toutes les écoles. Rappelons en particulier que le célèbre italien Guy d'Arrezo a inventé, vers 1030, un nouvel enseignement musical en codifiant la solmisation. La médecine à Chartres et ailleurs—les manuscrits médicaux en font foi—est toujours enseignée.

Cette "troisième renaissance carolingienne" se caractérise aussi par une forme d'humanisme.[14] À l'école des Anciens, on compose des poèmes qui ne sont pas d'inspiration religieuse. En Allemagne du Sud, au monastère de Tegernsee, est composé un long poème, le *Ruodlieb*, où la rencontre de deux amants tient une grande place. Et comment ne pas citer l'*Invitatio amicae*, contenu dans un manuscrit de Cambridge, mais écrit aussi en Allemagne: "Viens douce amie, toi que j'aime de tout mon cœur entre dans ma chambre ornée avec luxe. Là sont des sièges recouverts de tapis et une pièce ornée de rideaux. Des fleurs sont mêlées aux herbes parfumées", etc. Nous reconnaissons là l'"Invitation au voyage" de Baudelaire, ce dernier ayant connu le poème latin par la traduction du Méril en 1847. Certains ont vu là une paraphrase du Cantique des Cantiques, mais il est certain qu'Ovide n'est pas loin. Nous sommes au début du lyrisme profane du Moyen Âge latin.

Si enfin nous nous tournons dans le domaine des arts, même constatation.[15] Il n'a pas fallu attendre l'an mille, comme le voulait Raoul Glaber, pour que "le monde se couvre d'une robe blanche d'églises". À la fin du Xᵉ siècle, les chantiers de constructions sont ouverts et après l'an mille, les architectes continuent à travailler.

Ils s'inspirent souvent des plans carolingiens et le traité *De architectura* de Vitruve (Iᵉʳ siècle après J.C.) se trouve dans les bibliothèques; le maître d'œuvre de Saint-Michel d'Hildesheim, construite par l'évêque Berward (†1022) en possédait un et il n'était pas le seul.[16] De même, les ivoires, les pièces d'orfèvre et même les miniatures s'inspirent de modèles carolingiens.[17]

2

Vers 1030 et jusqu'au milieu du siècle, nous assistons à une transformation de la société européenne. C'est la fin d'une génération d'hommes politiques et religieux. Étienne I, premier roi chrétien de Hongrie meurt en 1035, la même année que Knut le Grand. Avant eux sont mort l'empereur Henri II (1024), Guillaume d'Aquitaine (1030), Robert le Pieux (1031). Guillaume de Volpiano, qui avait fondé de nombreux monastères en Normandie, meurt lui aussi en 1031, et Fulbert de Chartres l'a devancé en 1028. Notons enfin qu'Adalbéron de Laon, celui qu'on a appelé le "vieux traître" est mort presque qu'octogénaire en 1031.

Nous assistons à une transformation sociale. Ce n'est pas "l'anarchie féodale" dont on parlait autrefois, mais celui des Châtellenies qui profitent de l'amoindrissement des pouvoirs politiques pour s'affranchir. Ceux qui gardaient autrefois des châteaux pour le prince ou le comte, deviennent autonomes et se créent des clientèles. La justice ne dépend plus du comte ou du vicomte, mais du châtelain. Des châteaux se construisent partout particulièrement sur les "mottes féodales".[18] Le droit coutumier s'impose dans la législation.

Les dévastations de bandes armées, que déjà Fulbert redoutait, se multiplient et les évêques doivent réunir à nouveau les "assemblées de paix" et même décréter au concile d'Arles en 1041 la "Trêve de Dieu" (*Non militia sed malitia*).

L'Église, en effet, souffre de ces transformations sociales. Raoul Glaber, mort vers 1048, condamne dans une page célèbre de ses *Histoires* les prélats qui s'enrichissent par des moyens honteux. Il dénonce la simonie des prélats et des rois :

> À la lumière, des enseignements de la parole sacrée, on voit claire-
> ment que dans les jours nouveaux qui arrivent, le refroidissement de
> la charité au cœur des hommes et le foisonnement de l'iniquité vont
> rendre imminents des temps périlleux pour les âmes.
>   La raison de notre préambule, c'est que, presque tous les princes
> étant dès longtemps aveuglés par l'amour des vaines richesses, le mal a
> gagné à la ronde tous les prélats des églises disséminées par le monde.
> Du don gratuit et vénérable du Christ tout puissant, ils ont fait, comme
> pour rendre plus sûre leur propre damnation, une marchandise, chère
> à leur cupidité. De tels prélats paraissent d'autant moins capables
> d'accomplir l'œuvre divine qu'on sait bien qu'ils n'y ont point accédé
> en passant par la porte principale. Et l'audace de telles gens a beau être
> flétrie par maints textes des saintes Écritures, il est certain que de nos
> jours elle sévit plus que jamais dans les divers ordres de l'Église. Même
> les rois, qui auraient dû être les juges de la dignité des candidats aux
> emplois sacrés, corrompus par les présents qui leur sont prodigués.[19]

La papauté ne montre pas l'exemple. Les papes sont des aristocrates de la région romaine, de véritables princes qui achètent plus ou moins leur tiare. Benoît IX

(1032–1044), un homme très jeune et laïc de surcroît, est chassé par une émeute. Il est remplacé par Sylvestre III, lui aussi chassé. Bientôt, le trône de Saint-Pierre est aux mains de trois papes et il faut l'intervention de l'empereur Henri III au concile de Sutri en 1046 pour imposer l'évêque de Bamberg, sous le nom de Clément II.

Il était inévitable que dans cette décomposition de l'Église, n'apparaissent des hérésies. Comme disait H. Grundmann, l'hérésie naît d'un besoin de réforme de l'Église: "Tous les hérétiques du Moyen Âge étaient convaincus qu'ils réalisaient mieux le christianisme que l'Église qui les condamnait".[20]

La première grande hérésie est due à des écolâtres d'Orléans, dont l'un était même le confesseur de l'épouse de Robert le Pieux. En 1022, ces hérétiques sont brûlés, premier bûcher qui, hélas, sera suivi de bien d'autres. À la même époque, des hérétiques sont jugés à Arras et une autre hérésie naît en 1028 près d'Asti, en Italie. Les chroniqueurs de l'époque mentionnent des hérésies et même Adhemar de Chabannes (†1034) parle du manichéisme en Aquitaine. C'est également ce mot qu'emploie l'évêque de Châlons, Roger II, dans sa lettre à Wason de Liège en 1044. Tous ces hérétiques rejettent les sacrements, en particulier celui du mariage, ne reconnaissent plus l'autorité de l'Église, mais s'en remettent à l'Esprit Saint, forment leur propre église en voulant revenir à la vie évangélique, etc. On voit partout des hérétiques et comme dit Wason de Liège, "il suffit d'avoir un visage pâle pour être accusé d'hérésie".

L'hérésie peut avoir une autre origine, cette fois intellectuelle, l'usage abusif de la dialectique dans le commentaire des textes sacrés. Il faut alors présenter la crise de l'école dans les années 40–50.

Celui qui en parle le mieux est Pierre Damien.[21] Élève de l'école de Parme au début du xie siècle, il se destinait à être avocat. Mais à vingt-huit ans, en 1035, il décide de quitter le monde et de se faire ermite à Fonte Avellane. Cet ermite est au courant de ce qui se passe dans le monde, sa réputation d'ascète et de savant est telle qu'il est nommé Cardinal en 1057. Tout en priant dans son ermitage, il se rend compte que l'enseignement des arts libéraux et particulièrement de la dialectique, ont accablés les jeunes chrétiens. Toute son œuvre et sa correspondance, qui compte près de 200 lettres, sont un appel à la réforme et de l'Église et de l'école. Il fustige les évêques simoniaques qui ne pensent qu'aux honneurs et à l'argent, et dans son traité *Liber Gomorrianus*, il condamne les mœurs de certains clercs.

Pierre Damien dénonce les clercs de cours qui ne pensent qu'aux dignités et qui, à peine formés, deviennent avocats ou médecins, professions bien plus rémunérés. Il écrit un traité, *Contre l'incurie et l'ignorance des clercs*:

> J'estime à propos de t'exprimer à toi tout particulièrement la douleur
> qui me torture l'esprit au sujet des prêtres. Car l'incurie et la torpeur
> des évêques faits qu'on trouve aujourd'hui des prêtres si ignorants des
> lettres que non seulement ils n'arrivent pas à comprendre ce qu'ils

lisent, mais encore qu'ils peuvent à peine balbutier, en les parcourant syllabes par syllabes, les éléments qu'ils trouvent écrits. Mais quelle supplication peut donc adresser pour le peuple dans ses prières celui qui ignore comme un étranger ce qu'il dit lui-même? Il est écrit: "Celui qui ignore sera ignoré", et l'Apôtre nous prescrit de rendre à Dieu un "Culte raisonnable". Comment ce culte sera-t-il raisonnable si celui qui l'offre ne conçoit pas de sens à son offrande? Le mal s'étend bien au-delà de la personne du prêtre. Le peuple, privé de son ministère et de son enseignement, périra.

Dans son désir de réforme, il se rend compte que tout doit commencer par l'école. On étudie trop les disciplines profanes et pas assez les textes sacrés.

Sans doute, l'évêque Fulbert de Chartres avait encouragé dans son école l'étude la science religieuse, ce qui était assez nouveau à l'époque. Il connaissait les Pères de l'Église, avait une grande dévotion pour la Vierge, faisait des sermons, écrivait des poèmes religieux que l'on chantait et connaissait admirablement le droit canon. Bref, le Dieu de Fulbert était le Dieu d'Abraham, d'Isaac et de Jacob, alors que pour Gerbert d'Aurillac, c'était le Dieu des philosophes et des savants.[22]

Mais c'était là une exception. Dans les écoles, la tradition de l'enseignement des seuls arts libéraux se poursuivait. Alors, Pierre Damien de s'écrier: "Platon scrute les secrets de la mystérieuse nature, étudie les cours des astres, je le rejette avec dédain, Pythagore divise les latitudes et la sphère céleste, j'en fais peu de cas, Euclide se penche sur le problème embrouillé des figures géométriques, je le con-gédie également. Quant à tous ces rhéteurs avec leurs syllogismes et la cavillation sophistique, je les disqualifie comme indignes de traiter ces questions".

Mais c'est surtout à la dialectique que Pierre Damien s'attaque.[23] Un jour, il a découvert que des moines du Mont-Cassin discutaient sur la toute puissance de Dieu à partir des arguments de dialectique. Il leur répondit par un traité, *Lettre sur la toute puissance de Dieu*. Par ailleurs, il écrivit un opuscule "de la sainte sim-plicité préférable à la science qui enfle"; "Demeure assis dans ta cellule comme dans un paradis. Il n'y a qu'une voie dans les psaumes, ne la quitte jamais. Celui qui cherche Dieu n'a pas besoin de lumière étrangère pour contempler la vraie lumière"; "Ma grammaire, c'est le Christ", écrit Pierre Damien dans une formule qui sera souvent reprise.

Ancien avocat, Pierre Damien sait l'importance de la *disputatio* et de la controverse, véritable combat du clerc, mais il veut que les chrétiens utilisent les armes que leur donnent l'Écriture et la foi: "C'est une grande honte, dit-il, qu'un membre de l'Église se taise par ignorance pendant que ceux qui sont au-dehors lancent des fausses accusations et qu'un chrétien, ne sachant pas rendre raison du Christ, se retire vaincu et confus sous les insultes des ennemis". Le chrétien ne doit pas se servir de cette dialectique profane que son adversaire, l'hérétique, utilise. Et de penser, comme quelques Pères de l'Église, que "les dialecticiens sont les pères des hérétiques". L'exemple de Béranger de Tours, dont je parlerai plus loin, en est une illustration.

Un autre témoin de la crise de l'école est un vieux professeur de Liège, Gozzechin de Mayence, à son ancien élève Valcher. Je cite le passage presque *in extenso*, comme je le fais souvent car il représente bien les réactions du maître effrayé par la situation des jeunes. J'ai d'ailleurs découvert ce texte à Nanterre en 1968:

> Une avarice infernale usurpe toutes les récompenses de la vertu et, dans ce royaume de l'argent, l'ambition tarife ses marchandises. De cette racine empoisonnée, de cette semence pestilente, naît et pullule chaque jour la ruine des mœurs et de l'instruction. On résiste à tout système régulier, et la sévérité, la férule de nos pères, sont passées de mode. Si, en voyant suivre les tortueux sentiers du vice, vous étendez la baguette pour diriger ou retenir, aussitôt vient en aide aux plus âgés la foule de ceux qui pratiquent les mêmes habitudes et reçoivent une liberté prématurée ou se délivrent par une fuite aussi rapide que s'ils n'avaient des ailes. . . . Ceux qui devraient encore s'instruire sous la férule de l'école, ils se sont abandonnés à la paresse, à l'indolence; ils ont fait leur Dieu de leur ventre. Rebelles à l'enseignement grave de la morale, ils se laissent emporter comme une paille légère au vent de toute doctrine. Ils se font esclaves de vaines et pernicieuses nouveautés de langage ou de système. Eux qui, argile encore molle et pure, sur la route de l'instruction, devaient être façonnés en vases de gloire par le doigt d'un ouvrier avec actif et habile, se rejetant brusquement en arrière, ils dégénèrent en vases d'ignominie. Recueillent-ils par hasard quelques fragments d'une science infime et bavarde, dans de prétendues écoles savantes, ils errent çà et là sans pouvoir se fixer à rien. Comme il n'y a pas de place pour la morale dans leur éducation, ils rentrent dans leurs familles, après avoir secoué de leur front indompté le joug de la crainte, après avoir brisé le frein de la discipline. Ils tombent dans l'abîme, par les désordres de leur vie, et ils y précipitent les autres en leur communiquant la corruption. Il s'est élevé quelques faux professeurs de ces doctrines inventées par eux-mêmes, qui n'ayant pas d'asile assuré et ne pouvant pas se retirer dans leurs domaines, parce qu'ils n'en possèdent pas, vagabondent çà et là dans les campagnes, les bourgs et les villes, donnent de nouvelles interprétations des psaumes, des lettres de saint Paul, de l'Apocalypse, et entraînent après eux dans le sentier glissant des plaisirs une jeunesse avide de nouveautés, folle de légèretés qui a pris en aversion la grave discipline de l'étude.[24]

Et Gozzechin de citer ces faux professeurs qui sortent de l'école de Tours, qui est présidée par cet "apôtre de Satan" Béranger.

Béranger était un élève de Fulbert qui avait mal tourné. Son ami Adelman, dans la lettre où il parle de "l'Académie de Chartres sous notre vénérable

Socrate", le met en garde. Il imagine Fulbert priant pour ses élèves du ciel "pour que nous nous hâtions de tout notre zèle dans la voie royale, marchant sur la trace des Saints Pères sans nous engager dans des nouveaux sentiers et trompeurs".[25] Adelman était déjà au courant des idées de Béranger.

Ce dernier était un professeur remarquable qui avait beaucoup de succès et d'autorité, comme en témoigne son épitaphe.[26] Mais il avait surtout retenu des leçons de Fulbert tout ce qui était relatif à la dialectique.

N'avait-il pas écrit: "Nul ne contestera, à moins d'être stupidement aveugle, que dans la recherche de la vérité, la raison est incontestablement le meilleur des guides. Le propre d'un grand cœur est de recourir toujours à la dialectique. Y recourir, c'est recourir à la raison et qui ne le fait pas renonce à ce qui l'honore le plus en lui, car ce qui est en lui l'image de Dieu est sa raison".[27]

Béranger appliqua sa doctrine au dogme de l'eucharistie et reprenant sa thèse de moines carolingiens, il refusait d'admettre que le pain et le vin puissent devenir le corps du Christ, puisqu'après la consécration, les "accidents" du pain (couleur, goût, consistance) subsistaient. L'eucharistie était une figure spirituelle du Christ et non pas réellement son corps et son sang. Cette thèse eut quelques succès en France et en Italie.

3

Ainsi, l'école comme l'Église est en crise. Il faut une réforme générale. Ce sera la réforme grégorienne dans la seconde moitié du siècle. Mais avant de l'étudier, il faut rappeler les mutations qui se produisent dans tous les domaines à cette époque. L'Occident est en pleine transformation. La population augmente rapidement, les défrichements commencent partout, de nouvelles techniques apparaissent, tel le fléau articulé et la place du cheval dans l'agriculture. La "broderie de Bayeux" nous le représente tirant une herse. Les moulins à eau se multiplient et même les moulins à marée apparaissent. On utilise les dérivations pour la force motrice.

Dans les villes, pareilles transformations, "l'air de la ville rend libre" disait un proverbe médiéval. De fait, la population urbaine augmente surtout en Italie et dans le nord de la France. Arras, Bruges, Amiens se repeuplent. En Angleterre également et en Espagne du Nord. Des artisans, surtout des tisserands, jouent un rôle important dans les villes de Flandre. Les notables prennent conscience de leur rôle, non seulement économique mais politique. À partir de 1050, les *burgenses*, comme on disait, voudraient jouer un rôle politique. En 1070 est proclamée, au Mans, la première commune, mais elle est vite réprimée. Ailleurs, nous voyons des mutations semblables, à Verdun, à Liège, Cambrai, Worms, d'où l'évêque doit s'enfuir en 1073.[28]

Dans son livre *La société féodale*, Marc Bloch faisait commencer le "deuxième âge féodal" vers 1050 et il analysait les transformations de "ceux qui combattent". Les maîtres des châteaux profitent de la faiblesse des Grands pour usurper une partie de l'autorité publique. Les châtelains sont maintenant des "chevaliers" avec de nouvelles techniques guerrières et une grande autorité sur toute une région.

Les premières chansons de gestes célèbrent les exploits de ces *milites*. On croit même qu'à la veille de la bataille d'Hastings, 1066, les troupes guerrières de Guillaume le Conquérant chantaient la première version de la "Chanson de Roland".

Guillaume, avec la bénédiction de la papauté, s'empare de l'Angleterre et l'aristocratie normande trouve de quoi satisfaire son esprit guerrier. Mais d'autres Normands vont plus loin et avec Robert Guiscard conquièrent l'Italie du Sud. Robert se proclame duc en 1057, s'empare de la Calabre byzantine et même de la Sicile musulmane.

C'est à cette époque que débute la grande réforme de l'Église, véritable "révolution européenne", a-t-on dit.[29] Elle commence bien avant Grégoire VII, puisque dès 1049 le pape Léon IX, entouré de réformateurs lorrains, engage le combat contre les maux de l'Église, simonie, clérogamie, etc. Il préside le concile de Reims, s'entoure de réformateurs, ses compatriotes lorrains tel Humbert de Moyen-Moutier, qui écrit un *Adversus simoniacos*. Il voyage dans toute l'Europe: en 1049 à Reims, en 1050 à Ivrée et Rome, en 1051 à Trèves, au Mont-Cassin, l'année suivante encore au Mont-Cassin, à Mayence, en Alsace, en 1053 à Augsbourg et dans le Bénévent.

Léon IX cherche à soumettre les Normands qui menacent ses états, il est battu et fait prisonnier en 1053. Six ans après, la papauté fait la paix avec les Normands qui deviennent les fidèles de l'Église romaine. Lorsque Étienne IX est élu pape en 1057, il profite de la régence de l'impératrice Agnès, de ne pas aviser les souverains allemands, comme c'était autrefois l'usage. Il a auprès de lui le clerc Hildebrand, futur Grégoire VII, installé à Rome en 1049 et Pierre Damien, qui est fait cardinal et évêque d'Ostie. Son successeur, Nicolas II, va plus loin, et en 1059 décide que dorénavant les laïcs ne joueront aucun rôle dans l'élection pontificale. On avisera les princes après coup. C'est une véritable révolution. Cette procédure se maintient jusqu'à nos jours. En 1061, des troubles graves affectent Milan. C'est l'affaire de la *Pataria*. Des laïcs, qui veulent la réforme de l'Église, se révoltent contre l'archevêque et refusent de recevoir les sacrements de prêtres indignes. Ce mouvement, qui d'abord est considéré comme hérétique, sera utilisé par la suite par les papes réformateurs. Sous le pontificat d'Alexandre II (1061–1073) la réforme progresse. Pierre Damien est chargé de missions. Dans une lettre à Alexandre II, Pierre Damien considère que le pape est l'évêque universel, le premier des hommes, le prince des empereurs. On soupçonne dans l'ombre le rôle d'Hildebrand qui, en 1073, monte sur le trône de Saint Pierre, le nouveau pape, Grégoire VII, qui donne son nom à la réforme de l'Église, affirme vite son autorité.

Les fameux *Dictatus papae*, en vingt-sept propositions, sont resté célèbre. Donnons en quelques extraits significatifs:

I.	L'Église romaine a été fondée par le Seigneur seul.
II.	Seul le pontife romain est dit à juste titre universel.
III.	Seul, il peut déposer ou absoudre les évêques.
IV.	Son légat, dans un concile, est au-dessus de tous les évêques, même s'il leur est inférieur par l'ordination, et il peut prononcer contre eux une sentence de déposition.
VIII.	Seul, il peut user des insignes impériaux.
IX.	Le pape est le seul homme dont tous les princes baisent les pieds.
X.	Il est le seul dont le nom soit prononcé dans toutes les églises.
XI.	Son nom est unique dans le monde.
XII.	Il lui est permis de déposer les empereurs.
XIII.	Il lui est permis de transférer les évêques d'un siège à un autre, selon la nécessité.
XVI.	Aucun synode général ne peut être convoqué sans son ordre.
XVII.	Aucun texte et aucun livre ne peut prendre une valeur canonique en dehors de son autorité.
XVIII.	Sa sentence ne doit être réformée par personne et seul il peut réformer la sentence de tous.
XIX.	Il ne doit être jugé par personne.
XX.	Personne ne peut condamner celui qui fait appel au Siège apostolique.
XXII.	L'Église romaine n'a jamais erré; et selon l'Écriture, elle n'errera jamais.

Qui aurait pu imaginer de telles prétentions quelques décennies avant 1050?

Il était inévitable que l'empereur Henri IV, devenu majeur, s'oppose à la papauté, appuyé par une partie du clergé allemand, fidèles au principe de la *Reichskirche*, c'est-à-dire de l'entente entre prince et évêque, Grégoire VII n'admet pas que les princes donnent leur investiture aux évêques, d'où la fameuse querelle qui porte ce nom. Henri IV doit faire mine de se soumettre à Canossa, mais bientôt reprend le combat contre l'Église romaine. Il se fait couronner à Rome par un antipape et Grégoire VII doit chercher asile chez les Normands. Il meurt à Salerne en 1085.

La réforme grégorienne eut d'importantes conséquences. D'une part, c'est la naissance de la curie pontificale avec consistoire, administration financière, chancellerie, etc. Les légats romains parcourent l'Europe pour faire appliquer les principes grégoriens. D'autre part, c'est l'opposition entre clercs et laïcs. Il y a deux sortes de Chrétiens: les clercs adonnés à l'office religieux et à la prière, ce sont les élus; les laïcs qui possèdent les biens temporels, qui peuvent se marier—

concession à la faiblesse humaine—ils peuvent être sauvés en pratiquant le vertus et évitant les vices. Cette séparation clercs-laïques est celle de l'Église enseignante et Église enseignée, telle qu'on la connaîtra en Occident, non seulement pendant le Moyen Âge, mais même jusqu'au xxᵉ siècle. En Orient les laïcs étaient admis à faire de la théologie et des recherches religieuses.

Puisque je parle de l'Orient byzantin, il faut rappeler que c'est sous Léon IX qu'a eu lieu ce qu'on appelle le "schisme byzantin" de 1054. Humbert de Moyen-Moutier, représentant du pape, et le patriarche Michel Cérulaire se lancent réciproquement des anathèmes. On a exagéré l'importance de ce schisme, mais il montre bien que déjà l'Église romaine cherche à faire reconnaître partout son autorité. D'ailleurs Paul VI et le patriarche Athénagoras lèveront ces anathèmes en 1965.

D'autre part, c'est à cette époque que l'Église romaine combat les hérésies, en particulier celle de Béranger. L'écolâtre est condamné au concile de Rome en 1059 et doit affronter l'abbé du Bec-Hellouin, l'abbé Lanfranc, dans une célèbre discussion d'où il ne sort pas vainqueur.³⁰ Toujours dans cette période, les papes encouragent la lutte contre l'Islam. Alexandre II soutient les chrétiens d'Espagne dans leur *reconquista* et peu à peu les Musulmans doivent reculer. En 1085, date importante, Tolède l'ancienne capitale des Wisigoths, tombe aux mains des Chrétiens. Mais l'arrivée des Almoravides arrête un moment la reconquête.

L'Islam recule également, nous l'avons dit, en Italie du Sud et même en Sicile où les Normands jettent les bases de leur puissance. Enfin, après la victoire des envahisseurs turcs seldoucides à Mantzikek et leur installation dans le Moyen Orient, les papes décident de lancer les chevaliers occidentaux contre l'Islam pour reconquérir les Lieux saints. C'est la première croisade prêchée par Urbain II au concile de Clermont en 1095.

La réforme grégorienne eut des conséquences dans le domaine culturel. Les sciences religieuses l'emportent sur les sciences profanes et l'Église tient en main l'organisation de l'enseignement, qu'elle gardera pendant des siècles. On signale des maîtres qui abandonnent leurs recherches philosophiques pour étudier l'Écriture, tel Conrad d'Hirschau et surtout Lanfranc. Un contemporain écrit que Lanfranc "autrefois très savant en dialectique, maintenant explique avec beaucoup de subtilités les Épîtres de saint Paul et les Psaumes". Lanfranc a eu un disciple. C'est son compatriote italien, Anselme, devenu abbé du Bec-Hellouin en 1060 fut le premier, avec le *Monologion* puis le *Proslogion* (1077), qui affirmait comme saint Augustin autrefois une foi étayée par la raison: *Fides quaerens intellectum*. La théologie médiévale était née. Autre conséquence, les fondations monastiques qui se multiplient. Jean Gualbert fonde Vallombreuse, près de Florence. Le monastère souabe d'Hirschau se libère de l'autorité impériale et soutient les luttes du pape en Allemagne. En Angleterre, de nombreux monastères sont fondés en relation avec ceux de Normandie et l'appui de Guillaume le Conquérant, partisan des réformes. En Auvergne, la Chaise-Dieu, d'abord ermitage, devient siège d'une congrégation sous Grégoire VII. Cluny, gouverné par Hugues de Semur de 1049 à 1109, est toujours le grand monastère qui multiplie ses prieurés. Hugues est présent à Canossa mais reste très discret dans le conflit entre pape et empereur. Il fait commencer la construction de la grande abbaye de Cluny III, avec de nouvelles techniques (1088).

Mais la puissance de Cluny inquiète. À la fin du xiᵉ siècle, de nouveaux monastères, Molesmes en 1075, La Chartreuse en 1084 et Cîteaux en 1098, adoptent une vie religieuse plus exigeante. C'est ainsi que le bourguignon Bernard préfère aller à Cîteaux plutôt qu'à Cluny.

Autre innovation dans le monde monastique, la fin de l'oblation de jeunes enfants telle qu'on le connaissait depuis des siècles. Ainsi, les contrats passés entre familles et moines précisent que l'enfant peut, à la puberté, revenir à la vie laïque ayant reçu une bonne éducation religieuse.[31]

Enfin, à côté des monastères, des congrégations de chanoines réguliers sont créées. Ils doivent abandonner tout bien et s'adonner à la prière, tout en ayant un rôle pour la conversion du peuple. Signalons que le futur évêque de Chartres, Yves, est chanoine jusqu'à sa nomination épiscopale. On sait que ce savant canoniste jouera un rôle déterminant pour l'apaisement de la querelle des investitures (Concordat de Worms en 1122).

La deuxième moitié du xiᵉ siècle est, et pour l'Occident et pour l'Église en particulier, une période décisive. Nous sommes déjà engagés dans le xiiᵉ siècle.

Notes

1. Pierre Riché, *Les grandeurs de l'an mille* (Paris, 1999), 11 et suivantes.

2. Jean-François Lemarignier, *Le gouvernement royal aux premiers temps capétiens (987–1108)* (Paris, 1965), 37 et suivantes.

3. Adalbéron de Laon, *Poème au roi Robert*, éd. C. Carozzi (Paris, 1979), 23; G. Duby, *Les trois ordres ou l'imaginaire du féodalisme* (Paris, 1978).

4. Pierre Riché, "Image de l'évêque en France et dans l'Empire autour de l'an mille", dans *Histoire, Fiction, Représentation*, Colloque d'Aix en Provence 2006, éd. Graduate School of Letters (Nagoya University, 2007), 7–13.

5. Pierre Riché, *Abbon de Fleury, un moine savant et combatif (vers 950–1004)* (Turnhout, 2004), 217 et suivantes.

6. Riché, *Les grandeurs*, 83–84.

7. Cécile Treffort, "Le comte de Poitiers duc d'Aquitaine et l'Église aux alentours de l'an mil (970–1030)", dans *Regards croisés sur l'an mil—Cahiers de civilisation médiévale* (Poitiers, 2000), 395 et suivantes.

8. Adalbéron de Laon, *Poème*, vers 285–94.

9. Riché, *Les grandeurs*, 167 et suivantes.

10. Pierre Riché, *Écoles et enseignement dans le Haut Moyen Âge: Fin du Vᵉ siècle-milieu du XIᵉ siècle*, 3ᵉ éd. (Paris, 1999), 119 et suivantes.

11. Fulbert de Chartres, *Œuvres: Correspondances, controverses, poésies* (Chartres, 2006), lettre 9, 52.

12. Cf. les discussions à propos du poème de Gerbert étudié par Clyde Brockett, et cf. Flavio Nuvolone, *Archivum Bobiense* 24 (2002) et d'autre part E. Poulle, "Gerbert homme de sciences", dans *Gerbert d'Aurillac—Silvestro II, Archivum Bobiense Studia* 25 (2005), 95 et suivantes.

13. R. Halleux, "L'école mathématique lotharingienne et l'introduction de la science arabo-latine aux xie et xiie siècles", dans *Histoire des Sciences en Belgique de l'Antiquité à 1815* (Bruxelles, 1988), 27–35.

14. Riché, *Les grandeurs*, 214.

15. Ibid., 221.

16. Carol Heitz, "Vitruve et l'architecture du Haut Moyen Âge", dans *La cultura antica nell'occidente latino dal* vii *all'*xi *secolo*, Settimane di studio (Spoleto, 1975), t. II, 726–52. Sur l'architecture de cette époque, cf. J.-P. Caillet, dans *L'Europe et l'an mil*, dir. Pierre Riché (Paris, 2001), 149 et suivantes. De même, "Le Mythe du renouveau architectural roman", dans *Cahiers de civilisation médiévale* (2000), 342 et suivantes.

17. E. Palazzo, "*L'Art des manuscrits enluminés autour de l'an mil*" et D. Gabory-Chopin, "Les arts précieux de l'an mil", dans *L'Europe de l'an mil*, ed. Pierre Riché (Paris, 2001), 81 et suivantes.

18. Jan Dhondt, *Le Haut Moyen Âge*, édition française de Michel Rouche (Paris, 1976), 229 et suivantes; Jean-Pierre Poly et Eric Bournazel, *La mutation féodale: x^e–xiie siècles* (Paris, 1991), 105.

19. Raoul Glaber, *Historiae*, 1.6.

20. Sur ces hérésies, cf. Poly et Bournazel, *La mutation féodale*, 382 et suivantes.

21. Cf. en dernier lieu, André Cantin, *Saint Pierre Damien (1007–1072)* (Paris, 2006).

22. Claude Genin, *Fulbert de Chartres* (Chartres, 2003) et le volume publié à l'occasion du millénaire de Fulbert, *Œuvres: Correspondances, controverses, poésies*, par la Société archéologique d'Eure-et-Loire.

23. André Cantin, *Foi et dialectique au* xie *siècle* (Paris, 1997).

24. R. B. C. Huygens, ed., *Epistola ad Walcherum*, CCCM 62 (Turnhout, 1985), 11–43.

25. Pierre Riché, "Autour du millénaire de Fulbert: Le Maître et ses disciples", *Société archéologique d'Eure-et-Loir* 92 (2007), 9.

26. Baudri de Bourgueil, *Carmina*, 1.27, éd. J.-Y. Tillette (Paris, 1998), 46.

27. Cantin, *Foi et dialectique*, 70–71.

28. Dhondt, *Le Haut Moyen Âge*, 281 et suivantes.

29. Pierre Riché, *Grandeurs et faiblesses de l'Église au Moyen Âge* (Paris, 2006), 159 et suivantes.

30. Jean de Montclos, *Lanfranc et Béranger: La controverse eucharistique au* xie *siècle* (Louvain, 1971).

31. Pierre Riché, "Les moines bénédictins maîtres d'école (viiie–xie siècles)", dans *Benedictine Culture, 750–1050* (Leuven, 1983), 112, et les références au Cartulaire de Sauxillange, édité en 1864 et qui mériterait une réédition. Cf. aussi Nora Berend, "La subversion invisible: La disparition de l'oblation irrévocable des enfants dans le droit canon", dans *Médiévales* 36 (1994), 123 et suivantes.

PART 4

Visions and Voices

CHAPTER 13

Patterns of Miracle:
Four Late Antique Stories

GISELLE DE NIE

It is June 18 in the year 386, the day after an event that had profoundly impressed the beleaguered Christian community in Milan: their bishop Ambrose's discovery of the remains of two up-to-then-unknown local martyrs, Gervasius and Protasius, authenticated by the cries of the possessed at that moment. Significantly, this took place at the very moment that the Catholic bishop needed to be seen as receiving divine support in his struggle against the ambitions of the heretical Arian empress and her court, then resident in the city. As the martyrs' remains were being ceremonially carried to their final resting place in a newly built church, a blind man touched the cloth covering them and, in the sight of all, was suddenly healed. After the installation ceremony, Ambrose addresses his enthusiastic community with the following words:

> Not without reason do many call this the resurrection of the martyrs;
> for us certainly the martyrs have risen. You know—you have yourselves
> even seen—that many are cleansed from evil spirits, [and] that very
> many also, having touched the robe of the saints with their hands, are
> freed from those ailments which oppressed them; you see that *the mir-*
> *acles of ancient times are renewed now that through the coming of the Lord*
> *Jesus a greater grace is poured upon the earth*, and you see that many are
> healed through a certain shadow of the holy bodies. How many hand-
> kerchiefs are thrown [upon them]! How many pieces of clothing, laid
> upon the most sacred relics and through that very touch having become
> endowed with healing power, are reclaimed! All rejoice at touching
> their last thread, and whoever touches it, will be healed. [italics added][1]

Although, as Ambrose's words seem to indicate, this is not the first miracle in the then burgeoning martyr cult in Italy—as the bishop certainly knew, martyrs' miracles were then already commonly accepted in the East—for his community the phenomenon of miracle is evidently still something of a novelty. For after the apostolic period, the church authorities had shown great reserve over against miracles, also claimed by competitive pagans and not easily distinguishable as they were from magic. Accordingly, although there are vague general statements that Christian miracles continued to happen in modest numbers, there are very few descriptions of specific ones after the early second century.[2] This must be the reason that Ambrose associates what he calls the "renewal" "of ancient miracles" with an outpouring of grace preceding the now seemingly more imminent return of Christ. This New Testament notion, long in abeyance, provided a likely explanation for the new phenomenon, enabled church authorities to accept it, and is likely to have increased popular enthusiasm.[3]

The kind of miracles that the bishop here points to as being "renewed" are, of course, the healings through the apostle Peter's "shadow" (Acts 5:15), through Paul's handkerchiefs and aprons (Acts 19:12), and through the touching of the hem of Jesus's robe (Mk 5:25–34). Perhaps the restorational power emanating from the dead prophet Elisha's bones (2 Ki 13:21) was also remembered. Contact is central. Later in the same address, however, Ambrose puts the events into a more earthly context: he asserts that the recent miracles are a proof of the martyrs' power to defend the (Catholic) Church at a time when it is being threatened by a hostile military power.[4] It was a theme that would later be taken up by many other bishops in the increasing insecurity of the disintegrating Roman Empire.[5]

Not surprisingly, Ambrose's Arian enemies retorted by denying the authenticity of the relics and their ostensible cures. In a subsequent sermon he addresses the problem:

> What then is it that they do not believe: whether anyone can be visited by the martyrs? This is the same thing as not to believe in Christ, for he himself said: "You shall do greater things than these" [Jn 14:12]. Or by those martyrs whose merits have long been efficacious, whose bodies were long since found? Here I ask, do they bear a grudge against me, or against the holy martyrs? . . . If it be against the martyrs . . . , they show that the martyrs were of another faith than that which they believe. For otherwise they would not have any feeling against their works. . . . The demons said today, yesterday and during the night: "We know that you are martyrs." And the Arians say: "We know not, we will not understand, we will not believe." The demons say to the martyrs: "You are come to destroy us." The Arians say: "The torments of the demons are not real but false and invented ridiculous nonsense." I have heard much being made up, but no one has ever been able to

feign being an evil spirit. What is it which we see in those upon whom hands are laid? What room is there for fraud? What room for suspicion of simulation? But I shall not make use of the voice of demons to support the martyrs. Their sacred suffering is proven by the benefits which they confer. They have judges: the ones who are cleansed [of illness]; they have witnesses: those who are released [from demons].[6]

This evidence of disbelief and skepticism and of the bishop's defense against it is precious evidence of the conflicted situation in which miracles began to happen in Milan and of their function in it. Were there also Catholics who doubted? Ambrose's sermons do not mention them. Whereas—*pace* Ambrose—it is indeed possible to suspect a stage managing of the ostensibly possessed, a sudden real cure attested by reliable witnesses, such as that of the blind man, cannot be similarly dismissed.

Ambrose's sermon bringing miracles into prominent public notice again helped to initiate a momentous shift in Christian mentality. Thereafter, not only in Milan but in many other places miracles eventually began to take place—and to be recorded, if only in public memory—at the shrines of newly discovered martyrs.[7] It was the beginning of a miracle-expecting mentality that would last far into the Middle Ages. How did this new kind of event crystallize and how was it experienced? The experiential kind of truth in an event perceived as a "miracle" is best represented in the narrative form that invites empathy.[8] In what follows I shall examine four of the most elaborate stories of miraculous healings surviving from this period: first, in 387, an at-home cure through prayer recorded by Augustine as an eye-witness; then, in 426, the first-person account of a new-style public cure at a shrine of the martyr Stephen; finally, in the same period, an anonymous clerical editor's detailed account of two personal testimonies of cures involving visions of this same martyr.

Early Augustine: "A flood of tears, groans and sobs"

Although Augustine had been present in Milan when the relics were discovered, he was initially not impressed and continued for a long time to hold the traditional view that miracles had ceased after apostolic times because the world now believed.[9] A distaste for the current popular excesses of the miracle-mongering heretical Donatists in north Africa will also have played a role in his reserve. Thus he reported his witnessing a miraculous cure in a private home through prayer in 387[10] only forty years after the fact, when he had finally changed his mind about contemporary miracles. In the story he tells us that after his return to Africa from Milan, he stayed in Carthage with a friend, Innocentius, who had just undergone extremely painful surgery for fistulae in the rectum. It was then

discovered, however, that one had been overlooked, and that another operation—an anaesthetic is not mentioned—was necessary, to be carried out the next
day. When the doctor who had made the diagnosis had left, Augustine writes,
the whole household broke out in wailing as though at a funeral. And he lets the
image of death return when he says that Innocentius, terrified, asked Augustine
and other pious men who had been visiting him daily to be present the next day
at what he judged to be his death rather than his suffering:

> For such was the terror his former pains had produced, that he had
> no doubt but that he would die in the hands of the surgeons. They
> comforted him, and exhorted him to put his trust in God, and nerve
> his will like a man. Then we went to prayer; but while we, in the usual
> way, were kneeling and bending to the ground, he cast himself down,
> as if some one were hurling him violently to the earth, and began to
> pray; but in what a manner, with what earnestness and emotion, with
> what a flood of tears, with groans, sobs, and shakings of his whole body
> that he almost lost consciousness, who can describe it in words! . . .
> I could not pray at all. This only I briefly said in my heart: "O Lord,
> what prayers of your people do you hear if you don't hear these?" For
> it seemed to me that nothing could be added to this prayer, unless he
> expired in praying.

> [When] the dreaded day dawned, the servants of God were present, as
> they had promised to be; the surgeons arrived, all was prepared that
> was demanded by the hour, the frightful instruments are produced;
> all look on in wonder and suspense. . . . the knots of the bandages are
> untied; the part is bared; the surgeon examines it, and, with knife in
> hand, looks attentively and intently for the fold of tissue that is to be
> cut. He searches for it with his eyes; he feels for it with his finger; he
> applies every kind of scrutiny—but finds only a perfectly firm cicatrix.
>   No words of mine can describe the joy, and praise, and thanksgiv-
> ing to the merciful and almighty God which was poured from the lips
> of all, with tears of gladness. Let the scene be imagined rather than
> described.[11]

It looks as though the patient directly addressed God or Christ, either with or without a concomitant mental image of Christ as a personal healer. As Augustine hints
through his repeated allusions to death, however, the whole event, including Innocentius's violent prostration and his prolonged gut-wrenching sobbing and groan-
ing—all precipitated by his fear of expiring during surgery—was itself a kind of
death-experience from which he emerged, as it were, regenerated. The same kind of
experience is described as preceding miraculous cures in the subsequent centuries.[12]
As so-called liminal or transgressive experience it also figures in anthropologists'
reports of the healing rituals of present-day non-Christian traditional societies.

Such an experience dissolves the person's internal disharmonies that have been expressing themselves in the physical affliction, and makes a new, harmonious alignment of energies possible that allows the body to return to its natural health. The anthropologist and psychologist René Devisch, for instance, describes this as the leaving behind of an old, conflicted, debilitating, and unauthentic sense of self to repose in peace in a vital center, already there but until then obfuscated or undiscovered, that is perceived as being infused with creative, healing energies directly from a greater Source.[13] Since everyone in this period was convinced of the reality of the spirit world and its power, the comparison of late antique individual healing "ritual" to symbolic healing ritual in a nonliterate society taking the spirit world equally seriously is valid. This is less likely to be the case with the comparison of sociopolitical rituals which, depending upon group consent, are likely to function differently in more and less homogeneous societies.[14]

Paul of Caesarea: "I suddenly fell to the ground"

It was only by the middle 420s, when the relics of the first martyr Stephen—already precipitating miracles in other places—had arrived in Hippo, perhaps brought there by Augustine himself, that the bishop finally changed his mind about contemporary miracles through what must have been the force of circumstances. He tells us that at the moment of his writing, two years following the relics' arrival in the city in 424, almost seventy miracles had been recorded in writing.[15] In his *City of God* he gives concise, matter-of-fact descriptions of cures taking place through the sacraments, prayer, and indirect contact with the relics; they look like summaries of the more detailed personal testimonies in writing—*libelli* or pamphlets—which he now urged everyone to have made so that they could be read regularly in church—a 180-degree change of position on the subject.[16] This was not simply a caving in to popular pressure; his purpose was didactic: to convince the remaining pagans with visible proofs that the martyrs had risen and that therefore the faith they had died for is true.[17]

The miracles now beginning to happen around the remains of a long-dead martyr contained a new element: the accessing of Christ's power through a fellow human being—presumed to be in heaven—whose presence on earth was mediated through a physical object that might be, indirectly, touched.[18] The best-documented case of this happening takes place on Easter Sunday 426 in Hippo, when an eastern visitor, Paul, and two days later his sister Palladia—whose bodies had been afflicted with a constant tremor—were suddenly cured at Stephen's shrine in Augustine's church.[19] Augustine describes the event in his *City of God* and refers to it in his sermons to his congregation after it had happened.[20] The transcription of his sermons, however, also includes the text of the young man's own testimony—or *libellus*—of the cure that was read to the congregation two days after the event.[21] Augustine mentions that Paul had told his story to him at dinner on the evening after his cure; the next day, he tells his congregation that the text was "being prepared (*parabitur*),"[22] presumably by the same notary who recorded his sermons daily; it was read the day after that. This lapse of time but also the text's emphasis upon divine action rather than upon that of the saint— Augustine often stresses this[23]—appear to point to perhaps not inconsiderable editing. Although the pamphlet tells Paul's story in the first person, it appears to have been read by a lector while brother and sister, the one already healed and the other still trembling, stood on a raised platform facing the people.[24]

In their home town of Caesarea in Cappadocia, the text tells us, their elder brother had mistreated their recently widowed mother physically and the other, younger, children had not protected her. Disoriented by her grief, the mother prayed for a divine curse upon all her children, and in the course of the ensuing year they all incurred a debilitating tremor. Seeing the consequence of her ill-considered request, she then fell prey to such a desperate remorse that she hanged herself, and her children dispersed into other lands. Paul and his sister Palladia sought a cure in many places, including Stephen's shrine in Uzalis in north Africa, where a friend of Augustine's was bishop, and where as will be seen below many miracles had already taken place. Three months before Paul's cure, however, both he and his sister were admonished in visions. To Paul appeared "a certain man with a shining appearance and venerable through his white hair"[25] who told him that he would be cured within three months. The text does not identify this figure. In the book of Acts, there is no description of Stephen's physical appearance except that his face looked like that of an angel while he preached (Acts 6:15). Although Paul's image—shining and with white hair—resembles that of Christ in Revelation (Rev. 1:14), I would suggest that, at the time, he probably assumed it be the martyr. Paul's sister Palladia, however, saw "an effigy in which Augustine seemed to be present"[26]—did this one identify himself, or did she recognize Augustine when she met him? They understood these visions to indicate that they should come to Hippo to be healed. Later, Paul says, he saw Augustine again and again. Is this an implicit reference to an expectation that Augustine's own intercession—not explicitly mentioned anywhere in the text—would also play a role in the cure? In his sermon after the reading, Augustine discounts his own role and wonders how he could have visited them in a dream and told them to come to his city without being aware of it.[27]

Having arrived in Hippo two weeks before Easter, they came to the church daily and visited the relics; Augustine mentions that their condition had attracted everyone's attention and concern.[28] Paul's pamphlet describes the moment of transformation: "Every day, I prayed with many tears in the place where the *memoria* [shrine] of the most glorious martyr Stephen is. On Easter day, however, as those who were present saw, while holding onto the railing [around the altar and reliquary], praying and weeping strenuously, I suddenly fell to the ground. Robbed of my sensory awareness, I did not know where I was.[29] After a while, I stood up and no longer found that tremor in my body."[30] Similar phenomena are still occurring today in the context of charismatic healing sessions.[31] The text concludes by asking for everyone's thanksgiving for his cure and prayers for his still ailing sister. Did Paul perhaps visualize the heavenly figure he had seen in his dream-vision as the saint while he held on to the railing, all the while praying and weeping strenuously—much as Innocentius had done forty-odd years earlier?

After the reading, when Augustine had dismissed the brother and sister, had commented that children should always respect their parents, and was beginning to relate a recent miracle of Stephen's in Uzalis, cries were heard from the nearby shrine of the martyr. People came running to Augustine and told him that Palladia, after having touched the railing, had also collapsed and then arisen healed.[32] As she was led into the main part of the church, he reports, "such a shout of wonder rose from men and women together that the exclamations and the tears seemed like never to come to an end. . . . They shouted God's praises without words, but with such a noise that our ears could scarcely bear it."[33] When silence had finally been obtained, Augustine responded to the situation by quoting Psalm 31:5 (in an older translation): "I said: 'I will confess my transgression against myself to the Lord my God,' and you forgave the impiety of my heart."[34]

Augustine, then, appears to have regarded their cures as a purification of the heart that extended to the body, a forgiving of their sin of not protecting their mother, that removed its divine physical punishment. If this was also their own experience, the bishop's sermons in the foregoing days may have helped them to reach this state. Just before Easter, these are likely to have pointed to Christ's crucifixion and resurrection.[35] But as one of Augustine's—undated—sermons about Stephen[36] records, it was the church's custom also to read the book of Acts, containing Stephen's passion, around Easter,[37] and Augustine's sermons about Stephen repeatedly exhort his audience to imitate his forgiveness of his attackers.[38] He made his audience experience Stephen's passion and forgiveness in their hearts by enlisting their affective imagination, saying: "Listen, and you see shows in your heart. The sound is in your ears, the sight in your minds. You see the great strife of the holy Stephen, who is stoned in this fight."[39] Then he turns it into their own experience: "If you wish to avenge yourself upon your enemy, turn to your own anger: for this is your enemy, who is killing your soul!"; "Acknowledge with whom you are fighting in the theatre of your heart!"[40]

If Augustine had preached about Stephen's martyrdom with words like these in the weeks before Easter 426, one might imagine that they inspired Paul and Palladia to put aside their anger and to become reconciled to their mother's memory, as well as confident of divine forgiveness for themselves. If we follow Augustine's view, purification of the heart and thereby liberation from a physically debilitating sense of guilt and anger may thus be an essential pattern in this cure. Considering the evidence of other contemporary cures, such as those written up in Uzalis (two of which will presently be considered), however, it is likely that—in addition—a visualization of the shining heavenly figure played a greater role as a catalyst of the transformation than appears in what looks like Augustine's redaction of Paul's testimony.

Restitutus and Florentius: "A new countenance, bright and shining"

For that the perceiving of such an image could transform the beholder becomes very clear in the last two stories to be examined. *The Miracles of the First Martyr Stephen*[41] is the earliest independent collection of miracle stories around a Western Christian shrine.[42] More or less contemporary with Augustine's summaries of the events in Hippo, its anonymous clerical author describes the martyr's miracles in and around the north African town of Uzalis, now El Aliya, about seventy miles northwest of present-day Tunis at the command of the city's bishop Evodius, who had been urged by Augustine to have this done.[43] The author says that he is concerned to present the events as they were experienced by the persons in question and therefore professes to relate the events in the same words in which they were told to him.[44] The fact that the stories' later recitation to the whole community elicited much enthusiasm appears to show that they were recognized to be truthful accounts.[45] The collection is unique too in that half of its twenty-two stories include visions and they appear, at least at first, to be arranged in a roughly chronological order. In what the author presents as the progressively increasing specificity and detail of these visions we seem to see an imaginative process taking place: initial doubts about the indeterminate, faceless bits of dust that came their way as indeed those of the apostle are overcome, and a living visionary image gradually appears of a reassuring and healing saint whose smiling face and caring words are experienced as bringing about miracles.[46] And all this, as the author is clearly concerned to show, eventually brings about the city's acceptance of the martyr as their powerful new patron, implicitly as interpreted, of course, by the clerical community through its bishop.[47] What we see happening here again is that miracles happening to individuals could become the means to a collective loyalty.

The first miracle from this collection which we shall look at is a cure that took place after a number of visions and miracles had dispelled the community's initial doubts. The blacksmith Restitutus, from another city, who was paralyzed and had also lost his power of speech, was brought to the martyr's shrine at his own request.[48] Although it was winter, Restitutus spent many days praying while prostrated upon the cold mosaic floor of what was probably the chapel containing Stephen's shrine.[49] This may be the first evidence of Christian incubation, on the model of that traditionally occurring in the temples of Asclepius, but perhaps also already in churches of the saints Cosmas and Damian.[50] Restitutus, however, appears to be increasing his discomfort intentionally by lying on the cold floor, contrary to the usual therapies for this ailment, as our author points out. After about twenty days of this torture, "he said that there appeared to him in a dream a certain youth, beautifully dressed and elegant in bearing" (per somnium noctu apparuisse sibimet indicavit quemdam iuvenili forma praeditum, speciosa etiam veste et habitu decorum),[51] who, surprisingly, commanded him to walk on his own two feet up to the elevated place where the shrine was. In other words, he is ordered to believe in his cure and to exert himself to bring it about—presumably repeating the walk at least once every day. After this, not only his mobility gradually improved but his voice also slowly came back. When, after four months of what must have been very painful exertion and very gradual improvement but not yet full recovery, he was about to go home, another dream (not further described) told him to be patient and to stay for another four months to be completely healed—which happened just as foretold.

I would suggest that what we see in this remarkable story is again someone who—consciously or not—transgressed his normal everyday state of mind through extreme physical hardship. As in death and rebirth rituals in traditional societies, this cure may have taken place—be it incrementally—in successive moments of a liminal or trance state that produced a cathartic abreaction, releasing whatever energy sources were blocked and thereby restoring Restitutus's connection with his vital source or health. His cultural conditioning made him experience this as a command by and support from an inspiring image of a beautiful youth in a precious robe. This is a clear instance of what the well-known anthropologist Clifford Geertz called "belief reality."[52] A psychologist said similarly: "The world we perceive is a dream that we learn to have from a script we have not written."[53] Rejecting the views of such a dream as myth that result in the theoretical positions of archaism (taking it at its face value), cultural relativity and limited rationality, Gianni Vattimo proposes a positive concept of it: "having discovered the human, all too human basis of the systems of value, human culture can develop only if the creation of values continues, also with the new consciousness of their earthly essence; we have to keep on dreaming, while conscious of the fact that all is a dream."[54] This approach to truth wishes to remember and re-create in an aesthetic way narrative texts presenting historical experience as now the only criterion for finding and formulating human values.[55] Ihab Hassan similarly wrote: "I do not know how to give literature or theory or criticism a new hold on the world, except to remythify the imagination, at least locally, and bring back the reign of wonder into our lives. In this, my own elective affinities remain with Emerson: 'Orpheus is no fable: you have only to sing, and the rocks will crystallize; sing, and the plant will organize; sing, and the animal will be born.'"[56]

All this seems singularly relevant to the study of miracle stories: they sing of healing transformations. I hope that the modern writers quoted would agree that our late antique ones are myths or dreams in the positive sense, and that we need not share the specific ideological certainties of the authors whose writings we examine to appreciate their affective truth.

To return to Restitutus: the saint's elegance is likely to have reflected what was in this period increasingly being imagined as the heavenly court.[57] The visionary image of the martyr, then, appears to point to the martyr's assimilation to Christ. Restitutus's affective assimilation to the dynamic and beautiful image he saw is likely not only to have given him confidence but also to have transformed his image of himself and thereby inspired his body to conform.

The last story in the Uzalis collection is the most detailed report of a vision of a saint of all the accounts in this period. We might characterize it, in modern terms, as a psychic cure through the seeing/experiencing of an image. Florentius, the dispenser of public monies of the city of Carthage, we are told, was accused of a capital offense, summarily seized, and brought to the proconsul's court. Surrounded by executioners ready to apply the customary Roman judicial torture,[58] Florentius heard the judge lash out at him with terrible accusations, and "the terrified man's mind having left him out of fear, he could not find what to say nor what to respond."[59] However, our author assures his readers, God, looking down from heaven, "sent his angel as a man to liberate him, the angel of which has been written: 'The angel of the Lord will surround those who fear him, and will liberate them'" (Ps 33:8).[60] For then Florentius suddenly felt a tap on his back. Covertly looking backwards, he saw what seemed to be one of the executioners standing around him admonishing him: "Call upon the holy Stephen!"[61] This is the first vision or apparition, thought (at least by the editor) to have been an angel in the appearance of an executioner.

The next one is that of Stephen himself, although Florentius is only later sure of this through a dream that night in which the martyr identified himself:[62]

> Having seen and heard [the executioner and his message], Florentius, *restored to his mind and senses*, and *comforted after his soul's long flight*, did not cease to pray to and call upon the glorious Stephen inside himself. Finally, lifting his face a bit towards the judge who was questioning him, he saw the assessor of the judge [sitting behind him].[63] And he saw him glowing with a new face, a new countenance, bright and shining, not the one he knew very well but another, unknown and

wonderful counselor of the judge: the one he had noticed previously
had been withered of face by the deformity of senile old age, and the
one who [now] appeared to him shone with the beauty of a youthful
face and brightness. Seeing this, the afore-mentioned Florentius, *much
and long moved, no longer doubtful but firm and certain*, believed the
glorious Stephen to be present there—and himself to be seeing him
with a seeing faith—sitting as judge in his case, or rather as his asses-
sor. For the manner in which he *received confidence even more fully and
perfectly from so great a vision* and affirmation of presence of the Friend
of God was that he saw that same defender of his, his most merciful
counsel-at-law, even gesturing to him with his hand, and so that he
would fear no longer, making this clear with his right hand and joyful
face, smiling at him—thereby promising him the fullest safety. What
more is there to say? Gradually, those furious attacks by the judge and
his anger began to be converted into total peace and mildness: so that
[Florentius] did not fear the judge but recognized him as his father.
[italics added][64]

Florentius was acquitted. In this story, the author explicitly points to the overwhelming effect that the seeing of the heavenly image of forgiveness as "a new
face, a new countenance, bright and shining," "smiling at him," had upon Florentius. The vision is said to have transformed his anxious state to one of trust and
confidence: he was restored in his mind and senses, refreshed and re-created after
his soul's long flight—a phrase that reminds of the shamanic notion of illness as a
"loss of soul."[65] A spontaneous image of the saint's smiling, confidence-inspiring,
face, then, in this case projected upon the sensory environment, induced psychic
healing. Today, there is overwhelming scientific and clinical evidence that the
meditative visualization of a vitalizing image induces a replication of its dynamic
pattern in the subject, and that the body translates this energy pattern into an
analogous bio-chemical command to its autonomous systems.[66] Perhaps the
essential dynamic pattern of a smiling spiritual healer and protector had always
been hidden in Florentius's heart of hearts, waiting to be discovered, projected
and approached, waiting to make him blossom through the experience of an as-
it-were embracing, compassionate love.[67] One articulate mystic has called this
latent image the inner Christ.[68]

To conclude, I return now to our original question: what do these experiences tell us about the new phenomenon of miracle in this period? The miraculous transformations which we have just examined are psychic revitalizations
preceded by a purifying affective experience, and in at least two of the four cases,
the effective transformation appears to have been precipitated by the seeing of
an image. Innocentius experienced a total self-emptying while addressing and
trusting an invisible healer; Paul similarly emptied himself and simultaneously

achieved forgiveness and utter confidence in his cure through a human being who could be visualized as well as felt to be present through physical contact; for Restitutus, a self-mortification followed by a face-to-face encounter inspired him to expect and to work on his own healing; and for Florentius, utter trust in the supporting, protecting presence of a heavenly human being with a loving smile transformed what initially looked like a personal disaster. In their cases, then, fear, dismay and physical affliction disappeared through a psychic regeneration induced by hoping for and imagining—potentially visualizable—dynamic patterns that generated a new trust and confidence. If something "works," it must be in some way "true."

In his famous classic, *The Varieties of Religious Experience*, the philosopher-psychologist William James suggested that, in these transformational experiences, affectively patterned images arising from unconscious modes of awareness or perceived in the visionary mode that intimate truths of a higher order of existence are experienced as more truly real and powerful than the data of sensory perception.[69] Augustine, however, had already surmised the existence of what he called as yet undiscovered dynamic patterns or "seeds," placed in human minds and bodies by God at Creation, as being responsible for miracles, including cures, that seem to be breaches of "nature."[70] One way to look at what we have seen happening in these stories of late antique cures is that of an extremely erudite present-day Catholic priest and psychotherapist, Eugen Drewermann. He regards dynamic affective patterns, imaged or not, such as those which we have seen coming into awareness in the cures we have looked at, as inborn, latent dynamic configurations (similar to Augustine's "seeds") whose discovery and internal assimilation can connect the subject effectively with the workings of the creative Source that put them there for that purpose.[71]

Notes

1. "Non immerito autem plerique hanc martyrum resurrectionem appellant, videro tamen utrum ibi nobis certi martyres resurrexerint. Cognovistis immo vidistis ipsi multos a daemoniis purgatos, plurimos etiam, ubi vestem sanctorum manibus contigerunt his quibus laborabant debilitatibus absolutos, reparata vetusti temporis miracula, quo se per adventum domini Iesu gratia terris maior infuderat, umbra quadam sanctorum corporum plerosque sanatos cernitis. Quanta oraria iactitantur, quanta indumenta super reliquias sacratissimas et tactu ipso medicabilia reposcuntur! Gaudent omnes extrema linea contingere et qui contigerit salvus erit" (*Sancti Ambrosi opera*, pars 10: *Epistulae et Acta*, ed. Michael Zelzer, CSEL 82.3 [Vienna, 1982], ep. 77.9, lines 81–92 [131–32]; hereafter cited as Ambrose, *Epp.*, by ep. and line number, followed by page number from this edition). On the events mentioned see John Moorhead, *Ambrose: Church and Society in the Late Roman World* (London, 1999), pp. 150–54, and N. B. McLynn, *Ambrose of Milan: Church and Court in a Christian Capital* (Berkeley and Los Angeles, 1994), pp. 209–19.

2. See on this Morton T. Kelsey, *Psychology, Medicine and Christian Healing*, rev. ed. (San Francisco, 1973), and R. J. S. Barrett-Leonard, *Christian Healing after the New Testament* (Lanham, MD, 1994).

3. The same notion may underlie a statement in the early fifth-century letter by Bishop Severus of Minorca in 418: "Forsitan enim iam illud praedictum ab Apostolo venit tempus, ut plenitudine gentium ingressa omnis Israel salvus fiat" (Rom. 11:25); *Epistola Severi*, 31.3, ed. Scott Bradbury, *Severus of Minorca, Letter on the Conversion of the Jews*, Oxford Early Christian Texts (Oxford, 1996), 124, lines 3–5.

4. Ambrose, *Epp.*, 77.10, lines 93–95 (132).

5. See Raymond Van Dam, *Saints and Their Miracles in Late Antique Gaul* (Princeton, 1993), 18–21.

6. "Sed quaero quid non credant, utrum a martyribus possint aliqui visitari—hoc est Christo non credere, ipse enim dixit: *Et maiora his facietis* [Jn 14:12]—an ab istis martyribus, quorum merita iam dudum vigent, corpora dudum reperta sunt? Quaero hic utrum mihi an sanctis martyribus invideant? . . . Si martyribus . . . ostendunt alterius fidei fuisse martyres, quam ipsi credunt. Neque enim aliter eorum operibus inviderent. . . . Dicebant hodie et superiore die vel nocte daemones: *Scimus quia martyres estis*, et Arriani dicunt: *Nescimus, nolumus intelligere, nolumus credere*. Dicunt daemones martyribus: *Venistis perdere nos*, Arriani dicunt: *Non sunt daemonum vera tormenta, sed ficta et composita ludibria*. Audivi multa componi, hoc nemo umquam fingere potuit ut daemonem se esse simularet. Quid illud quod ita exagitari eos videmus quibus manus imponitur? Ubi hic locus fraudi est, ubi suspicio simulandi? Sed non ergo ad suffragium martyrum usurpo vocem daemoniorum, beneficiis suis sacra passio comprobetur. Habet indices sed purgatos, habet testes sed absolutos" (Ambrose, *Epp.*, 77.19–20, lines 199–204, 206–9; 22–23, lines 227–39 [138–40]).

7. The status of miracle had always been more or less problematic; for that in the preceding centuries see Marc van Uytfanghe, "La controverse biblique et patristique autour du miracle, et ses répercussions sur l'hagiographie dans l'Antiquité tardive et le haut Moyen Âge latin," in *Hagiographie, cultures et sociétés: IVᵉ–XIIᵉ siècles* (Paris, 1981), 205–33 (208–13). The seminal study of the rise of the martyr cult is that of Peter Brown, *The Cult of the Saints: Its Rise and Function in Latin Christianity* (Chicago, 1981). It has recently been shown that in the high and later Middle Ages ordeals and patently improbable miracles—but not necessarily cures such as those to be discussed here—were perceived as necessarily counterintuitive and hence could be viewed with various degrees of skepticism; see on this Steven Justice, "Did the Middle Ages Believe Their Miracles?," *Representations* 103 (2008): 1–29. As will be shown in my forthcoming study *Poetics of Wonder*, Studies in the Early Middle Ages 31 (Turnhout, 2012), in the late antique period the notion and experience of the new miracles was greatly differentiated and not necessarily "contrary to nature."

8. Paul Ricoeur, *Time and Narrative*, trans. Kathleen Blamey and David Pellauer, 3 vols (Chicago, 1988), 3:184: "Reenactment is the telos of the historical imagination."

9. Augustinus, *De utilitate credendi*, 16.34, ed. Joseph Zycha, CSEL 25 (Prague, 1891), 42–44, and *De vera religione*, 25.47, ed. K.-D. Daur, CCSL 32 (Turnhout, 1962), 216–17; cited in D. P. de Vooght, "La théologie du miracle selon saint Augustin," *Recherches de théologie ancienne et médiévale* 11 (1939): 197–222 (221). An overview of Augustine's two opposed positions in D. P. de Vooght, "Les miracles dans la vie de saint Augustin," ibid., 5–16.

10. The older Christian tradition of curing by prayer in the home, insofar as one can

tell from the very scarce evidence, followed the advice in the letter of James 5:14 to "call the elders of the church and let them pray over him, anointing him with oil in the name of the Lord."

11. "Tantus enim eum metus ex prioribus invaserat poenis, ut se inter medicorum manus non dubitaret esse moriturum. Consolati sunt eum illi et hortati, ut in Deo fideret eiusque voluntatem viriliter ferret. Inde ad orationem ingressi sumus; ubi nobis ex more genua figentibus atque incumbentibus terrae ille se ita proiecit, tamquam fuisset aliquo graviter inpellente prostratus, et coepit orare: quibus modis, quo affectu, quo motu animi, quo fluvio lacrimarum, quibus gemitibus, atque singultibus succutientibus omnia membra eius et paene intercludentibus spiritum, quis ullis explicet verbis? . . . Ego tamen prorsus orare non poteram; hoc tantummodo breviter in corde meo dixi: "Domine, quas tuorum preces exaudis, si has non exaudis?" Nihil enim mihi videbatur addi iam posse, nisi ut expiraret orando. . . . Inluxit dies qui metuabatur, aderant servi Dei, sicut se adfuturos esse promiserant, ingressi sunt medici, parantur omnia quae hora illa poscebat, tremenda ferramenta proferuntur adtonitis suspensisque omnibus. . . . solvuntur nodi ligamentorum, nudatur locus, inspicit medicus et secandum illum sinum armatus atque intentus inquirit. Scrutatur oculis digitisque contrectat, temptat denique modis omnibus—invenit firmissimam cicatricem. Iam laetitia illa et laus atque gratiarum actio misericordi et omnipotenti Deo, quae fusa est ore omnium lacrimantibus gaudiis, non est committenda meis verbis; cogitetur potius quam dicatur" (Augustinus, *De civitate Dei*, 22.8.106–12, 113–20, 123–26, 128–35, ed. Bernard Dombart and Alphons Kalb, CCSL 48 [1955]; all citations of *De civitate Dei* refer to this edition).

12. Most clearly in Gregory of Tours, *De virtutibus sancti Martini*, 3.prol., MGH SS rer. Merov. 1.2; see Giselle de Nie, "History and Miracle: Gregory's Use of Metaphor," in *The World of Gregory of Tours*, ed. Kathleen Mitchell and Ian Wood (Leiden, 2002), 273–79.

13. René Devisch, *Weaving the Threads of Life: The "Khita" Gyn-Eco-Logical Healing Cult among the Yaka* (Chicago, 1993).

14. As is rightly argued by Philippe Buc in *The Dangers of Ritual: Between Early Medieval Texts and Social Scientific Theory* (Princeton, 2001).

15. Augustinus, *De civitate Dei*, 22.8.356–57. Cf. Victor Saxer, *Morts, martyrs, reliques en Afrique chrétienne aux premiers siècles*, Théologie historique 55 (Paris, 1980), 270.

16. Augustinus, *De civitate Dei*, 22.8.400–402.

17. Ibid., 22.9.1–9.

18. Brown, *Cult*, 50–68, 106–27.

19. See on this church and the shrine Othmar Perler, "L'église principale et les autres sanctuaires chrétiens d'Hippone-la-Royale d'après les textes de saint Augustin," *Revue des études augustiniennes* 1 (1955): 321–26.

20. Augustinus, *Sermones*, 320–24 (PL 38, cols. 442–47).

21. It is contained in Augustinus, *Sermones*, 322 (PL 38, cols. 1443–45).

22. Augustinus, *De civitate Dei*, 22.8.450–52; cf. Augustinus, *Sermones*, 321.9 (PL 38, col. 1443).

23. As in Augustinus, *Sermones*, 319.8 (PL 38, col. 1442): "Per conservum [Stephanus] beneficia sumamus, honorem et gloriam Domino demus." Cf. C. Mayer, "'Attende Stephanum conservum tuum' (*Serm.* 317, 2, 3)," in *"Fructus centesimus": Mélanges offerts à Gerard J. M. Bartelink*, ed. A. A. R. Bastiaensen et al., Instrumenta patristica 19 (Steenbrugge, 1989), 217–37.

24. Augustinus, *De civitate Dei*, 22.8.454–61; cf. Augustinus, *Sermones*, 322.4–5.

25. "[Q]uidam aspectu clarus, et candido crine venerabilis" (Augustinus, *Sermones*, 322.68–69; PL 38, col. 1444).

26. "[I]n visione Sanctitas tua in ea effigie, in qua te praesentes videmus, apparuit" (Augustinus, *Sermones*, 322.70–72; PL 38, col. 1444).

27. Ibid., 323.2 (PL 38, col. 1445).

28. Augustinus, *De civitate Dei*, 22.8.420–26.

29. This phenomenon, still occurring today, is discussed in M. F. G. Parmentier, *Rusten in de Geest: God houdt ons een spiegel voor* (Hilversum, 1992).

30. "Orabam ego cotidie cum magnis lacrymis in loco ubi est memoria gloriosissimi martyris Stephani. Die autem dominico Paschae, sicut alii qui praesentes erant, viderunt, dum orans cum magno fletu cancellos teneo, subito cecidi. Alienatus autem a sensu, ubi fuerim nescio. Post paululum assurexi, et illum tremorem in corpore meo non inveni" (Augustinus, *Sermones*, 322.83–89; PL 38, col. 1445).

31. See on this Parmentier, *Rusten in de Geest*.

32. Augustinus, *Sermones*, 323.4 (PL 38, col. 1446); Augustinus, *De civitate Dei*, 22.8.468–69.

33. "Tum vero tantus ab utroque sexu admirationeis clamor exortus est, ut vox continuata cum lacrimis non videretur posse finiri. Exultabant in Dei laudem voce sine verbis, tanto sonitu, quantum nostrae aures ferre vix possent" (Augustinus, *De civitate Dei*, 22.8.472–74, 478–79).

34. "Dixi, Proloquar adversum me delictum meum Domino Deo meo, et tu dimisisti impietatem cordis mei" (Augustinus, *Sermones*, 323.81–83; PL 38, col. 1446).

35. Cf. Augustin d'Hippone, *Sermons pour la Pâque*, ed. and trans. S. Poque, Sources chrétiennes 116 (Paris, 1966).

36. On the more general history of the relics: Victor Saxer, "Aux origines du culte de saint Étienne protomartyr," in *Les miracles de saint Étienne*, ed. Jean Meyers, Hagiologia 5 (Turnhout, 2006), 37–46; S. Vanderlinden, "Revelation S. Stephani (BHL 7850–56)," *Études Byzantines* 4 (1946): 178–217; Josef Martin, "Die revelatio Stephani und Verwandtes," *Historisches Jahrbuch* 77 (1958): 419–33. On the whole corpus of the Stephen tradition: François Bovon, "The Dossier on Stephen, the First Martyr," *Harvard Theological Review* 96 (2003): 279–315; François Bovon, "Beyond the Book of Acts: Stephen, the First Martyr, in Traditions outside the New Testament Canon of Scripture," *Perspectives of Religious Studies* 32 (2006): 93–107. See also A. A. R. Bastiaensen, "Augustine on the Deacon-Preacher-Martyr Stephen," *Augustiniana* 54 (2004): 103–27 (123).

37. Augustinus, *Sermones*, 315.1 (PL 38, col. 1426).

38. Ibid., 315.2 (PL 38, col. 1427).

39. "Audistis, et spectacula cordis vidistis. Sonus erat in auribus, visio in mentibus. Spectastis magnum agonem sancti Stephani, qui in agone lapidabatur" (ibid., 315.5; PL 38, col. 1428).

40. "Si vindicare te vis de inimico tuo, ad ipsam iram tuam te converte: quia ipsa est inimica tua, quae occidit animam tuam" (ibid., 315.9); "[A]gnosce cum qua pugnas in theatro pectoris tui" (*Sermo* 315.10; PL 38, cols. 1430 and 1431).

41. *De miraculis sancti Stephani protomartyris* (hereafter MS), in *Les miracles de saint Étienne*, ed. Meyers, 266–368. Cf. Hippolyte Delehaye, "Les premiers 'Libelli miraculorum,'" *Analecta Bollandiana* 29 (1910): 427–34, and Hippolyte Delehaye, "Les recueils antiques de miracles des saints," *Analecta Bollandiana* 43 (1925): 80–85; and Saxer, *Morts*, 246–54.

42. Delehaye, "Les recueils antiques," 81.

43. Meyers, *Les miracles de saint Étienne*, 306. Other articles in the same volume discuss various aspects of the source and its context. An earlier briefer analysis and still very useful commentary of the text and its historical context in Saxer, *Morts*, 245–54. A still useful older overview in H. Leclercq, "Étienne (Martyre et sépulture de saint)," in *Dictionnaire d'archéologie chrétienne et de liturgie (DACL)*, ed. F. Cabrol and H. Leclercq, 15 vols. (Paris, 1907–53), vol. 5.1, cols. 624–71. On the site of Uzalis: Taher Galia, "Le site d'Uzalis: recherches récentes en archéologie et en épigraphie," in *Les miracles de saint Étienne*, ed. Meyers, 81–87. On Evodius: Paul Monceaux, *Histoire littéraire de l'Afrique chrétienne*, 7 vols. (Paris, 1912–23), 7:42–45, and G. de Plinval, "Évode," *Dictionnaire de spiritualité: Ascétique et mystique, doctrine et histoire*, 17 vols. (Paris, 1932–95), 4.2:1788–89. Augustine refers to their common history in his *Confesssiones*, 9.8.17.2–7 (ed. Lucas Verheijen, CCSL 27 [1981]). For his correspondence with Augustine on visions and other subjects, see *S. Aureli Augustini Hipponensis episcopi epistulae*, 158–61, 163, 164, 169 (ed. Aloysius Goldbacher, CSEL 44 [1904]). About the probable date of the collection see Meyers, *Les miracles de saint Étienne*, 11–25.

44. MS, 1.prol. 14–17.

45. Ibid., 2.1.1–28.

46. My article detailing part of this development, "Dreaming a Saint in Early Fifth-Century Africa," will appear in a volume containing the collected papers of a workshop entitled *Dynamic Patterns in Imagery and Images*, edited by Thomas F. X. Noble and myself.

47. MS, 1.14.17–20.

48. Ibid., 1.11.

49. See on this Y. Duval, "Les monuments du culte d'Etienne à Uzalis," in *Les miracles de saint Étienne*, ed. Meyers, 89–100. The shrine was usually referred to as *memoria*; see H. Lerclerq, "Memoria," in *DACL*, vol. 11.1, cols. 296–324.

50. Martine Dulaey, *Le rêve dans la vie et la pensée de saint Augustine* (Paris, 1973), 186–88.

51. MS, 1.11.10–11.

52. Clifford Geertz, "Religion as a Cultural System," ch. 4 in *The Interpretation of Cultures* (New York, 1973), 87–125.

53. Silvan S. Tomkins, *Affect, Imagery and Consciousness*, vol. 1, *The Positive Affects* (New York, 1962), 13.

54. Gianni Vattimo, "Myth and the Fate of Secularization," *Social Research* 52 (1985): 347–62 (360).

55. Gianni Vattimo, *La fin de la modernité: nihilisme et herméneutique dans la culture post-moderne*, trans. C. Alunni (Paris, 1985), 181.

56. Ihab Hassan, *The Postmodern Turn* (Columbus, 1987), 182.

57. Imagined in most detail in the late sixth century by Venantius Fortunatus in his *Vita sancti Martini* (ed. and trans. Solange Quesnel, Collection Budé [Paris, 1996]).

58. Meyers, *Les miracles de saint Étienne*, 367n87.

59. "At pavefacti hominis fugata mens metu, nec quid diceret nec de quo diceret inveniebat" (MS, 2.5.20–21).

60. "Sed ecce Deus ill magister e caelo prospiciens ad liberandum eum hominem angelum suum misit, de quo dictum est: *Immittet angelus Domini in circuitu timentium eum, et eruet eos*" (MS, 2.5.25–32).

61. "Invoca sanctum Stephanum" (ibid., 2.5.32).

62. Ibid., 2.5.79–85.

63. Meyers, *Les miracles de saint Étienne*, 367n88.

64. "Quo viso auditoque, Florentius, suae menti ac sensui redditus et fuga dudum retracto animo recreatus, gloriosum Stephanum intra semetipsum orare atque invocare minime desistebat. Deinde elevata parumper facie ad interrogantem iudicem, oculos intendit in iudicis assessorem. Quem cum nova facie novoque vultu micantem fulgentemque conspiceret, neque illum sibimet notissimum sed alium incognitum atque mirificum iudicis consiliarium cerneret, ita ut cum esset assessoris antea nota in omnibus et marcida aevo in vultu deformitas et senilis aetas, in illo vero qui ei apparebat, iuvenili decore vultus et candore fulgebat; hoc viso memoratus Florentius, diu multumque permotus, non iam dubius sed firmus et certus, gloriosum Stephanum ibi praesentem credebat adesse, ipsumque oculata fide intendere se, et in sua causa iudicem sedere vel iudici adsistere. Nam quo plenius perfectiusque de tali visione ac praesentatione amici Dei fiduciam caperet, videt Florentius eumdem suum suffragatorem suique iudicis misericordissimum consiliatorem etiam manu sua sibimet annuentem, et ne quidquam prorsus timeret per manum dexteram significantem, vultuque hilari sibi arridentem ac spem salutis plenissimam pollicentem. Quid multa? Sensim coepere illi furiales impetus iudicis tumentesque animi ad omnem tranquillitatem lenitatemque deduci, ita ut non formidaret iudicem sed agnosceret patrem" (MS, 2.5.32–50).

65. As Jeanne Achterberg, *Imagery in Healing: Shamanism and Modern Medicine* (Boston, 1985), 18, 48.

66. See Achterberg, *Imagery*, and Candace B. Pert, *Molecules of Emotion* (New York, 1997). If affective visualizations work for modern patients, why not also for ancient ones, who moreover believed in the powerful reality of the visualized?

67. See on the notion of inborn "archetypes," Jolande Jacobi, *Complex, Archetype, Symbol in the Psychology of C. G. Jung*, trans. Ralph Manheim, Bollingen Series 57 (Princeton, 1959), 31–73.

68. As T. R. Kelly, *A Testament of Devotion* (New York, 1941), 29.

69. William James, *The Varieties of Religious Experience* (1902; repr. New York, 1958), 392–97.

70. Augustine, *De Trinitate*, 3.9.17, ed. W. J. Mountain, CCSL 50 (Turnhout, 1968), 140.

71. Eugen Drewermann, *Tiefenpsychologie und Exegese II. Die Wahrheit der Werke und der Worte: Wunder, Vision, Weissagung, Apokalypse, Geschichte, Gleichnis*, 2 vols. (Olten, 1984–85), 2:769.

 CHAPTER 14

Representing the Saint:
The Structure of Heiric of
Auxerre's *Miracula sancti Germani*

AMY K. BOSWORTH

Scholars have long recognized the importance of the study of the saints in understanding the Carolingian world. Historians utilize the multitude of *vitae*, *miracula*, and *translationes* written in the eighth to tenth centuries to broaden our understanding of this critical time in European history.[1] Heiric of Auxerre's *Miracula sancti Germani* (BHL 3462), written in the 870s, exemplifies this flourishing ninth-century hagiographical tradition. Focusing primarily on the activities of St. Germanus in the Carolingian world, Heiric's work complemented and added to the preexisting literary tradition surrounding the holy man. The *Miracula* presented Germanus as a powerful, active, and contemporary figure. Historians have begun to recognize the richness of this text and its usefulness in understanding the cult of the saints in the ninth century, the political landscape of the Carolingian world, and the interaction between the sacred and the profane.[2] Yet the most recent printed version of the complete work dates to 1863 and is itself a reprint of an eighteenth-century edition. Even more problematic, most of the versions of the *Miracula* in print (including the two accessible online) omitted the original ninth-century organizational structure in favor of chapter headings and chapter breaks devised by modern editors. Although the printed versions faithfully reproduced the contents of the *Miracula*, their omission of the original chapter headings and the inclusion of an artificial organizational scheme distorted the ninth-century conception of the work and interjected modern editorial and historiographical biases into the text. A comparison of the original chapter headings found in the ninth-century manuscript with those found in the modern printed versions will highlight the need to consider the Carolingian-era organizational scheme in any study of this miracle collection and underline the necessity for a new, easily accessible edition of Heiric of Auxerre's *Miracula sancti Germani* that reincorporates the ninth-century structure and chapter headings into the text.[3]

The Monk and the Saint

Heiric of Auxerre's life and work reflected the scholarly trends of the ninth century and a personal concern for the edification of his community. He was born in 841, entered the monastery of St. Germanus in Auxerre at the age of nine, and received his primary education under the master of the monastic school, Haimo of Auxerre, known in Carolingian intellectual circles for his prolific exegetical scholarship.[4] As a teenager, he traveled to Ferrières to study with its abbot Lupus and then to Soissons to study with John Scottus or one of his students. By the time he returned to Auxerre in 865, Heiric possessed an enviable ninth-century education and had become part of a group of interconnected scholars all participating in the Carolingian "Renaissance." Heiric authored two hagiographical texts dedicated to his holy patron, the prose *Miracula sancti Germani* and the verse *Vita sancti Germani*. His other works included a number of homilies for his fellow monks and the *Collectanea*, a collection of notes the monk took during his time as a student of Haimo and Lupus, dedicated to Bishop Hildebold of Soissons.[5] Louis Holtz called the latter collection "truly a very precious work" and "a key to authenticate the writings of the theologians of Auxerre."[6] Heiric ended his life as the master of the monastic school at Auxerre in 876 or 877.[7]

The two-book *Miracula sancti Germani*, written in the 870s, chronicled the life and posthumous activities of the fifth-century bishop Germanus of Auxerre. Heiric chose not to reproduce the miracles contained in the earlier fifth-century *Vita sancti Germani* written by Constantius of Lyon, although he knew the text. Instead he recorded a few "new" tales of the saint's wonders prior to his death and over fifty posthumous miracles. Heiric's work added to the centuries-old hagiographical tradition surrounding the saint and crafted a richer and more diverse portrait of Germanus's deeds as Auxerre's bishop and posthumous patron.[8] The work not only reinforced the saint's status as one of the Christian holy dead, but it also portrayed him as a relevant figure in the ninth-century Carolingian world through Heiric's inclusion of a number of contemporary wondrous events. Heiric organized the *Miracula sancti Germani* into two books. The first provided a brief look at the activities of Germanus prior to his death and the events surrounding the return of the saint's body from Ravenna to Auxerre for burial. Heiric included a discussion of the saint's Merovingian patrons, especially the building and decorating of a church in his honor that occurred in the first half of the sixth century. This brief Merovingian interlude continued with the inclusion of two miracles credited to St. Germanus and recorded by Gregory of Tours, one occurring in Auxerre, the other in Moissat. Heiric then described a series of ninth-century miracles the saint performed posthumously in Auxerre and beyond. He organized these accounts geographically, beginning with the saint's primary shrine (and Heiric's community) at Auxerre and then moving to various churches dedicated to Germanus throughout Francia. The first book concluded with a story about Germanus's miraculous and political interventions in Britain.[9] Book 2 focused on the political events surrounding the translations of the saint's body to renovated tombs at Auxerre in 841 and 859 and the miracles and events that transpired during and immediately after these years. In particular, Heiric noted the participation of Count Conrad of Auxerre and King Charles the Bald in the promotion and support of the holy places of Auxerre. He also included a discussion of the acquisition of the relics of several other saints by the monks of Auxerre and a detailed description of the shrines housed in the church dedicated to Germanus. The *Miracula* concluded with a sermon addressing the brothers at Auxerre, reminding them of their responsibilities as monks. The majority of the miraculous deeds Heiric included he dated to the ninth century, emphasizing the holy man's continued power and influence on contemporary Carolingian society. He portrayed Germanus as active in Auxerre, but not exclusively. In the *Miracula*, the saint cured or punished men and women in over a dozen different locations. Neither time nor geography bound the holy man. St. Germanus also assisted and received the support of some of the Carolingian ruling family and nobility. Through the miracles Heiric selected for the *Miracula sancti Germani*, books 1 and 2 presented a specific, deliberate, and carefully crafted image of St. Germanus.

The *Miracula sancti Germani* as Seen by Its Editors

The only extant manuscript of Heiric's *Miracula sancti Germani* dates to the late ninth century and is today housed in the Paris, Bibliothèque nationale de France, MS lat. 13757 (hereafter P).[10] It contains Heiric's metric *Vita sancti Germani* (folios 2r–87r), his prose *Miracula sancti Germani* (folios 88r–151v), an untitled sermon by Heiric to his monks (folios 152r–155v), a miracle of unknown authorship occurring during the life of St. Germanus and witnessed by the empress Galla Placidia (folio 156r–v), and a homily, *Omelia in die sancto paschae Beatum Augustinum*, credited by modern editors to Augustine (folios 156v–158r).[11] The complete text of the *Miracula sancti Germani* appears in four printed collections and select passages in five other works.[12] In 1657 Philippe Labbe (1607–67) published the first complete edition of Heiric's *Miracula* in *Novae bibliothecae manuscrit, librorum tomus primus*.[13] It contained the entirety of books 1 and 2 and the miracle of unknown authorship recorded in P, folio 156r–v. Labbe incorporated the wondrous tale into the miracle collection itself, placing it toward the end of book 1 in the chapter "About the reverence of a monastery called Mons Falconis," rather than as an independent entity after book 2 as in P.[14] Nearly a century later in 1731 the editors of the *Acta Sanctorum* produced a second full edition of the *Miracula sancti Germani*. Appearing in volume 7 of the month of July, it included all of books 1 and 2 and the sermon written by Heiric (fols. 162r–155v). Two reprints of the complete miracle collection appeared in the mid-nineteenth century. Volume 124 of Migne's Patrologia Latina (published in 1852) contained books 1 and 2 and Heiric's sermon. Eleven years later, Louis Maximilien Duru (1804–69) included books 1 and 2 of the *Miracula sancti Germani* along with Heiric's sermon as part of his *Bibliothèque historique de l'Yonne*. Both Migne and Duru faithfully reproduced the *Acta Sanctorum* version of the *Miracula sancti Germani*.[15] Duru's version represents the most recent full edition of the *Miracula* to appear in print. The complete text of the *Miracula* remains untranslated with only partial translations available.[16]

The printed versions of the *Miracula sancti Germani* are consistent in their presentation of the text itself, although Labbe omitted Heiric's sermon to the monks of Auxerre and the *Acta Sanctorum* group did not include the Germanus-Placidia miracle.[17] All maintained the order of the narrative found in the earliest manuscript and also the separation of the text into two books. Slight variations in spelling appear between the extant manuscript and the printed versions and among the versions themselves, with the variant spellings for place and personal names being the most common examples.[18] Only the Labbe edition of the *Miracula* changed the order of some phrases, omitted words, and substituted one word for another. These variations alter the content of the *Miracula* in no significant way. There appears to be no preferred edition of the *Miracula sancti Germani* used by historians. The contributors to *Abbaye Saint-Germain: Intellectuels et artistes dans l'Europe carolingienne IXᵉ–XIᵉ siècles* utilized Labbe's edition, while Van Egmond and Crook favored the *Acta Sanctorum*, and Quadri, Nelson, and Barré used the Patrologia Latina. Roumailac, Louis and Moreau, and Sapin all cited Duru. Some referenced more than one edition such as Janin, who worked with Labbe and Duru; Sassier, who preferred the Patrologia Latina and Labbe; and Contreni, who referenced the Patrologia Latina and P.[19] Yet Heiric's *Miracula sancti Germani* found in the ninth-century manuscript P contains elements not available in most printed versions of the work. The manuscript tradition and printed editions of the work diverge in the chapter headings and overall organizational scheme. Labbe maintained the original organizational structure and chapter headings as found in P, while the editors of the *Acta Sanctorum* (and Duru and Migne in their reprints) replaced them both with a new system of their own design. Several historians have noted the discrepancy between the chapter headings found in P and the modern editions in the *Acta Sanctorum* group.[20] Yet, many continue exclusively to utilize these later editions without consulting P or Labbe and are therefore not reading the work as it appeared to ninth-century readers.

The *Miracula sancti Germani* through Carolingian Eyes

Heiric of Auxerre carefully arranged and organized the *Miracula sancti Germani*. The miracles appeared chronologically, beginning with a few examples of the saint's activities in life before focusing on his posthumous wonders and shrine in Auxerre. He split the work into two books, each beginning with an untitled prologue justifying and introducing the subsequent text. The phrase "prior libellus explicuit," written in all capitals, denoted the end of book 1. In P the book was subdivided into chapters—book 1 containing fifty-four, and book 2 seventeen, each with a short sentence or phrase, written in capitals, that acted as chapter headings and described the text that followed. Most of the chapters were between one-quarter of a folio and two folios in length. Longer chapters, three to six folios in length, emphasized the importance of a particular place or event. Heiric's description of miracles occurring after the translation of the saint's relics to a new shrine in Auxerre filled nearly six folios. The number of examples found in this chapter highlighted the importance of the event and Germanus's acceptance of it.[21] To further divide some of the chapters the ⌐ symbol appeared in the manuscript separating multiple miracles or distinct topics occurring in the same chapter. In a chapter concerning miracles performed in the villa of Pouilly this symbol appeared fourteen times, each before the tale of a new wonder.[22] The ⌐ was also used on occasion to indicate the insertion of an authorial aside. For instance, in the chapter "The evidence revealed in the same church in the words of the same [man]," a ⌐ appeared after a miracle taken from the *Liber in gloria confessorum* of Gregory of Tours. Heiric then noted that he would now record some more recent miracles.[23] In the *Miracula sancti Germani* Heiric recorded the wondrous events that surrounded St. Germanus in life and death. The Carolingian manuscript used a sophisticated system of books, chapters, and subchapters to organize information. Each break in the text had meaning, whether it represented a change in subject, chronology, or location. The organizational scheme found in the earliest extant manuscript constructed acted as a complement to the miracles by placing emphasis on and leading the reader toward certain themes. The organization of the story of St. Germanus thus reinforced the message communicated by the miraculous tales themselves.

Recognizing the sophistication and deliberateness of the ninth-century organizational scheme, historians must read the *Miracula sancti Germani* as intended. In particular, the chapter headings constituted a vital part of the work.[24] These headings highlighted Germanus's role as a bishop, a man connected to the wider political world in life and death, a relevant ninth-century Carolingian holy man, and a worker of miracles. The Carolingian-era chapter headings shaped the reader's image of the text and the holy man behind the miracles. They provide historians with a glimpse into how the early medieval audience was introduced to the saint. They are an integral part of the *Miracula*. Only one edition of the *Miracula sancti Germani*—the earliest by Labbe—included the original ninth-century chapter headings found in P.[25] He preserved the chapter headings without rearranging or altering them, thus reflecting the *Miracula* as found in the earliest surviving manuscript. The second edition of the text, published in the *Acta Sanctorum*, and its reprints by Migne and Duru contained an entirely new structure. Although the division into two books remained, the editors omitted all of the seventy-two original chapter headings.[26] They split book 1 into twelve chapters and book 2 into four. Each of these new chapters received a new heading that described the text that followed, but they in no way reflected the chapter headings contained in the actual manuscript. The placement of the original chapter headings within the body of the *Miracula* and the division of many of these headings into several paragraphs negated any organizational scheme from the ninth century. The reduced number of chapters in the *Acta Sanctorum* group removed the emphasis on the individual miracles and the importance each played in strengthening St. Germanus's holiness. Instead the modern printed versions, excepting Labbe, grouped the miracles into broad categories based on chronology, geography, and relic translations.

This entirely new organizational structure, in particular the omission of the ninth-century chapter headings and the creation of new ones, is puzzling, since the descriptive chapter headings in the manuscript provided key pieces of information about the text—for example, "About Michomere a monk and follower of his [Germanus]," "About a dead man brought back to life on the road," and "A brief mention of Patrick appointed to Ireland because of blessed Germanus."[27] The original headings also revealed crucial details within each chapter. In reading the manuscript, one finds the following chapter headings (in this order) in folios 111r–119v,

> About a deaf man having been cured while sleeping
> About the church in the estate of Ladriacus

About a blind woman cured in that place
About the recovery of a certain invalid
About a horse impetuously allowed into the meadow of [Ger-
    manus's] church
About miracles occurring in the church at Pouilly
About a mute girl cured as witnessed by a group of people
About the chapel constructed by blessed Remigius in his honor
About the church in Soissons constructed in his honor
About the rashness of Count Vivian who was punished via his
    falcons in Cadriacus
And also the rashness of perjury was punished here
About the miraculous cure of a certain girl
About a place in the Morvennicos forest

These chapter headings communicate to the reader, without having to read a
single miracle, that Germanus's power reached to Ladriacus, Pouilly, Soissons,
Cadriacus, and Morvennicos. The saint interacted with men, women, and animals. He cured the sick and castigated the wicked. Germanus even punished
a count for his "rashness." In comparing these chapter headings to the ones
provided in the *Acta Sanctorum* group for the same paragraphs—for example,
"Miracles done throughout Gaul in other churches of St. Germanus" and "The
continuation of miracles performed in various places dedicated in his name at
the same time"—it is clear that while the chapter headings in the *Acta Sanctorum* group reflected the general feeling of the *Miracula*, they failed to project the nuances found in the ninth-century chapter headings.[28] Ignoring the
manuscript's chapter placement and headings distorted the meaning of the text.
These passages of the *Miracula sancti Germani* did not simply reflect vague miracles performed in unnamed locations "throughout Gaul." Instead, the chapter
headings themselves highlighted the types of miracles, specific locations, and
the variety of recipients.

The chapter headings of book 1 also stressed both the miracles performed
by Germanus in his lifetime and in his role as bishop. For instance, the headings
from folios 95r–100r read:

About a clear revelation made known in the church of the
    martyr Alban
And the church of his see enriched in many ways by [Germa-
    nus's] generosity
A brief mention of Patrick appointed to Ireland because of
    Blessed Germanus

> About a monk's cell that knew intimately the torments of
>   that one [Germanus]
> A summary of his glorious death
> And he continued to Ravenna as planned and the cause of
>   the departure itself
> And as he departed [Germanus] was indeed aware of his
>   imminent death
> About the most remarkable preparation of his sacred funeral

Here the manuscript chapters described Germanus's behavior as bishop of Auxerre, the events leading up to his death, and even note a relationship between the holy man and St. Patrick. They emphasized these behaviors and relationships as important in the life of Germanus. Yet the chapter headings found in the *Acta Sanctorum* group neglected this almost entirely, instead noting only the saint's miracles. In the *Acta Sanctorum* group the corresponding heading reads "Other kinds of miracles with respect to his life all the way to his death and funeral."[29] The artificial chapter heading found in the *Acta Sanctorum* group for this same section of the *Miracula* suggests none of the elements noted in the earliest extant manuscript.

In book 2 Heiric's focus shifted to the spiritual enhancement of Germanus's shrine in the Carolingian era through translations of relics and the aid of the saint's monks and secular patrons. Miracles remained an important element in this second book. Folios 128r to 131v of P included the following headings:

> A mention of the elder Conrad and his generosity
> About the restored sight of Count [Conrad]
> About the most distinguished idea for the eastern building
> About the suitability and setting of this place
> About the departure of the monks [of Auxerre] into the
>   countryside to acquire marble stones

They highlighted the association between the tomb of St. Germanus, Auxerre, and Count Conrad in these headings. Conrad was not only himself the count of Auxerre, but his namesake also became count of the city in the time of Heiric, and yet another son the abbot of the monastery of St. Germanus in Auxerre. The elder Conrad was also the grandfather of King Charles the Bald via his daughter, the empress Judith. He and his family patronized St. Germanus's holy places in the second half of the ninth century and also actively participated in secular politics. By connecting Germanus to this family Heiric sought to make the holy man and his monks more relevant in contemporary Carolingian society. The headings showed the importance of more than just miracles in maintaining the reputation of a saint. Political connections and secular politics mattered, too. The chapter headings in the *Acta Sanctorum* group also stressed the pivotal role of wondrous deeds, yet they ignored the political elements seen in the ninth-century manuscript. Book 2, chapter 1, of the *Acta Sanctorum* group reads "The new construction of a church of St. Germanus in the monastery of Auxerre, both having been begun and completed with miracles."[30] The *Acta Sanctorum* group omitted mention of Count Conrad, instead noting only the new construction and the miracles surrounding it.

In a similar vein, the *Acta Sanctorum* group labeled chapters 2 and 3 of book 2 as "The translation of St. Germanus made famous with miracles; also the relics of the holy bishop Amator, and of the Martyrs Urbanus and Tiburtius having been brought to his church" and "The signs made during the translation of SS Urbanus and Tiburtius MM; also of SS Mauritius and Innocentius; a list of saints buried in the crypts of St. Germanus of Auxerre," respectively.[31] While these chapter headings called attention to several events centered on the three saints Amator, Urbanus, and Tiburtius, and accurately reflected the subsequent texts, these chapter headings nevertheless dramatically shifted the original tone of those passages. The manuscript provided the following chapter headings in folios 133v–144r (which correspond to book 2, chapters 2 and 3, of the *Acta Sanctorum* group):

> About the transfer of the holy body and a mention of the
> distinguished translation
> A mention of the war between kings
> How the aforementioned king translated the same holy body
> How the king drove away his enemies with God himself
> protecting him
> A list of miracles [occurring] after the second translation of
> the holy body
> How the same place acquired the bones of the holy martyrs
> brought from Rome
> A brief report about the miracles performed
> About the renowned acquisition of the saints
> How the bodies of the saints were translated and a concise
> mention of the bishops of Auxerre

Nowhere do these headings mention the names of Amator, Urbanus, and Tiburtius. Instead, the ninth-century manuscript focused on the king (Charles the Bald), his political crises (three of the six chapters), and the translation of the body of Germanus. Rather than highlighting the three saints, they brought to the reader's attention a series of contemporary political events book-ended by relic translations. The chapter headings found in P reflected both the secular and the sacred. They indicated an interest in both realms and an assumption that hagiography could encompass both the miraculous and the mundane. The later editors of the *Miracula sancti Germani* removed this duality and sought only to highlight the saints and the celestial events described in the text that followed. The reworking and reorientation of the meanings of the chapters found in the *Acta Sanctorum* group more clearly reflected eighteenth- to twentieth-century attitudes toward hagiography than ninth-century concerns. The editors of the *Acta Sanctorum* and the compilers of the subsequent reprints saw little scholarly value in hagiography beyond the few facts buried in the lives and deaths of the saints. Their chapter headings reflected this attitude by focusing on the miracles of Germanus and other "religious" activities, while completely suppressing the more secular or political elements of the text—elements purposefully highlighted in the ninth-century manuscript of the *Miracula sancti Germani*. The Carolingian chapter headings also stressed how the translation of the unnamed saints enhanced the shrine dedicated to Germanus. The omission of their names only emphasized that St. Germanus and the shrine at Auxerre were the primary focus of the author. The *Acta Sanctorum* group shifted focus away from Germanus and towards saints Amator, Urbanus, Tiburtius, Mauritius, and Innocentius. The new chapter headings accurately reflected the contents of the text, but they altered the ninth-century emphasis on St. Germanus, his power, and his relevance to Carolingian society.

Historians seeking to utilize Heiric of Auxerre's *Miracula sancti Germani* find themselves in the enviable position of having four modern printed versions of the text from which to choose, including several now available online. Each provides an accurate duplication of the only extant manuscript of the work, BnF lat. 13757 (P). Yet three of the four versions omitted the original ninth-century organizational scheme and chapter headings of the *Miracula*, replacing them with a new, artificial structure. Although the changes did not alter Heiric's narrative, they nonetheless present the unsuspecting modern reader with a skewed vision of the miracle collection. While the Carolingian text stressed a rich variety of cures, punishments, places, and people with whom the saint interacted, the modern versions of the *Miracula* (excluding Labbe) present only generic mentions of wondrous deeds. More importantly, through the chapter headings, the ninth-century manuscript reflected an image of Germanus as a worldly and pious bishop in life and a politically active saintly entity in death. These chapters noted the holy man interacting with kings, counts, and other bishops, and mentioned his own austere lifestyle and fiscal generosity toward the church. The new chapters created by the editors of the *Acta Sanctorum* (and perpetuated by the Patrologia Latina and Duru) neglected to include any of these details. St. Germanus remains the primary focus of Heiric's work and the chapter headings reinforce this, especially in the chapters concerning the ninth-century translation of relics from Rome. The manuscript's chapter headings note these "new" saints being brought to Auxerre, yet they remain unnamed. This strategy allows for the cult of Germanus to be enhanced but not overshadowed. The *Acta Sanctorum* group chose the opposite tactic by naming the saints who were brought to Auxerre, thus detracting from Germanus and his shrine. By crafting an entirely new set of chapter headings and reducing the number of chapters, the editors of the *Miracula sancti Germani* significantly altered the Carolingian vision of the work. The easily accessible versions of the *Miracula* have maintained the miracles and the vignettes about the life and death of the holy man featured in the manuscript. Yet by omitting the ninth-century organizational structure they have altered Heiric's work and diminished his message. In view of the valuable information Heiric of Auxerre's *Miracula sancti Germani* has provided and will continue to provide about the cult of saints, the early medieval period, and the Carolingian world, it is clear that scholars would benefit greatly from a new edition of this important text—one that includes not only the valuable editorial insights included in the current printed versions, but also the ninth-century organizational structure and chapter headings. Only then will we be able to see St. Germanus through Carolingian eyes.

Appendix
Comparative Chapter Headings in the *Miracula sancti Germani*

Paris, BnF, MS lat. 13757 (P)		*Acta Sanctorum* July 7: 255B–258C	
Folio	Heading	Line	Heading
		255B	Prologus auctoris
90v	De mychomeree monacho et discipula eius	256D	Liber primus caput primum. S. Germani colloquium cum discipulo defuncto, mortui resuscutatio, aliaque miracula
91v	De altaris dedicatione mirabili	257A	
92r	Quod ei revertenti ad urbem suam sanctus anianus per spiritum instructus occurrerit	257B	
92v	De mortuo in itinere suscitato	257C	
93r	Quod ruensnparies obiectu signi salutaris restiterit	257D	
94r	De Corylo humi defixa	257F	
94r	De fago singularis magnitudinis	258A	
94v	De corporibus martyrum praesulatus eius tempore revelatis	258A	
95r	De revelatione perspicua in basilica albani martyris declarata	258D	Caput II. Alia quaedam ad ejus vitam spectantia usque ad obitum et exsequias
96r	Quod suae sedis ecclesiam multimoda largitate ditaverit	258F	
97r	Succincta mentio patricii per beatum germanum in hiberniam destinati	259B	
97v	De cellula crucibus illius familiariter conscia	259C	
98r	Recapitulatio gloriosi transitus eius	259D	

Appendix *(continued)*
Comparative Chapter Headings in the *Miracula sancti Germani*

Paris, BnF, MS lat. 13757 (P)			*Acta Sanctorum* July 7: 255B–258C	
Folio	Heading		Line	Heading
98r	Quod non fortuitu ravennam perrexerit et causa profectionis eiusdem		259E	
98v	Quod etiam cum proficisceretur imminentem excessum non ignotaverit		260A	
100r	De nobilissimo sacri funeris apparatu		260B	
100r	De ecclesia vercellis per mortuum mirabiliter dedicata		260F	Caput III. Translatio corporis ejus in Gallias; ejusdem receptio ac sepultura
101v	De fervore instantissimo accurrentium populorum		261C	
102r	Qualiter sancti excessus ponitificis saturno innotuerit		261D	
102v	De quinque sororibus sacrum corpus ardentissime prosecutis		261E	
103r	De sacri exceptione corporis et splendidissimo sepulcri apparatu		261F	
103v	Quid muneris in relatione sacri corporis collatum putetur per apostropha		262A	
104v	Retractatio exceptionis supradictae		262B	
104v	Ut sacrum sorpus sepulturae traditum sit et de loco sepulcri		262C	
105v	De extructione basilicae beatissimi germani		263C	Caput IV. Basilicae S. Germani et sepulcri magnificentia regia, miraculis assiduis decorata

Appendix *(continued)*
Comparative Chapter Headings in the *Miracula sancti Germani*

Paris, BnF, MS lat. 13757 (P)		*Acta Sanctorum* July 7: 255B–258C	
Folio	Heading	Line	Heading
105v	De ornatu sacrae memoriae eius	263D	
106r	Quod locus idem miraculorum semperdote floruerit	263E	
106v	Quid gregorius turonics in miraculorum libris	263E	
107r	Quid evidentiae in eadem basilica declaratum sit ex verbis eiusdem	264A	
107v	De esopo puero ab angelis visitatio	264B	
108r	De eo qui pomum furto sublegit	264C	
108v	De adulescente debilitate dampnato	264E	
109r	De eo qui bibens noctu correptus est a demone	264E	
109v	Quod in perioros quoque evidentem exerat ultionem	265A	
110r	Quanta virtus sanctissimo sepulcro assit	265B	
110r	Quid diligentiae a sacri custodibus corporis exigatur	265B	
110v	De virtute panis eius nomine insignitit	265C	
111r	De surdo inter dormiendum curato	266B	Caput V. Miracula in aliis S. Germani per Galliam ecclesiis facta
111r	De ecclesia ladriaci fundi	266C	
111v	De mulier caeca inbib curata	266D	

Appendix (*continued*)
Comparative Chapter Headings in the *Miracula sancti Germani*

Paris, BnF, MS lat. 13757 (P)			*Acta Sanctorum* July 7: 255B–258C	
Folio	Heading		Line	Heading
112r	De invalidi cuiusdam reparatione		266E	
112r	De equo in pratum ecclesae violenter admisso		266E	
112v	De miraculis apus ecclesiam pauliaci gestis		266F	
115r	De puella muta generalis conventus testimonio curato		267E	
115v	De oratorio beati remigii manibus in eius honore extructo		268B	Caput VI. Continuatio miraculorum variis locis ibidem ejus nominee dicatis patratorum
116v	De basilica suessionis euis honore constructa		268C	
118r	De temperitate viviani principis apud cadriacum in falconibus punita		269B	
119r	Quod hinc periurii temeritas puniatur		269C	
119r	De cuiusdam puellae mirabili restauratione		269D	
119v	De locis morvennicis		269E	
120v	De reverentia coenobii quod mons falconis dicitur		270B	Caput VII. Miracula facta apud coenobium S. Germani Monfalconense
124r	De oratorio eius inter alpium summa constructo		271D	Caput VIII. Miracula ejus quae in Alpibus et in Britannia contigerunt

Appendix (*continued*)
Comparative Chapter Headings in the *Miracula sancti Germani*

Paris, BnF, MS lat. 13757 (P)			*Acta Sanctorum* July 7: 255B–258C	
Folio	Heading	Line	Heading	
124v	Quod in partrandis miraculis secraetum sempter praetulerit	271F		
125r	De britannis sancto Germano speciali cultu obnoxiis deque subulci hospitio et rege abiecto	272A		
127v	Prior libellus explicut	273A	Liber secundus prologus	
128r	Commemoratio Chuinradi Mairois et de munificentia eius	273C	Caput primum. Nova ecclesiae S. Germani in coenobio Antissiodorensi fabrica, miraculis et coepta et confecta	
129r	De lumine principis reparatio	273E		
130r	De prima orientalis fabricae conceptione	274A		
130v	De oportunitate ac positione loci	274B		
131v	De fratrum profectione in provintiam marmorum causa	274E		
133v	De transmutatione sacri corporis et commemoratio primariae translationis	275E	Caput II. S. Germani translationes miraculis illustratae; sanctorum quoque Amatoris episcopi, et Urbani ac Tiburtii martyrum reliquiae ad ejus ecclesiam delatae	
135r	Commemoratio per duellii inter reges	276C		
135v	Qualiter praefatus rex idem corpus sacrum transtulerit	276D		
136v	Qualiter hostes deo se protegente pepulerit	276F		

Appendix (*continued*)
Comparative Chapter Headings in the *Miracula sancti Germani*

Paris, BnF, MS lat. 13757 (P)		*Acta Sanctorum* July 7: 255B–258C	
Folio	Heading	Line	Heading
136v	Ad breviatio miraculorum post secondam sacri corporis translationem	276F	
139v	Qualiter sanctorum pignora martyrum ab urbe delata locus idem merverit	278A	
140v	De patratis miraculis compensiosa relatio	278D	Caput III. Prodigia facta in translatione SS. Urbani et Tiburtii MM; item SS. Mauritii et Innocentii MM; catalogus sanctorum in cryptis S. Germani Antissiodori sepultorum
142v	De celebri exceptione sanctorum	279D	
144r	Qualiter sanctorum corpora translata et pontificum autisioderensium succincta commemoratio	280A	
147v	De dignitate loci toti sanctorum memoriis cumlati	281F	Caput IV. Elogium ecclesiae S. Germani Antissiodorensis, et pia S. Heirici ad fraters exhortatio
148r	Adversus eois qui sanctorum scriptus necant suis corporibus esse praesentis	282C	
149r	Commonitorium sanctis fratribus	282E	

Notes

1. See Michel Rouche, "Miracles, maladies et psychologie de la foi à l'époque carolingienne en France," in *Hagiographie cultures et sociétés IVᵉ–XIIᵉ siècles: Actes du Colloque organisé à Nanterre et à Paris (2–5 mai 1979)* (Paris, 1981), 319–37; Roman Michalowski, "Le don d'amitié dans la société carolingienne et les 'Translationes sanctorum,'" ibid., 399–416; C. M. Gillmor, "Aimoin's *Miracula sancti Germani* and the Viking Raids on St. Denis and St. Germain-des-Prés," in *The Normans and Their Adversaries at War*, ed. Richard P. Abels and Bernard S. Bachrach (Woodbridge, 2001), 103–27; Jean Roumailhac, "Saint Germain d'Auxerre et Charles le Chauve: Un exemple du culte des reliques au IXᵉ siècle," in *Memoriam sanctorum venerantes: Miscellanea in onore di Monsignor Victor Saxer* (Vatican City, 1992), 711–23; Janet Nelson, "The Franks, the Martyrology of Usuard, and the Martyrs of Cordoba," in *Rulers and Ruling Families in Early Medieval Europe: Alfred, Charles the Bald, and Others*, ed. Janet Nelson (Brookfield, 1999), 67–80; Julia M. H. Smith, "The Hagiography of Hucbald of Saint-Amand," *Studi medievali* 35 (1994): 3–37; Julia M. H. Smith, "A Hagiographer at Work: Hucbald and the Library at Saint-Amand," *Revue bénédictine* (1996): 151–71; Frantisek Graus, "Sozialgeschichtliche Aspekte der Hagiographie der Merowinger- und Karolingerzeit: Die Viten der Heiligen des südalemannischen Raumes und die sogenannten Adelsheiligen," in *Mönchtum, Episkopat und Adel zur Gründungszeit des Klosters Reichenau*, ed. Arno Borst (Sigmaringen, 1974), 130–76; and Ian Wood, "Missionary Hagiography in the Eighth and Ninth Centuries," in *Ethnogenese und Uberlieferung: Angewandte Methoden der Frühmittelalterforschung*, ed. Karl Brunner and Brigitte Merta (Vienna, 1994), 189–99.

2. See for instance John J. Contreni, "'And Even Today': Carolingian Monasticism and the *Miracula sancti Germani* of Heiric of Auxerre," in *Medieval Monks and Their World: Ideas and Realities*, ed. David Blanks, Michael Frassetto, and Amy Livingstone (Leiden, 2006), 35–48; John Crook, *The Architectural Setting of the Cult of Saints in the Early Christian West c.300–1200* (Oxford, 2000), 74, 141–43; John Crook, "The Enshrinement of Local Saints in Francia and England," in *Local Saints and Local Churches in the Early Medieval West*, ed. Alan Thacker and Richard Sharpe (Oxford, 2002), 220; Janet L. Nelson, *Charles the Bald* (London, 1992), 189–90; and Wolfert S. Van Egmond, *Conversing with the Saints: Communication in Pre-Carolingian Hagiography from Auxerre*, Utrecht Studies in Medieval Literacy 15 (Turnhout, 2006). The present author has also completed a dissertation on the *Miracula*: Amy K. Bosworth, "Criminals, Cures, and Castigation: Heiric of Auxerre's *Miracula sancti Germani* and Ninth-Century Carolingian Hagiography" (PhD dissertation, Purdue University, 2008).

3. Rosamond McKitterick argued for the importance of going back to the manuscripts in her study of the *Chronicon universale—741*. She noted that the editors of the Monumenta Germaniae Historica "omitted the first twenty-one folios (forty-two pages) and thus created a totally erroneous impression of the character of the history" in *Perceptions of the Past in the Early Middle Ages* (Notre Dame, IN, 2006), 26.

4. Heiric himself left these dates for posterity in a ninth-century manuscript. For a discussion of this document and a more comprehensive list of dates see Riccardo Quadri, *I Collectanea di Eirico di Auxerre* (Friburgo, 1966), especially p. 28; Riccardo Quadri, "Heiric," in *Abbaye Saint-Germain d'Auxerre: Intellectuels et artistes dans l'Europe carolingienne IX–XI siècles* (Auxerre, 1990), 38–39; B. de Gaiffier, "Le calendrier d'Héric d'Auxerre du manuscript de Melk 412," *Analecta Bollandiana* 77 (1959): 392–425; and Contreni, "'And Even Today,'" 37.

5. For Heiric's homilies see *Heirici Autissiodorensis: Homiliae per circulum anni*, ed. Richardi Quadri, CCCM 116 (Turnhout, 1992). The full text can be found in Quadri, *I Collectanea*. See also Quadri, "Heiric," 38–39.

6. Louis Holtz, "L'École d'Auxerre," in *L'École carolingienne d'Auxerre: De Murethach à Remi 830–908*, ed. Dominique Iogna-Prat, Colette Jeudy, and Guy Lobrichon (Paris, 1991), 131–46 (132).

7. Although no exact date is recorded for Heiric's death, the most accepted date is 876/77. For this argument see for instance Quadri, *I Collectanea*, 28; Édouard Jeauneau, "Dans le sillage de l'Erigène: Une homélie d'Héric d'Auxerre sur le prologue de Jean," *Studi medievali* 2 (1970): 938; and Pierre Janin, "Heiric d'Auxerre et les *Gesta pontificum Autissiodorensium*," *Francia* 4 (1976): 89–106 (105). M. Cappuyns questioned this generally accepted chronology but failed to provide an alternative in "Publications de sources et travaux," *Revue d'histoire ecclesiastique* 62 (1967): 720–21. Henri Barré noted that Heiric's death could be placed after 883. See *Dictionnaire de spiritualité: Ascétique et mystique, doctrine et histoire*, 17 vols. (Paris, 1932–95), 7:282–83. Contreni also took up this question suggesting that he may have lived into the early 880s. See Contreni, "'And Even Today,'" 38. Both Contreni and Barré based their arguments on evidence from the *Collectanea*.

8. Heiric utilized Constantius's work in his discussion of the saint's final words to his friend Senator, but did not reproduce the miracle noted in the vita. See Heiric of Auxerre, *Miracula sancti Germani* (*Acta Sanctorum* [hereafter AS], July 7: 260A–B); Constantius of Lyon, *Vita sancti Germani*, 29, ed. F. R. Hoare *Soldiers of Christ: Saints' Lives from Late Antiquity to the Early Middle Ages*, ed. Thomas F. X. Noble and Thomas Head (University Park, PA, 1995), 97.

9. This story parallels one found in the *Historia Brittonum* commonly credited to Nennius. Although the general narrative is the same in each (i.e., Germanus brings a calf back to life, deposes a king, and elevates a generous swineherd to the throne) and the holiness of Germanus is always highlighted, the details and overarching themes differ. Heiric's version emphasizes the importance of hospitality, while Nennius focuses on Christianity and conversion. See Nennius, *British History and the Welsh Annals*, 32, ed. John Morris (Totowa, NJ, 1980), 26–27.

10. Georg Waitz, "Hericus (Heiricus)," *Neues Archiv* 4 (1879): 528–31.

11. The origins of the miracle included after the *Miracula* in BnF lat. 13757 (P) are unknown. It tells the story of St. Germanus resurrecting an ass in the presence of the empress Galla Placidia. The *Vita sancti Germani* of Constantius, the *Historia Brittonum* of Nennius, and the *Miracula sancti Germani* of Heiric attest to Germanus's ability to resurrect humans and animals. See Constantinus of Lyon, *Vita sancti Germani*, 38, ed. Hoare, 102–3; Nennius, *British History and the Welsh Annals*, 32, ed. Morris, 26–27; Heiric of Auxerre, *Miracula sancti Germani* (AS, July 7: 256E–257A); and Heiric of Auxerre, *Miracula sancti Germani*, P, fols. 90v–91v, fol. 156r–v. This particular miracle may have occurred during the saint's final trip to Ravenna, where the hagiographical tradition notes his interaction with the empress. The homily that follows this miracle and ends the manuscript appears in (Augustine of Hippo?), *Sermo CLX, De Pascha, II* (PL 39, 2059–61).

12. Works that include a portion of the *Miracula* include Jean Gremaud, ed., *Documents relatifs à l'histoire du Vallais*, vol. 1, 300–1255 (Lausanne, 1875), 28–29; Pierre-François Chifflet, ed., *Histoire de l'abbaye royale et de la ville Tournus* (Dijon, 1664), 204–5; Jean Du Bouchet, ed., *La veritable origine de la seconde et troisiesme ligne de la maison royale de France* (Paris, 1646), 347–50; Georg Waitz, ed., MGH, SS 13, 401–4; Martin Bouquet, ed.,

Recueil des historiens des Gaules et de la France, 24 vols. in 25 (Paris, 1738–52), 7:355–56 and 8:402.

13. Heiric of Auxerre, *Miracula sancti Germani*, *Novae bibliotheca manuscript, librorum tomus primus*, ed. Philippe Labbe (Paris, 1657), 531–69.

14. Ibid., 553: "De reverential coenobii quod mons falconis dicitur." Labbe provided no explanation for the discrepancy.

15. Heiric of Auxerre, *Miracula sancti Germani* (PL 124, 1207C–1272D) and Louis Maximilien Duru, ed., *Bibliothèque historique de l'Yonne ou Collection de legends, chroniques et documents divers, pour servir a l'histoire des differentes contrées qui forment aujourd'hui ce department* (Auxerre, 1863), 114–92. Since Migne and Duru reprinted the *Acta Sanctorum* edition of the *Miracula sancti Germani*, I will refer to all three collectively as the "*Acta Sanctorum* group.*" The *Acta Sanctorum* is cited below when discussing the group's version of the *Miracula*.

16. See Jean-Charles Picard, "Les *Miracula sancti Germani* d'Heiric d'Auxerre et l'architecture des crypts de Saint-Germain: Le témoignage des texts," in *Abbaye Saint-Germain d'Auxerre: Intellectuels et artistes dans l'Europe carolingienne IXe–XIe siècles* (Auxerre, 1990), 97–101; Van Egmond, *Conversing with the Saints*, 144 and 166; and René Louis and Henri Moreau, "Les crypts de Saint-Germain d'Auxerre: État de la question," *Bulletin de la Société des fouilles archéologiques de l'Yonne* 3 (1986): 27–28.

17. The *Acta Sanctorum* and Patrologia Latina note Labbe's decision to include this fragment, but both editors found the story itself incongruous with the surrounding text and omitted it. See Heiric of Auxerre, *Miracula sancti Germani*, 1.76, note 61 (PL 124, 1241D–1242D): "Huc illa sane imperite intrusa fuit contra apertum Herici contextum ac fidem codicum nostrorum omnium"; and note c (AS, July 7: 271D): "Huc illa sane imperite intrusa fuit contra apertum Herici contextum ac fidem codicum nostrorum omnium: imo multo opportunius aptiusque supra Vitae Constantianae inseri posset inter numerous 73 & 74."

18. For instance, the Patrologia Latina version spells Auxerre "Antissiodorensis," while all the other printed versions and P use "Autissioderensis." Labbe refers to Count Conrad's wife as "Adheleis," while Waitz uses "Adheleid" and the remaining versions and P "Adheleidh." Minor differences in spelling also occur between the printed versions and the manuscript, such as "numquam" versus "nunquam" and "coelestibus" versus "caelestibus" and "celestibus."

19. Quadri, *I Collectanea*; Nelson, *Charles the Bald*; Henri Barré, "Héric d'Auxerre," in *Dictionnaire de spiritualité*, 7:282–85; Christian Sapin, ed., *Archéologie et architecture d'un site monastique: 10 ans de recherché à l'abbaye Saint-Germain d'Auxerre* (Paris, 2000); Yves Sassier, "Les Carolingiens et Auxerre," in *L'École carolingienne d'Auxerre*, ed. Iogna-Prat, Jeudy, and Lobrichon, 21–36.

20. Contreni: "the chapter headings and numbered divisions of the printed editions of the Miracula (i.e., PL and Duru) are modern confections and do not appear in the earliest surviving manuscript of the text BnF lat. 13757" ("'And Even Today,'" 41n23); Janin: "Le texts de reference le plus sûr est celui des Bollandistes (AA. SS. Bolland., julii t.7, 2nd ed., pp. 255–83; 3rd ed., pp. 266–94), mas il présente l'inconvénient de sub-stituer à la division en chapitres des deux livres, qui remonte aux manuscripts anciens, une division factice en paragraphes, numerates de façon continue pour l'ensemble de l'ouvre. Seule l'édition du P. Labbe dans sa Nova bibliotheca manuscriptorum, t. 1, Paris 1657, pp. 532–68, respecte la division originelle des *Miracula*" ("Heiric d'Auxerre," 89–90n5); Van

Egmond, "A drawback of this edition [the Acta Sanctorum] is that it contains a continuous chapter numbering rather than the original numbering which starts afresh in the second book of the Miracula" (Conversing with the Saints, 1n1).

21. Heiric of Auxerre, Miracula sancti Germani, P fols. 136v–139v. For additional examples, see fols. 112v–115r (concerning miracles in the villa of Pouilly), folios 116v–118r (concerning miracles in the Soissons), and fols. 144r–147v (a discussion of the bishops of Auxerre).

22. Ibid., fols. 112v–115r.

23. Ibid., fol. 107r–v.

24. See the appendix for a complete list of these headings.

25. The printed versions found in Du Bouchet, Chifflet, and Waitz all included the chapter headings found in P and Labbe. Bouquet utilized the chapter numbering system inserted by Labbe, but not the chapter headings. Gremaud included his own chapter heading ("Translation des reliques des saints Urbain et Tiburce") in the one short passage he reprinted.

26. The Acta Sanctorum edition only hints at the original chapter structure and titles by incorporating the ninth-century chapter headings within the text itself, but enclosing them in brackets. For instance, "Illud sane, quod apud urbem Aquilisimam, sive, [de altaris dedicatione mirabili] ut usus frequentior Egolismam cognominat." The original organizational scheme of the Miracula was clouded, however, by the editors' decision to often split the ninth-century headings and spread them out over several paragraphs. See for instance Heiric of Auxerre, Miracula sancti Germani (AS, July 7: 257D–257F) where the original heading was split in half and spread over two paragraphs and (AS, July 7: 266F–267E) where the original heading was split into four parts.

27. Heiric of Auxerre, Miracula sancti Germani, P fols. 90v, 92v, and 97r: "de Michomere monacho et discipulo eius," "de mortuo in itinere suscitato," and "succincta mentio Patricii per beatum Germanum in Hiberniam destinati."

28. Heiric of Auxerre, Miracula sancti Germani (AS, July 7: 266B–266C and 268B–C): "Miracula in aliis S. Germani per Galliam ecclesiis facta" and "Continuatio miraculorum variis locis ibidem ejus nomine dicatis patratorum."

29. Ibid., AS, July 7: 258D.

30. Ibid., AS, July 7: 273C.

31. Ibid., AS, July 7: 275E and 278D.

CHAPTER 15

Why Did Eriugena Write?

PAUL EDWARD DUTTON

Socrates never wrote a book. Epictetus only taught. Shakespeare wrote plays but never published them. Early medieval authors wrote books, but can have had little expectation of achieving a large audience or much fame; there were few copies of their books and those few were housed in restricted spaces. In short, we cannot assume that ancient and medieval writers ever collectively or even individually shared the same attitude toward writing that we do.

In the midst of the explosion of book writing in the Carolingian Empire, Eriugena, the Irish-born speculative thinker who taught at the palace school of King Charles the Bald in the 850s and 860s, knew a great deal about books: how they were made, something of their history and specific features, and the imperfection of handmade products. He translated seven Greek works and wrote glosses and commentaries on the Bible and works of the liberal arts. He published poems, an exquisitely refined homily, a controversial monograph, and a sweeping synthetic treatise. We also know his handwriting and can see where he worked to revise copies of his work, even restoring diphthongs and correcting orthography. But, for all his published brilliance, he seems never to have believed that writing was a great and glorious thing, a worthy end in itself. To approach the graphical dimension of his life and thought, let us work our way up from the material surface of the manuscript pages he touched to his studied philosophical subordination of writing.

The Physical

For all writers, writing is both an intellectual and physical process, one that proceeds from the immaterial to the material. When we strike the keys on a computer keyboard, insert paper into a printer, and hand-correct printed pages, we are physically producing thought. The great Eriugena was no different, though his tools of production were.

Johannes Scottus (as he was known) or Eriugena (as he singularly called himself) left evidence of his handwriting in five manuscripts that survive: a short letter on folio 1r of Laon, Bibliothèque municipale (BM), MS 24; annotations to Dubthach's Priscian Codex (Leiden, Bibliotheek der Rijksuniversiteit, BPL 67); a rewritten Greek phrase in the bottom margin of Paris, Bibliothèque nationale de France (BnF), MS lat. 13345, folio 96v; the extensively revised draft copy of his masterwork the *Periphyseon* in Reims, Bibliothèque municipale, MS 875; and his corrections and additions to portions of his commentary on the Gospel of John in Laon, Bibliothèque municipale, MS 81.[1]

To write in the ninth century, a writer such as Eriugena needed to know how to write on both parchment and waxed tablets, to wield a pen and stylus as appropriate for each medium, to prepare the shaft of a goose feather pen, to make ink, to test a pen, to erase with knife and pumice on parchment and to smooth incised wax with his thumb and the blunt end of a stylus, to use a short knife to hold down the thick and resistant surface of Carolingian parchment with one hand while he wrote upon it with the other, to scrape wax shavings to the side of a tablet, to apply ink without splattering and blotting (particularly on erased surfaces where ink tends to bleed), and to assemble quires and a codex. There is no denying that Eriugena, the soaring speculative thinker, possessed all of these graphical skills, the evidence for which is to be found in his work on the draft copy of the *Periphyseon*.

The manuscript of that work in Reims 875 is the best example of the workshop of Eriugena and of his own hands-on work as a writer. There we can detect the full range of his physical engagement with a codex.[2] To produce his manuscript, he employed the students of his school to copy the drafts of his work. To the version of the text being laid down, he made changes: additions, subtractions, and corrections. His working method was to hand his student-scribes small pieces of parchment or, more likely, waxed tablets with additions he had written or dictated and wanted inserted into the text; he placed signs (*signes de renvoi*) in Reims 875 and the same signs on the text additions so that his student-scribes would know exactly where to insert the new material in the manuscript. Eriugena himself also went over the manuscript several times, adding materials with his own hand, erasing (presumably, that is, since erasure is a negative graphic phenomenon and can only be tentatively assigned to a writer by associating an erasure with the positive changes he made there), and making on-the-spot changes and corrections to the text. He verified some of the work of his student-scribes and made corrections where they had erred, but he was not a perfectly attentive copyeditor, often missing or ignoring scribal mistakes.[3] He was more interested in the developing text, entering changes and additions of his own, often spontaneous, creation to both the established and added texts. His overriding concern was to perfect his thought rather than to fuss over the scribal flaws of the Reims codex.

His involvement in production was not just confined to the text. The codex as a whole was under his direct control. He marked the quires with Greek numbers to keep them in order as the manuscript was being prepared. It was also presumably Eriugena who made the decision to terminate the manuscript where it now ends in midsentence on folio 358v by removing the next quire, which would have been the forty-sixth. He did this as he abandoned his original plan to compose the *Periphyseon* in four books and extended the work to five books. Reims 875, thus, is that rarest of early medieval manuscript specimens, a draft copy of a work with the author's own handwriting and active participation in its production.[4]

The Intellectual

Eriugena would never have thought of himself as a *scriptor*, but rather as an *auctor*. In the Middle Ages an *auctor* was not just a writer, as an author is today,[5] but rather an originator, creator, inventor, and source, God being the greatest *auctor* of all.[6] A *scriptor* was a scribe, copyist, or secretary, whose work and station in life were less highly regarded.[7] Eriugena conceived of a higher form of engaged writing, as he put it succinctly in his commentary on Martianus Capella: "WRITE WELL: read well, understand what you write, approve what you understand."[8] Thus, his advice to his students and readers on how to write well was to read over the inscribed work, comprehend fully what they had written, and then to endorse rational and perfected thought.

On the few occasions when Eriugena mentions a *scriptor*,[9] it is often to assign blame for an error in the manuscripts of the texts upon which he was commenting. "There seems to be an error of the scribe at this point," he says in one version of his glosses on Martianus.[10] He made such comments not only about Latin texts, but about a Greek one as well, allowing for the possibility of error by Greek scribes. When commenting on the *Celestial Hierarchy* of the Pseudo-Dionysius, he wondered "if the scribe of the Greek codex did not err, writing ZΩA for ONTA."[11] This may seem an unlikely mistake for a scribe to commit, the forms of the words bearing no similarity to each other in shape or sound, but Eriugena was ready to blame an unknown scribe rather than a sainted author as the source of textual confusion. Such an approach gave him an additional tool for massaging the meaning of texts that were difficult or faulty without blaming authors for errors of composition and thought.

As a commentator Eriugena was aware of textual variance. In his various glosses and commentaries, he frequently cited unspecified other codices that contained different readings from the ones he was currently engaging.[12] He realized that textual variance was a product of the transmission of texts, the effect of poor readings passed down to and contained in the manuscripts he was consulting, and of the plasticity of text in general. He was prepared to emend flawed texts. In the short letter preserved in Laon BM 24, he invited Lord Winibert to lend him for a short time the copy of Martianus Capella that they had been reading and said that he would emend it in those places that they had neglected when they were together.[13]

Eriugena did appreciate that not all textual difficulties were caused by scribes; some were mistakes by authors, including himself. With Priscian he granted that "if any errors occur in my writing, I do not succumb to despair. I console myself that I have a human nature and that I am not alone in erring, as the distinguished authors, whom I emend, also erred."[14] Eriugena believed in correcting himself, but when he asked Wulfadus, abbot of St-Médard of Soissons and later the archbishop of Bourges, to read over the *Periphyseon*, he was not requesting that he copyedit the text, but rather that he point out matters that had not been fully treated or had been neglected.[15]

Eriugena had a vast knowledge of the liberal arts, and in his glosses he occasionally touched upon, as those works required, the history and character of books and their production. He knew that books (*libri*) were so called because the ancients had first made books from the bark of trees.[16] He also knew that the ancients had called the rocks on which they wrote the history of their gods *stelae* and that they inscribed in rock because inscriptions there were more visible.[17] *Neniae* were songs written on the tombs of the dead and sung to cithara music.[18] Antiquarians write of old things,[19] *a commentariis* (1 Chron. 18:15) refers to the recorders who make charters,[20] an archive is a library, called so from archon or secret,[21] a *pagella* is a little page,[22] and so on.

Eriugena made a few passing remarks on writing tools and materials. "Papyrus, smeared with the sap of a cedar, is incorruptible," he said.[23] Here we should bear in mind that Eriugena glossed the obscure and abstruse, not the obvious things he expected that his students already knew. Hence papyrus smeared with cedar oil wanted explanation, but obvious words such as parchment, which he could have glossed if he so chose, he ignored. When he did choose to gloss a common word such as *quaternion*, it was probably so that he could point out that it was used both to refer to a commander of four soldiers (as in Acts 12:4) and a quaternion (or four sheets) of parchment.[24] Similarly he felt it worth glossing Martianus's strange description of wax being made from gall and gum resin precisely because it was contrary to local experience. Wax prepared in this way was suitable for writing upon, he said, but he himself chiefly worked upon waxed tablets[25] and would have known that gall and gum were unnecessary for the preparation of the wax for his own writing tablets.

A series of *-graph* words appear in Eriugena's works, including *psalmographus*, *catagraphus*, *zoographia*, *cosmographia*,[26] but the most interesting of these may be *chyrographus*, which for the ancients meant the autograph writing of anything. For Eriugena, however, the meaning was Irish and restricted in meaning: "Chyrographus, a composition (*scriptio*) or law (*scriptum*) which is divided [in half]; because it has elongated letters and no one can read it unless it is joined together again. The lord and his servant possess such."[27] That is to say that a lord and his man each possessed half of the document. Thus, for Eriugena, whose autograph writing we do possess, a chyrograph was a legal instrument or charter.

If many of his learned etymologies and explanations of exotic bookish things seem strained, we do occasionally encounter moments when more spontaneous explanations suggest his everyday graphic experience. Thus to gloss Martianus's "ADAMANTINI CACVMINIS IMPRESSIONE" (with the steely hard impression of a point), he wrote "duri stili" (of a hard stylus).[28] Remigius of Auxerre, whose glosses on Martianus sometimes read as though they are glosses on Eriugena's glosses, says of the same phrase: "of a hard stylus, for nothing is harder than steel. He says that the CACVMEN is the acute part of the stylus with which letters are formed."[29] At another point Eriugena's gloss on "ACVMEN" or sharpness states that "it signifies the point of the art of grammar or pens."[30]

In his treatise on predestination, he makes several graphical comparisons. Thus, to mock Gottschalk's substantial doubling of God's will, he says, "as if from the impressing of one signet-ring many marks could not be made in wax."[31] At another point, he invites us to consider the beautiful iron stylus with which he writes in wax. Made by an artisan, it is perfectly designed to fill two purposes. One end of the stylus is used for writing, the other for deleting. If someone should reverse the ends, using the deleting end for writing and the writing end for deleting, the action itself would be bad, but the stylus would not be.[32] Thus, did the graphic nature of a scholar's daily life inform his higher thought.

Voice

Though Eriugena knew a good deal about the physical, historical, and philological aspects of writing, indeed much more than he wanted to explain in his specialized glosses, as a philosopher he ranked writing an inferior thing.

He denied the claim of some grammarians that voice was said to be articulated because of the way in which it was written: "Therefore, it is called an articulated voice because it is corroborated by its arts and grasped by the rational intellect, and not, as some of the grammarians think, that it is called an articulated voice because it is written with the joints (*articulis*) of the fingers; rather [it is so called] because it exists with its own parts and is brought together by the understanding of a rational mind."[33]

Instead, for Eriugena, voice is primary. Born of fire, its matter being the finest air, voice has a fiery nature, one moved by the fiery soul.[34] "Three bodies, formed by the extraordinary work of nature, are born from the nature of fire: that is, light, heat, and voice."[35] Remarkably each of these three bodies pertains to a different bodily sense: voice to hearing, light to sight, and heat to touch.[36] He explains that while we hear a voice by means of the voice itself, we see a voice by means of an image or representation of that voice.[37]

Eriugena says that Priscian's observation that a letter is a voice that can be written should be understood in two ways. Voice is not written by means of itself, but by means of an image. No voice can be written as a voice just as no light can be written by means of itself.[38] "Not only, however, does the writing of the voice pertain to the image, which is represented in images in wax or on skin, but also to the writing itself of the mouth. For a voice is written in two ways: one properly, the other improperly. A voice is written properly when it is divided into letters, syllables, and even distinct parts of speech, the soul being at work through the instruments of the tongue and palate. It is, however, written improperly when it is represented and formed by means of certain images of letters."[39] There are two forms of written voice. The first, which he calls writing or a composition of the mouth, is its division vocally into letters, syllables, and the parts of speech. Thus, the articulation of voice into speech constitutes the first form of writing. The second form of writing, which cannot occur before the first has taken place, is its inscription or representation in the form of images on a surface. Oral writing (the composition of the mouth) is guided by the soul and the instruments of the mouth; graphic writing stands at further remove from voice, and so is inferior and dependent, a mere image or approximation.[40]

Eriugena signals the inferiority of inscriptional or graphic writing by his use of the word *pingere* (that is, to represent in pictures; to paint, color, or adorn) to characterize graphic writing. In his treatise on predestination, he drew the same connection: "[F]or every false thing seeks under some likeness of truth to be what it is not. An example of this from the nature of things is the image of voice (*uocis imago*) which the Greeks call an echo (HXω), and [another] the shadow of bodies, and indeed in art the figures in pictures, and other things of that kind. In fact, likeness (but not every one) appears to be the cause of falsity."[41] Eriugena cites echo in five of his works as a natural example of the unreliability of sensory perception.[42] An echo is an image of voice because it comes to hearing indirectly or circuitously, resounding off the rocky surfaces of hillsides.[43] Voice properly comes directly to hearing without a mediating surface. Likewise, inscribed letters are images or representations of mediated voice, transformed improperly or irregularly into painted images and received by the sense of sight, which is not the proper or primary sense receptor of voice.

For Eriugena, the speculative thinker, oral writing or articulation was secondary to voice itself. Voice comes first, is pure and primary, preceding the word not in time, but in cause, he says, just as formless matter precedes the formed body; and, just as cause precedes effect and fire the conflagration, so voice precedes the word.[44] Voice, however, does occur in time before the mental processing of the hearer, before mental conception.[45]

The first Voice (the equivalent of cause and fire) is the Voice of God. For Eriugena, the divine Voice is akin to the primary light or illumination of God. The conception of a first, divine, immaterial, and transcendent Voice assumed a significant place in Eriugena's thought. "Voice is the interpreter of the spirit. For everything, that the spirit first thinks and orders invisibly within itself, it brought forth sensibly through the voice into the sense of the hearers."[46] But, just as Eriugena delimited human talk of God, restricting what can be said about God, so he never defines the Voice of God—it just is or exists. He never describes the divine Voice as articulated, a feature that belongs to human voice and its first form of writing.

The opening lines of Eriugena's homily, *Vox spiritualis*, express the idea of Voice that he had been developing since his work on Prisican and Martianus, Voice as divine truth, pure thought, and beyond human words. The homily opens with an arresting compression of ideas: "The voice of the mystic eagle [John] pulses against the hearing of the church. Let exterior sense receive the surpassing sound, interior spirit penetrate the enduring meaning. This is the voice of the high-flying winged one, not of the one that soars above the material air, ether, and the circumference of the entire sensible world, but of him who, by the rapidly beating wings of the deepest theology and with gazings of the sharpest and loftiest contemplation, surpasses all speculation, beyond all things that are and that are not."[47] It is the Voice of God that the evangelist, whose symbol is the eagle, transmits. Eriugena does not here talk about interpreting the written words of the Gospel, but about trying to catch the sound of the Voice in which divine truth abides. That Voice contains the very reasons of things. Human grammar and the inscribed word, while necessary for human argument and dialectic, are imperfect human constructions, mere images of the Truth, not the Truth itself.

        This line of reasoning is to be found elsewhere in Eriugena's thought. Late
in the *Periphyseon*, as the master takes up examples of the Return to God, first from
the sensible world and then the intelligible, he turns to the liberal arts in which
rational minds seek out their first principles, which are also their last. Thus, for
instance, the Monad stands as the beginning and end of arithmetic.[48] The student
wonders aloud why the master neglected to mention grammar and rhetoric in his
survey.[49] The master answers: "Know then, that they are omitted not for one reason
only; firstly, because many philosophers, not without reason, think that these two
arts are in some sort branches of Dialectic; secondly, for the sake of brevity; and
lastly, because Grammar and Rhetoric do not deal with the nature of the Universe,
but either with the laws of human speech, which Aristotle and his school show
to be not a natural phenomenon but one arising out of the behavior of articulate
beings, or are concerned with particular causes and persons, which has no relation
to the nature of the Universe."[50] Grammar and rhetoric are not even necessary for
the rational soul to discourse with itself says the student,[51] but the critical point
for Eriugena was that while correct speaking and writing contribute to the human
capacity to form arguments and explore the truths of the universe, they are insuf-
ficient and auxiliary arts for the philosopher's profounder search for Truth.
        Eriugena regarded writing as inferior to speech, just as all human language
fails in its attempt to signify the divine essence.[52] He quotes the apostle's maxim
that "[t]he letter kills, the spirit gives life" (2 Cor. 3:6) to argue that those who
pursue the letter are those who take the perceptible as true when it is false, and
who neglect the spirit or true understanding of the letter. By letter, the apostle
meant not only that which is the image of the voice, but all the figures found
in Scripture, which do contain spiritual truths and the hidden meaning of the
celestial things if understood by the interior spirit.[53] God speaks with intelligible
Voice about the things that are and are not.[54] The human mind, in its ascent,
encounters verbal symbols from the Voice to which, by charity, Voice imparts
inner understanding.[55] The full weight of this Eriugenian theme deserves more
attention than we can give it in this short essay, but it may help us to understand
something of Eriugena's philosophical subordination of and skepticism about
writing, both the graphic and the oral.
        Though as a master of the liberal arts, Eriugena had obviously spent some
time teaching and thinking about Virgil, he dismissed the pagan poets. They
played at making fanciful fictions of burning cities and conquering heroes, but
told lies and passed them off as truths. He longed for the abiding Truth of things
communicated by the Voice that ignites the transparent constellations of our
minds.[56] As a philosopher he regarded writing as inferior to thought, subsequent
to the Truth, and only a degraded image of it, just as an echo resounds voice, but
indirectly and imperfectly.

Yet he wrote. He took pen and stylus in hand, printed a perfectly readable script, handled manuscripts, knew something of the history of the book and its physical properties, and could produce the beautiful Latin prose of his ethereal homily. But he subordinated written letters to the primacy of speech. Indeed, all of Eriugena's works except his translations can be thought of as voice or spoken books, having an oral setting and context.

His glosses and commentaries presumably derive from the lectures he once gave to students in the palace school. The modern reader needs to recall the setting of these exercises. The master expounded upon the generalities and specifics of great books while students followed along with one finger on the text while their other hand scribbled notes on a waxed tablet. The margins of an Irish master's copy of Horace and Servius in Bern, Burgerbibliothek, MS 363 are covered with brief citations (some of them mentioning Eriugena), which probably served as his aide-mémoire, or prompt book, as he glossed the texts for his students.[57] Eriugena's glosses belong to the magisterial inquiry of a classroom. His great homily, the *Vox spiritualis*, was obviously meant for oral delivery, probably to a distinguished audience of men such as the king and high ecclesiastics like Wulfadus. Some of his poems were meant to be spoken to the king at Easter and other high occasions in the Carolingian calendar.[58]

The treatise on divine predestination is a fascinating amalgam of the written and spoken or rather it is a written treatise that keeps trying to break into a purer form of oral discourse. Yet he acknowledges that he is writing a book, many of whose chapters begin in expository mode with logical arguments set out in systematic fashion. At one point, he even states that his first task is to convince readers of the validity of his writings, if any think that they are worth reading.[59] For much of the treatise, however, Eriugena attempts to engage in a pointed conversation with Gottschalk: "Where, therefore, Gottschalk, are the necessities of your two predestinations?" "But rather you say, you heretic . . . " "Say, therefore, Gottschalk, where those two predestinations which you assert can be found." "Tell me, I ask, for what reason did you take up the argument of God's divided work?"[60] That artificial conversation fitted with the dialectical model of philosophical inquiry proposed at the start of the work.[61] The problem, of course, was that Gottschalk was not there for him to debate and Eriugena knew only so much about the missing man's predestination doctrines. Eriugena's real audience of listeners and readers were the sponsors of his book: Pardulus of Laon, Hincmar of Reims, and, standing in the background, King Charles the Bald. As such he could never sustain a true voice book in his early treatise, but one can hear him trying.

The *Periphyseon* is a different matter. It is a pure dialogue between a master and student that makes no reference to anything written by the two speakers. They talk. Only in the letter of dedication to Abbot Wulfadus that follows the dialogue does Eriugena speak as an author. For this reason, in his critical edition of the work, Édouard Jeauneau moved the dedication-letter outside the dialogue proper.[62] In that letter Eriugena refers to what he had written (*nos . . . scripsisse*) and beseeches his readers (*lecturos*) to accept the work on its own terms. He knew that his book was a graphic product, an image of the truth, whereas the Truth, as pursued by the dialectician and philosopher, was a matter of Voice. Writing was but its pale image and an inadequate representation of the Truth.

By teaching rather than writing the Stoic Epictetus aimed at individual human improvement, both his own and his students'. For Shakespeare the play was the thing; his plays lived and died in the oral, aural, and visual experience of the actors and the audience in the theater. Socrates preferred dialectical speech over graphic writing as the best means for discerning truth. In the *Phaedrus* (274b–279a) Plato's Socrates spurns declamatory or read speeches and criticizes writing (particularly its hieroglyphic and published form) because it produces images of the truth, is frozen and not open to questioning and improvement, may be misunderstood and misused by ignorant and willful readers, and undermines human memory.[63] It is difficult to ascertain the living Socrates's specific thoughts on writing and written culture from the Platonic representation of them in the *Phaedrus*, but there is no escaping the fact that Socrates chose not to write books. Eriugena wrote many and yet had a philosophical, indeed metaphysical, disdain for writing. He subordinated all writing, both its oral and inscriptional forms, as inferior representations of divine reality. He preferred to listen to the sound of the pulsating Voice of the divine.

We are left with a perplexing question. Why did someone who thought that graphic writing was such an imperfect representation of truth write so much, so well, and with such care? That question may lead us back to the Carolingian classroom, a subject on which Professor Contreni has long enlightened us. It may also lead us to wonder if Eriugena's insistence on dialectic and his doubts about writing were not at some level a rejection of the wordy, writerly world the Carolingians had so suddenly created. But just as the fuller story of Socrates's critique of written culture eludes us, Eriugena's thoughts on the written culture of his time still remain to be situated. Yet we cannot ignore that Socrates chose not to write and Eriugena did. In any rethinking of the Carolingians and the written word, we shall have to ponder why Eriugena wrote.

Notes

1. For a history of the identification of Eriugena's script, a description of the codices, the particulars of Eriugena's handwriting, and plates of the specimens of his script, see Édouard Jeauneau and Paul Edward Dutton, *The Autograph of Eriugena*, Corpus Christianorum Autographa Medii Aevi 3 (Turnhout, 1996). On the manuscripts of Laon, see

John J. Contreni, *The Cathedral School of Laon from 850 to 930: Its Manuscripts and Masters*, Müchener Beiträge zur Mediävistik und Renaissance-Forschung 29 (Munich, 1978).

2. For a full treatment of this, see Paul Edward Dutton, "Eriugena's Workshop: the Making of the *Periphyseon* in Rheims 875," in *History and Eschatology in John Scottus Eriugena and His Time: Proceedings of the Tenth International Conference of the Society for the Promotion of Eriugenian Studies, Maynooth and Dublin, August 16–20, 2000*, ed. James McEvoy and Michael Dunne (Leuven, 2002), 141–67.

3. One can now examine the full range of these Caroline anomalies in the synoptic edition of the first four books of the *Periphyseon* edited by Édouard Jeauneau. The fifth book, in the same series, relies upon later manuscripts since Reims 875 ends in book four. For the full series, see *Iohannis Scotti seu Eriugenae Periphyseon*, ed. Édouard Jeauneau, CCCM 161–65, 5 vols. (Turnhout, 1996–2003).

4. For two medieval authors whose direct work on autograph copies of their work has been established, see Jason Glenn, *Politics and History in the Tenth Century: The Work and World of Richer of Rheims* (Cambridge, 2004), 128–65, 285–300; Monique-Cécile Garand, *Guibert de Nogent et ses secrétaires*, Corpus Christianorum Autographa Medii Aevi 2 (Turnhout, 1995), and Jay Rubenstein, *Guibert of Nogent: Portrait of a Medieval Mind* (New York, 2002), 212–16.

5. In current English to say that "X is an author" means that X is a writer. Variant uses of "author" require a qualification such as "the prime minister is the author of the peace plan." On medieval meanings of author, see Patrick J. Geary, "Medieval Archivists as Authors: Social Memory and Archival Memory," in *Archives, Documentation, and Institutions of Social Memory: Essays from the Sawyer Seminar*, ed. Francis X. Blouin Jr. and William G. Rosenberg (Ann Arbor, 2006), 106–13.

6. For the sake of economy, the examples below are taken from one work of Eriugena, but similar usages can be found in his other works. *Iohannis Scotti De diuina praedestinatione liber*, 5.2.43–46, ed. Goulven Madec, CCCM 50 (Turnhout, 1978), 35: "ita deus omnia quorum ipse auctor est praescit nec tamen omnium quae praescit ipse auctor est. Quorum autem non est malus auctor iustus est ultor"; 11.4.89–90, 69: "Quoniam uero sanctus pater Aurelius Augustinus, eloquentiae christianae copiosissimus auctor." See also Marie-Dominique Chenu, "Auctor, Actor, Autor," *Bulletin Du Cange* 3 (1926): 81–86.

7. See Paul Edward Dutton, *Charlemagne's Mustache and Other Cultural Clusters of a Dark Age* (New York, 2004), 88–89.

8. "Scribe recte [85.10] lege bene, intellige quod scribis, approba quod intelligis": *Iohannis Scotti Annotationes in Marcianum*, ed. Cora E. Lutz, Medieval Academy of America Publication 34 (Cambridge, MA, 1939), 77.2–3. The section numbers given in Lutz's edition to the lemmata refer to the page and line numbers of *Martianus Capella*, ed. A. Dick (Stuttgart, 1975).

9. In his glosses on Priscian, he notes, somewhat skeptically, that it is said that a Latin grammatical case (*casus*) is so called from writing, "because it falls from the pen of the scribe into letters and lines." *In Priscianum*, Barcelona, Archivo de la Corona de Aragón (ACA), MS Ripoll 59, fol. 279r: "eo quod cadit de penna scriptoris in litteras et lineas." For a similar case of skepticism, see n. 33, below. On the attribution of the work to Eriugena, see Paul Edward Dutton, "Evidence That Dubthach's Priscian Codex Once Belonged to Eriugena," in *From Athens to Chartres: Neoplatonism and Medieval Thought; Studies in Honour of Edouard Jeauneau*, ed. Haijo Jan Westra (Leiden, 1992), 15–45; and Paul Edward Dutton and Anneli Luhtala, "Eriugena in Priscianum," *Mediaeval Studies* 56

(1994), 153–63. Editions of portions of the text appear in those two articles and also in Anneli Luhtala, "Early Medieval Commentary on Priscian's *Institutiones grammaticae*," *Cahiers de l'Institut du Moyen-Âge Grec et Latin* 71 (2000), 115–88.

10. "Videtur esse error in hoc loco scriptoris," at "Item ex septem" (26.13), ed. Édouard Jeauneau, *Glosae Martiani*, in Jeauneau, *Quatres thèmes érigéniens*, Conférence Albert-le-Grand 1974 (Montreal, 1978), 147.17–18.

11. *Iohannis Scoti Eriugenae Expositiones in Ierarchiam Coelestem*, 4.156–57, ed. J. Barbet, CCCM 31 (Turnhout, 1975), 69. In this case Eriugena does not simply accept his proposed emendation of the faulty text, but expends much effort in trying to understand the wrong reading of the manuscript: see Paul Rorem, *Eriugena's Commentary on the Dionysian "Celestial Hierarchy,"* Studies and Texts 150 (Toronto, 2005), 28–33.

12. For a partial list of these mentions of different readings in other books and codices, see: *Glosae Martiani*, ed. Jeauneau, 108.9, 120.26, 135.3, 135.13–14; *Annotationes*, ed. Lutz, 207.10 (104), 208.2 (105), 228.9 (117), 267.13 (127), 271.14 (127), 279.11 (23), 287.17 (135), 443.20 (176), 463.10 (184), 470.14 (186), 470.14 (186), 473.5 (188), 475.8 (189), 476.18 (190), 476.21 (191), 501.3 (208); *Iohannis Scotti Commentarius in evangelium Iohannis*, ed. and trans. Édouard Jeauneau, in Jean Scot, *Commentaire sur l'évangile de Jean*, Sources Chrétiennes 180 (Paris, 1972), 1.23 (106.25–26), 1.25 (126.3).

13. "Domine Vuiniberte commodate nobis Felicem Capellam paruo tempore et, si uultis, illum emendabo in illis partibus quas, dum simul eramus, praetermissimus. Vtinam in uno loco essemus etiam paruo tempore! Sidera, si sparsim speciali lumine fulgent, O quam collectim ΦΩΣ animosa foret!" For a photograph of the inscription, see Jeauneau and Dutton, *Autograph of Eriugena*, plate 73. On the identification of this letter, see John J. Contreni, "A propos de quelques manuscrits de l'école de Laon: Découvertes et problèmes," *Le Moyen Âge* 78 (1972): 5–39 (10); Bernhard Bischoff, *Irische Schreiber*, in *Jean Scot Érigène et l'histoire de la philosophie: Laon 7–12 juillet 1975*, Colloques internationaux du Centre national de la recherche scientifique 561 (Paris, 1977), 47–58 (56) (repr. in Bischoff, *Mittelalterliche Studien: Ausgewählte Aufsätze zur Schriftkunde und Literaturgeschichte*, 3 vols. [Stuttgart, 1966–81], 3:39–54); Édouard Jeauneau, "Les écoles de Laon et d'Auxerre au IXᵉ siècle," in *La scuola nell'occidente latino dell'alto medioevo*, Settimane di stuido del Centro italiano de studi sull'alto medioevo 19 (Spoleto, 1972), 495–522 (505) (repr. in Jeauneau, *Études érigénniennes* [Paris, 1987], 57–84 [67]); Paul Edward Dutton, "Minding Irish Ps and Qs: Signs of the First Systematic Reading of Eriugena's *Periphyseon*," in *A Distinctive Voice: Medieval Studies in Honor of Leonard E. Boyle, O.P.*, ed. Jacqueline Brown and William P. Stoneman (Notre Dame, IN, 1997), 14–31 (29n18).

14. *In Priscianum*, ACA Ripoll 59, fol. 280v: "DE VERBI QVOQVE [194.14] . . . si aliquid humani erroris in meis scriptis acceserit, non cado in disperationem. Sicut consolor me ipsum, quia humanum ingenium habeo, et quia non solus errans, sicut etiam praecipui auctores errauerunt, quos emendo." The lemmata numbers given refer to the page and line numbers of Priscian, *Institutiones grammaticae*, ed. Martin Hertz, 2 vols., *Grammatici latini*, 2–3, ed. Heinrich Keil (1855; repr. Hildesheim, 1961).

15. *Iohannis Scotti seu Eriugenae Periphyseon*, 5.7367–82 (1022A–B), ed. Jeauneau, 227–28.

16. "PHILLIORVM [59.15] foligerum; arbor de cuius <foliis> faciebant primo ueteres libros, ΦΥΛΛΝ folium": *Annotationes*, ed. Lutz, 65.10–11. See also the fuller gloss of Remigius of Auxerre, which contains a version of Eriugena's gloss: *Remigii Autissiodorensis Commentum in Martianum Capellam: Libri I–II*, ed. Cora E. Lutz (Leiden, 1962), 174.20–26.

17. *Annotationes*, 59.20, ed. Lutz, 65.18–19.

18. *Annotationes*, 491.6, ed. Lutz, 203.29–30, and *Glossae divinae historiae: The Biblical Glosses of John Scottus Eriugena*, 3, ed. John J. Contreni and Pádraig P. Ó Néill, Millennio medievale 1: Testi 1 (Florence, 1997), 90.

19. *In Priscianum*, ACA Ripoll 59, fol. 287rv: "Antiqvarivs [2.40.23], qui uetera scripsit."

20. *Glossae divinae historiae*, 518, ed. Contreni and Ó Néill, 188.

21. Ibid., 557, ed. Contreni and Ó Néill, 194; and *Glosae Martiani*, ed. Jeauneau, 153.7: "'Archium,' custos librarii."

22. Ibid., 327, ed. Contreni and Ó Néill, 151.

23. "Papyrvs [59.12] de suco cedri linitus imputribilis est": *Annotationes*, ed. Lutz, 65.8. See also *Remigii Autissiodorensis Commentum in Martianum Capellam*, ed. Lutz, 174.14–17.

24. *In Priscianum*, ACA Ripoll 59, fol. 275v: "Qvaternio [146.5], dux quatuor militum et quaternio de percameno."

25. *Annotationes*, 83.14, ed. Lutz, 76.13–14. On Eriugena's use of waxed tablets, see Dutton, "Eriugena's Workshop," 144–46.

26. See *De diuina praedestinatione*, 18.41, ed. Madec, 112; *In Priscianum*, ACA Ripoll 59, fols. 279r, 284r; *Annotationes*, 59.17, ed. Lutz, 65.13–14.

27. *Glossae divinae historiae*, 626, ed. Contreni and Ó Néill, 205; *Annotationes*, 218.13, ed. Lutz, 112.7: "Scripta leges uel cyrographum." See Bernhard Bischoff, "Zur Frühgeschichte des mittelalterliche Chirographum," in *Mittelalterliche Studien*, 1:118–22.

28. *Annotationes*, 46.19, ed. Lutz, 59.5, and see *Remigii Autissiodorensis Commentum in Martianum Capellam*, ed. Lutz, 154.14–16.

29. *Remigii Autissiodorensis Commentum in Martianum Capellam*, 46.19, ed. Lutz, 154.16.

30. *Annotationes*, 83.1, ed. Lutz, 76.3–4.

31. *De diuina praedestinatione*, 3.7.229–30, ed. Madec, 26.

32. Ibid., 16.5.164–70, ed. Madec, 99.

33. *In Priscianum*, ACA Ripoll 59, fol. 261r: "Articulata igitur uox dicitur, quia suis artibus confirmatur et rationabili quodam intellectu complectitur, non sicut quidam grammaticorum putant, ut ideo articulata uox diceretur quia articulis digitorum scribitur, sed quia suis propriis membris constat et sensu rationabilis mentis colligitur."

34. See the edition in Dutton, "Evidence," 31–33.

35. *In Priscianum*, ACA Ripoll 59, fol. 259v: "Tria enim corpora mirabili naturae opere formata de natura ignis nascuntur, id est lux, et calor, et uox." On Eriugena's wider thoughts on fire, see Édouard Jeauneau, "Jean Scot et la métaphysique du feu," in Jeauneau, *Études érigénniennes*, 299–319.

36. *In Priscianum*, ACA Ripoll 59, fol. 259v: "Item mirandum quod haec tria, cum de una natura ignis nasci manifestum est, non ad unum sensum corporeum pertinent, sed ad tres, id est uox ad auditum, lux ad oculos, calor ad tactum."

37. Ibid., fol. 260r: "Audimus enim uocem per ipsam uocem; uidemus uocem, sed per imaginem ipsius uocis. Cum enim uidemus figuram alicui [sic] litterae per illam figuram quasi per quandam imaginem, quodammodo uocem uideo."

38. Ibid., fol. 262r: "POSSVMVS ET SIC DIFINIRE: LITTERA EST VOX, QVAE SCRIBI POTEST INDIVIDVA [6.10]. Duobus modis intelligi potest. QVAE ideo uox dicitur SCRIBI propter imaginem ipsius uocis. Vox enim scribi dicitur, non per se, sed per imaginem suam. Nulla enim uox scribi potest quantum uox est. Sicut enim nulla lux

scribi potest quantum lux est, sic etiam nulla uox. Scribi tamen uox dicitur, quia imago eius scribitur, quae proprie littera uocatur. QVAE autem dixit INDIVIDVA, satis et sufficienter demonstrauimus."

39. Ibid., fol. 262r–v: "Non solum autem scriptura uocis ad imaginem pertinet, quae pingitur in cera aut in membrana, sed etiam ad ipsam scripturam oris. Duobus namque modis scribitur uox: uno proprio, altero abusiuo. Proprie enim scribitur uox, cum distinguitur in litteras et syllabas atque etiam distinctas orationis partes, anima per instrumenta linguae palatique operante; abusiue autem, cum per quasdam imagines linearum pingitur atque figuratur."

40. Ibid., fol. 262v: "De illo igitur primo modo Priscianum dixisse manifestum est. Cum enim naturaliter uox profertur et in artheriis promitur, tunc quasi quaedam materies informis esse uidetur. Cum autem in litteras et syllabas partesque distinguitur, tunc quodammodo scribi uidetur. Ideoque dictum est: LITTERA EST VOX, QVAE SCRIBI POTEST INDIVIDVA, id est scribi potest, quantum ad uocem corporalem indiuidua, quantum ad substantiam rationabilem uel magis uere corpus, tamquam aperte dixisset magis dicendum est uocem esse corpus quam esse similitudinem corporis. Dicit enim primum QVASI CORPVS ALIQVOD [6.16], non enim dixit corpus aliquod, sed quasi corpus aliquod, propter eos qui putant uocem non esse corpus."

41. *De diuina praedestinatione*, 3.1.38–43, ed. Madec, 19. See also John Scottus Eriugena, *Treatise on Divine Predestination*, trans. Mary Brennan, Notre Dame Texts in Medieval Culture 5 (Notre Dame, IN, 1998), 18.

42. *Iohannis Scotti seu Eriugenae Periphyseon*, 4.1733–37 (784A), ed. Jeauneau, 62; *Iohannis Scotti seu Eriugenae Periphyseon*, 5.2442–45 (914A), ed. Jeauneau, 77. See also *Iohannis Scotti Eriugenae Periphyseon (De diuision naturae): Liber quartus*, ed. Édouard Jeauneau, Scriptores Latini Hiberniae 13 (Dublin, 1995), 302n115. For sources, see Marius Victorinus, *Aduersum Arium*, 1.55, ed. Paul Henry and Pierre Hadot, in *Marii Victorini opera: Pars prior; opera theologica*, CSEL 83 (Vienna, 1971), 153–54.6–7; *Isidori hispalensis episcopi: Etymologiarum sive originum, libri XX*, 16.3.4, ed. W. M. Lindsay, 2 vols. (Oxford, 1911), 2:188; Augustine, *Soliloquia*, 2.6.10, ed. W. Hörmann, CSEL 89 (Vienna, 1986), 58.10–13, 60.7–19.

43. *In Priscianum*, ACA Ripoll 59, fol. 258r: "Ex his uerbis apparet uocem duobus sensibus accidere, id est auribus et oculis, sed quia per litteras oculis, per se autem auribus, ideo proprie auribus accidit. Ad circumposita loca et corporea uox accidit, nam echo, id est uocis imago, de lignis et saxosis collibus resultat"; *Glossae divinae historiae*, 573, ed. Contreni and Ó Néill, 197, here "Eecho, imago uoics" is a gloss on Sap. 17:18, "resonans de altissimis montibus echo"; *Expositiones*, 2.901–5, ed. Barbet, 44, which does not use the word *echo*, but does have "imago uocis ex rupe quadam seu aliqua concauitate."

44. *Iohannis Scotti seu Eriugenae Periphyseon*, 3.3329–45 (699B–D), ed. Jeauneau, 115–16. And see *Iohannis Scotti seu Eriugenae Periphyseon*, 1.1719–22, ed. Jeauneau, 57.

45. *Iohannis Scotti Commentarius in evangelium Iohannis*, 1.28.15–16, ed. Jeauneau, 144: "Vox uocatur quia, sicut uox praecedit mentis conceptum"; and see 145n3.

46. Ibid., 1.28.72–74, ed. Jeauneau, 138.

47. *Vox spiritualis*, 1, ed. Édouard Jeauneau, *Jean Scot, Homélie sur le Prologue de Jean*, Sources Chrétiennes 151 (Paris, 1969), 200–204.

48. See *Iohannis Scotti seu Eriugenae Periphyseon*, 5.348–96 (868C–869B), ed. Jeauneau, 13–15.

49. See ibid., 5.397–402 (869D), ed. Jeauneau, 15.

50. Eriugena, *Periphyseon (the Division of Nature)*, trans. I. P. Sheldon-Williams, rev. John J. O'Meara (Montreal, 1987), 533, and see *Iohannis Scotti seu Eriugenae Periphyseon*, 5.403–11 (869D–870A), ed. Jeauneau, 15.

51. *Iohannis Scotti seu Eriugenae Periphyseon*, 5.432–36 (870B–870C), ed. Jeauneau, 16.

52. Ibid., 1.587–89 (456A), ed. Jeauneau, 23.

53. *Expositiones*, 2.1167–78, ed. Barbet, 51–52.

54. *Iohannis Scotti seu Eriugenae Periphyseon*, 3.1035–43 (643D–644A), ed. Jeauneau, 37–38.

55. *De diuina praedestinatione*, 3.1.22–26, ed. Madec, 18. On charity or love as God, see 1 John 4:8 and 4:16, and *De diuina praedestinatione*, 3.5.127, ed. Madec, 22.

56. Eriugena, *Carmen*, 2.1.1–18, ed. Ludwig Traube, *Poetae Latini aevi Carolini III*, MGH Poetae 3, 527–29. See also *Iohannis Scotti Eriugenae Carmina*, ed. Michael Herren, Scriptores Latini Hiberniae 12 (Dublin, 1993), 58–63. On this poem and Eriugena's poetry in general, see Paul Edward Dutton, "Eriugena, the Royal Poet," in *Jean Scot Écrivain: Actes du IVe Colloque international, Montréal, 28 août–2 septembre 1983*, ed. G.-H. Allard (Montreal, 1986), 51–80.

57. See Dutton, "Minding Irish Ps and Qs," 21–22 and 30nn25–26. See also John J. Contreni, "The Irish in the Western Carolingian Empire (According to James F. Kenney and Bern, Burgerbibliothek 363)," in *Die Iren und Europa im früheren Mittelalter*, ed. H. Löwe, 2 vols. (Stuttgart, 1982), 2:766–98.

58. See Dutton, "Eriugena, the Royal Poet," 61–69.

59. *De diuina praedestinatione*, 11.1.9–12, ed. Madec, 67.

60. Ibid., 2.1.4–5, 2.2.27, 2.6.161–62, 3.7.212–13, ed. Madec, 9, 11, 17, 25.

61. Ibid., 1.1–3.4–75, ed. Madec, 5–8.

62. *Iohannis Scotti seu Eriugenae Periphyseon*, 5.7338–94 (1021B–1022C), ed. Jeauneau, 226–28; Édouard Jeauneau, "La conclusion du *Periphyseon*: Comment un dialogue devient monologue," in *Divine Creation in Ancient, Medieval, and Early Modern Thought: Essays Presented to the Reverend Dr. Robert D. Crouse*, ed. Michael Treschow, Willemien Otten, and Walter Hannam (Leiden, 2007), 223–34 (227).

63. See Ronna Burger, *Plato's Phaedrus: A Defense of a Philosophic Art of Writing* (Tuscaloosa, AL, 1980), 90–114. See also Irene van Renswoude, "'The Word Once Sent Forth Can Never Come Back': Trust in Writing and the Dangers of Publication," in *Strategies of Writing: Studies on Text and Trust in the Middle Ages*, ed. Petra Schulte, Marco Mostert, and Irene van Renswoude, Utrecht Studies in Medieval Literacy 13 (Turnhout, 2008), 393–413.

 CHAPTER 16

The *libera vox* of Theodulf of Orléans

JANET L. NELSON

Theodulf of Orléans was an intellectual jack-of-many-trades, and as a result his output has tended to be studied in parts rather than as a whole and in context. There has been no overall account for over a century, despite many important contributions on particular aspects.[1] This essay obviously has no pretensions to comprehensiveness, but tries to make some connections. Theodulf has often been seen as a representative figure of the Carolingian Renaissance, one of the learned advisers assembled by Charlemagne, a typical court scholar.[2] In the historiography of recent decades, Theodulf is increasingly coming to be seen as distinctive as well as, even rather than, representative. First, the scope and design-audacity of Charlemagne's house of many mansions accommodated Theodulf's Spanish intellectual formation and brand of reformist rigor without smoothing away the sharp edges of either. The late Ann Freeman's demonstration of Theodulf's role in the authorship of the *Libri Carolini*, or *Opus Caroli regis contra synodum*, has been a signal transforming contribution here.[3] Further, there has been a shift away from a mainly literary focus on Theodulf's poetry and towards a cultural-historical approach to his oeuvre at large. Among many scholars involved in this re-envisioning,[4] John Contreni put his finger on the significance of Theodulf's episcopal statutes in the educational, hence reforming, thrust of Charlemagne's project.[5] In this paper, as an offering to these essays in John's honor, I trace a line of reforming continuity through a series of Theodulf's works datable to Charlemagne's reign: works which were not, or not only, commissioned, or offered to gain patronage, but written from the author's own urgent, lifelong, concerns as political critic, teacher, and pastor.

Theodulf's career nearly ended when hardly begun, in or soon after 778. Charlemagne's one foray into Spain was a response to invitations from local Muslim rulers in Ebro valley cities including Zaragoza, Theodulf's likely home.[6] These dissidents provoked fierce retaliation from the emir of Cordoba, and Christian communities hitherto left in relative peace were now expelled by the emir's forces.[7] This scenario provides a plausible explanation for Theodulf's leaving Spain around 780. His days reading the Bible and the works of Isidore and the Spanish poets Prudentius and Juvencus in the peace of Zaragoza's cathedral library were brusquely ended. He would never again hear the familiar Visigothic liturgy in the cathedral church. He might well have died a displaced person. As it turned out, he emigrated to that region of southern Gaul known to the Franks in Charlemagne's reign as Gothia or Septimania, which had been part of the Visigothic kingdom until 711 and where Visigothic law and liturgy continued in use. Here Theodulf resettled and honed his skills.[8] From here, within a decade, he moved to begin a new career at the court of Charlemagne, where he was first famed, apparently, before 791 as a poet who, along with his Frankish colleague Angilbert, "shone wonderfully in the style of Juvencus," meaning that they both wrote in the genre of epic verse.[9] In this milieu, Theodulf would also have attracted attention as an all-rounder, learned in Scripture and the Fathers, knowledgeable in rhetoric and logic: credentials that qualified him to be entrusted by Charlemagne with the writing of the *Libri Carolini*.

Perhaps he had already written a major work of moral instruction for bishops. The epic-poem nowadays called *Ad episcopos* survives only in fragmentary form, as *Carmina* 1 and 2 in Dümmler's edition.[10] These apparently lacked titles in the manuscript Jacques Sirmond used for his 1646 edition of Theodulf's works, and in entitling them *Paraenesis ad episcopos*, he explicitly followed the model of the title given by Pierre Daniel to the much better known *Carmen* 28 in his 1598 edition, *Paraenesis ad iudices*.[11] Evidently Sirmond saw a resemblance between the two; and Elisabeth Dahlhaus-Berg, who classes them together as poems of instruction (*Lehrgedichten*), moves smoothly to a suggestion that they are close in date of composition.[12] The poem on justice (*Carmen* 28) was certainly written after 798 (it describes the poet's activities as a royal superintendant, or *missus*, in Septimania in that year) and before 801: most scholars date it to 799–800.[13] The advice to bishops was written by Theodulf before he became a bishop himself—that is, before, or in, 798. Dahlhaus-Berg's conjecture would bring the composition of *Ad episcopos* too as near that date as possible. But it could have been written a decade earlier. While *Carmen* 2's words, "Parva sed in magna cum sim levitate turba pars" (Though I am a small part of a large priestly crowd) may constitute a humility topos,[14] they do not exclude the possibility that the poem was a youthful work either predating Theodulf's arrival at court, or perhaps, like the acrostic *Carmen* 23, a test piece set for the "débutant at court" by the king himself.[15]

Theodulf's lowly rank in the clerical hierarchy constituted a vantage point from which he could view superiors dispassionately, and speak out with a free voice of his own. To grasp that paradox is to retrieve, but now on contextual rather than strictly chronological grounds, the idea of an earlier generation of scholars that *Ad episcopos* was written before the *Libri Carolini*.[16] Dahlhaus-Berg rightly perceived that both *Ad episcopos* and *Ad iudices* were poetic works that connected with capitularies—which she considered to be the *same* capitularies. I think, though, that each connected with a *different* one. The theme of *correctio* runs through all Charlemagne's capitularies. At the same time, different emphases are apparent in the two poems which to my mind reflect not stages in the poet's development, but the different circumstances of distinct reforming moments.[17]

The earlier of these occurred in 789, with the summoning (probably) to Aachen and on March 23 of an assembly of bishops and counselors.[18] Donald Bullough thought there was "a reasonable possibility" that Theodulf had a hand in the prefatory letter to the *Admonitio generalis*, sent out to inform the bishops at large of the measures agreed at this assembly. If that is accepted, it seems an equally reasonable inference that Theodulf was there.[19] The mood of the preface is a blend of confident relief and anxious concern. This ambivalent tone is struck repeatedly. God's protection has been granted hitherto, but its continuation has to be secured by "continued practice of good works" for which the bishops's "care and admonition" will be required. The bishops are "shepherds and guides of Christ's flock and brightest luminaries of the world" (pastores . . . et ductores . . . et clarissima mundi luminaria), yet the king fears for the safety of straying sheep at risk of being devoured by the prowling wolf: a risk that can be averted only by episcopal admonition, exhortation, and constraint. Charlemagne assures the bishops that his efforts will cooperate with theirs and that he is sending out *missi* "to correct, with you, and by the authority of our name, what must be corrected." Yet the king fears that his admonition may sound presumptuous and urges those who receive it to do so in a spirit of charity. Biblical authority is invoked to justify royal intervention: "[F]or we read in the Books of Kings that the holy Josiah strove to recall, by traveling around it, and by correcting and by admonishing it, the kingdom given to him by God to the worship of the true God—not that I am making myself in any way Josiah's equal in holiness, but because the examples of holy men are always those we must follow."[20]

This particular example goes to the root of the king's anxiety. Josiah had indeed become king of Judah after the reigns of evil kings who had reverted to idol-worship, not heeding the book of the law, and Josiah had read out to the assembled people "a parvo usque ad magnum" the newly rediscovered Law of God, restored the temple of the Lord and slain the idolatrous priests, broken the images in pieces and put away all the wizards and the images and the idols and all the abominations that were spied in the land of Judah, and turned to Lord with all his soul, according to the law of Moses.[21] But anyone familiar with their Bible knew that Josiah had been slain in battle and succeeded by unworthy sons that did evil in the sight of the Lord, and that within a couple of generations Jerusalem had been destroyed by Nebuchadnezzar.[22] Old Testament history showed, as usual, how hard it was to assuage the Lord's anger and how necessary it was to maintain eternal vigilance, not least where the conduct of priests was concerned. Here, the *Admonitio* followed through: the final section of the preface re-emphasized the necessity of pastoral admonition which might be rewarded (*remuneretur*) by almighty God; fifty-nine ensuing *capitula* set out a selection of laws of universal councils for bishops especially, but also priests and, instructed by them, the laity, to follow; a second, even more urgent, admonition (c. 60) was given to the bishops (*dilectissimi*) that they should keep to the law; and twenty-two further *capitula* spelled out, with a string of biblical injunctions from the New Testament and the Old, a program of moral reform of doctrine and practice, concluding with impassioned recommendation of preaching to be undertaken by priests under the supervision of their bishops (addressed twice more as *dilectissimi* in the final *capitulum*). The *Admonitio*, in short, was a warning to bishops to understand their duties in terms more exacting than ever before.

Even if it remains no more than a likely hypothesis that Theodulf actually attended the Aachen assembly, I think his *Ad episcopos* was programmatically connected with the *Admonitio*'s agenda. It was as much a pièce d'occasion as the (later) poems on the court. It was designed to be read and heard in the same setting—a court assembly—as the decrees of universal councils and the injunctions to preaching on adherence to truth and shunning of vices. Poetry and law were distinct as genres, but their messages were entirely consonant. Two scenarios can be imagined: one, that Theodulf wrote *Ad episcopos* in the south, and sent it northwards as self-recommendation to solicit a summons to court; the other, I think to be preferred, that Theodulf had already been invited to Charlemagne's court and that he wrote "wonderfully, with Iuvencan art," in Francia on the basis of perceptions gained in Gothia.[23] Either way, what surely motivated Theodulf's writing was an urgent sense of bishops's deficiencies and the need to remake the episcopal cadre in light of scriptural and patristic teaching. Charlemagne as legislator had countered any charge of presumption by appealing to a holy king as exemplar: Theodulf met any analogous charge against himself by pleading that "[n]o presumptuous mind compelled the writing of this work / Nor do I put myself forward as a teacher for holy bishops / whose life inspires me as a norm of salvation; / Yet small part as I am of a large priestly crowd, / may I help the fathers [i.e., the bishops] in whatever way I can!"[24]

The *Admonitio generalis* was the fruit of Charlemagne's desire to admonish his *dilectissimi*, his bishops, about following the canonical rules essential to attaining eternal felicity. Correct and appropriate episcopal conduct was central to both parts of the *Admonitio*, involving law and morals alike. *Carmen 2*'s early lines include a list of the bishop's correct clothing and equipment, which must be kept clean. This is the prelude to an account of order disrupted. Short passages from the Old and New Testaments, versified and elaborated in Juvencan style, castigate blind leaders, unlearned teachers, a whole battery of lookouts without lights, a pack of dogs without any powers of barking.[25] One after another, antitheses and oxymorons reinforce a message about the gap between the requirements of office and inadequate incumbents: dirty bishops can't clean, sleepy bishops give no wake-up calls, sick bishops can't cure, drunken bishops won't preach sobriety. The actions of good shepherds, *turba felix*, are sketched (lines 141–64), only to be violently contrasted with "this crowd / which pants with mouth agape after its own gain, not the Lord's gain" (lines 165–66; [turba] ista / Quae sua non domini lucra inhianter adit). "Not the job but the money, not the responsibility but the honor, is what pleases that mob" (line 175; Non opus, heu, sed opes, nec onus, sed honor placet illi). Four verses from the prophet Ezechiel 34:2–5 are rendered into sixteen lines (183–98) decrying the evil pastors of Israel, before the poem assumes a more positive tone: "Why won't I prepare to put on purity of life, if [even] now I won't wear clothing that has a stain on it?" (lines 209–10; Vitae et munditiem cur non adhibere parabo / Cum modo si sordem non fero vestis habet?). High ecclesiastical rank is a heavy burden: *Honos* is *onus* (line 254). "The image of divine goodness abides in that in which it is impressed, if it is well conjoined in holy conduct. If an analogy from small things can be used, the ring impresses a likeness in the same way on you, O wax!" (lines 268–69; In qua divinae exprimitur bonitatis imago, / Moribus in sanctis si huic bene iuncta manet. / Si licet exemplum de rebus sumere parvis, / Annulus effigiem sic tibi, cera, premit). After this metaphor neatly chosen to impress men invested *ex officio* with seal-rings and engaged in everyday use of these in authenticating documents, the poem ends as it began, with reminders about episcopal decorum. Whether in Gothia or in Francia, or both, Theodulf had evidently encountered bishops behaving badly and performing badly. His assessment of bishops' importance to the reform project was every bit as high as Charlemagne's.

The second great moment of reforming energy that came a decade or so later was associated with the enhanced aspirations aroused by Charlemagne's imperial title, and perhaps too with apocalyptic speculations at court.[26] Theodulf accompanied Charlemagne and the young Charles to Rome in 800–801.[27]

Alcuin's student Candidus had been there too, and on his return to Tours in mid-April he reported back to Alcuin, and then Alcuin relayed appreciation back to Theodulf, on the fine outspoken speech—"quam libera voce . . . testimonia protulisses!"—that Theodulf had made at the Rome assembly in early December, how greatly he impressed those he met, and how conscientiously he had pursued his ecclesiastical business.[28] Theodulf had apparently prolonged his stay in Italy and had still to make his way home,[29] when Alcuin wrote to congratulate him on the increase in his ecclesiastical status and Pope Leo's personal conferment on him of a personal pallium signifying archiepiscopal rank.[30] Alcuin recalled for him that since "the tongue of episcopal dignity [*sacerdotalis dignitatis lingua*] is the key of the heavenly realm and the most shining trumpet of the citadels of Christ," he was "not to be silent, nor fear to speak out," but to "'lift up your voice like a trumpet,'" urging him to "'set the trumpet to your mouth like an eagle over the house of God,'" to be mindful of his task as preacher, "and, like a wise banker [*trapazeta sapiens*], multiply the Lord's account, so that you may be worthy of your pay." Here, with exquisite tact, Alcuin inserted a couple of lines from Juvencus's Gospel epic, adapting them for this, Juvencus's literary heir, to wish that his work too might, as Juvencus had hoped for himself, "save you from hell-fire and give you a place in heaven."[31]

Several points emerge strongly here. The first is that Candidus, in reporting the impression made by Theodulf's *libera vox* at the Rome assembly, and Alcuin, in urging the continued sounding of Theodulf's trumpetlike voice, surely had in mind the frank speech (*parrhesia*) which ancient authors had admired in philosophers who fearlessly spoke out against potentates, which Christ and the apostles presented in the New Testament, which late antique Christians saw in holy men and spiritual advisers who dared to criticize emperors and give good counsel, and which now commended itself as the critical style appropriate to a new imperial court. Theodulf himself knew the relevant texts; and at Rome, in the most public of settings, he assumed the parrhesiast's role.[32] His self-positioning and rhetorical talents too had made Theodulf the most effective advocate for Alcuin's solution to the problem of judging the one who could not be judged, namely, that the pope should clear himself by voluntary self-purgation of the charges laid against him: a certain abnegation was required on Leo's part, and the grant of the pallium to Theodulf (as agreed, no doubt, with Charlemagne) signaled the pope's personal acknowledgment of his concession to the parrhesiast.[33] Second, Theodulf had articulated a key argument for Charlemagne's coronation, and thanks to the evidence of the Lorsch Annals, that argument can be identified: "[T]he name of emperor was at that time in a state of cessation in the land of the Greeks and they had a woman's rule among them."[34] There was, in other words, an imperial vacancy to be filled. This was a variant of an important

argument that Theodulf had presented in the *Libri Carolini* against the validity of
the decrees of the Council of Nicaea, namely that a woman had summoned the
council and participated in its deliberations: Theodulf likened Eirene to the Old
Testament queen Athaliah, "who destroyed nearly all of the royal seed because
with unfitting desire she had an appetite for command over men."[35] In the imagined vision of a female *institutrix* or *doctrix*, Theodulf, aghast, saw a breach of the
law of nature: "For frailty of sex and mutability of mind do not allow a woman to
put herself in supreme authority over men in matters of doctrine or command."
He also saw a breach of the law of God: "For it is laid down by divine laws that
whatever vows women make may be declared null by a man's judgment." Finally,
he saw a transgression of human law: "Women unmarried [in this case, without
a husband because of widowhood] although of mature years must remain in tute-
lage because of their inherent shallowness of mind."[36] All these passages could
well have resurfaced as *testimonia* on December 23, 800. The man who a few
years before had declared Eirene gender-disqualified from supreme authority was a
natural choice in 800 to declare *femineum imperium* no rule at all, and some form
of *translatio imperii* therefore not merely justified but required. Of the strong team
he had brought to Rome, Charlemagne, with so much at stake, and a difficult
wicket, put his best man in to bat.

A further inference is that Theodulf had remained in Lombardy while the
emperor and his entourage were still busy securing the political position (in April
Charlemagne sent Pippin of Italy to campaign in Benevento, while he himself was
occupied in doing justice and making peace at Ravenna in "early summer")[37] and
that the "ecclesiastical business" which Theodulf had taken the chance to pursue
included the collection of information about manuscripts available in Lombardy
that would be required for his editorial labors on a definitive text of the Bible.[38]
These points add up to good evidence for Theodulf's enhanced position at court,
indeed a new high point in his career so far.[39] If he had been a trusted counselor
already in 789 and the early 790s, he stood out now as more influential than ever.

Theodulf's role in 800–801 can be further contextualized. Thanks to the
work of Peter Godman, and above all Lawrence Nees, Theodulf's *Ad iudices*
emerges as a political intervention in the discussions that preceded and ensued
from the momentous journey of Charlemagne and his son to Rome, accompanied by other members of the royal family and elite advisers and power brokers.[40]
Again, Theodulf's response took the form of a programmatic epic, this time on
the theme of justice, and the implicitly associated demand that judges be free
of corruption which in this context meant bribery; and again, these were fore-
shadowed in 789. In the *Admonitio*, Charlemagne had likened himself to Josiah:
in Theodulf's *Ad iudices*, Josiah is praised for making strict observance of religious duties his priority: "For you, O Josiah, what mattered first and foremost was

observing [the laws], and this raised your famous name to the heights. You are the one who removes the impious monuments of ancient crime, and, as far as you can, renews the ancestral laws—you, who were given as a pious glory to the declining kingdom, and whom the course of evening-time gave."[41] Yet, significantly, Theodulf does not neglect the "evening time" that Josiah's kingdom represented in the kingdom's history. Theodulf's personal situation had now changed. In 798, he was himself a bishop-designate, already invested with the authority of a judge as one of Charlemagne's *missi dominici*. For him, the temptations of bribery had become familiar at first hand. Even before the first great set piece of the poem, Theodulf paused to consider the temptations presented to judges by people offering bribes. "I often try to dissuade those who want to succumb . . . but when I do so, they secretly say to themselves that I am just the same as they are. / I am often suspected of this, even though I am not a man of this kind. / I have many faults, but I shall be free from this stain."[42] Theodulf's aim in this poem went far beyond merely personal experiences of temptation and self-exculpation. He launched a general attack on the prevalence of bribery: "Everyone was putting their trust in a gift, / and no-one thinks they can have anything unless they give something. O foul stain, spread through all parts, / O crime, O madness, O thing most cruel, which so wickedly claims to hold the whole world captive to itself!" (fidebant munere cuncti, / Nec se quis quiddam, ni det, habere putant. O scelerate lues, partes diffusa per omnes / O scelus, o furor, o res truculenta nimis, / Quae sibi captivum totum male vindicate orbem).[43] *Munera*, gifts, were perfectly correct in many social contexts; but when used to pervert the course of justice, they became evil. The same word served in both contexts: evaluation depended on circumstances, motives, and scale. The probably exactly contemporary capitulary *De villis* interestingly showed royal estate-managers vulnerable to similar temptations. For them, and for his own counselors and *missi*, Charlemagne prescribed similar ways of resolving moral dilemmas, and remaining on the virtuous side of the gift.[44]

The temptation went with the office, and hence went far beyond the personal. As Charlemagne extended his governmental project, made increasing use of *missi*, and depended more and more heavily on their integrity and impartiality, he needed to impress on them the moral point. It now becomes more plausible to imagine an audience for the work that Theodulf had written: an elite of office-holders made hyper-receptive to charges of corruption by the events of 799–800. Theodulf called on judges to make God rule their minds, and make mind rule the flesh.[45] Later in the poem, Theodulf chose the unambiguously pejorative word *merces* to hammer home his message that both the giver and receiver of the bribe was morally dead: "O bribe, bribe, bribe that does more harm than any other, / because that one thing kills two, both giver and taker" (O merces, merces, mercede nocentior omne, / Dantem et captantem quae necat una duos).⁴⁶ The poem moves to a lengthy and powerful consideration of the system in which judges, and *missi* as judges, work. Flawed as it is, it may have good effects. "Let condemnation be first, let mercy come next, yet never let bribes / be there in the judgment: Christ is there also" (Sit censura prius, pietas post, praemia numquam / sint in iudicio, est quoque Christus ibi).⁴⁷ This strategic mention of Christ signals a new attentiveness to an idea of justice that excludes corruption and values mercy, while implicitly accepting the inevitability of punishment. For, like Augustine, Theodulf acknowledges the demands of *lex prisca*, hence the cruel dilemmas of the judge, and the need to settle for *mediocre bonum*.⁴⁸ Theodulf begs the judge to aspire to be, as he himself aspires to be, an imitator of Christ: "May I be the one who redeems many battalions of wretched people, / May I be the one who raises up many by the cross, from disaster" (Ille ego sim, redimam miserorum qui agmina multa, / Ille ego sim, plures qui cruce, clade levem).⁴⁹ But Theodulf never abandons his starkly Augustinian view of a postlapsarian world inherently characterized by violence and oppression.⁵⁰ Not to be forgotten is the plight of the weak and the needy, oppressed by the rich: "Whoever you are who has responsibility for the poor, be very gentle, and know yourself to be equal to them by nature. The subjection of them to you yourself has been imposed, not by the human condition, but by sin" (Pauperibus quicumque praees, mitissimus esto, / Teque his natura noveris esse parem. / Non hos condicio tibimet, sed culpa subegit, / Quae dedit ut homini subditus esset homo).⁵¹ The poem ends with a brief vision of the life to come, in which Christ "summons to his gifts, according to merits, you and those for whom he is, dead, the creator of life."⁵²

The giver of *consilium in hoc carmine* demands a hearing.⁵³ He repeats that the judge must serve. According to the author of the Lorsch Annals, under the year 802, "Charlemagne, remembering his mercy concerning the poor people who lived in his realm and could not have their rights to the full, refused, because of bribes, to send out from the palace his poorer vassals to do justice, but [instead] chose in his kingdom archbishops and other bishops and abbots together with dukes and counts who now had no need to receive to take bribes [*munera*] at the expense of the innocent, and he sent them out throughout his whole kingdom to do justice to churches, to widows and to orphans, and to the poor and the whole people."⁵⁴ There may well be a ring of irony here; yet the author, like the emperor himself, recognized that countering corruption meant increased reliance on powerful magnates. Later in 802, Charlemagne at a great assembly publicly announced a moral campaign, enlisted in it "dukes, counts and the rest of the Christian people together with those who declared the law [*cum legislatoribus*], and he caused all the laws in his realm to be read out, and delivered to each man his law . . . and said that the judges must judge in accordance with what was written and not accept gifts [*munera*], but all men, poor and rich, should have justice in his realm."[55] I think Theodulf's counsel can be heard behind this announcement, and this staging, of a reforming agenda. The receptiveness of the judges, not to say the assembled Christian people, had been enhanced by the barrage of rhetoric in *Ad iudices*, a work expressly written to generate self-criticism and constructive discussion at court, and at assemblies that were extensions of the court, involving men who, once back home, would participate in delivering justice. The man had met the moment.

By way of conclusion, I want briefly to review Theodulf's role as a counselor, and role model, after 802 and for the remainder of Charlemagne's reign. Five texts ring with a now-familiar voice. First, Theodulf's theological opinion on the procession of the Holy Spirit, given along with those of other experts to an assembly summoned by Charlemagne to Aachen to consider the problem in 809, echoes the selection of patristic texts which he deployed in the *Libri Carolini*.[56] Second, the will Charlemagne made in 811 in the presence of *amici et ministri sui*, with Theodulf as one of its eleven episcopal witnesses (along with four abbots and fifteen counts) in a roll call of the emperor's most influential advisers, seems to resonate with Theodulf's quite particular concerns in stipulating "that the books which he has collected in his library in great numbers shall be sold for a fair price [*iusto pretio*] to those who might want them, and the money received given to the poor."[57] Third, Theodulf gave a sonorously distinctive, and in places distinctively Spanish, response to Charlemagne's request for explication of the baptismal liturgy.[58] Fourth, Theodulf's episcopal statutes datable to the years before 813, while part of a broader pastoral symphony, accord with the particular tones of his teaching and preaching priorities.[59] Fifth, the decrees of the Council of Chalon in 813 echo so strongly the Theodulfian themes of the episcopal statutes and also those of and the *Carmina* considered in detail above, that they too have to be heard (and read) as Theodulf's work.[60]

The years of Charlemagne's reign after 802, which I have called elsewhere the Aachen years,[61] saw the unfolding of an extraordinarily ambitious project best characterized—to end where I began, with John Contreni—as educational. Now, more easily than earlier, a court can be seen in action. Charlemagne has been generally recognized as the project's main mover, and certainly the project could never have been put into any sort of effect without his material resources and driving force. But it is equally true that he could never have achieved so much without exceptional advisers and right-hand men. Of these, Alcuin has attracted most scholarly attention.[62] But Alcuin was very seldom at the Aachen court after 796, and he died in April 804. It has been my aim in this paper, not to diminish Alcuin's contribution but to highlight Theodulf's. Sometimes rivals, these men were also colleagues who sang, most of the time, from the same hymn-sheet. In their different approaches to editing the text of the Bible, as on the *Libri Carolini*, they are probably best seen as complementing each other. Setting apart the *Libri Carolini*, as a peculiarly time-bound work of much greater interest to modern scholars than to any contemporary readership, and given the predominance, with few exceptions, of literary specialists in evaluating the *Carmina*, Theodulf's oeuvre has been relatively underappreciated by historians. If he was "champion of the Old Testament,"[63] Theodulf was an equally close devotee of the New, and indeed he understood the two as inseparably linked: *nova antiquitas et antiqua novitas*.[64] The combination of diversity and consistency, of genres and of themes, resounds insistently; and a willingness to listen, stereophonically as it were, for both *antiquitas* and *novitas* can make even more clearly audible what Alcuin (perhaps echoing Candidus) called Theodulf's *libera vox*.

Notes

1. Charles Cuissard, *Théodulfe, éveque d'Orléans: Sa vie et ses oeuvres*, Mémoires de la société archéologique et historique de l'Orléanais 24 (Orléans, 1892). This very substantial study by Bishop Charles Cuissard of Orléans is a monument to provincial piety, identity and erudition. While modern work on Theodulf has been segmented and patchy, that on Alcuin has been full and extensive. Reasons for this contrast would deserve a study in themselves. Meanwhile for a brief, useful, survey of his life and work, see Christian Ménage, "Théodulfe d'Orléans," in *Histoire littéraire de la France* 42 (2002): 237–67.

2. Joseph Fleckenstein, "Karl der Große und sein Hof," in *Karl der Große: Lebenswerk und Nachleben*, ed. Wolfgang Braunfels, 5 vols (Düsseldorf, 1965), 1:24–50; Joseph Fleckenstein, "Alcuin im Kreis der Hofgelehrten Karls des Großen," in *Science in Western and Eastern Civilization in Carolingian Times*, ed. Paul Leo Butzer and Dietric Lohrmann (Basel, 1993), 3–21. For healthy scepticism about Charlemagne's "court" or "court-circle" (which does not, however, quite address the sociological and psychological aspects of scholars' collective self-perception), see Rosamond McKitterick, *Charlemagne: The Formation of a European Identity* (Cambridge, 2008), 345–78. Cf. Peter Godman, *Poetry of the Carolingian Renaissance* (London, 1985), esp. 6–26, and Peter Godman, *Poets and Emperors* (Oxford, 1986), 44–45, 52–55, 64–70, 77–82, with pertinent observations on the way that poetry lent itself to rhetorical expression of rivalries. See further Mary Garrison, "The Emergence of Carolingian Latin at the Court of Charlemagne," in *Carolingian Culture: Emulation and Innovation*, ed. Rosamond McKitterick (Cambridge, 1994), 111–40; Mary Garrison, "English and Irish at the Court of Charlemagne," in *Karl der Große und sein Nachwirken*, ed. P. L. Butzer, M. Kerner, and B. Oberschelp (Turnhout, 1997), 97–124; and Mary Garrison, "The Social World of Alcuin: Nicknames at York and at the Carolingian Court," in *Alcuin of York: Scholar at the Carolingian Court*, ed. L. A. J. R. Houwen and A. A. MacDonald, Germania latina 3 (Groningen, 1999), 59–79. Charlemagne's court, despite some relevant contributions in Catherine Cubitt ed., *Court Culture in the Early Middle Ages*, Studies in the Early Middle Ages 3 (Turnhout, 2003), has received less attention than the courts of his successors: for the high Carolingian court as "a frame of mind," see Janet L. Nelson, "History-Writing at the Courts of Louis the Pious and Charles the Bald," in *Historiographie im frühen Mittelalter*, ed. Anton Scharer and Georg Scheibelreiter

(Vienna, 1994), 435–42 (438–39) (repr. Janet L. Nelson, *Rulers and Ruling Families in Early Medieval Europe* [Aldershot, 1999], ch. 9); also Stuart Airlie, "Bonds of Power and Bonds of Association in the Court Circle of Louis the Pious," in *Charlemagne's Heir: New Perspectives on the Reign of Louis the Pious*, ed. Peter Godman and Roger Collins (Oxford, 1990), 191–204; Stuart Airlie, "The Carolingian Court as a Political Centre," in *Courts and Regions in Medieval Europe*, ed. S. Rees Jones, R. Marks, and A. J. Minnis (Woodbridge, 2000), 1–20; and Stuart Airlie, "Ansegis and the Writing of Carolingian Royal Authority," in *Early Medieval Studies in Memory of Patrick Wormald*, ed. Stephen David Baxter et al. (Farnham, 2009), 219–35; see further Eric J. Goldberg, "*Regina nitens sanctissima Hemma*: Queen Emma (827–876), Bishop Witgar of Augsburg and the Witgar-Belt," and Simon MacLean, "Ritual, Misunderstanding, and the Contest for Meaning: Representations of the Disrupted Royal Assembly at Frankfurt (873)," in *Representations of Power in Medieval Germany 800–1500*, ed. B. Weiler and Simon MacLean, International Medieval Research 16 (Turnhout, 2006), 57–95, 97–120.

3. Theodulf, *Opus Caroli regis contra synodum*, ed. Ann Freeman [with Paul Meyvaert], MGH Conc. 2, Supp. 1; also the papers collected in Ann Freeman, *Theodulf of Orléans: Charlemagne's Spokesman against the Second Council of Nicaea* (Aldershot, 2003).

4. Among pathbreaking works, Elisabeth Dahlhaus-Berg, *Nova antiquitas et antiqua novitas: Typologische Exegese und isidorianisches Geschichtsbild bei Theodulf von Orléans* (Cologne, 1975), and Lawrence Nees, *A Tainted Mantle: Hercules and the Classical Tradition at the Carolingian Court* (Philadelphia, 1991) deserve special mention, as does the brilliant vignette of Theodulf in J. M. Wallace-Hadrill, *The Frankish Church* (Oxford, 1983), 217–25, drawing wisely on the work of Freeman and Dahlhaus-Berg. Fundamental on Theodulf's poetic output is Dieter Schaller, "Philologische Untersuchungen zu den Gedichten Theodulfs von Orléans," *Deutsches Archiv* 18 (1962): 13–92; and on Theodulf as a writer in several genres, see Franz Brunhölzl, *Geschichte der lateinischen Literatur des Mittelalters*, 2 vols. (Munich, 1975), 1:288–99.

5. See John J. Contreni, "The Pursuit of Knowledge in Carolingian Europe," in *"The Gentle Voices of Teachers": Aspects of Learning in the Carolingian Age*, ed. Richard E. Sullivan (Columbus, OH, 1995), 106–41, esp. 111, 112; and John J. Contreni, *Carolingian Learning, Masters and Manuscripts* (Aldershot, 1992).

6. Theodulf in the poem he himself entitled *De libris quos legere solebam* (The books I used to read), *Carmen*, 45, ed. Ernst Dümmler, MGH Poetae 1, 543, refers to Prudentius as *noster parens*, which has been taken to suggest that Theodulf too came from Zaragoza: see Ann Freeman, "Scripture and Images in the *Libri Carolini*," ch. 7 in *Theodulf of Orléans*, 163–88 (179). Though Dahlhaus-Berg, *Nova antiquitas*, 6, prefers to read this as testimony to a sense of shared "consciousness of literary and spiritual tradition," and Godman, *Poetry of the Carolingian Renaissance*, 169, translates, "fellow-countryman," Prudentius does not identify the other Spaniard on his author-list, Juvencus, as *parens*. Prudentius was born in the province of Tarraconensis, and Zaragoza is one of two cities suggested as his birthplace: see Anne-Marie Palmer, *Prudentius on the Martyrs* (Oxford, 1989), 21 and n. 3. Though other poets of the Carolingian Renaissance knew Prudentius and Juvencus, Theodulf seems exceptional in the extent of his citations from both, especially Prudentius: see Dümmler's "Addenda," MGH Poetae 2, 694–97, to his edition of Theodulf's *Carmina* in MGH Poetae 1, and compare similar evidence for Paulinus, Alcuin, or Hibernicus Exul (ibid., 690–94).

7. On the 778 campaign, see Robert-Henri Bautier, "La campagne de Charlemagne

en Espagne (778): La réalité historique," ch. 3 in his *Recherches sur l'histoire de la France médiévale: Des Mérovingiens aux premiers Capétiens* (Aldershot, 1991), 1–47, with careful discussion of the Muslim sources (4 and n. 4), and pertinent comment on the reactions of local Muslim elites, and of the emir of Cordoba, as reported in the anonymous compilation Akhbār Majmūʿa, more probably assembled in the tenth century than the ninth (14–15, 43–44); for the date, see Ann Christys, *Christians in Al-Andalus* (Richmond, Surrey, 2002), 18. See also more briefly, Ann Freeman, "Theodulf of Orléans: A Visigoth at Charlemagne's Court," ch. 8 in her *Theodulf of Orléans*, 185–94 (185–86). I confess to not finding persuasive the argument of Yitzhak Hen, "Charlemagne's Jihad," *Viator* 37 (2006): 33–51, esp. 45–49, that the transmission of a Muslim notion of forced conversion was "Theodulf's contribution" to Charlemagne's treatment of Saxony in the 790s.

8. Ann Freeman, "Further Studies in the *Libri Carolini*," *Speculum* 40 (1965): 274–78; Dahlhaus-Berg, *Nova Antiquitas*, 5–7.

9. *Versus Fiduciae ad Angelramnum presulem*, ed. Ernst Dümmler, MGH Poetae 1, 76–77. The poem is preserved in a late eighth-century manuscript (ibid., 32), including poems apparently by Peter of Pisa. "Fiducia" asks *Anghelramus*, presumably Bishop Angilramn of Metz, who died in 791, to help him get the king's patronage, and evokes a court where "Teudulfus rutilat mire de arte Iuvenci / Atque Angelpertus, divini ambo poetae." For Theodulf's familiarity with Juvencus, see above, n. 6. Godman, *Poets and Emperors*, 63 and n. 133, thinks the reference to Juvencus should be read as echoing Theodulf's *Carmen*, 45, and implying that *that* poem itself "would then antedate 791," but the inference is uncertain. Juvencus's retelling of the Gospels' story in Virgilian hexameters is well discussed by Roger P. H. Green, *Latin Epics of the New Testament* (Oxford, 2007), 1–134, with too-brief comment at 359 on his influence on Theodulf.

10. *Carmen* 1, MGH Poetae 1, 445–52, is an account of the battle between virtues and vices, modeled on Prudentius's *Psychomachia*, and *Carmen* 2, ibid., 452–58, a work of admonition to bishops. *Carmen* 1 is apparently a fragment of book 3, and *Carmen* 2 the whole of book 4, of a four-book work, which survives, in this truncated form, only in Jacques Sirmond's edition of Theodulf's *Opera*.

11. *Carmina* 1–2, ed. Jacques Sirmond, in *Theodulfi Aurelianensis episcopi opera* (Paris, 1646), 227, 237; Dümmler, MGH Poetae 1, 445, 452, with comment on Sirmond and Daniel at 443. Dümmler, ed., *Carmen* 28, MGH Poetae 1, 493, noted the lack of any manuscript title, and having mentioned the title *Ad iudices* suggested in a handwritten note on the manuscript by D. Pétau, and the title *Paraenesis ad iudices* suggested by Sirmond, *Theodulfi opera*, 131, supplied his own title, *Versus Teudulfi episcopi contra iudices*. Godman, *Poetry*, 14–15, 162, offers brief but thought-provoking comments on *Carmen* 28, with translated extracts at no. 16, and cf. Godman, *Poets*, 70–74. See further, Nees, *Tainted Mantle*, 18–143, for excellent discussion. Neither Godman nor Nees considers *Carmina* 1–2, however. Unfortunately, I have been unable to consult N. A. Alexandrenko, "The Poetry of Theodulf of Orléans: A Translation and Critical Study" (PhD dissertation, Tulane University, 1970), cited extensively by Nees. All translations in what follows are my own, although I have often learned a great deal from others' translations, and have been greatly helped by the generous advice and expertise of Francis Davey and David Ganz, who kindly commented on and sometimes corrected my efforts.

12. Dahlhaus-Berg, *Nova antiquitas*, 70n48, and 183–84.

13. Nees, *Tainted Mantle*, 69 and n. 12, and 111, pointing out that at line 102, Charles is called "king," not "emperor." See further below, pp. 294–97.

14. Dahlhaus-Berg, *Nova antiquitas*, 183, commenting on *Carmen 2*, as cited below, p. 291 and n. 23. It may be that the word *levite* suggests Theodulf's relative youth as well.

15. Donald A. Bullough, *Carolingian Renewal: Sources and Heritage* (Manchester, 1991), 141, thought this acrostic poem datable to the late 780s/790. Following Dieter Schaller, "Die karolingischen Figurengedichte des Cod. Bern. 212," in *Medium aevum vivum: Festschrift für Walter Bulst*, ed. H. R. Jauss and Dieter Schaller (Heidelberg, 1960), 38–40, Godman, *Poets*, 60, calls this "one of [Theodulf's] earliest productions as a poetic débutant at court." See also Dahlhaus-Berg, *Nova antiquitas*, 184–85. If the idea of an acrostic contest for *Carmen 23* is accepted, then in light of the reconstruction of Joseph's career by Donald A. Bullough, *Alcuin: Reputation and Achievement* (Leiden, 2003), ch. 7, the years immediately before 790 would offer a likelier date than any later context. Bullough, *Alcuin*, 373, dates the poem collection to 788–90. David Ganz kindly informs me (pers. comm.) that the late Donald Bullough considered the compilation "certainly from the court." The title of *Carmen 23*, "Teudulfus episcopus hos versus conposuit," was presumably added by the copyist at the beginning of the ninth century (for the date of the manuscript, Bern, Burgerbibliothek, MS 212, see Bernhard Bischoff, "Das geistige Leben," in the catalogue of the exhibition, *Karl der Grosse: Werk und Wirkung* [Aachen, 1965], 204). Commentators have stressed the autobiographical significance of pages 480, 482, lines 28–29: "Annuit is mihi, qui sum inmensis casibus exul/Talia prolato ut promam nunc carmina tractu" (He ordered that I, who am an exile through great misfortunes, should now sing out such songs at extended length, cf. above p. 289 for the dire circumstances of Theodulf's becoming an "exile"), but they have not picked up the dating implications of lines 33–35: "Nunc laeto ingens spes cum mira coniuge rege / Omnibus augebit conatum et proemia sanctis, / Ruricolis tribuendo annonam temporis actu" (Now huge hope in the happy king with his wondrous wife will enhance efforts and rewards for all the holy, providing corn-supplies for the countryfolk in the passage of time), where the *mira coniunx* seems more likely to refer to Fastrada (queen 784–94) than to Liutgard (cf. Nelson, "Charlemagne—*pater optimus?*," in *Am Vorabend der Kaiserkrönung*, ed. Peter Godman, J. Jarnut, and P. Johanek [Stuttgart, 2002]; repr. as ch. 15 in Janet L. Nelson, *Courts, Elites and Gendered Power in the Early Middle Ages* [Aldershot, 1999], 277–79) and the reference to "the efforts and rewards of holy men" evokes the deployment of prayers and fasts in time of famine in 779 and again in 791 in time of military emergency (capit. no. 21, 51–52, recently redated to 779 by Hubert Mordek, "Karls des Großen zweites Kapitular von Herstal und die Hungersnot der Jahre 778/779," *Deutsches Archiv* 62 [2005]: 1–52, and Charlemagne's letter to Fastrada [September 791], ed. Dümmler, MGH Epp. 4, *Epistolae variorum Carolo magno regnante scriptae*, no. 20, 528–29). See further below, p. 291.

16. Dümmler, "Prooemium," 444–45; Schaller, "Philologische Untersuchungen," 29; Dahlhaus-Berg, *Nova antiquitas*, 32, very helpfully sets out the contrast between Sirmond's ordering of the *Carmina* following his (lost) ninth-century source, and Dümmler's reconstructed chronological ordering; cf. her comments, *Nova antiquitas*, 182–84.

17. Earlier phases can be seen in the capitularies of Pippin and in the Capitularies of Herstal: Mordek, "Karls des Großen." I endorse Dahlhaus-Berg's rejection, *Nova antiquitas*, 28–31, of Dümmler's (and others') account of Theodulf's literary development as moving from an initial theologically driven "schoolmasterly" phase to a more varied, lively, personal, and "courtly" form of poetic expression: these were styles and genres in which Theodulf could excel throughout his career.

18. Ed. Alfred Boretius, MGH Capit. 1, no. 22, 52–62. The date and place are

generally accepted on the basis of those given in MGH Capit. 1, no. 23, 62–64, which complements no. 22 and accompanies it in many manuscripts: Hubert Mordek, "Kapitularien und Schriftlichkeit," in his *Studien zur fränkischen Herrschergesetzgebung* (Frankfurt a.m., 2000), 307–39 (314); see further Steffen Patzold, "Normen im Buch," *Frühmittelalterliche Studien* 41 (2007): 331–50; also more briefly on the *Admonitio generalis*, Rosamond McKitterick, *The Frankish Church and the Carolingian Reforms* (London, 1977), 1–10; Wallace-Hadrill, *Frankish Church*, 259–60; Donald A. Bullough, "Alcuin and the Kingdom of Heaven," ch. 5 in *Carolingian Renewal* (Manchester, 1991), 161–240 (175) and 217–18n46; Peter Brown, *The Rise of Western Christendom* (Oxford, 1996), 285–86; and, for the wider context, Thomas M. Buck, *Admonitio und praedicatio: Zur religiös-pastoralen Dimension von Kapitularien und kapitulariennahen Texten (507–814)* (Frankfurt a.m., 1997).

19. Bullough, *Alcuin*, 380, with the comment that the *Admonitio* was "a collaborative effort involving notaries or chaplains and more than one of the resident 'international' scholars." Here Bullough's evidence for Theodulf's involvement consists the mention of Josiah, in the preface and also in *Ad iudices*, and the use of the very rare word *aequiparabilis* in the comparison with Josiah in the preface, and in another work, combined with his judgment that "the Old Testament exemplar is unlikely to be due to Alcuin." For further discussion see below, p. 294 and n. 38. The argument is very attractive, if not compelling. For the collaboration of *consiliarii*, *capellani* and notaries, though without specific reference to capitulary-production, see Philippe Bernard, "Benoît d'Aniane est-il l'auteur de l'avertissement 'Hucusque' et du Supplément au sacramentaire 'Hadrianum'?," *Studi medievali* 39 (1998): 1–120 (55–61).

20. MGH Capit. 1, no. 22, pref., 53–54. The significance of this passage is captured by Airlie, "Ansegis," 229–30.

21. 4 Reg. (= 2 Kings), 23:2, 5, 12, 24–25.

22. 4 Reg. (= 2 Kings), 23:24–37; 24; 25. The ambivalence of the story of Josiah is noted by Nees, "Carolingian Art and Politics," in *"Gentle Voices of Teachers,"* ed. Sullivan, 186–226 (206–7), in the context of Charles the Bald; but I think the "subversive" side of the model must have occurred to Theodulf and his contemporaries as apposite for Charlemagne as well—a point not made by Nees in *Tainted Mantle*. In this light, it is worth reflecting on what might have been Theodulf's take on eighth-century Iberian history.

23. *Carmen 2*, MGH Poetae 1, 452, lines 13–17, refers back to *Carmen 1* (= book 3; see above, n. 10), but if not wholly metaphorical, could evoke southern cities: "socios qua valet arma armat ope. / Fundamen fidei, fabricae incrementa salubris, / Hi bene componunt, dant pia iura loco. / Obsistunt vitiis, cives virtutibus armant, / Componuntque urbem milite, lege, fide. / Ipse sacerdotes ad moenia nostra vocato" (it [*Carm*. 1] arms comrades [i.e., bishops] with the resources they need. They construct well the foundation of faith, the building-up of a sound structure, they give religious laws for the place. They resist vices, they arm the citizens with virtues, they build the city with soldiery, law, and faith. Let it [*Carm*. 1] call the bishops to our ramparts).

24. *Carmen 2*, MGH Poetae 1, 452–53, lines 28–32: "Mens nec praesumptrix cogat ad istud opus. / Nec me praesulibus doctorem praefero sanctis, / Quorum vita mihi norma salutis inest, / Parva sed in magna cum sim levitide turba / Pars, placet ut patres qua queo sorte iuvem." See further, below, n. 40.

25. *Carmen 2*, MGH Poetae 1, 453–58, lines 53–66, drawing on and spinning out Luke 6:39 and Isaiah 56:10. This and the quotations that follow are at 453–58.

26. Wolfram Brandes, "*Tempora periculosa sunt*: Eschatologisches im Vorfeld der

Kaiserkrönung Karls des Großen," in *Das Frankfurter Konzil von 794*, ed. Rainer Berndt, 2 vols. (Mainz, 1997), 1:49–79.

27. This is an inference from a little group of Alcuin's letters, especially Ep. 214, 357–58, written perhaps in February or March 801, in which he thanks Abbess Gisla of Chelles, Charlemagne's sister, for her letter and rejoices at the news of Charlemagne's "exaltation" and the pope's well-being; Ep. 216, 359–60, written after Easter (April 4), in which he tells Abbess Gisla and her niece Rotrude, Charlemagne's daughter, that Candidus is back from Rome (for the dating inference, see Dümmler, 362n8); and Ep. 225, 368–69, addressed to Theodulf, also dating from after April 4, expressing joy at the news brought by Candidus about Theodulf's activities at Rome. On the Rome assembly on December 23, most of the huge historiography is in German, but for a digest, see Janet L. Nelson, "Why Are There So Many Different Accounts of Charlemagne's Imperial Coronation?," ch. 12 in *Courts, Elites, and Gendered Power*, 1–27. The only source to give the date, December 23, of Leo's oath is the *Annales Laurissenses minores*, s.a. 800, also known as the *Chronicon laurissense breve*, ed. H. Schnorr von Carolsfeld, *Neues Archiv* 36 (1911): 35 (for the early ninth-century date of this compilation, see Rosamond McKitterick, *History and Memory in the Carolingian World* [Cambridge, 2004], 35). The author(s) of the *Annales regni francorum*, s.a. 800, ed. Friedrich Kurze, MGH SS rer. Germ. 6, 112, place the arrival of messengers from Jerusalem on "the same day" without saying which day that was. The author(s) of the *Annales Laureshamenses* (Lorsch Annals), s.a. 800, ed. Georg H. Pertz, MGH SS 1, 38, stress the size of the assembly (*conventus maximus*) before which Leo swore his oath, but fail to clarify the day, and leave implicit the fact that the arguments spelled out in the first sentence of the annal for 801 were those put forward at that assembly: nevertheless these annals are critically important in exposing how Charlemagne's assumption of the imperial title was justified to contemporaries. On the manuscript evidence and its implications, see McKitterick, *History and Memory*, 104–10.

28. Ep. 225, 368: "filius noster Candidus, vester fidelis famulus, plurima bonitatis insignia nobis de vestrae beatitudinis nomine narrare solet: vel quam libera voce in conventu publico veritatis testimonia protulisses; vel quam honestis moribus inter maiores minoresque personas tuae beatitudinis foret conversatio; etiam quam pia et religiosa sedulitate ecclesiastica coleres officia; vel qualiter impias disceptationes odio haberes." It was Alcuin who had urged what he regarded as the canonically correct option of self-purgation in Leo's case: Alcuin, Ep. 179, 29.

29. I infer this from the references in Ep. 225 to "Christ being the companion of your journey," to "filling the routes of your journey with the flowers of preaching," to "leaving the footprints of your arrival in every place," and to himself as "at St. Martin following your route with prayers, asking God's good angel to travel with you so that you go prosperously and return safely to us." The importance of Theodulf's travels in Italy for his interest in art and knowledge of mosaics in Rome is very well grasped by Ann Freeman and Paul Meyvaert, "The Meaning of Theodulf's Apse Mosaic at Germigny-des-Prés," *Gesta* 40 (2001): 125–39 (126), though my own interest in, and inferences from, Alcuin's Ep. 225 are somewhat different from theirs.

30. Ep. 225, 368: "Gaudens gaudebo de augmento honoris vestri et de sigillo sacerdotalis dignitatis, quod apostolica vobis superaddidit auctoritas." Years later, Theodulf himself recalled this to Moduin: "ego accepi pallia sancta manu" (*Carmen 72*, MGH Poetae 1, 565).

31. Alcuin, Ep. 225, 368–69. The biblical citations are from Isaiah 58:1 and Hosea 8:1.

32. Fundamental is Michel Foucault, *Fearless Speech*, lectures given at the University of California, Berkeley, in 1983, published and ed. Joseph Pearson (Los Angeles, 2001), which in one way or another lies behind Peter Brown, *Power and Persuasion in Late Antiquity: Towards a Christian Empire* (Madison, WI, 1992), 61–72, esp. 65–67, 72, on good counsel exemplified by Ambrose's admonition of Theodosius; Claudia Rapp, *Holy Bishops in Late Antiquity: The Nature of Christian Leadership in an Age of Transition* (Berkeley and Los Angeles, 2005), 67, 83 (on prayer as parrhesia in the case of the holy man's intercessory power, and Origen's influence here on Cassian), 220–21, 266–73; and Irene van Renswoude's introduction to her University of Utrecht doctoral thesis, 2010, "Licence to Speak: The Rhetoric of Free Speech from Ambrose to Rather," esp. 17–27. I am very grateful indeed to Irene van Renswoude for letting me read unpublished work, for her assurance that Theodulf was acquainted with the anonymous *Rhetorica ad Herennium* (early first century BC, attributed by early medieval scholars to Cicero) and the work of John Chrysostom, where parrhesia was discussed, and for her intriguing suggestion that Alcuin warned the newly elevated Theodulf against loss of the parrhesiast's freedom to criticise. For parrhesia in the Bible, and as underlying an Augustinian attitude, see A. P. Carriker, "Augustine's Frankness in His Dispute with Jerome over the Interpretation of Galatians 2:11–14," in *Nova doctrina vetusque: Essays on Early Christianity in Honor of Frederic W. Schlatter*, ed. Douglas Kries and Catherine Brown Tkacz (New York, 1999), 121–38. My thanks also go to the anonymous reader of a draft of the present paper for invaluable bibliographical suggestions. I hope to return elsewhere to the relationship between Alcuin and Theodulf.

33. Alcuin, Ep. 179, 297; Verena Epp, "499–799: von Theoderich dem Grossen zu Karl dem Grossen," in *Am Vorabend der Kaiserkrönung*, ed. Godman, Jarnut, and Johanek, 219–29 (225–26), observes that Alcuin's canonical base was in fact a forgery.

34. *Annales Laureshamenses*, s.a. 801, 38.

35. Theodulf, *Opus Caroli*, 3.13 (pp. 390–91), citing 4 Reg. 11:1, 16.

36. Ibid., 3.13 (p. 386), with citations from 1 Petr. 3:7; Num. 30:4–5; Isidore, *Etymologiae*, 9.7.30. This chapter of the *Libri Carolini* would merit fuller discussion elsewhere. Meanwhile see Janet L. Nelson, "Women at the Court of Charlemagne: A Case of Monstrous Regiment?," ch. 13 in *The Frankish World 750–900* (London, 1997), 223–42 (228–30).

37. Ep. 224, 367; cf. *Annales Laureshamenses*, s.a. 801, 38: *aestivo tempore*; cf. *Annales regni francorum*, s.a. 801, 114: in fact Charlemagne remained in Italy until late June (ibid., 116).

38. For Theodulf's editorial achievement, see Bonifatius Fischer, "Bibeltext und Bibelreform unter Karl dem Grossen," in *Karl der Grosse*, ed. Braunfels, 2:156–216, esp. 176–82; Dahlhaus-Berg, *Nova antiquitas*, part 1, esp. 44–46; and now Veronika von Büren, "La place du manuscrit Ambr. L 99 sup. dans la transmission des *Étymologies* d'Isidore de Seville," in *Nuove ricerche su codici in scrittura latina dell'Ambrosiana*, ed. Mirella Ferrari and Marco Navoni (Milan, 2007), 35–36.

39. Dahlhaus-Berg, *Nova antiquitas*, 11.

40. Godman, *Poets*, 70–74; Nees, *Tainted Mantle*, 21–143, esp. 110–12, 117, 120–24. See also Charles Witke, *Latin Satire: The Structure of Persuasion* (Leiden, 1970), ch. 7, "Theodulf of Orleans and the Carolingian Renaissance," 168–99 (176–99); and Manfred Fuhrmann, "Philologische Bemerkungen zu Theodulfs *Paraenesis ad iudices*," in *Das Profil des Juristen in der europäischen Tradition: Symposion aus Anlaß des 70. Geburtstags von Franz*

Wieacker, ed. Klaus Luig and Dieter Liebs (Ebelsbach, 1980), 257–77, esp. 273, 277, stressing the poem's topicality as an intervention in public discourse.

41. Theodulf, *Carmen* 28, *Ad iudices*, 495, lines 77–82: "Haec tibi, Iosias, fuit observantia princeps / Haecque celebre tulit nomen ad alta tuum, / Impia qui sceleris demis monumenta vetusti / Et patrias leges qua potes usque novas, / Qui decedenti datus es pia gloria regno / Quem vespertini temporis ordo dedit." Cf. Wittke, *Latin Satire*, 182. Hereafter Dümmler's edition of *Carmen* 28 is cited simply as *Ad iudices*.

42. *Ad iudices*, 496, lines 93–95: "Saepe ego dum pravos de talibus arguo rebus, / Hac sibi clam dicunt me quoque sorte parem. / Saepe etiam talis cum non sim, suspicor esse, / Cum mihi sint plures, hac lue liber ero."

43. Ibid., 253–57.

44. See Janet L. Nelson, "The Settings of the Gift in the Reign of Charlemagne," in *The Languages of Gift in the Early Middle Ages*, ed. Wendy Davies and Paul Fouracre (Cambridge, 2010), 116–48, and Janet L. Nelson, "*Munera*," in *Les élites et la richesse dans le Haut Moyen Âge*, ed. J.-P. Devroey et al. (Brussels, 2010), 383–401, esp. 394–400.

45. *Ad iudices*, 508, lines 571–72: "Praesideat mente deus, haec quoque provida carni."

46. Ibid., 514, lines 807–8.

47. Ibid., 515, lines 845–46.

48. Ibid., line 852, and cf. line 877 ("lex hos prisca trucidat"). The echoes of *De civitate Dei*, 19.6 and 12, are audible. For profound reflections on these chapters, see R. A. Markus, *Saeculum: History and Society in the Theology of St Augustine* (Cambridge, 1970), 68–71, and esp. 98–100; also Nees, *Tainted Mantle*, ch. 4, esp. 90–93, and 128.

49. *Ad iudices*, 515, lines 881–82.

50. Theodulf in *Carmen*, 29, MGH Poetae 1, 517–20, a poem often taken to have been written at about the same time as, and possibly in conjunction with, *Ad iudices*, with which it survives, untitled, in a single late medieval manuscript (Dümmler, "Prooemium," 441–42), contrasts the *novum lumen* and *quieta lex* of Christianity (lines 61, 79–80) with the savage cruelties inflicted by contemporary laws ("iura moderna"; line 28) and also with Old Testament law ("lex antiqua dei [which] veteres . . . tum docuit homines"; line 59). Here Theodulf contrasts secular law, "old" or "modern," with what the Christian "law of peace" teaches but which it can never make prevail *in saeculo*. The contorted comments of Godman, *Poets*, 73–74, and cf. Nees, *Tainted Mantle*, 127–28, suggest difficulty in reconciling Theodulf's message here with what might seem *Ad iudices*' more positive one. Yet Theodulf's Augustinian starkness is evident in *Ad iudices* too, even when he urges the judge to combine law with mercy.

51. *Ad iudices*, 516, lines 895–98.

52. Ibid., 517, lines 953–54: "Ut pro te vitae est, pro his quoque mortuus auctor, / Quemque et pro meritis ad sua dona vocat."

53. Ibid., 515, line 859.

54. *Annales Lauueshamenses*, s.a. 802, 38–39. Note the echo of Luke 1:54 in the opening phrase of this passage. For propagandistic irony here, see Jürgen Hannig, "*Pauperiores vassi de infra palatio?* Zur Entstehung der karolingischen Königsbotenorganisation," *Mitteilungen des Instituts für Österreichische Geschichtsforschung* 91 (1983): 309–74.

55. Ibid., 39.

56. Harald Willjung, *Das Konzil von Aachen*, 809, MGH Conc. 2, Supp. 2, with Theodulf's *Libellus de processione spiritus sancti*, the largest of these treatises, at 314–82, and the editor's comments, 170–213; see Rosamond McKitterick, "History, Law and

Communication with the Past in the Carolingian Period," *Settimane di studio del Centro italiano di studi sull'alto medioevo* 52 (2005): 941–79; and McKitterick, *Charlemagne*, 314–15.

57. Einhard, *Vita Karoli Magni*, ed. Oswald Holder-Egger, MGH SS rer. Germ. 25, ch. 33, 40. See the comment of Harald Siems, *Handel und Wucher im Spiegel frühmittelalterliche Rechtsquellen* (Hannover, 1992), 476; Matthew Innes, "Charlemagne's Will: Inheritance, Ideology and the Imperial Succession," *English Historical Review* 112 (1997): 833–55. Theodulf, among "those who might want," and was in a position to bid for, some of Charlemagne's books, could satisfy at once his bookish interests and his pastoral concerns. Cf. more or less contemporaneous with the will, capitularies denouncing the derelictions of bishops and affirming New Testament values. See Nelson, "The Voice of Charlemagne," ch. 13 in *Courts, Elites, and Gendered Power*, 76–88.

58. Susan A. Keefe, *Water and the Word*, 2 vols. (Notre Dame, IN, 2002), vol. 2, with Theodulf's *Liber de ordine baptismi* as text 16, 279–321. See esp. Dahlhaus-Berg, *Nova antiquitas*, 99–168, esp. 116–35 for Isidore of Seville's particular influence here.

59. Theodulf's two sets of episcopal statutes are edited by Peter Brommer, MGH Capit. episc. 1, "Theodulf I," 73–142, and "Theodulf II," 142–84.

60. Dahlhaus-Berg, *Nova antiquitas*, 221–35, for the connection between these and the decrees of the Council of Chalon-sur-Saône (813). For Theodulf's concern with educational provision, cf. p. 289 and n. 5, above.

61. Janet L. Nelson, "Aachen as a Place of Power," ch. 14 in *Courts, Elites, and Gendered Power*, 1–23.

62. Bullough, *Alcuin*, and Philippe Depreux and Bruno Judic, eds., "Alcuin de York à Tours," *Annales de Bretagne et des Pays de l'Ouest* 111 (2004), indicate the weight of scholarship.

63. Wallace-Hadrill, *Frankish Church*, 225: "as champion of the Old Testament [Theodulf] made a vital contribution to the Carolingian concept of a Christian society."

64. This watchword of complementarity was Theodulf's own, in *Opus Caroli*, 2.27 (p. 295), as first highlighted by Dahlhaus-Berg, *Nova antiquitas*, 36. Among the marginal annotations of the unique manuscript which Ann Freeman, "*Opus Caroli regis contra synodum*: An Introduction," ch. 1 in *Theodulf of Orléans*, 1–123 (70–74) (following W. von den Steinen, as cited, ibid., 70n328), accepted as Charlemagne's own comments, against *nova antiquitas et antiqua novitas* is written: "*acute*" (spot on).

Contributors

Amy K. Bosworth received her Ph.D. from Purdue University in 2008, working under the direction of John J. Contreni. Her dissertation, "Criminals, Cures, and Castigation: Heiric of Auxerre's *Miracula sancti Germani* and Ninth-Century Carolingian Hagiography," explores the creation of and uses for the miracle collections in the ninth-century Carolingian world. Dr. Bosworth is an assistant professor of history at Muskingum University in New Concord, Ohio, where she teaches courses in the Middle Ages, ancient history, and world history.

Cullen J. Chandler joined the Department of History at Lycoming College in 2003 and serves as chair of the department. His research, including articles published in *Early Medieval Europe*, *Studies in Medieval and Renaissance History*, and the *International History Review*, focuses on how Carolingian rulers invented new ways of making their power felt in Catalonia through political appointments, religious policy, and legal maneuvers. He is currently completing a book on the Carolingian Spanish March.

Martin A. Claussen is at the University of San Francisco. His interests focus on Carolingian church history and early medieval monasticism. He is currently working on a series of articles on Benedict on Aniane.

Marcia L. Colish, Frederick B. Artz Professor of History emerita, Oberlin College and Lecturer in history at Yale University, is a Fellow and Past President of the Medieval Academy of America, which awarded its Haskins Medal in 1998 to her *Peter Lombard*. She has published widely on intellectual history from the church fathers to the Renaissance humanists, on topics such as medieval epistemology and sign theory, the Latin tradition of Stoicism, Carolingian thought, scholastic philosophy and theology, and Machiavelli. Her *Medieval Foundations of the Western Intellectual Tradition, 400–1400* has been published in Italian and Chinese translations. Her current work is on debates in medieval baptismal thought.

GISELLE DE NIE taught history at the University of Utrecht and is currently associated with the Center for Patristic Research in the Netherlands. Her work has focused on miracles and the religious mentality of the late antique period through the sixth century, and her latest book, *Poetics of Wonder: Testimonies of the New Christian Miracles in the Late Antique Latin World*, appeared in 2012.

PAUL EDWARD DUTTON is the Jack and Nancy Farley University Professor in History at Simon Fraser University. He is a Fellow of the Medieval Academy of America and the Royal Society of Canada, and the author, co-author, or editor of eight books including *The Politics of Dreaming in the Carolingian Empire* (Nebraska, 1994) and *Charlemagne's Mustache and Other Cultural Clusters of a Dark Age* (Palgrave, 2004). One of his continuing interests is the cultural and intellectual setting of Eriugena in Carolingian civilization. With Edouard Jeauneau, he wrote *The Autograph of Eriugena* (Brepols, 1996), which informs his contribution to this volume.

DAVID GANZ studied Carolingian history in Oxford and taught palaeography at the University of North Carolina and at King's College, London. In 2011 he gave the Lowe lectures in palaeography at Corpus Christi College, Oxford. He was Visiting Professor of Palaeography at the Medieval Institute, University of Notre Dame, in 2012.

ERIC J. GOLDBERG is associate professor of history at the Massachusetts Institute of Technology. He is currently working on a book about hunting and elite culture in the early Middle Ages.

JOHANNES HEIL is Executive Rector and Ignatz Bubis Professor of History, Religion and Culture at the Hochschule für Jüdische Studien Heidelberg, and honorary professor at Heidelberg University. His research interests are Jewish history with a focus on the late classical and early medieval period, history of texts, historiography, and Jewish-Christian relations (medieval and modern).

ROSAMOND MCKITTERICK is Professor of Medieval History in the University of Cambridge and Fellow of Sidney Sussex College. Her current research interests are the migration of ideas in the early Middle Ages, the implications and impact of the historical and legal texts produced during the sixth and seventh centuries in Rome, and Rome's transformation into a Christian city. In addition to over one hundred and twenty articles and chapters in books, her recent monographs and edited collections include *History and Memory in the Carolingian World*; *Perceptions of the Past in the Early Middle Ages*; *Charlemagne: The Formation of a European Identity/Karl der Grosse*, published in English and in German; and *Rome across Time and Space: Cultural Transmission and the Exchange of Ideas, c. 500–1400* (with C. Bolgia and J. Osborne).

LAWRENCE NEES has taught at the University of Delaware since 1978, where he is professor in the Department of Art History. He is the author of *From Justinian to Charlemagne, European Art 565–787: An Annotated Bibliography* (G. K. Hall, 1985), *The Gundohinus Gospels* (Medieval Academy of America, 1987), and *A Tainted Mantle: Hercules and the Classical Tradition at the Carolingian Court* (University of Pennsylvania Press, 1991), *Early Medieval Art* (Oxford, 2002), and editor of *Approaches to Early-Medieval Art* (Medieval Academy of America, 1998), He recently completed a book manuscript "Perspectives on Early Islamic Art in Jerusalem," and is working on a book on art and architecture during the time of Charlemagne. He is currently serving as president of the International Center of Medieval Art.

DAME JANET L. NELSON is Emerita Professor of History and Fellow at King's College London and past president of the Royal Historical Society. She has published over two hundred articles, chapters, and books on early medieval politics, religion, and gender, and is currently preparing a new biography of Charlemagne. Her scholarly work is featured in four collections, including *Politics and Ritual in Early Medieval Europe* (Hambledon, 1986), *The Frankish World* (Hambledon, 1996), *Rulers and Ruling Families in Early Medieval Europe* (Ashgate, 1999), and *Courts, Elites and Gendered Power* (Ashgate, 2007).

THOMAS F. X. NOBLE is professor of history at the University of Notre Dame and a former director of the Medieval Institute and chair of the history department. He has won three awards for excellence in teaching. His research has focused on Rome, the papacy, and the Carolingians. He is the author, most recently, of *Images, Iconoclasm, and the Carolingians* (University of Pennsylvania Press, 2009), which won the Otto Gründler Prize in 2012.

Pierre Riché earned the Docteur ès Lettres at the Sorbonne (1962) and after teaching posts in Algeria, Tunisia, and Rennes, France, taught at the University of Paris X–Nanterre from 1967 until his retirement in 1989. His landmark *Education et culture dans l'Occident barbare, VIe–VIIIe siècles* (conveyed into English by John Contreni in 1976), *Daily Life in the World of Charlemagne* (1973; English trans. 1978), and *The Carolingians: A Family Who Forged Europe* (1983; English trans. 1993) have all become staples in North American classrooms. His edition of the *Liber manualis* (1975; English trans. 1991) established a cottage industry around Dhuoda, female culture, and lay aristocratic values, and many other works have likewise opened new perspectives on the barbarian invasions, children, pedagogy, the tenth century, and the medieval Church. He was elected Corresponding Fellow of the Medieval Academy of America in 2012.

Wesley Stevens is professor of classics at the University of Manitoba, visiting scholar at St. Paul's College, and professor emeritus of history at University of Winnipeg, Canada. He has published fourteen books and over one hundred articles, of which the most recent are "Ars computi: quomodo inventa est" (2010), "Walahfrid Strabo's Study of the Computus" (2012), and "Zero: A Roman Numeral at Murbach, 814–820" (2013). He is director of LEXICA LATINA: mathematical and scientific terminology missing from Latin dictionaries.

Steven A. Stofferahn is associate professor of history at Indiana State University, where he also serves as a Faculty Fellow in the Center for Community Engagement. Specializing in intellectual and political culture, he has authored numerous articles in *Early Medieval Europe*, *Réflexions Historiques*, *The Historian*, *Magistra*, and other journals, and continues his research on exile in the Carolingian era, as well as on monastic missionary endeavors on the American Great Plains.

Index

Typeset in 10/13 Goudy
Composed by Tom Krol
Manufactured by McNaughton & Gunn, Inc.

Medieval Institute Publications
College of Arts and Sciences
Western Michigan University
1903 W. Michigan Avenue
Kalamazoo, MI 49008-5432
http://www.wmich.edu/medieval/mip

 WESTERN MICHIGAN UNIVERSITY